Children, Human Rights and Temporary Labour Migration

This book focuses on the neglected yet critical issue of how the global migration of millions of parents as low-waged migrant workers impacts the rights of their children under international human rights law.

The work provides a systematic analysis and critique of how the restrictive features of policies governing temporary labour migration interfere with provisions of the Convention on the Rights of the Child that protect the child-parent relationship and parental role in children's lives. Combining social and legal research, it identifies both potential harms to children's well-being caused by prolonged child-parent separation and State duties to protect this relationship, which is deliberately disrupted by temporary labour migration policies. The book boldly argues that States benefitting from the labour of migrant workers share responsibility under international human rights law to mitigate harms to the children of these workers, including by supporting effective measures to maintain transnational child-parent relationships. It identifies measures to incorporate children's best interests into temporary labour migration policies, offering ways to reduce interferences with children's family rights.

This book fills a gap that emerges at the intersection of child rights studies, migration research and existing literature on the purported nexus between labour migration and international development. It will be a valuable resource for academics, researchers and policymakers working in these areas.

Rasika Ramburuth Jayasuriya has worked for two decades across government, multilateral and civil society organisations on policy issues related to migration and children's rights. She has a PhD from the University of Melbourne's Law School and was a doctoral associate at the University of Toronto. Rasika has held positions as a migration policy specialist at UNICEF and IOM-UN Migration in Geneva and as a senior policy officer at the Department of Premier and Cabinet in Victoria, Australia. She is lead author of 'The Migration of Women Domestic Workers from Sri Lanka: Protecting the Rights of Children Left Behind' (2015).

Routledge Research in Asylum, Migration and Refugee Law

Available titles in this series include:

Refugee Protection and the Role of Law
Conflicting Identities
Edited by Susan Kneebone, Dallal Stevens and Loretta Baldassar

Gender in Refugee Law
From the Margins to the Centre
Efrat Arbel, Catherine Dauvergne, and Jenni Millbank

Asylum-Seeker and Refugee Protection in Sub-Saharan Africa
The Peregrination of a Persecuted Human Being in Search of a Safe Haven
Cristiano D'Orsi

Migrant Rights at Work
Law's Precariousness at the Intersection of Immigration and Labour
Laurie Berg

Unaccompanied Children in European Migration and Asylum Practices
In Whose Best Interests?
Edited by Mateja Sedmak, Birgit Sauer and Barbara Gornik

European Asylum Law and the Rights of the Child
Ciara Smyth

Asylum Law in the European Union
Francesco Cherubini

Forthcoming in this series:

The Socio-Economic Rights of Asylum Seekers
Liam Thornton

Children, Human Rights and Temporary Labour Migration

Protecting the Child-Parent Relationship

Rasika Ramburuth Jayasuriya

Routledge
Taylor & Francis Group
LONDON AND NEW YORK

First published 2021
by Routledge
2 Park Square, Milton Park, Abingdon, Oxon OX14 4RN

and by Routledge
605 Third Avenue, New York, NY 10158

Routledge is an imprint of the Taylor & Francis Group, an informa business

British Library Cataloguing-in-Publication Data
A catalogue record for this book is available from the British Library

Library of Congress Cataloging-in-Publication Data
Names: Jayasuriya, Rasika Ramburuth, author.
Title: Children, human rights and temporary labour migration : protecting the child-parent relationship / Rasika Ramburuth Jayasuriya.
Description: Abingdon, Oxon ; New York, NY : Routledge, 2021. |
Series: Routledge research in asylum, migration and refugee law | Based on author's thesis (doctoral - University of Melbourne, Law School, 2019) issued under title: Protecting the child-parent relationship : the place of children's rights in temporary labour migration. | Includes bibliographical references and index.
Identifiers: LCCN 2021005989 (print) | LCCN 2021005990 (ebook) |
ISBN 9780367462994 (hardback) |
ISBN 9781032037868 (paperback) | ISBN 9781003028000 (ebook)
Subjects: LCSH: Children of foreign workers–Legal status, laws, etc.. |
Children (International law)
Classification: LCC K3274 .J39 2021 (print) | LCC K3274 (ebook) |
DDC 341.4/8572–dc23
LC record available at https://lccn.loc.gov/2021005989
LC ebook record available at https://lccn.loc.gov/2021005990

ISBN: 978-0-367-46299-4 (hbk)
ISBN: 978-1-032-03786-8 (pbk)
ISBN: 978-1-003-02800-0 (ebk)

Typeset in Galliard
by Taylor & Francis Books

For my children, who remind me each day about why this matters.
Thank you.

Contents

Illustrations

Figures

Table

Acknowledgements

My deepest thanks go to John Tobin, Susan Kneebone and Helen Rhoades for their invaluable guidance, support and encouragement in the research for and drafting of this book. I'd particularly like to thank you John for your continued mentorship. I greatly appreciate having had the opportunity to work with and learn from you.

To each of the key informants who participated in my research, I am ever grateful to you for so generously, willingly and openly sharing your invaluable insights with me. Your contributions to this research have not only strengthened its depth but also my resolve to continue working to address this issue. Similarly, I am extremely grateful to those researchers working with children, families and communities around the world to better understand the social implications of temporary labour migration, whose studies I have relied on heavily to bring people's voices and experiences to the fore.

I wish to express my gratitude to Melbourne Law School and the University of Melbourne for providing me with the funding and support that made this research possible. My sincere thanks also go to Michelle Foster and Kirsty Gover for their valued input at key points throughout this process, including affirming the pressing need for this research.

For their ongoing mentorship, generous support and continued interest in my research, I wish to convey my greatest appreciation to Deborah Brennan, Sara Charlesworth, Elizabeth Hill, Ito Peng, Sonya Michel, Rianne Mahon, Matt Withers, Brian Opeskin and Josef Szwarc. I would also like to thank the Centre for Global Social Policy at the University of Toronto and the Social Policy Research Centre at the University of New South Wales for their support for this research.

Lastly, my heartfelt thanks to my treasured friends and family for their constant encouragement and belief in me. Particular thanks go to my mother, for showing me what is possible as a woman and a mother; and to my father, for always keeping me grounded and connected to my roots. But most of all, I wish to thank my husband for making this possible. Without your patience, motivation, encouragement and advice – and your care for our children – I could not have undertaken this endeavour. Thank you for your unwavering love and support.

Preface: COVID-19

Since the drafting of this book, we have witnessed a pandemic that has changed the status quo for migrant workers and their families. While this book does not examine the ramifications of COVID-19, the fall-out from the pandemic highlights the urgency of the need to address the impacts of the design and structure of temporary labour migration programmes and policies on children, parents and families across the globe.

At the individual level, loss of employment and wages during the pandemic has significant ramifications for both migrant workers and their families. Globally, remittances have not declined during the pandemic to the extent originally projected, dropping only 1.6 per cent from US$548 billion in 2019 to US$540 billion in 2020. However, this is largely because migrant workers were driven to continue supporting their families by drawing on their savings or cutting their consumption.[1] Importantly, remittances earned by an estimated 164 million migrant workers worldwide provide financial support to at least 800 million family members in low- and middle-income countries (LMIC), including millions of children.[2] States have given little attention to the massive impact that this loss of household income will have on the families of migrant workers, many of who are dependent on remittances to meet their basic needs. This includes meeting costs associated with their children's health and education, a common motivation for parents to migrate for temporary low-waged work in the first place.

Labour-receiving countries have largely disregarded the socioeconomic impacts that the mass return of hundreds of thousands of migrant workers in the face of the pandemic will have on their families, children and labour-sending countries. For example, by early October 2020, over 230 000 migrant workers had been repatriated to the Philippines, representing one-tenth of overseas Filipino workers (OFWs) and 50 per cent of Filipino workers who lost their jobs in the wake of the pandemic.[3] This demonstrates the fragility of depending on remittances alone as a livelihood strategy, particularly when labour-receiving States assume few to no

1 World Bank, 'Resilience: COVID-19 Crisis Through a Migration Lens' (KNOMAD, Migration and Development Brief 34, May 2021) x.

2 IFAD and the UN Network on Migration (UNNM), 'The Impact of COVID-19 on Family Remittances: A Lifeline Cut for Migrant Families' (UNNM Policy Brief, June 2020) 2.

3 Philippine Overseas Labor Office, cited in World Bank Migration and Remittances Team, above n 1, 4.

legal and social responsibilities towards the families and children of migrant workers in ways that would if they were nationals. In other words, as Newland states, 'the cracks in the relationship between migration and development' have been revealed in the wake of COVID-19.[4]

The pandemic has also exposed the huge dependency that labour-receiving countries have on migrant workers, with many at the front lines of COVID-19 responses and deemed to be essential workers in sectors including healthcare, childcare, aged care, agriculture, food production, cleaning and transport. However, at the same time, migrant workers are frequently excluded from social assistance, including unemployment benefits and COVID-19 social protection measures,[5] that would have a flow-on benefit to their families when workers are faced with unemployment.

Instead, migrant workers who have lost their jobs during the pandemic are being returned home without support, placing an unrealistic burden on labour-sending countries to absorb the economic and social costs associated with supporting these workers and their families. This, again, reflects the structurally uneven nature of how low-waged temporary labour migration operates at present. However, as the International Labour Organization has reiterated in the context of seasonal agricultural work, the COVID-19 pandemic provides an opportunity to redesign foreign worker schemes and develop bilateral labour migration agreements that are rights-based to 'potentially reduce the power imbalances between origin and destination countries'.[6]

To this end, it is urged that in the design and redesign of temporary labour migration programmes and policies going forward, children's rights are brought to the fore and given the due consideration that they not only deserve, but that States are obligated to give. This book goes some way to understanding a number of children's rights that are affected by temporary labour migration, and it is strongly welcomed that the ideas and analysis presented here be further developed and built upon by researchers and policymakers alike.

4 Kathleen Newland, 'Will International Migration Governance Survive the COVID-19 Pandemic?' (MPI Policy Brief, October 2020) 2.

5 CMW Committee and UN Special Rapporteur on the human rights of migrants, *Joint Guidance Note on the Impacts of the COVID-19 Pandemic on the Human Rights of Migrants* (26 May 2020) 1.

6 International Labour Organization (ILO), 'Seasonal Migrant Workers' Schemes: Rethinking Fundamental Principles and Mechanisms in light of COVID-19' (ILO Brief, May 2020) 6.

Abbreviations

ASEAN	Association of Southeast Asian Nations
ASEAN Consensus on the Rights of Migrant Workers	ASEAN Consensus on the Protection and Promotion of the Rights of Migrant Workers (2018)
ASEAN Declaration on the Rights of Migrant Workers	ASEAN Declaration on the Protection and Promotion of the Rights of Migrant Workers (2007)
CMW Committee	Committee on the Protection of the Rights of All Migrant Workers and Members of their Families
CRC	Convention on the Rights of the Child (1989)
CRC Committee	Committee on the Rights of the Child
ECD	early childhood development
ESC	economic, social and cultural
Global Compact for Migration	Global Compact for Safe, Orderly and Regular Migration (2018)
ICCPR	International Covenant on Civil and Political Rights (1966)
ICESCR	International Covenant on Economic, Social and Cultural Rights (1966)

ICRMW	International Convention on the Protection of the Rights of All Migrant Workers and Members of their Families (1990)
ILO	International Labour Organization
IOM	International Organization for Migration
LCP	Live-in Caregiver Program
Maastricht Principles	Maastricht Principles on Extraterritorial Obligations of States in the Area of Economic, Social and Cultural Rights (2013)
New York Declaration	New York Declaration for Refugees and Migrants (2016)
OHCHR	Office of the High Commissioner for Human Rights
PICS	Pacific Island Countries
SAWP	Seasonal Agricultural Workers Program
SDGs	Sustainable Development Goals
Siracusa Principles	Siracusa Principles on the Limitation and Derogation Provisions in the International Covenant on Civil and Political Rights (1984)
Sustainable Development Agenda	The 2030 Agenda for Sustainable Development (2015)
SWP	Seasonal Workers Program (Australia)
TFWP	Temporary Foreign Worker Program (Canada)
TLM	Temporary Labour Migration
UDHR	Universal Declaration of Human Rights (1948)
UN	United Nations
UNDP	United Nations Development Programme
UNICEF	United Nations Children's Fund

Note on referencing style

This book has been referenced in accordance with the Australian Guide to Legal Citation (3rd edition). International treaties and declarations and official United Nations documents have been cited only once in full.

Introduction

Low-waged, temporary labour migration (TLM) is a global phenomenon that involves the migration of workers for months or years at a time generally *without* their dependent children. As States recruit migrant workers of prime child-rearing age,[1] it is inevitable that many are parents of dependent children at the time of their migration. As a result, millions of children are now growing up with the prolonged absence of one or both of their parents.[2] This gives rise to foreseeable potential harms that are associated with child-parent separation for this group of children. However, the dominant discourse surrounding TLM has, to date, focused on the potential economic benefits of TLM to both 'labour-sending' and 'labour-receiving' States[3] and the families of migrant workers *without* considering

1 Migrant workers are typically in their early twenties to mid-forties at the time of their recruitment. For example, Australia's Pacific Labour Scheme recruits migrant workers from Pacific Island countries aged 21–45 years to work for up to 3 years in low- and semi-skilled roles in rural and regional Australia. See Australian Government Department of Foreign Affairs and Trade, *Frequently Asked Questions about the Pacific Labour Scheme* (November 2018) <https://dfat.gov.au/geo/pacific/engagement/pacific-labour-mobility/Pages/frequently-asked-questions.aspx>.

2 These include children in labour-sending countries in Asia, Central and South America, Africa and Eastern Europe. To illustrate, it is estimated that there are over 9 million such children in the Philippines (which constitutes roughly 27 per cent of minors in the Philippines), 1 million in Sri Lanka, 100 000 in Moldova (which equates to 31 per cent of children in Moldova aged 0–14 living without at least one parent who is a migrant worker), 200 000 in the Ukraine and 300 000 in Ecuador alone. See Melanie M Reyes, *Migration and Filipino Children Left-Behind: A Literature Review* (UNICEF, 2007) 1; Committee on the Rights of the Child ('CRC Committee'), *Concluding Observations: Sri Lanka*, UN Doc CRC/C/LKA/CO/3-4 (19 October 2010) [44]; Liza Yanovich, *Children Left Behind: The Impact of Labor Migration in Moldova and Ukraine* (23 January 2015) Migration Policy Institute <http://www.migrationpolicy.org/article/children-left-behind-impact-labor-migration-moldova-and-ukraine>; United Nations (UN) Children's Fund (UNICEF), *Children and Migration* (13 October 2017) Global Forum on Migration and Development <https://www.gfmd.org/unicef-children-and-migration>.

3 The terms 'labour-sending' and 'labour-receiving' have been used in this book in the same fashion as Howe and Owens to capture the notion that certain States predominantly 'send' or 'receive' migrant workers on a temporary basis primarily to meet demands for low-waged labour in receiving countries and generate remittances to raise

how parental migration affects children's rights. This book seeks to counter this dominant approach by making visible the place of children's rights in TLM. These rights cannot continue to be overlooked given the sheer scale of parental migration being encouraged by States and the projected future growth of this form of migration.

Put simply, TLM need not be as potentially harmful to the child-parent relationship as it is at present. This book brings into focus children's rights that protect the child-parent relationship under the *Convention on the Rights of the Child (1989)* ('*CRC*')[4] and demonstrates how these rights continue to be unnecessarily subject to interference by TLM policies without justification by States. Building on existing knowledge about the potential harms of child-parent separation to children, both in the context of migration and more generally, it highlights potential impacts on children's rights caused by TLM policies that encourage prolonged parental migration. Importantly, the central proposition is that conditions associated with low-waged temporary labour migration create *potential* harms to children; and that reasonable policy measures are available to States to mitigate these foreseeable harms. These measures are grounded in universal norms and obligations that have been accepted by States under the CRC.

While it appears obvious that TLM policies premised on child-parent separation will have significant implications for children, nowhere has this issue been considered in light of State obligations under the CRC to protect the child-parent relationship. Not only does the CRC legally bind States parties to consider the impact of policies on children's rights and best interests,[5] it also heavily presumes that, unless shown otherwise, it is in children's best interests to have their relationship with their parents and family life protected.[6] As such, the Committee on the Rights of the Child ('CRC Committee') has emphasised the importance of strong mutual attachments between children and their parents/primary caregivers to meeting children's physical and emotional needs, stressing the essential role of parents/primary caregivers as 'the major conduit through which young children are able to realise their rights'.[7]

The near-universal commitment to the CRC, which has been ratified by all countries except for the United States,[8] reflects agreement by States about the

national income in sending countries. It is noted that this structure can be considered to embody neoliberal principles that reflect the existing global economic system that favours free market capitalism. See Joanna Howe and Rosemary Owens, 'Temporary Labour Migration in the Global Era: The Regulatory Challenges' in Joanna Howe and Rosemary Owens (eds), *Temporary Labour Migration in the Global Era* (Hart Publishing, 2016) 3, 3–4, 8.

4 *Convention on the Rights of the Child*, opened for signature 20 November 1989, 1577 UNTS 3 (entered into force 2 September 1990) ('*CRC*').

5 *CRC* art 3.

6 *CRC* arts 7, 18, 16, 5, 10(2), 27.

7 CRC Committee, *General Comment No 7: Implementing Child Rights in Early Childhood*, 40th sess, UN Doc CRC/C/GC/7/Rev.1 (20 September 2006) para 16 ('*General Comment No 7*').

8 The CRC currently has 196 States parties. See UN, *Treaty Collection* (21 October 2020) <https://treaties.un.org>.

applicability of the norms, rights and principles that it establishes.[9] The CRC also obliges States parties to give effect to its principles and standards in domestic policies and law.[10] This includes the norm that the child-parent relationship is central to children's upbringing and development and, therefore, to be protected and supported by States.[11]

Hence, the CRC is used here to develop a normative and conceptual framework for understanding the discrete issue of *how* State obligations under the CRC could be better fulfilled to reduce interferences by TLM policies with children's rights. It is important to recall that children's rights are held by children as individual rights-bearers and therefore *must* be considered by policymakers *irrespective* of the denial of family rights to their parents, which occurs when labour-receiving countries attach family rights to a worker's citizenship and migration status.[12]

Hence, while there are complex and intersecting social, economic and political issues that drive TLM – discussed briefly in the following chapter – *none* of these drivers affect the obligation on States under international human rights law to openly and comprehensively consider how TLM policies that separate children and parents affect children's rights. The discrete purpose of this book is to bring children's family rights into discussions about the development of TLM policies going forward.

Adopting a rights-based framework

A rights-based framework is used here to achieve three aims. First, to understand the duty of States under international human rights law to support the child-parent relationship in the context of TLM. Second, to identify potential harms to children's rights that protect the child-parent relationship caused by State-designed TLM policies. Third, to recommend measures to reduce interferences by TLM with children's rights by better supporting the child-parent relationship.

9 Sonia Harris-Short, 'International Human Rights Law: Imperialist, Inept and Ineffective? Cultural Relativism and the UN Convention on the Rights of the Child' (2003) 25(1) *Human Rights Quarterly* 130, 156.

10 *CRC* art 4; Mary Crock and Hannah Martin, 'First Things First: International Law and the Protection of Migrant Children' in Mary Crock and Lenni Benson (eds), *Protecting Migrant Children: In Search of Best Practice* (Elgar, 2018) 75, 82.

11 *CRC* Preamble para 6, arts 18, 27.

12 Children as individual rights-bearers and the significance of citizenship are discussed in Chapter 6 (see Sections 6.3.2 and 6.3.4). See also Susan Kneebone, 'Transnational Labour Migrants: Whose Responsibility?' in Fiona Jenkins, Mark Nolan and Kim Rubenstein (eds), *Allegiance and Identity in a Globalised World* (Cambridge University Press, 2014) 426, 426–8, 445–6; Nicola Piper and Stefan Rother, 'Editorial: Migration and Democracy: Citizenship and Human Rights from a Multi-level Perspective' (2015) 53(3) *International Migration* 3; Christl Kessler, 'Democratic Citizenship and Labour Migration in East Asia: Mapping Fields of Enquiry (2009) 8(2) *European Journal of East Asian Studies* 181; Mary Crock and Lenni B Benson, 'Central Issues in the Protection of Child Migrants' in Mary Crock and Lenni Benson (eds), *Protecting Migrant Children: In Search of Best Practice* (Elgar, 2018) 1, 21.

Each aim fills a void in the existing discourse surrounding TLM. Together, they are intended to improve understanding about ***how*** and ***why*** States must act to mitigate potential harms to children's rights arising from TLM policies.

i) Improving our understanding of State duties to support the child-parent relationship in the context of temporary labour migration (TLM)

To date, interferences with human rights in the context of TLM have been largely understood in relation to the violation of the rights of adult workers.[13] States have recognised the susceptibility of migrant workers to human rights abuses inherent in working conditions associated with low-waged work and temporary migration status.[14] However, there is a complete omission by States as to how TLM policies that require parental migration ***without*** dependent children may affect children's rights protected under international human rights law.

To ensure that children's rights are not arbitrarily interfered with, human rights law requires States to justify measures that limit children's rights. This involves showing that limitations on children's rights caused by structural features of TLM policies pursue a legitimate aim and are necessary, reasonable and proportionate to that aim.[15] The principle of proportionality requires there to be a rational connection between the measures employed and the aim being pursued;[16] ***and*** the use of those measures reasonably available that would least restrict the rights in question.[17] At present, *no* States – labour-receiving or labour-sending – have made any

13 See, eg, Amnesty International, 'Abusive Labour Migration Policies' (Submission to the UN Committee on Migrant Workers' Day of General Discussion on Workplace Exploitation and Workplace Protection, 7 April 2014); Human Rights Watch, *Exported and Exposed: Abuses against Sri Lankan Domestic Workers in Saudi Arabia, Kuwait, Lebanon, and the United Arab Emirates* (Human Rights Watch, 2007); Committee on the Protection of the Rights of all Migrant Workers and Members of Their Families ('CMW Committee'), *General Comment No 1 on Migrant Domestic Workers,* 13th sess, UN Doc CMW/C/GC/1 (23 February 2011); Nicola Piper, 'The "Migration-Development Nexus" Revisited from a Rights Perspective' (2008) 7(3) *Journal of Human Rights* 282; Stuart Rosewarne, 'Temporary International Labour Migration and Development in South and Southeast Asia' (2012) 18(2) *Feminist Economics* 63.

14 See, eg, Standing Committee on Human Resources, Skills and Social Development and the Status of Persons with Disabilities, Parliament of Canada, *Temporary Foreign Worker Program* (2016) 31; Sri Lankan Ministry for Foreign Employment Promotion and Welfare, National Labour Migration Policy for Sri Lanka (Government of Sri Lanka, October 2008) 10, 19, 45.

15 *Siracusa Principles on the Limitation and Derogation Provisions in the International Covenant on Civil and Political Rights,* UN ESCOR, 41st sess, UN Doc E/CN.4/1985/4 (28 September 1984) annex pt I A para 10 ('*Siracusa Principles*'); Human Rights Committee, *CCPR General Comment No 27: Freedom of Movement (Article 12)*, 67th sess, 1783rd mtg, UN Doc CCPR/C/21/Rev.1/Add.9 (1 November 1999) para 14 ('*CCPR General Comment No 27*').

16 John Eekelaar and John Tobin, 'Article 3. The Best Interests of the Child' in J Tobin (ed), *The UN Convention on the Rights of the Child: A Commentary* (OUP, 2019) 73, 97.

17 *Siracusa Principles*, UN Doc E/CN.4/1984/4, annex pt I A para 11.

attempt to recognise the interferences with CRC rights caused by TLM, let alone justify that the features of TLM that create prolonged periods of child-parent separation are necessary, reasonable or use measures of least interference reasonably available to States.[18]

There are several rights pertaining to the child-parent relationship under the CRC that are foreseeably impacted by TLM. They include children's rights to be cared for by their own parents as far as possible (Art 7); to maintain direct and regular contact and personal relations with their parents if separated transnationally (Art 10(2)); to receive direction and guidance from their parents (Art 5); to have their family life protected from arbitrary interference (Art 16); and to have their parents assisted by the State in the performance of their child-rearing responsibilities as primary caregivers (Art 18), including in securing conditions necessary for their children's overall development (Art 27). Together, these rights highlight both the centrality of the child-parent relationship in human rights law and the indivisibility of the rights of children and parents.[19] They also reflect a consensus by States about the primary role of parents in their children's upbringing and development and the duty of States to support parents to fulfil that role.[20]

TLM policies that cause the separation of children and parents for prolonged periods necessarily interfere with parental capacity to fulfil significant aspects of the primary caregiving role. They also fundamentally disrupt the normative expectation created by these CRC rights that, unless shown otherwise, it is in a child's best interests to be with and raised by their parents. The CRC Committee, together with the Committee on Migrant Workers ('CMW Committee'), have emphasised that States should maintain their duty to respect, protect and fulfil the rights of the children of migrants since 'States should ensure that children in the context of international migration are treated first and foremost as children.'[21]

Importantly, the CRC recognises that a parent's child-rearing responsibilities are broad and involve providing for children's *overall* development needs (including their psychosocial and emotional needs). By contrast, TLM policies encourage parents to migrate to provide for limited aspects of their children's needs (particularly their material, physical and educational needs), which can potentially (but

18 The requirement for limitations on rights to be necessary, reasonable and use measures of least interference is discussed throughout the book. See, eg, Chapter 3 (Section 3.2.1), Chapter 5 (Section 5.3.2) and Chapter 6 (Section 6.4).

19 *CRC* arts 5, 18, 27; See John Tobin, 'Fixed Concepts but Changing Conceptions: Understanding the Relationship Between Children and Parents under the CRC' in Martin D Ruck, Michele Peterson-Badali and Michael Freeman (eds), *Handbook of Children's Rights Global and Multidisciplinary Perspectives* (Routledge, 2017) 53.

20 UNICEF Office of Research (Innocenti), *Family and Parenting Support: Policy and Provision in a Global Context* (UNICEF, 2015) 21.

21 CMW and CRC Committees, *Joint General Comment No. 3 (2017) of the Committee on the Protection of the Rights of All Migrant Workers and Members of Their Families and No. 22 (2017) of the Committee on the Rights of the Child on the General Principles Regarding the Human Rights of Children in the Context of International Migration*, UN Doc CMW/C/GC/3-CRC/C/GC/22 (16 November 2017) para 11 ('*Joint General Comment on Children in the Context of International Migration*').

not necessarily) be better met with increased income.[22] This is at the expense of those psychosocial and emotional development needs best met through a strong parental presence in children's lives.[23] Hence, it is argued that States have a duty to support parents to provide for *all* of their children's development needs rather than systematically prioritising potential economic gains – without any consideration of children's rights – over other equally important and protected aspects of the parental role.

The book examines the abovementioned specific CRC rights that protect the child-parent relationship in light of general obligations and principles in human rights law.[24] These include the duty to give due consideration to children's best interests in all policies affecting them;[25] children's right to be heard in all matters affecting them in a manner appropriate to their age and maturity;[26] the principle that the family is the most fundamental unit in society entitled to protection by the State;[27] and the notion that the protection of children's rights is a shared responsibility between labour-sending *and* labour-receiving countries. The latter concerns the principle of international cooperation in human rights law, espoused in the CRC, which requires States with resources to contribute to the global implementation of children's rights beyond their own jurisdiction.[28] It is argued that while labour-sending States have a clear duty to protect the rights of

22 The promotion of TLM as a means by which parents can provide for their children's material needs, and the mixed evidence as to whether remittances improve children's material, physical and educational outcomes, are discussed in Chapter 4 (see Sections 4.2.3 and 4.2.4).

23 Potential negative impacts of parental migration on children's psychosocial development needs are discussed in Chapter 4 (see Section 4.3) and the recognised value of parental involvement in children's lives to their development and well-being is discussed in Chapter 7 (see Section 7.2).

24 These general principles are the focus of Chapter 3.

25 *CRC* art 3.

26 *CRC* art 12.

27 *CRC* Preamble para 6; *Universal Declaration of Human Rights*, GA Res 217A (III), UN Doc A/810 (10 December 1948) art 16(3) ('*UDHR*'); *International Covenant on Civil and Political Rights*, opened for signature 16 December 1966, 999 UNTS 171 (entered into force 23 March 1976) art 23(1) ('*ICCPR*'); *International Covenant on Economic, Social and Cultural Rights*, opened for signature 16 December 1966, 993 UNTS 3 (entered into force 3 January 1976) art 10(1) ('*ICESCR*'); *International Convention on the Protection of the Rights of All Migrant Workers and Members of their Families*, opened for signature 18 December 1990, 2220 UNTS 3 (entered into force 1 July 2003) art 44 ('*ICRMW*').

28 *CRC* Preamble para 12, art 4. See also CRC Committee, *Report on the Forty-sixth Session*, UN Doc [92] ('*Report on the Forty-sixth Session*'); CRC Committee, *General Comment No 5 on General Measures of Implementation for the Convention on the Rights of the Child*, 34th sess, UN Doc CRC/GC/2003/5 (3 October 2003) para 7 ('*General Comment No 5*'); CRC Committee, *General Comment No 19 (2016) on Public Budgeting for the Realization of Children's Rights (art 4)*, UN Doc CRC/C/GC/19 (20 July 2016) para 35 ('*General Comment No 19*'); *Maastricht Principles on Extraterritorial Obligations of States in the Area of Economic, Social and Cultural Rights* (ETO Consortium, January 2013) [31] *('Maastricht Principles')*.

children of migrant workers who continue to reside in their jurisdiction; the principle of international cooperation underpins the duties of labour-receiving States to also support measures to reduce potential harms to children.[29] This is particularly since labour-receiving States have greater resources and are primarily responsible for defining the terms of TLM policies.[30] These general principles must be considered in the justification of interferences with children's specific rights.

ii) Identifying potential harms caused by TLM to rights that protect the child-parent relationship

By analysing findings from social science studies within a children's rights-based framework, the book demonstrates *how* TLM is interfering with CRC rights that States are obligated to protect. Importantly, there is a significant alignment between the evidence from existing social science research on parental migration in the context of TLM and the concerns being raised here about interferences with CRC rights that protect the child-parent relationship. Thus, the significance of this approach is that while the focus of the book is on children's rights, the impact of TLM on these rights is not being considered in theory alone but in an applied and evidence-based manner.

For example, findings presented here are informed by the significant body of social science research that raises concerns about the psychosocial impacts of parental migration on children, particularly when the migration is for a prolonged period; the primary caregiver (usually the mother) migrates; there is infrequent communication between children and their absent parents; and when the children affected are young (with the CRC Committee defining early childhood as below eight years of age[31]).[32] Existing research has found that when children are separated from their primary caregiving parent(s) for prolonged periods of time, they often experience negative psychosocial impacts including a sense of loneliness and

29 *Maastricht Principles*, above n 28, [19]–[21].

30 Ibid [31]–[33].

31 *General Comment No 7*, UN Doc CRC/C/GC/7/Rev.1, para 4.

32 These social science studies are discussed in Chapter 4 (see Section 4.3) and Chapter 5 (see Section 5.4). See, eg, Graziano Battistella and Cecilia Conaco, 'The Impact of Labour Migration on the Children Left Behind: A Study of Elementary School Children in the Philippines' (1998) 13(2) *Sojourn: Journal of Social Issues in Southeast Asia* 220; Save the Children Sri Lanka and Kishali Pinto-Jayawardena, *Left Behind, Left Out: The Impact on Children and Families of Mothers Migrating for Work Abroad* (Save the Children Sri Lanka, 2006); Aree Jampaklay, 'Parental Absence and Children's School Enrolment: Evidence from a Longitudinal Study in Kanchanaburi, Thailand' (2006) 2(1) *Asian Population Studies* 93; Kusala Wettasinghe, Gethsie Shanmugam and Sarala Emmanuel, *Alternative Care Giving of Migrant Workers' Children* (Terre des Hommes, 2012) 32; Rasika Jayasuriya and Brian Opeskin, 'The Migration of Women Domestic Workers from Sri Lanka: Protecting the Rights of Children Left Behind' (2015) 48 *Cornell International Law Journal* 579; Yanovich, above n 2.

abandonment, even if well cared for by alternative caregivers.[33] In fact, recent studies have shown that some young adults who transitioned into adolescence and adulthood in the absence of their parents, who migrated to provide for them, are choosing not to migrate themselves, with the view that proximity is important to parenthood and because '(d)espite higher monetary gains overseas, the pain of family separation is too great'.[34]

Existing social science literature also demonstrates the positive impact that shorter periods of separation and frequent communication between children and parents can have on the capacity of migrant workers to engage successfully in 'transnational parenting'.[35] Recent research has reiterated the importance of communication as one of the key conditions affecting the well-being of children in this context, along with the child's environment and the specificities of the transnational child-raising arrangement.[36] Prolonged separation and a lack of communication, on the other hand, has been found to cause the breakdown of relationships between migrant workers and their children, even after children and parents are reunited.[37]

Hence, findings from social science studies reinforce and support the importance of States fulfilling their legal obligations to protect the child-parent relationship as demanded by the CRC. Such findings are used throughout to offer

33 Ibid. See also S T Hettige et al, *Understanding Psychosocial Issues Faced by Migrant Workers and their Families* (Sri Lankan Ministry of Foreign Employment Promotion and Welfare, 2012); Francisca Antman, 'The Impact of Migration on Family Left Behind' (Institute for the Study of Labor Discussion Paper No. 6374, March 2012); Oxford Policy Management, 'Impact of Labour Migration on "Children Left Behind" in Tajikistan' (Research Report to UNICEF Tajikistan, November 2011).

34 Bittiandra Chand Somaiah, Brenda S A Yeoh and Silvia Mila Arlini, '*Cukup* for Me to be Successful in this Country: 'Staying' Among Left-Behind Young Women in Indonesia's Migrant-Sending Villages' (2020) 20(2) *Global Networks* 237, 238.

35 Transnational parenting is discussed in Chapter 5 (see Section 5.4). See also CHAMPSEA Philippines, *In the Wake of Parental Migration: Health and Well-being Impacts on Filipino Children* (Scalabrini Migration Center, 2011) 37; Swarna Ukwatta, 'Sri Lankan Female Domestic Workers Overseas: Mothering their Children from a Distance' 27 *Journal of Population Research* 107, 123–5; Halahingano Rohorua et al, 'How do Pacific Island Households and Communities Cope with Seasonally Absent Members?' (2009) 24(3) *Pacific Economic Bulletin* 19, 21.

36 Karlijn Haagsman and Valentina Mazzucato, 'The Well-Being of Stay Behind Family Members in Migrant Households' in Tanja Bastia and Robert Skeldon (eds), *Routledge Handbook of Migration and Development* (Routledge, 2020) 181, 183.

37 The breakdown of child-parent relationships post-reunification is discussed in Chapter 5 (see Section 5.4.4). See also Phillip Kelly, 'Understanding Intergenerational Social Mobility: Filipino Youth in Canada' (IRPP Study No 45, Institute for Research on Public Policy, February 2014); Ofelia Becerril, 'Gendered Policies, Single Mothers and Transnational Motherhood: Mexican Female Migrant Farmworkers in Canada' in Zahra Meghani (ed), *Women Migrant Workers: Ethical, Political and Legal Problems* (Taylor and Francis, 2015) 154; Oishi Nana, 'Family Without Borders? Asian Women in Migration and the Transformation of Family Life' (2008) 14(4) *Asian Journal of Women's Studies* 54.

concrete examples of the types of interferences, and subsequent harms to children, that need to be proactively mitigated in TLM policies going forward.

iii) Recommending measures to reduce the degree of interference by TLM with children's rights

Importantly, it is not argued that TLM should be abolished, nor is this practice promoted or condemned. Such arguments are beyond the scope of this book. Rather, it is accepted that TLM will continue in coming decades. Hence, the purpose is to recommend measures for debate and development in future TLM policies that could reduce interference with children's rights by better supporting the child-parent relationship. To this end, the rights-based framework that has been adopted assists not only in mapping how specific children's rights are interfered with by TLM policies, but also in identifying measures needed to reduce interference with these rights.

While implementation of the CRC is mandatory for States parties, the CRC does not specify how States are to implement their obligations and States retain discretion in this regard.[38] However, they must take 'all appropriate' measures to implement CRC rights,[39] which entails that measures be both effective in implementing the right in question and consistent with all CRC provisions and principles.[40] Central to the argument in this book is the obligation on States under the CRC to provide appropriate assistance to parents to fulfil their recognised role as those adults with the primary responsibility for their children's upbringing and development.[41] This entitles parents to State assistance to meet their parenting responsibilities, if needed, in ways that are effective and consistent with all other CRC provisions. In this sense, the CRC requires States to take measures to strengthen parental capacity to fulfil their broad parenting role.[42] It also reflects the critical role that the CRC assigns States to assist parents to fulfil their child-rearing responsibilities.[43]

Noting that there is considerable variation between TLM policies and the contexts in which they operate, this book identifies a range of practical measures that States could adopt that require varying degrees of resourcing. It focuses particularly on the role of labour-receiving countries given their greater available resources and predominant role in defining TLM policies; and the limited alternatives for

38 Laura Lundy, Ursula Kilkelly and Bronagh Byrne, 'Incorporation of the United Nations Convention on the Rights of the Child in Law: A Comparative Review' (2013) 21(3) *International Journal of Children's Rights* 442, 443, 445.

39 *CRC* art 4.

40 'Appropriate' measures are defined in Chapter 4 (see Section 4.2.1). See also John Tobin, 'Article 4. A State's General Obligation of Implementation' in J Tobin (ed), *The UN Convention on the Rights of the Child: A Commentary* (OUP, 2019) 108, 111.

41 *CRC* arts 18 and 27.

42 *General Comment No 7*, CRC/C/GC/7/Rev.1, para 20.

43 Tobin, above n 19, 59.

many labour-sending countries that have become economically dependent on remittances.[44]

TLM policies that *require* the separation of dependent children and parents are by their very nature incongruous with a child's right to be cared for as far as possible by his or her own parents under Art 7 of the CRC. Presently, given the sheer scale of TLM globally, the number of children growing up in the absence of their parents has been described as a 'deprived generation' in all major labour-sending countries.[45] However, it is argued that there are measures available to States to support the children of migrant workers to maintain strong, continuous and meaningful relationships with their parents in the event of separation; and that under the CRC, States have a duty to adopt such measures to mitigate the potential negative impacts on children arising from the widespread disruption to child-parent relationships caused by TLM.

Using the CRC in the design, development and reform of TLM policies can improve State accountability and assist in the identification of reasonably available measures to reduce potential harms to children. To this end, CRC provisions provide useful criteria for auditing State actions.[46] Each measure identified in this book offers States an opportunity to reduce the degree of interference by TLM policies with CRC rights that protect the child-parent relationship.

Defining the scope

The book considers the impact of TLM on the rights of the *children* of migrant workers residing *in labour-sending countries* whose parents have migrated *overseas* for low-waged employment. To this end, it does not consider other groups of children of migrant workers or rights violations against adult migrant workers themselves. It also utilises the CRC and its overarching principles to inform the conceptual framework that has been developed to analyse the issues raised, the limitations of which are discussed below.

i) Other groups of children of migrant workers

The Office of the United Nations High Commissioner for Human Rights ('OHCHR') has recognised that migration affects children in multiple ways, of which being 'left behind by one or both parents who migrate' is only one.[47]

44 The primary focus on labour-receiving countries is discussed below in relation to the method; and in Chapter 4 (see Section 4.2.4).

45 Nicola Piper, 'Contributions of Migrant Domestic Workers to Sustainable Development' (Policy Paper for the Pre-GFMD VI High-Level Regional Meeting on Migrant Domestic Workers at the Interface of Migration and Development, UN Women, 2013) 29.

46 Michael Freeman, 'The Value and Values of Children's Rights' in A Invernizzi and J Williams (eds), *The Human Rights of Children From Visions to Implementation* (Ashgate, 2011) 21, 27.

47 *Study of the Office of the United Nations High Commissioner for Human Rights ('OHCHR') on Challenges and Best Practices in the Implementation of the International Framework for the Protection of the Rights of the Child in the Context of*

Others include children who migrate with their parents, migrate independently without their parents or are born to migrant workers in labour-receiving countries.[48] While many factors compounding the vulnerability of these children are shared, different issues and obligations arise when children and parents are separated by migration processes and when the child remains in the labour-sending country. Hence, only those issues related to the rights of children of migrant workers residing in labour-sending countries are addressed here. This book does not seek to address issues, whether similar or not, affecting the children of migrant workers who reside with their parents in labour-receiving countries.

Importantly, the rights of children of migrant workers residing with their parents are also protected by the *International Convention on the Protection of the Rights of All Migrant Workers and Members of their Families (1990)* ('*ICRMW*'), which affords these children rights to, for example, birth registration and education.[49] Together with Arts 44 and 45 of the ICRMW – which protect the unity of families and the rights of family members to access education, health and social services – the ICRMW demonstrates an assumption in human rights law that migrant workers and their dependent children are entitled to move and reside together.[50]

Additionally, millions of low-waged adult workers move from rural to urban areas for employment *within* their country of nationality each year. These parents also experience lengthy periods of separation from their children, and their children face many of the challenges addressed in this book. As Castles explains:

> Internal migration attracts less political attention, but its volume in population giants like China, India, Indonesia, Brazil and Nigeria is far greater than that of international movements, and the social and cultural consequences can be equally important.[51]

In China alone, there are an estimated 58 million children being raised predominantly by their grandparents following their parents' migration for work in urban areas.[52] According to the UN Children's Fund (UNICEF), this amounts to

Migration, UN GAOR, 15th sess, Agenda Items 2 and 3, UN Doc A/HRC/15/29 (5 July 2010) [7] ('*OHCHR Study on the Protection of the Rights of the Child in the Context of Migration*').

48 Ibid.

49 *ICRMW* arts 29, 30.

50 *ICRMW* arts 44, 45; CMW Committee, *Working Paper: Terminology in the International Convention on Migrant Workers: A Comparison With Other International and Regional Instruments*, 2nd sess, UN Doc CMW/C/2/L.1 (22 March 2005) [5].

51 Stephen Castles, 'The Forces Driving Global Migration' (2013) 34(2) *Journal of Intercultural Studies* 122, 123.

52 UNICEF, United Nations Global Compact and Save the Children, *Children's Rights and Business Principles* (UN, 2012) 21; Xiang Biao, 'How Far are the Left Behind Left Behind? A Preliminary Study in Rural China' (2007) 13(3) *Population, Place and Space* 179. See also Sonya Michel and Ito Peng, 'Introduction' in Sonya Michel and

30 per cent of all children living in rural China and over 40 million of these children are below 14 years of age.[53] However, while there is certainly an overlap with issues raised by transnational parental migration, matters of internal migration are beyond the scope of this book. This is because transnational TLM impacts the obligations of States differently and depends on international arrangements between States to support the child-parent relationship effectively. This requires the construction of an argument, based largely on the principle of international cooperation in international human rights law, as to why labour-receiving States must share responsibility for supporting the rights of children who are *not* their nationals.

ii) Rights violations against migrant workers

The extensive and well-documented human rights abuses against migrant workers themselves[54] are also not addressed beyond those abuses that directly impact their parenting role and responsibilities. Moreover, this book is limited to the consideration of dedicated low-waged labour migration regimes that States use to move large numbers of migrant workers, which differ from other regular migration streams. Hence, factors that result in many other migrants in labour-receiving countries also being employed in low-waged work with precarious working conditions[55] are beyond the scope of this book. Importantly, the *New York Declaration for Refugees and Migrants* (2016) ('*New York Declaration*') has reiterated that 'large movements' of migrants must be met with 'comprehensive policy support, assistance and protection' that is consistent with the obligations of States under international law.[56] This supports the context within which this book is framed.

Ito Peng (eds), *Gender, Migration, and the Work of Care: A Multi-Scalar Approach to the Pacific Rim*' (Palgrave Macmillan, 2017) 3, 4.

53 UNICEF, United Nations Global Compact and Save the Children, above n 52, 21.

54 See, eg, Human Rights Watch, above n 13; Amnesty International, above n 13; Elizabeth Frantz, 'Jordan's Unfree Workforce: State-Sponsored Bonded Labour in the Arab Region' (2013) 49(8) *Journal of Development Studies* 1072; Amrita Pande, '"The Paper that You Have in Your Hand is My Freedom": Migrant Domestic Work and the Sponsorship (Kafala) System in Lebanon' (2013) 47(2) *International Migration Review* 414.

55 This includes factors such as limited local language abilities, lack of recognition of qualifications and fear of ramifications for one's immigration status. See, eg, Laurie Berg, *Migrant Rights at Work: Law's Precariousness at the Intersection of Immigration and Labour* (Routledge, 2016) 63–106.

56 *New York Declaration*, UN Doc A/RES/71/1, para 11. The Declaration states that, '"Large movements" may be understood to reflect a number of considerations, including: the number of people arriving, the economic, social and geographical context, the capacity of a receiving State to respond and the impact of a movement that is sudden or prolonged. The term does not, for example, cover regular flows of migrants from one country to another. "Large movements" may involve mixed flows of people, whether refugees or migrants, who move for different reasons but who may use similar routes'. See *New York Declaration*, UN Doc A/RES/71/1, para 6.

iii) How the CRC has been utilised

The CRC has been utilised in this book as an established set of rights, norms and principles recognised and committed to by governments. However, it is recognised that while the CRC provides a comprehensive framework for the protection of children's rights, it is frequently coupled with a lack of political commitment needed for its effective implementation.[57] This is compounded for children affected by migration, who enjoy the same fundamental rights as citizen children but remain largely invisible in international law. As Bhaba explains, this is largely due to:

> two enduring defects in the international migration system as it impinges on children: the absence of supervisory jurisdiction regulating state compliance with the plethora of international norms protecting children in the migration context, and the continuing political invisibility of children within their own states.[58]

Hence, it is understood that the positioning of the State as the primary guarantor of the rights embodied in the CRC gives rise to a tension between State obligations to support the universality of child rights and the CRC's overarching principles – including of the best interests of the child and non-discrimination – and a State's sovereign interests towards its citizens.[59] It is also recognised that, as Thronsen argues, national immigration laws systemically deny children agency by narrowly defining them as passive objects whose rights and interests are controlled by their relationship with their parents.[60] This, again, gives rise to a significant gap between the expressed commitment of States to children's rights and agency under the CRC and the challenges children face in enjoying their 'universal' rights in the context of migration.[61]

However, it must be noted that this book is not intended to provide a critical assessment of the CRC and its development. Rather, the intended purpose is to use the CRC as a framework that has been accepted and endorsed by governments and policymakers – and one that is currently utilised and applied in international law and governance – to structure an argument as to why children's rights should be considered in policymaking in relation to labour migration. In this sense, the CRC provides an invaluable tool for elevating children's interests in an area in

57 Jacqueline Bhabha, '"More Than Their Share of Sorrows": International Migration Law and the Rights of Children' (2003) 22(2) *Saint Louis University Public Law Review* 253, 258.

58 Ibid 275.

59 Boyden and Hart (2007) cited in Julia O'Connell Davidson, 'Moving Children? Child Trafficking, Child Migration, and Child Rights' (2011) 31(3) *Critical Social Policy* 454, 471.

60 David B Thronson, 'You Can't Get Here from Here: Toward More Child-Centered Immigration Law' (2006) 14(1) *Virginia Journal of Social Policy and the Law* 58, 67–69.

61 O'Connell Davidson, above n 59, 455.

which they have been rendered invisible, offering a framework for mitigating the potential harms or unintended consequences of TLM. A critical analysis of the CRC and its limitations embodies a different purpose and is beyond the scope of this book.

Explaining the method

The issues raised in this book emerge at the intersection of different (often competing) policy agendas. These include human rights law, child-development psychology, migration and citizenship policies, labour rights and the international development agenda. This generates a degree of complexity that is best addressed through an interdisciplinary research approach, which permits consideration of multiple factors that contribute to both the problems and solutions being considered. Hence, the book is based on socio-legal research,[62] integrating a legal framework with qualitative social science research methodologies to understand the issues being examined in an *applied* manner.

i) A note on socio-legal research

The benefit of a socio-legal approach is its capacity to utilise multiple research methods to better understand the complexities of TLM in practice. This is because particular social science methodologies lend themselves to understanding issues in an in-depth, context-specific and nuanced way. These include key informant interviews and case studies, both of which allow policy issues to be considered in real-world settings. This inevitably enhances the value of subsequent policy recommendations, which are strengthened by the legal analysis of relevant human rights law within which they are framed. As such, a socio-legal approach combines methodologies from the social sciences with an understanding of the significant impact that international law has on national policy agendas,[63] making it fitting for law reform research that combines legal arguments with social science evidence to strengthen recommendations for policy reform.[64]

The rights-based normative and conceptual framework, outlined in Chapter 2, provides the structure for understanding how the data collected through social science methodologies relates to the children's rights in question. As the primary legal instrument informing this book, the doctrinal legal analysis in this book is largely restricted to a consideration of the relevant principles, rights and

62 A socio-legal approach to research involves blending research methods and evidence from different disciplines into legal reasoning to enhance recommended reforms. See, Terry Hutchinson, 'The Doctrinal Method: Incorporating Interdisciplinary Methods in Reforming the Law' (2015) 3 *Erasmus Law Review* 130, 130.

63 Terry Hutchinson, 'Developing Legal Research Skills: Expanding the Paradigm' (2008) 32 *Melbourne University Law Review* 1065, 1084.

64 H W Arthurs, 'Law and Learning: Report to the Social Sciences and Humanities Research Council of Canada by the Consultative Group on Research and Education in Law' (Social Sciences and Humanities Research Council of Canada, 1983).

obligations under the CRC.[65] These are, however, considered in light of other legal instruments that provide context for the interpretation of the specific CRC rights being examined[66] and the legal obligations under international law of both labour-sending and labour-receiving States.

There exists a wealth of other legal sources that support a legal presumption in favour of preserving the child-parent relationship, including in domestic family law doctrines. However, given limits in scope, it was only practical to address these doctrines briefly and as part of the context for interpreting the CRC rights being considered. The doctrinal analysis of specific CRC rights provides a solid legal foundation for the normative framework that is used to inform and structure this book. In contrast, the qualitative research component explores the more complex, nuanced and variable policy issues arising from TLM in practice. Being sensitive to the broader context in which these CRC rights are being interpreted is necessary to conceive of how these rights can realistically be implemented in light of existing socio-political realities and constraints.[67]

ii) Qualitative research component

Qualitative research offers an invaluable methodology for examining the complex and intersecting issues that arise in the context of TLM and practical challenges concerning the implementation of the CRC. This is important if a full picture of the potential impacts of TLM on children's rights and the child-parent relationship is to be generated. The spectrum of issues that need to be considered for this full picture to emerge not only cross disciplines, but also vary between countries and forms of TLM. Qualitative methods are suited to acquiring a nuanced understanding of issues in complex policy settings like TLM, particularly as they value the collection, integration and presentation of data from a variety of sources.[68]

To this end, the qualitative research in this book is based on evidence compiled from three data sources: i) key informant interviews; ii) secondary social science literature; and iii) primary policy documents (national, regional and international). It was considered vital to interview key informants with significant experience across the range of organisational sectors engaged with TLM; and from the countries/regions being considered. Hence, a purposive sampling technique was used to source 20 experts from relevant organisational sectors and countries/

65 Doctrinal research involves first identifying the primary legal sources after which their text is interpreted and analysed. See, Terry Hutchinson and Nigel Duncan, 'Defining and Describing What We Do: Doctrinal Legal Research' (2012) 17(1) *Deakin Law Review* 83, 110.

66 This approach ensures coherence with the broader international law system. See, John Tobin, 'Seeking to Persuade: A Constructive Approach to Human Rights Treaty Interpretation' (2018) 23 *Harvard Human Rights Journal* 201, 234–7.

67 Ibid 240–8.

68 Robert K Yin, Qualitative Research from Start to Finish (The Guilford Press, 2nd ed, 2016), 11.

regions, each with deep knowledge of their area of expertise and an established reputation in her or his field. A de-identified table of key informants is provided at Appendix II.

The three organisational sectors represented by key informants comprised the government sector (relevant federal and provincial departments), from which there were six key informants; research and policy institutes engaged in research on TLM, from which there were seven key informants; and peak non-government and multilateral organisations providing specialist services to, or advice to governments on, migrant workers and their families, from which there were seven key informants. This spread of key informants allowed for the identification of policy challenges facing governments, the incorporation of emerging knowledge on the effects of TLM and an understanding of how TLM policies are being actualised at the grassroots level.

It is recognised that the sample size does not permit assertions of representativeness or statistical significance to be made based on the interview data, which is not attempted. Rather, the purpose of the key informant interviews is to draw on the knowledge of people with significant experience in and understanding of TLM policies in practice, in order to understand the implications of these policies in applied settings. Data from these interviews was used to complement and illustrate issues emerging in social science studies and across a range of policy instruments relating to TLM.

Secondary social science literature provided evidence of the potential psychosocial impacts of parental migration on children in labour-sending countries, with significant fieldwork having already been conducted by social science researchers in the context of TLM.[69] Social science studies drawn on throughout the book also provided invaluable first-hand accounts from children and parents, and helped to situate this book within existing scholarship on both TLM regimes and child-parent separation.

Primary policy documents incorporated in the data include national, regional and global policy statements and instruments. These include, for example, domestic laws and policies in which governments reiterate commitments to human rights norms and the non-separation of children and parents; national labour migration policies in major labour-sending countries; bilateral agreements between labour-receiving and labour-sending countries; regional policies and declarations; and global policy agendas such as the New York Declaration, the recently adopted *Global Compact for Safe, Orderly and Regular Migration* ('*Global Compact for Migration*')[70] and the UN's 2030 Sustainable Development Agenda.[71] These

69 Examples of studies from labour-sending countries are provided in Chapter 4 (see Section 4.3).

70 *Global Compact for Safe, Orderly and Regular Migration*, GA Res 73/195, UN GAOR, 73rd sess, Agenda Items 14 and 119, UN Doc A/RES/73/195 (11 January 2019) ('*Global Compact for Migration*').

71 *Transforming Our World: The 2030 Agenda for Sustainable Development*, GA Res 70/1, UN GAOR, 70th sess, Agenda Items 15 and 116, UN Doc A/RES/70/1 (21 October 2015) ('*Sustainable Development Agenda*').

documents illustrate public commitments to the human rights norms and child development principles reflected in the conceptual framework and establish a general acceptance by governments of the value of these principles.

An examination of primary policy documents enabled comparisons between government commitments under different policy agendas and an analysis of how these may be inconsistent both with each other and with State obligations under the CRC. It also served to situate this book within very *public* concerns being raised at all levels about the potential social impacts of current TLM practices, including by governments themselves. This is important because of the role that States themselves are assigned in human rights law to 'limit their own actions and policies in accordance with the human rights norms that they recognize and respect'.[72]

iii) Case study approach

The value of utilising case studies in this research is their capacity to focus on context, allowing issues to be examined in 'relation to environment'.[73] Canada was selected as the primary case study for this research, largely because it is a labour-receiving country that is frequently identified as having best practice immigration models[74] and a strong commitment to human rights norms.[75] However, because TLM regimes vary considerably in their design and the political contexts within which they operate, comparative labour-receiving countries were also examined to address aspects of TLM policies that are not present in the Canadian context. These include Australia, which has assigned a dual international development goal to its TLM policies; and TLM regimes within Asia and between Asia and the Gulf States, which present different human rights challenges due to weaker protections of the rights of migrant workers. These contexts are discussed briefly in the following chapter.

Suffice to say that while there is considerable variation between the structure of these TLM regimes and the contexts in which they operate, shared features include: the targeting of workers of prime child-rearing age who are foreseeably

72 Joseph Carens, *The Ethics of Immigration* (Oxford University Press, 2013) 7.

73 Flyvbjerg Bent, 'Chapter 17: Case Study' in Norman K Denzin and Yvonna S Lincoln (eds), *The Sage Handbook of Qualitative Research* (Sage, 4th Edition, 2011) 301, 301.

74 See, eg, Jenna Hennebry and Kerry Preibisch, 'A Model for Managed Migration? Re-Examining Best Practices in Canada's Seasonal Agricultural Worker Program' (2012) 50(1) *International Migration* 49, 55–56; Richard Curtain et al, *Pacific Possible: Labour Mobility: The Ten Billion Dollar Prize* (Pacific Possible Series, World Bank, July 2016) 23–4; The World Bank, *Expanding Employment Pathways for Pacific Islanders in the Australian and New Zealand Aged Care Sectors* (The World Bank Group, 2017) 71.

75 *Canada Act 1982* (UK) c 11, sch B pt I ('*Canadian Charter of Rights and Freedoms*'); *Canadian Human Rights Act*, RSC 1985, c H-6; Hannah Dawson, 'The Role of Canada in the International Promotion of Human Rights', *McGill Blogs* (6 March 2016); Rhoda E Howard-Hassmann, *Compassionate Canadians: Civic Leaders Discuss Human Rights* (University of Toronto Press, 2003).

parents of dependent children; explicit or implicit policy features that generate significant periods of child-parent separation; the absence of processes for assessing the impact of TLM policies on children's rights; and a failure on the part of labour-receiving States to share responsibility for supporting transnational child-parent relationships that are created by their policies.

Outlining the structure

i) Part A

Part A of this book comprises Chapters 1–3, which provide a brief overview of the contextual landscape of TLM and present both the normative and conceptual framework and the general legal principles that have informed this research.

Chapter 1 provides an overview of the contemporary context of TLM and explains the comparative regional and national TLM contexts that are of focus in the book – Canada, Australia and the Asia-Pacific/Gulf regions. It highlights critical perspectives on TLM that account for how a landscape that ignores the centrality of the child-parent relationship to children's well-being has been able to emerge. These include a focus in the dominant discourse on the notion of remittance-based development, as well as dual efforts by States to encourage the transnational movement of migrant workers while relying on their sovereignty to restrict both the mobility of these workers (and their families) and their rights as non-nationals. It highlights particular challenges emerging from the gendered aspects of TLM associated with the increased feminisation of this form of migration.

The rights-based normative and conceptual framework is presented in Chapter 2. This framework is used for organising the research findings in Part B and understanding the interrelationship between the CRC rights that protect the child-parent relationship that are being analysed. This chapter provides the foundation for understanding *why* these rights are important to children's development and well-being; and explains the interdependence of these specific rights. That is, it discusses how interference with one of the rights in the conceptual framework will inevitably interfere with the other interconnected rights; just as improved support for one right will inevitably enhance the capacity of children to realise the others.

Chapter 3 provides an overview of relevant general legal principles that are drawn on throughout the book to inform the analysis of the specific rights pertaining to the child-parent relationship identified in the normative and conceptual framework. These include the CRC's overarching principles, which the CRC and CMW Committees have clearly stated must guide all State actions in the context of children affected by migration.[76] These principles are that the best interests of the child must be a primary consideration in *all* matters affecting children;[77]

76 *Joint General Comment on Children in the Context of International Migration*, UN Doc CMW/C/GC/3-CRC/C/GC/22, para 19.

77 *CRC* art 3.

children must not be arbitrarily discriminated against;[78] States must recognise every child's right to life, survival and development;[79] and children have a right to be heard in all matters affecting them in a manner appropriate to their age and maturity.[80] Chapter 3 also outlines the principles of international cooperation and the fundamental role of the family in human rights law as they apply in the context of children and migration.

ii) Part B

Part B engages in an analysis of how TLM impacts each of the rights identified in the normative and conceptual framework. The analysis draws on findings from three sources of qualitative data: key informant interviews, secondary social science studies and primary policy documents. Together, the chapters comprising Part B demonstrate the interferences with the child-parent relationship that are currently generated by TLM policies and identify measures that could reduce the degree of these interferences.

Chapter 4 argues that children's right to a standard of living necessary for their *overall* development – and parents' entitlement to be assisted by States if needed to provide this standard of living – under Art 27 of the CRC are interfered with by TLM policies that encourage parents to migrate to provide only for their children's *financial* needs. It argues that this inappropriately shifts the entire burden of providing for children's material needs to parents who have limited alternatives to migration; and ignores the potential impact of prolonged parental absence on children's psychosocial development and well-being.

Chapter 5 highlights how *unnecessarily* restrictive features of TLM policies create conditions that interfere with the capacity of children and parents to maintain a transnational relationship. It argues that this limits children's right under Art 10(2) to maintain direct and regular contact and personal relations with their parents if separated transnationally, *as well as* the enjoyment of their right under Art 5 to receive direction and guidance from their parents. It reveals the ease by which these interferences could be reduced through reasonable measures such as creating opportunities for more frequent return home visits for migrant workers; and simple, affordable and practical measures to support regular and frequent communication between migrant workers and their children. It argues that if parents are not supported to continue key elements of their parenting role during the period of separation, including providing direction and guidance to their children, then the child-parent relationship can break down even upon reunification.

Chapter 6 argues that the structural features of TLM policies that unnecessarily and unreasonably prolong the period of child-parent separation create arbitrary interferences with children's right to have their family life protected under Art 16. These features include the deliberate encouragement of the remigration of

78 *CRC* art 2.
79 *CRC* art 6.
80 *CRC* art 12.

workers over years and even decades; and restrictive visa regimes that prevent the free movement of workers. It highlights that even if parents 'choose' to migrate for low-waged employment, they frequently do not anticipate the length of separation from their children, which is often protracted by factors outside their control such as debt and restrictive visa conditions. This chapter identifies measures that can help reduce and manage periods of child-parent separation, drawing on learnings from other fields that regularly manage the separation of children and parents such as family law and military deployment. It also highlights how the failure by States to justify the differential treatment of the children of *low-waged* temporary migrants – with other groups of temporary migrants such as skilled workers and international students being entitled to family accompaniment – amounts to discrimination against these children.

While measures identified in Chapters 4, 5 and 6 can assist in mitigating the negative impacts of TLM on children's relationships with their parents, Chapter 7 argues that children's right to be cared for by their own parents under Art 7 is fundamentally undermined by TLM policies that separate children and parents. Similarly, so is the interconnected right of their parents to be supported by States to fulfil their role as their children's primary caregivers under Art 18. This chapter grounds the recommended measures identified throughout the book in the existing value of the child-parent relationship in domestic settings for children who reside in labour-receiving countries. This includes understanding about the benefits of strong child-parent relationships in fields such as family law and child development. It argues that the importance of the child-parent relationship to children's development and well-being is universal and protected for *all* children no matter where they reside.

Chapter 7 also argues that encouraging parental migration as an international development strategy presents significant challenges to the notion that strong and stable families are essential to both children's development and achieving sustainable development outcomes, which States have yet to reconcile. It concludes that without a more comprehensive measurement of social impacts on children and familial relationships, States cannot make informed decisions about how to promote TLM without significantly interfering with children's rights.

Together, the chapters in Part B shine light on a particular aspect of the 'profound social implications' associated with the movement of human beings across borders as labour.[81] This aspect is the undermining by TLM policies of a parent's role in raising their children, which is currently masked by what the ILO has described as 'misperceptions about the relationship between migration, jobs and development'.[82]

81 Ryszard Cholewinski, 'Migration for Employment' in Sir Richard Plender (ed), *Issues in International Migration Law* (Brill Nijhoff, 2015) 27, 28.

82 International Labour Organization (ILO) global estimates from 2013 cited in ILO, *Report IV: Addressing Governance Challenges in a Changing Labour Migration Landscape*, International Labour Conference, 106th sess, 2017 [2].

The CRC and CMW Committees have stressed the potential for the vulnerability of the children who are the focus of this book to be compounded by their parents' migration, highlighting that:

> In the context of international migration, children may be in a situation of double vulnerability as children and as children affected by migration who … remain in their country of origin while one or both parents have migrated to another country.[83]

While TLM is considered a form of voluntary migration on the part of parents,[84] parental migration is often driven by poverty, which States have a broader duty to work together to address. This is recognised in the Sustainable Development Agenda as well as the emerging framework for the global governance of migration that features the New York Declaration and the Global Compact for Migration.[85] However, given that the end of poverty is not near, the factors driving TLM will continue and migrating for work will remain the only option for many people to improve life chances for themselves, their families and, most importantly, their children.[86] This means that parents will continue to migrate, generally not out of genuine choice but out of necessity for the survival and sustenance of their families and children.[87]

While this continues to leave parents in a position where they must fracture their physical relationships with their children in order to provide for them, there are numerous measures that can be put in place to reduce the degree of disruption to the child-parent relationship caused by TLM. These measures are needed irrespective of whether one believes that it is a parent's 'choice' to migrate in the face of poverty or limited alternatives under conditions that restrict their capacity to continue fulfilling their parenting role in their children's lives. At present, restrictive conditions placed on low-waged migrant workers both directly and indirectly limit rights that are held by their children *in their own right*.

Given that labour-receiving States are significantly wealthier than labour-sending countries and benefit greatly from the cheap labour that they gain through TLM, they must not shy away from the sharing of responsibility for reducing harm

83 *Joint General Comment on Children in the Context of International Migration*, UN Doc CMW/C/GC/3-CRC/C/GC/22, para 3.

84 Parental 'choice' to migrate for TLM is discussed in Chapter 4 (see Section 4.2.2), Chapter 5 (see Section 5.2.2) and Chapter 6 (see Section 6.3.4).

85 *New York Declaration*, UN Doc A/RES/71/1; *Global Compact for Migration*, UN Doc A/RES/73/195; *Sustainable Development Agenda*, UN Doc A/RES/70/1. The significance of these legally non-binding instruments is discussed in Chapter 7 (see Section 7.3.4).

86 UN Development Programme (UNDP), *Human Development Report 2009: Overcoming Barriers – Human Mobility and Development* (UNDP, 2009) 1.

87 Kneebone, above n 12, 439. See also Eve Lester, 'Socioeconomic rights, human security and survival migrants: Whose rights? Whose security?' in Alice Edwards and Carla Ferstman (eds), *Human Security and Non-Citizens: Law, Policy and International Affairs* (Cambridge University Press, 2010) 314.

to children caused by features of TLM policies that they institute. Rather, States should work towards improving coherence between migration policies and procedures that govern migrant workers and State obligations to support the rights of children affected by migration.[88] Significant improvements can be achieved even with labour-receiving countries maintaining their sovereign interests in immigration control.[89] Importantly, labour-receiving countries themselves recognise and espouse the absolute importance of the child-parent relationship to children's development and well-being for their own citizen children. The importance of this relationship does not disappear simply because a parent has no other option for earning a viable living to support their family other than to migrate for significant periods of time.

Rather, TLM policies give rise to a spectrum of possible negative consequences for children in labour-sending countries that exacerbate their vulnerability by undermining child-parent relationships and disrupting children's family life. These consequences – unintended or not – have yet to be recognised or addressed by those States responsible for the design of these migration policies. The emerging framework for the global governance of migration identifies the review of migration policies and practices – using approaches that are human-rights based and child-sensitive – as instrumental to ensuring that States understand the 'possible unintended negative consequences'[90] of their migration policies, and 'do not create, exacerbate or unintentionally increase vulnerabilities'.[91] This offers an invaluable opportunity to incorporate the concerns raised here into the review and future development of TLM policies that can promote, rather than hinder, a child's continued relationship with his or her parents as protected under human rights law.

88 Crock and Benson, above n 12, 9.
89 Ibid.
90 *New York Declaration*, UN Doc A/RES/71/1, para 45.
91 *Global Compact for Migration*, UN Doc A/RES/73/195, [23.a].

Part A

1 Understanding the landscape

TLM in context

1.1 Introduction

While the movement of people for low-waged labour is not new and bears significant resemblance to indentured labour of the colonial past,[1] the current scale of TLM – driven by deepening economic inequality and an increasing *demand* for low-waged workers[2] – is unprecedented. There are now an estimated 150 million migrant workers worldwide[3] and this number is only expected to increase with ageing populations and purported labour shortages in labour-receiving countries.[4]

1 Joanna Howe and Rosemary Owens, 'Temporary Labour Migration in the Global Era: The Regulatory Challenges' in Joanna Howe and Rosemary Owens (eds), *Temporary Labour Migration in the Global Era* (Hart Publishing, 2016) 3, 3; See also John Connell, 'From Blackbirds to Guestworkers in the South Pacific: Plus ça Change …?'(2010) 20 *Economic and Labour Relations Review* 111; Laurie Berg, *Migrant Rights at Work: Law's Precariousness at the Intersection of Immigration and Labour* (Routledge, 2016) 53; Mary E Crock, 'Contract or Compact: Skilled Migration and the Dictates of Politics and Ideology' (2001) (16) *Georgetown Immigration Law Journal* 133, 137.

2 Michael J Piore, 'Comment' (1980) 33(3) *Industrial and Labor Relations Review* 312.

3 International Labour Organization (ILO) global estimates from 2013 cited in ILO, *Report IV: Addressing Governance Challenges in a Changing Labour Migration Landscape*, International Labour Conference, 106th sess, 2017 [13]. See also OECD, *International Migration Outlook 2019* (OECD, 2019). This report demonstrates, for example, the narrowing of pathways to permanency in the OECD, with 583 000 labour migrants entering OECD countries in 2017 on permanent visas while 4.9 million entered through temporary channels, with the latter group growing almost twice as fast year-on-year.

4 See, eg, Patrick A Taran, 'Clashing Worlds: Imperative for a Rights-Based Approach to Labour Migration in the Age of Globalization' in Vincent Chetail (ed), *Globalization, Migration and Human Rights: International Law Under Review* (Bruylant, 2007) vol 2, 405–7; Ryszard Cholewinski, 'Migration for Employment' in Sir Richard Plender (ed), *Issues in International Migration Law* (Brill Nijhoff, 2015) 27; International Organization for Migration (IOM), *World Migration 2008: Managing Labour Mobility in the Evolving Economy* (IOM, 2008) 36–8; UN Population Fund, *State of World Population 2006: A Passage to Hope: Women and International Migration* (UNFPA, 2006) 7; Zahra Meghani, 'Women on the Move' in Zahra Meghani (ed), *Women Migrant Workers: Ethical, Political and Legal Problems* (Taylor and

This means that in coming decades, we are likely to see *increasing* numbers of children whose parents migrate without them for low-waged employment under State-designed TLM policies. While it is recognised that parental migration is influenced by factors at multiple scales – familial, community, national, regional and global[5] – each of these is impacted to some degree by State policies that either constrain or enable parents' capacity to continue fulfilling their parental role in the context of TLM. This chapter provides a brief overview of some of the key forces at play in contemporary TLM and situates the regional and national TLM contexts of focus in this book – Canada, Australia and the Asia-Pacific/Gulf regions.

It is recognised that TLM operates in complex and context-specific policy environments in which multiple (often competing) policy agendas intersect. These include, for example, the sovereignty of States to control immigration, labour regulation, business interests tied to the free movement of capital, international development agendas and gender policies, in addition to human rights law. This book focuses on *one* aspect of TLM – how TLM policies impact children's rights that protect the child-parent relationship – which has been significantly understudied in relation to other disciplinary perspectives. This is in part because of the overwhelming focus by States on immigration restriction, which frequently reduces any focus on human rights.[6] It has also been ignored because TLM has been deliberately framed in the dominant discourse as being beneficial to people (including children) in labour-sending countries, based on the contested notion of remittance-based development,[7] which is understood by economic measures alone.[8] These issues, together with the impact of the increased feminisation of TLM, are discussed briefly below to provide an understanding of how a landscape that ignores the centrality of the child-parent relationship to children's well-being has been able to emerge in the context of TLM.

Francis, 2015) 5; *Report of the Special Rapporteur on the Human Rights of Migrants, François Crépeau: Banking on Mobility Over a Generation: Follow-up to the Regional Study on the Management of the External Borders of the European Union and its Impact on the Human Rights of Migrants*, UN GAOR, 29th sess, Agenda Item 3, UN Doc A/HRC/29/36 (8 May 2015) [77]–[78].

5 See Sonya Michel and Ito Peng, 'Introduction' in Sonya Michel and Ito Peng (eds), *Gender, Migration, and the Work of Care: A Multi-Scalar Approach to the Pacific Rim*' (Palgrave Macmillan, 2017) 3.

6 Mary Crock and Lenni B Benson, 'Central Issues in the Protection of Child Migrants' in Mary Crock and Lenni Benson (eds), *Protecting Migrant Children: In Search of Best Practice* (Elgar, 2018) 1, 19.

7 'Remittance-based development' is discussed in Chapter 4 (see Section 4.2.2).

8 See Rosalia Cortes, 'Remittances and Children's Rights: An Overview of Academic and Policy Literature' (Division of Policy and Practice Working Paper, UNICEF, January 2007); Robert E B Lucas, 'Migration and Economic Development: An Introduction and Synopsis' in Robert E B Lucas (ed), *International Handbook on Migration and Development* (Edward Elgar Publishing, 2014) 1; *Resolution on International Migration and Development*, GA Res 71/237, UN GAOR, 71st sess, Agenda Item 21(b), UN Doc A/RES/71/237 (23 January 2017) ('*Resolution on International Migration and Development*').

1.2 Remittances and development

The role of remittances in improving certain outcomes for children (and achieving development outcomes in labour-sending countries) is a matter of controversy that draws significantly divergent views.[9] To date, there are mixed findings about whether remittances improve material, education and health outcomes for children[10] or generate sustainable development outcomes for communities.[11] As Withers contends:

> The 'wins' accruing to migrant-receiving economies are clear: host countries can leverage temporary labour migration schemes to tap into an eminently exploitable global reserve army of labour and care. The returns to migrant families and their countries of origin, meanwhile, are far more equivocal.[12]

Arguments in favour of so-called 'triple-win' TLM schemes are based on the notion that remittances generate personal income for migrant workers and their families that aggregate as a major source of foreign capital for labour-sending countries, which assumes that remittances will alleviate poverty, facilitate entrepreneurship through personal savings and enhance a country's creditworthiness at the macroeconomic level.[13] However, as researchers have highlighted, empirical findings – such as those drawn on in Part B – reflect a different reality, one in which outcomes for migrants and labour-sending countries generated by remittances and TLM are largely 'determined by the interplay of individual circumstances and prevailing structural constraints to development'.[14]

The studies drawn on in Part B support the notion that without addressing the structural drivers of migration, remittances alone are unlikely to generate sustainable development in labour-source countries.[15] This is because development depends predominantly on structural reforms undertaken by States rather than reliance on individuals and markets to generate social, political and economic change in a country.[16] This is evidenced by the fact that major labour-sending countries that have been exporting low-waged labour for decades,

9 This is discussed in Chapter 4 (see Section 4.2.5) and Chapter 7 (see Section 7.3). See also Lucas, above n 8, 1; Hein de Haas, 'The Migration and Development Pendulum: A Critical View on Research and Policy' (2012) 50(3) *International Migration* 8; Matt Withers, *Sri Lanka's Remittance Economy: A Multiscalar Analysis of Migration-Underdevelopment* (Routledge, 2019).

10 These mixed findings in relation to children's material, education and health outcomes are discussed in Chapter 4 (see Section 4.2.5).

11 The relationship between TLM and sustainable development outcomes for communities is discussed in Chapter 7 (see Section 7.3.3).

12 Matt Withers, 'Temporary Labour Migration and Underdevelopment in Sri Lanka: The Limits of Remittance Capital' (2019) 8(3) *Migration and Development* 418, 420.

13 World Bank (2006), cited in Withers, above n 12, 20.

14 Withers, above n 12, 421.

15 de Haas, above n 9, 19–20.

16 Ibid.

such as Sri Lanka and the Philippines, have not experienced leaps in their development.[17]

Scholars such as de Haas have urged researchers to adopt a broader framework for understanding the relationship between migration and development that considers social and political aspects together with the economic.[18] This encapsulates a spectrum of development outcomes that ranges from traditional economic measures through to political participation and more subjective measures that include happiness and well-being.[19] This approach is reflective of how children's development needs are conceived in the CRC,[20] which protects a parent's broad role in their children's upbringing and development, in which providing for their children's economic needs is only *one* aspect.[21]

At present, poverty and limited viable employment options in labour-sending countries are creating conditions where parents often have to 'choose' between migrating to provide for their children's economic needs and being physically present to raise their children.[22] The Committee on the Rights of the Child ('CRC Committee') has recognised that the situation of parents being 'forced to work far away from their families' as a result of economic pressures has an 'impact on parents' capacities to fulfil their responsibilities towards children'.[23] This is because many parental responsibilities, including those relating to children's psychosocial development and primary care, require parents and children to be together particularly (but not only) when children are young.[24] This, once again, highlights the limits of understanding human development and the child-parent relationship purely from an economic perspective, as has been done to date in the context of TLM.

17 See, eg, Withers, above n 9; Waoma G Nwaogu and Michael J Ryan, 'FDI, Foreign Aid, Remittance and Economic Growth in Developing Countries' (2015) 19(2) *Review of Development Economics*, 19(1) (2015) 100; Rebecca J Calzado, Department of Labor and Employment Philippines, 'Labour Migration and Development Goals: The Philippine Experience' (Paper presented at International Dialogue on Migration, Geneva, 8 October 2007) 5–6; Jeffrey H Cohen, 'Remittance Outcomes and Migration: Theoretical Contests, Real Opportunities' [2005] (Spring) *Studies in Comparative International Development* 88, 93–9; Asia Pacific Mission for Migrants, *Labour Export Program and Further Commodification of Migrants as Prescriptions for Development* (19 September 2014) <http://aprnet.org/?p=196>.

18 Hein de Haas, 'Migration and Development: A Theoretical Perspective' (2010) 44 (1) *International Migration Review* 227.

19 Lisa Andersson and Melissa Siegel, 'Empirical Assessments of the Development Impacts of Migration' (MIGNEX Background Paper, Peace Research Institute Oslo, 2019) 19–21.

20 See Chapter 4 on art 27 of the CRC as it relates to children's physical, mental, spiritual, moral and social development.

21 *CRC* arts 27, 18, 5.

22 See Chapter 4 (Section 4.2) and Chapter 6 (Section 6.3.4).

23 CRC Committee, *General Comment No 7: Implementing Child Rights in Early Childhood*, 40th sess, UN Doc CRC/C/GC/7/Rev.1 (20 September 2006) para 19 ('*General Comment No 7*').

24 The significance of a child's age is discussed in Chapter 4 (see Section 4.4).

However, importantly, this book argues that children's rights affected by TLM must be addressed by States *irrespective* of whether policymakers believe that TLM serves the economic and development interests of migrant workers, their families and labour-sending countries. This is because the CRC requires policymakers to consider children's rights and best interests in *all* processes and decision-making that affects them[25] and to give due consideration to children's views in matters that concern them.[26]

Studies from the social sciences have reiterated the importance of understanding how young people view the costs and benefits of parental migration, highlighting that some who have experienced this separation view 'migration-as-development' as an 'incoherent strategy that works against rather than for the family'.[27] In a recent study of children of Indonesian migrant workers who have transitioned into adulthood, participants expressed that their families had had 'enough' of migration, with this notion used:

> (F)irst, as an affective plea for rewarding work that is consistent with proximate family life; second, as a careful attempt to redress a history of absent family life; and third, as a combined (familial and individual) resistance to risqué developmentalist desires to uplift the family economically through the quick-fix of migration.[28]

Such findings are complemented by the *World Happiness Report*, which reiterates that for the families of migrants left behind in countries of origin, 'there is a rise in negative affect (sadness, worry, anger), especially if the migrant is abroad on temporary work'.[29] The report highlights that while family members may view their quality of life more positively than those families without a household member living abroad, 'they do not benefit from migration in terms of emotional well-being'.[30] These mixed outcomes are attributed to the likelihood of families assessing their quality of life based on economic gains rather than their own affective experiences.[31] Regarding the latter, the report holds that family members often suffer emotionally from the separation for reasons including not being able to share the responsibility of nurturing children.[32]

25 *CRC* art 3. See also Mary Crock and Hannah Martin, 'First Things First: International Law and the Protection of Migrant Children' in Mary Crock and Lenni Benson (eds), *Protecting Migrant Children: In Search of Best Practice* (Elgar, 2018) 75, 89.
26 *CRC* art 12. The CRC's general principles, including under art 3 and art 12, are discussed in Chapter 3 (see Section 3.2).
27 Bittiandra Chand Somaiah, Brenda S A Yeoh and Silvia Mila Arlini, '*Cukup* for Me to be Successful in this Country: "Staying" Among Left-Behind Young Women in Indonesia's Migrant-Sending Villages' (2020) 20(2) *Global Networks* 237, 242.
28 Ibid.
29 John F Helliwell, Richard Layard and Jeffrey D Sachs (eds), *World Happiness Report 2018* (Sustainable Development Solutions Network, 2018) 8.
30 Ibid 58.
31 Ibid 56–7.
32 Ibid.

1.3 Transnationalism and State sovereignty

Transnational movement in the era of globalisation has been characterised by the mass movement of workers across borders with the simultaneous mass restriction of rights afforded to migrant workers and their families.[33] Such 'large-scale and unrelenting cross-border migrations' have forced questions as to how these movements impact children into migration policy discourse and debates.[34] At present, TLM policies undermine, rather than support, the child-parent relationship through structural features that create unnecessarily protracted periods of parental absence in children's lives. While some families are able to mitigate the potential harms to children that arise from policies that require children and parents to reside in different countries, it is currently with little to no support from those States responsible for these policies. Moreover, many families in the context of low-waged TLM do not have sufficient resources to adopt strategies to preserve strong child-parent relationships transnationally. This is compounded when the capacity of migrant workers to exercise their own agency is constrained by features beyond their control, such immigration restrictions.[35]

Hence, it is vital that, when considering low-waged TLM, the agency of migrants is not overstated[36] and due consideration is given to the 'protracted precarity' for migrant workers that is created by States through their management of TLM across the migration cycle.[37] That is to say that notions of migrant agency in the context of transnational activities cannot ignore the rigid constraints placed on low-waged migrants by States.[38] These constraints continue to fuel the 'durable inequalities'[39] experienced by migrants that relate to factors such as gender, ethnicity and class, which are not transformed in any significant way by the transnational movement.[40] Rather, low-waged migrants experience new inequalities in transnational social spaces, such as a lack of rights in subcontracted labour markets[41] and as non-citizens in labour-receiving countries.

33 Matt Withers and Nicola Piper, 'Transnationalism and Temporary Labour Migration' in Brenda S A Yeoh and Francis Collins (eds), *Handbook on Transnationalism* (Edward Elgar, 2021) (forthcoming).

34 Maruja M B Asis and Alan Feranil, 'Not for Adults Only: Toward a Child's Lens in Migration Policies in Asia' (2020) 8(1) *Journal on Migration and Human Security* 68, 68–69.

35 Other constraints such as financial debt and employer discretion are discussed in Chapter 5 (see Section 5.3).

36 Faist (2008) cited in Nicola Piper and Matt Withers, 'Forced Transnationalism and Temporary
Labour Migration: Implications for Understanding Migrant Rights' (2018) 15(5) *Identities* 558, 560.

37 Piper and Withers, above n 36, 560.

38 Ibid 562.

39 Tilly (1998), cited in Thomas Faist, *The Transnationalized Social Question: Migration and the Politics of Social Inequalities in the Twenty-First Century* (Oxford University Press, 2019) 95.

40 Ibid.

41 Ibid 96.

Bilateral arrangements between labour-sending and labour-receiving States reflect the balance of power between countries,[42] with labour-sending countries having little negotiating power because of a) their economic dependence on TLM; and b) intense competition for access to labour markets. This is the case even in the context of liberal, democratic labour-receiving countries.[43] Hence, prospects for achieving policy reforms are best understood in the context of labour-receiving countries, given that they are primarily responsible for the framing and regulation of TLM[44] and they determine which rights are afforded to workers based on their assigned migration status.[45] This includes those rights pertaining to the child-parent relationship. As Carling et al have observed in their study of transnational parenthood:

> [T]he separation of parents and children and the very formation of transnational families owe a great deal to the immigration policies of the receiving countries.[46]

That is to say that the sovereignty of the nation-state continues to be the defining factor in people's capacity to not only engage in transnational activities, but to enjoy and nurture transnational relationships. States determine who can be mobile, and the nature of that mobility, which has become blatantly apparent in the context of COVID-19 and the mass closure of borders and forced return of millions of migrant workers worldwide.[47] Hence, in an era of transnationalism, immobility – both in terms of people's ability to move and the portability of their rights – casts doubt over 'the linkages between migration and development that underlie much of international cooperation on migration'.[48] This begs the question, as posed by Merla et al:

> Where do care and family relations fit in such processes? This is a question of fundamental importance that is often overlooked in analyses of the 'immobility regime'.[49]

42 Susan Kneebone, 'Migrant Workers Between States: In Search of Exit and Integration Strategies in South East Asia' (2012) 40 *Asian Journal of Social Science* 367, 375.

43 Michelle R Gamburd, 'Advocating for Sri Lankan Migrant Workers: Obstacles and Challenges' (2009) 41(1) *Critical Asian Studies* 61, 85.

44 Howe and Owens, above n 1, 6.

45 Susan Kneebone, 'Transnational Labour Migrants: Whose Responsibility?' in Fiona Jenkins, Mark Nolan and Kim Rubenstein (eds), *Allegiance and Identity in a Globalised World* (Cambridge University Press, 2014) 426, 444.

46 Jørgen Carling, Cecilia Menjivar and Leah Schmalzbauer, 'Central Themes in the Study of Transnational Parenthood' (2012) 38(2) *Journal of Ethnic and Migration Studies* 191, 199. See also Kitty Calavita, *Immigrants at the Margins: Law, Race, and Exclusion in Southern Europe* (Cambridge University Press, 2005).

47 See Preface. See also UN Network on Migration (UNNM), 'The Global Compact for Migration (GCM): Well Governed Migration as an Essential Element of Effective COVID-19 Response' (UNNM Policy Brief, 2020).

48 Kathleen Newland, 'Will International Migration Governance Survive the COVID-19 Pandemic?' (MPI Policy Brief, October 2020) 1.

49 Laura Merla, Majella Kilkey and Loretta Baldassar, 'Introduction to the Special Issue "Transnational care: Families Confronting Borders"' (2020) (Early View) *Journal of Family Research* 1, 1.

1.4 The feminisation of migration

The gendered aspect of TLM has seen the increasing feminisation of this form of migration, with growing demand for low-waged labour in domestic and care work settings that are typically dominated by women.[50] This is of significance to this book because it has particular implications for children. That is, the impact of parental migration on children is exacerbated when their primary caregiver migrates and, globally, it remains that children's primary carers are predominantly their mothers and/or other women.[51] With women now comprising nearly half of all migrant workers,[52] it is inevitable that many migrant workers are their children's primary caregiver at the time of their migration.[53] The potential impacts of parental migration (including the migration of both mothers and fathers) on children's development needs is discussed in Chapters 4 and 5. [54] Suffice to say that the foreseeable ramifications for children of significant disruption to their primary attachment relationships remains unaddressed across TLM policies despite the CRC Committee having urged that:

> Young children are especially vulnerable to adverse consequences of separations because of their physical dependence on and emotional attachment to their parents/primary caregivers. They are also less able to comprehend the circumstances of any separation.[55]

50 The feminisation of migration is discussed in Chapter 4 (see Section 4.3.2). See Lise Widding Isaksen, Sambasivan Uma Devi and Arlie Russell Hochschild, 'Global Care Crisis: A Problem of Capital, Care Chains, or Commons?' (2008) 52(3) *American Behavioral Scientist* 405; Fiona Williams, 'Markets and Migrants in the Care Economy' (2011) 47 *Soundings* 22; Eleonore Kofman, 'Gendered Global Migrations' (2004) 6(4) *International Feminist Journal of Politics* 643; Sonya Michel and Ito Peng (eds), *Gender, Migration, and the Work of Care: A Multi-Scalar Approach to the Pacific Rim* (Palgrave Macmillan, 2017); Deborah Brennan and Elizabeth Adamson, 'Care and Migration' in Sheila Shaver (ed), *Handbook on Gender and Social Policy* (Elgar, 2018) 253.

51 See Chapter 4 (see Section 4.3.2). See also ILO, *Care Work and Care Jobs for the Future of Decent Work* (ILO, 2018); Catherine Hein, *Reconciling Work and Family Responsibilities: Practical Ideas from Global Experience* (ILO, 2005).

52 ILO, *Labour Migration: Facts and Figures* (26 March 2014) <http://www.ilo.org/global/about-the-ilo/media-centre/issue-briefs/WCMS_239651/lang–en/index.htm>.

53 See Chapter 4 (see Section 4.3.2). For example, the CRC Committee estimated in 2010 that of the more than one million women migrating from Sri Lanka predominantly as domestic workers, most were mothers who left behind children and half of these children were under six years old. See CRC Committee, *Concluding Observations: Sri Lanka*, UN Doc CRC/C/LKA/CO/3-4 (19 October 2010) [44].

54 See Chapter 4 (Section 4.3) on the potential impacts of parental migration on children's psychosocial development needs and Chapter 5 (Section 5.4) on transnational parenting and parental guidance.

55 *General Comment No 7*, UN Doc CRC/C/GC/7/Rev.1, para 18.

Feminist scholarship has brought to the fore notions of 'transnational motherhood' and global 'care chains' and 'care drains'.[56] Transnational motherhood can be understood as the alternative constructions of motherhood created by migrant women when they leave their children to take up domestic and care work abroad.[57] As Merla et al explain, placing the concept of transnational motherhood within the broader economic and political context of the international division of reproductive labour gave rise to what is referred to as global care chains: where women in labour-sending countries care for the children of women migrant workers, who migrate to care for the children of women in (wealthier) labour-receiving countries.[58] This, in turn, results in a care drain in labour-sending countries, where 'women who normally care for the young, the old and the sick in their own poor countries move to care for the young, the old, and the sick in rich countries'.[59] As market care services are largely unavailable or unaffordable in labour-sending countries, the burden of care largely falls on other women (usually relatives) when women who have caring responsibilities migrate.[60]

Care chains reflect the commodification of care that requires migrant women to sell their caregiving – which requires their physical presence in another country – in exchange for money that is returned home as remittances.[61] However, the commodification of care and labour provided by migrant workers ignores the social and economic ramifications of care chains and care drains for the families of migrant workers and labour-sending countries alike. As stressed by the International Labour Organization (ILO):

> The social costs of labour migration in terms of fractured families and communities are without a doubt at least as significant as those related to the more measurable economic costs. The effects are almost never gender-neutral.[62]

Additionally, we are reminded that paid employment does not necessarily equate to a way out of poverty or empowerment for women.[63] Rather, it must be

56 Merla, Kilkey and Baldassar, above n 49, 4.
57 Pierrette Hondagneu-Sotelo and Ernestine Avila (1997), cited in Merla, Kilkey and Baldassar, above n 49, 4.
58 Parreñas (2000), Ehrenreich and Hochschild (2004) and Hochschild (2000), cited in Merla, Kilkey and Baldassar, above n 49, 4.
59 Hochschild (2005), cited in Merla, Kilkey and Baldassar, above n 49, 4.
60 World Health Organization (WHO), *Women on the Move: Migration, Care Work and Health* (WHO, 2017), 49.
61 Loretta Baldassar and Laura Merla, 'Locating Transnational Care Circulation in Migration and Family Studies' in Loretta Baldassar and Laura Merla (eds), *Transnational Families, Migration and the Circulation of Care: Understanding Mobility and Absence in Family Life* (Routledge, 2014) 25, 29.
62 ILO, *Report VI: Towards a Fair Deal for Migrant Workers in the Global Economy*, International Labour Conference, 92nd sess, Agenda Item 6, 2004 [77].
63 Shahra Razavi and Laura Turquet, 'Progress of the World's Women 2015–2016: Transforming Economies, Realizing Rights' (2016) 16(1) *Global Social Policy* 86, 89.

coupled with gender-responsive migration, employment and social policies to address the structural constraints, power inequalities and discriminatory norms that limit women's capacity to realise their rights.[64] In the context of TLM, this pertains to women's rights as both workers and parents. As expressed by the UN Commission on Information and Accountability for Women's and Children's' Health:

> The health of a country's women and children is a moral, political, economic, and social imperative. When women move across national borders, this imperative remains. However, the question of who (which country) is responsible and can be held accountable arises, and needs to be addressed by multiple stakeholders, and transnationally.[65]

1.5 Comparative analysis of labour-receiving countries

There are a range of factors that contribute to the significant differences between TLM regimes, each of which are 'highly specific to country and time'.[66] These include the degree of control that a country has over immigration, which is never complete; domestic institutions, values and political regimes; international human rights systems; and labour market and welfare policies.[67] As Ruhs argues:

> Variation in objectives and constraints leads to different 'national policy spaces' and labour immigration policy regimes that vary both across countries and over time.[68]

These objectives and constraints are compounded when the complexities of family migration are also considered, which include the different aspects of child-parent relations.[69] As Orellana et al explain, this includes how children and parents are positioned in the law; divisions in labour based on gender, age and sector; and subsequent 'patterns of economic dependence'.[70]

The ILO has highlighted that just under half of the world's estimated 150 million migrant workers are concentrated in North America and Europe, just over a fifth in Asia and the Pacific and over one-tenth in the Arab States.[71] Moreover, in 2013, it was estimated that 11 per cent of migrant workers had jobs in the

64 Ibid 87–90.

65 UN Commission on Information and Accountability for Women's and Children's Health (May 2011) in WHO, above n 60, 45.

66 Martin Ruhs, 'Protecting the Rights of Temporary Migrant Workers: Ideals Versus Reality' in Joanna Howe and Rosemary Owens (eds), *Temporary Labour Migration in the Global Era* (Hart Publishing, 2016) 299, 305–6.

67 Ibid.

68 Ibid.

69 Marjorie Faulstich Orellana et al, 'Transnational Childhoods: The Participation of Children in Processes of Family Migration' (2001) 48(4) *Social Problems* 572, 578.

70 Ibid.

71 ILO, above n 3, [14].

agricultural sector, 18 per cent in industry and 71 per cent in services, including 8 per cent (12 million) employed as domestic workers.[72] Of those domestic workers, 75 per cent were women, often working in conditions that left them vulnerable to exploitation and abuse, including working long hours in private homes without being covered by labour laws.[73]

Together, these workers represent the three major types of TLM programmes that are utilised by States, which, as explained by Martin and Costa, are defined by the nature of the job and a migrant worker's status while employed.[74] These are, first, seasonal jobs filled by temporary workers, such as in agriculture, hospitality and other seasonal sectors, with these workers being cheaper for businesses than alternatives like investing in machines that are only used for a few months a year.[75] This approach is reflected in Canada and Australia's seasonal worker programmes. Second, are permanent jobs filled by temporary workers who are employed in year-round jobs on one- or two-year contracts, after which they must return home and re-migrate. These programmes are intended to prevent migrants from developing roots in labour-receiving countries and reduce labour and other rights to which permanent migrants would be entitled.[76] This approach is reflected in the low-wage stream of Canada's Temporary Foreign Worker Program, Australia's Pacific Labour Scheme and low-waged TLM across Asia and between Asia and the Gulf States. The third type of TLM programmes comprise permanent jobs filled by migrant workers who are able to renew work permits and are on a pathway to permanent residency, following probationary periods and meeting income thresholds required to support the subsequent migration of immediate family members (including dependent children).[77] This, for example, was the case with Canada's Live-in Caregiver Program prior to its reform in 2014.

Thus, consideration of TLM in the contexts of Canada, Australia and the Asian/Gulf regions reflects the spread of TLM regimes not only in terms of their global distribution, but also in relation to the types of TLM programmes in operation and the range of labour-receiving contexts. A contextualised understanding of how TLM regimes operate in these different labour-receiving environments allows for an applied understanding of how TLM impacts those human rights norms identified in the conceptual framework that is outlined in the following chapter.

1.5.1 Canada

Canada offers a rich context for considering issues concerning TLM. This is because it has well-established TLM regimes that have been operating and

72 ILO (2015), cited in Daniel Costa and Philip Martin, 'Temporary Labor Migration Programs: Governance, Migrant Worker Rights, and Recommendations for the UN Global Compact for Migration' (Economic Policy Institute Report, 1 August 2018) 6.

73 Costa and Martin, above n 72, 6.

74 Ibid 13.

75 Ibid.

76 Ibid 13–14.

77 Ibid.

researched for decades, providing a strong evidence base for analysing the impacts of TLM. Moreover, its regimes involve both seasonal agricultural TLM (with workers sourced primarily from Mexico and the Caribbean) and migration for care work (which is dominated by workers from the Philippines).[78] This permits the examination of different aspects of TLM models, including the shorter periods of child-parent separation characteristic of seasonal TLM and the migration of children's mothers that commonly occurs with caregiver migration. A further benefit of examining these issues in the Canadian context is that Canada has an authorising environment – or 'national policy space'[79] – that is open to considering human rights implications as grounds for policy reforms.[80] Moreover, the Canadian context demonstrates that even when TLM policies are developed in liberal, democratic countries with strong human rights values, transnational family arrangements are a structural feature of TLM policies.[81] That is, even a country that is considered to have best practice immigration models and a strong commitment to human rights has normalised the separation of dependent children and parents through explicit and implicit policy measures that govern its TLM programmes.

The Canadian experience offers invaluable learnings in relation to TLM policies operating in a range of contexts, from labour-receiving countries with similar authorising environments (such as Australia) to those that govern the large movement of workers between, for example, Asia and the Gulf. This is because Canada has highly regulated programmes that have been operating for decades to govern a significant number of workers. TLM regimes in comparative contexts may be highly regulated but manage significantly fewer numbers of workers (such as Australia); or have a greater number of workers but have less strict labour regulation (such as in Asia and the Gulf States). Hence, TLM regimes discussed in this book by way of comparison to the Canadian context can all draw something from an understanding of the implications of Canadian TLM policies in practice.

1.5.2 Australia

A significant contextual factor not captured in the Canadian context is the framing of TLM as having both labour market and international development policy goals. For this reason, examples from Australia's TLM programmes with Pacific Island Countries (PICs) (which draw heavily on New Zealand's TLM models) have been incorporated in this book. This provides a comparative context in which some

78 See Table 1.1.

79 Ruhs, above n 66, 306.

80 See, eg, *Canadian Charter of Rights and Freedoms*; Hannah Dawson, 'The Role of Canada in the International Promotion of Human Rights', *McGill Blogs* (6 March 2016); Rhoda E Howard-Hassmann, *Compassionate Canadians: Civic Leaders Discuss Human Rights* (University of Toronto Press, 2003).

81 Judith K Bernhard, Patricia Landolt and Luin Goldring, 'Transnationalizing Families: Canadian Immigration Policy and the Spatial Fragmentation of Care-giving among Latin American Newcomers' (2009) 47(2) *International Migration* 3, 4.

Table 1.1 Background on comparative TLM countries

Canada	Temporary Foreign Worker Program (TFWP)[1]	*Former Live-in Caregiver Program (LCP)*	Seasonal Agricultural Workers Program (SAWP)
Ratified CRC – 1991	• Created in 1973 with purpose being to permit the hiring of foreign nationals to temporarily fill labour market gaps • Administered jointly between Federal departments responsible for employment and immigration • Four streams (high-wage, low-wage, primary agriculture and support for permanent residency (PR)) – stream determines access to family rights • Requires Labour Market Impact Assessment to demonstrate shortage in the Canadian labour market • Transition plans identifying how the job will be filled by a Canadian or the migrant worker transitioned to PR to meet permanent shortage are only required for high-waged workers • Low-waged workers (eg, in accommodation, food services, fishing and retail sectors) are tied to employers through employer-specific work permits; can stay in Canada for one year unless the employer applies for a renewal; and employers do not need to provide transition plans for these workers • *Caregivers:* Since 2014, the TFWP includes workers in low-waged caregiving and medical support roles (including in-home care) who enter under the TFWP's Caring for Children Pathway and Caring for People with High Medical Needs Pathway[2] • Caregivers under these pathways must still work in Canada for two years before being eligible to apply for PR[3] and only 2750 PR applications will be processed under each stream yearly	• Created in 1993 to bring caregivers to Canada • Preceded by the Foreign Domestic Movement Program (1982–1993), which brought mainly Filipina workers to Canada;[4] and the post-war recruitment of caregivers from Jamaica and Barbados in 1945[5] followed by other Caribbean countries under the Caribbean Domestic Scheme in the 1950s[6] • From the mid-1980s, domestic and caregiver migration to Canada has been dominated by Filipinas[7] • Under the former LICP, caregivers could apply for PR after two years • LCP was reformed in 2014 and is no longer a standalone program – caregivers enter under the TFWP and do not *have* to live with employers	• Began over 50 years ago with recruitment of workers from Jamaica then Mexico in 1974[8] and now falls under the TFWP • In 2015, 59% of all positions approved under the TFWP related to primary agriculture (i.e. 53,303 migrant workers)[9] • Workers (aged 22 to 40 years[10]) are recruited from countries with which Canada has bilateral agreements (Mexico and 11 Caribbean countries)[11] • Bilateral agreements take the form of standard contracts (reviewed yearly) • SAWP workers stay in Canada for a maximum of eight months per year • SAWP workers are the only group of temporary workers in Canada *legally* barred from accessing PR[12]

Australia	Seasonal Worker Programme (SWP)	Pacific Labour Scheme (PLS)
Ratified CRC – 1990	• Began as a pilot in 2008 and became a permanent scheme in 2012 • Administered jointly by Federal departments responsible for employment and international aid and development, reflecting dual objective: to fill labour shortages and contribute to economic development in Pacific countries[13] • Initial cap of 5000 workers was lifted in 2015 and the SWP extended beyond horticulture and viticulture to include other agricultural sectors and *non-seasonal* sectors including accommodation and tourism in Northern Australia[14] • SWP workers from larger Pacific Island countries (PICs) can stay in Australia for up to six months and from smaller (PICs) for up to nine months (because of higher transportation costs that workers have to pay) • Uptake of the SWP has remained low and it employed only 3177 workers in 2014–15[15] (as this work is often filled by backpackers at an even lower cost to employers)	• Commenced in July 2018 to recruit Pacific Island workers to fill low and semi-skilled jobs in rural and regional Australia • Employer-sponsored scheme initially focused on non-seasonal labour in sectors including care (e.g. health, aged and disability), hospitality, forestry and fishing, but now opened up to all ANZCO three–five jobs in rural and regional Australia[16] • Positions are subject to labour market testing to identify labour shortages • Initial intake of 2000 workers from smaller PICs but the intake is now uncapped and participation is open to 10 countries (Kiribati, Nauru, Tuvalu, Solomon Islands, Samoa, Timor Leste, Tonga, PNG and Fiji) • Workers can stay for up to three years
Asia/Gulf	Two-year employment contracts/visas for low-waged jobs (including domestic work)	
E.g. of CRC ratifications[17] *Singapore – 1995* *Malaysia – 1995* *United Arab Emirates – 1997* *Saudi Arabia – 1996* *Sri Lanka – 1991* *Philippines – 1990*	• Low-waged TLM has been pursued as a deliberate economic strategy by Asian labour-sending countries since the mid-1970s[18] • Migration (predominantly by migrant workers) between Asia and the Gulf States and within South-East Asia has tripled since 1990, with an estimated 22 million migrant workers in the Gulf States in 2013 (mainly from South Asia, the Philippines, Egypt and Ethiopia);[19] and 1.1 million documented low-waged migrant workers in Singapore in 2014 (27% of Singapore's workforce)[20] *[Note: These figures and trends have been impacted at present by the COVID-19 pandemic]*[21] • Labour-receiving countries such as Singapore, Malaysia and Gulf States typically issue two-year employment visas to migrant workers • Workers are only contractually entitled to return home at the end of two-year contracts (that can be and frequently are extended)[22] • While some countries have bilateral agreements or MOUs, there remain significant enforcement issues in labour-receiving countries • Some Gulf States still adopt the kafala (employer sponsorship) system under which migrant workers' employment, residency rights and *right to exit the country* are tied to their employers[23] • Domestic work is the main category of employment for women migrant workers in the Gulf States and Asia[24] and domestic workers frequently reside with their employers	

1 Standing Committee on Human Resources, Skills and Social Development and the Status of Persons with Disabilities, Parliament of Canada (HUMA Committee), *Temporary Foreign Worker Program: Report of the Standing Committee on Human Resources, Skills and Social Development and the Status of Persons with Disabilities* (2016) 1, 3, 13–14 ('*Report on the Temporary Foreign Worker Program*').

2 HUMA Committee, *Report on the Temporary Foreign Worker Program*, above n 86, 3–4; Government of Canada, *Caregiver Program* (21 December 2018) <http://www.cic.gc.ca/english/helpcentre/results-by-topic.asp?top=28>.

3 CIC News, *Major Reforms to Caregiver Program Announced by Canadian Government* (5 November 2014) <https://www.cicnews.com/2014/11/major-reforms-caregiver-program-announced-canadian-government-114044.html>.

4 Phillip Kelly, 'Understanding Intergenerational Social Mobility: Filipino Youth in Canada' (IRPP Study No 45, Institute for Research on Public Policy, February 2014) 9.

5 Canadians for an Inclusive Canada, *The Story of the Live-In Caregiver Program* <http://www.inclusivecan.ca/learn/lcptimeline/>.

6 Glenda Tibe Bonifacio, 'Live-in Caregivers in Canada: Servitude for Promissory Citizenship and Family Rights' in Maria Kontos and Glenda Tibe Bonifacio (eds), *Migrant Domestic Workers and Family Life* (Palgrave Macmillan, 2015) 145, 146.

7 Geraldine Pratt, 'Between Homes: Displacement and Belonging for Second-Generation Filipino-Canadian Youths' [2003-04] (Winter) 140 *BC Studies* 41, 44.

8 Fay Faraday, 'Made in Canada: How the Law Constructs Migrant Workers' Insecurity' (Summary Report, Metcalfe Foundation, September 2012) 14.

9 HUMA Committee, *Report on the Temporary Foreign Worker Program*, above n 86, 7.

10 Ofelia Becerril, 'Gendered Policies, Single Mothers and Transnational Motherhood: Mexican Female Migrant Farmworkers in Canada' in Zahra Meghani (ed), *Women Migrant Workers: Ethical, Political and Legal Problems* (Taylor and Francis, 2015) 154, 158.

11 HUMA Committee, *Report on the Temporary Foreign Worker Program*, above n 2, 3.

12 Delphine Nakache and Leanne Dixon-Perera, 'Temporary or Transitional? Migrant Workers' Experiences with Permanent Residence in Canada' (IRPP Study No 55, Institute for Research on Public Policy, October 2015) 5.

13 John Gibson and David McKenzie, 'Development through Seasonal Worker Programs: The Case of New Zealand's RSE Program' in Robert E B Lucas (ed), *International Handbook on Migration and Economic Development* (Edward Elgar Publishing, 2014) 186.

14 Richard Bedford et al, 'Managed Temporary Labour Migration of Pacific Islanders to Australia and New Zealand in the Early Twenty-First Century' (2017) 48(1) *Australian Geographer* 37.

15 Australian Government Department of Employment, *Annual Report 2014–15* (Department of Employment, 2015) 21.

16 Australian Government, *Pacific Labour Mobility* (20 November 2020) <https://pacificlabourmobility.com.au/>; Australian Government Department of Foreign Affairs and Trade (20 November 2020) <https://www.dfat.gov.au/geo/pacific/engagement/pacific-labour-mobility>.

17 All countries in Asia and the Gulf region have ratified the CRC.

18 See, eg, A J Wadud, 'Sri Lanka Country Report: Situation Report on International Migration in East and South-East Asia' in Asia-Pacific RCM Thematic Working Group on International Migration and Human Trafficking (ed), *Situation Report on International Migration in East and South-East Asia* (IOM, Regional Office for Southeast Asia, Bangkok, 101–11.

19 ILO, above n 3, [9], [25]–[26].

20 Nicholas M. Harrigan and Koh Chiu Yee, 'Vital Yet Vulnerable: Mental and Emotional Health of South Asian Migrant Workers in Singapore' (Social Insight Research Series, Lien Centre for Social Innovation, 2015) 10; Singapore Ministry of Manpower 2014 cited in Anja Wessels, 'Home Sweet Home? Work, Life and Well-being of Foreign Domestic Workers in Singapore' (Research Report, Humanitarian Organisation for Migration Economics, March 2015) 10.

21 See Preface for a note on the implications of the COVID-19 pandemic.

22 Human Rights Watch, *Slow Reform: Protection of Migrant Domestic Workers in Asia and the Middle East* (Human Rights Watch, 2010), 9.

23 International Human Rights Clinic, *The Protection of the Rights of Migrant Domestic Workers in a Country of Origin and a Country of Destination: Case Studies of the Philippines and Kuwait* (International Law and Organizations Program and The Protection Project of The Johns Hopkins University, 2013) 28; UN Women, *Review of Laws, Policies and Regulations Governing Labour Migration in Asian and Arab States: A Gender and Rights Based Perspective* (UN Women, 2013) 126.

24 UN Women, above n 23, 42.

issues vary from the Canadian setting because of an explicit development objective built into the TLM policies by the labour-receiving country.

Moreover, Australia is in a unique position to benefit considerably from an understanding of the Canadian experience given that its dedicated TLM programmes have only recently been developed and are still being shaped (with Australia's Seasonal Worker Programme becoming a permanent scheme in 2012 and its Pacific Labour Scheme being launched in 2018). This provides space for policies to be moulded in response to learnings from Canada, particularly since Canada and Australia share a similar authorising environment in relation to policymaking and public commitments to human rights norms. Moreover, as Hugo explains, the Canadian experience is of particular relevance to Australia because of the challenges presented by similar demographic structures and their shared approach to managing and promoting immigration through substantial planned programmes.[82]

1.5.3 Asian and Gulf regions

A significant variable that was not captured in either the Canadian or Australian contexts is those TLM regimes that have been developed in an attempt to regulate existing, large-scale movements of migrant workers in certain migration corridors with poorly regulated recruitment and employment practices.[83] These types of regimes dominate TLM within Asia and between Asia and the Gulf States.[84] For this reason, examples from Asian labour-receiving countries (such as Singapore) and labour-receiving countries in the Gulf region have also been drawn upon throughout this book. This comparative context provides a very different environment from both Canada and Australia for considering some of the issues raised in relation the impact of TLM on children's rights. It contrasts starkly with the Australian programmes, which create new migration flows that are small-scale and highly regulated.[85] The Canadian programmes appear to sit somewhere in the middle in terms of their size and management of existing migration flows.

82 Graeme Hugo, 'Care Worker Migration, Australia and Development' (2009) 15 *Population, Space and Place* 189, 197.

83 ILO, above n 3, [9]; Piyasiri Wickramasekara, 'Migration Regimes and Their Linkages for Family Unity, Integrity and Development' in Marion Panizzon, Gottfried Zurcher and Elisa Fornale (eds), *The Palgrave Handbook of International Labour Migration: Law and Policy Perspectives* (Palgrave Macmillan, 2015) 146, 164–6.

84 ILO, above n 3, [9].

85 Wickramasekara, above n 83, 164–6.

2 Normative and conceptual framework

2.1 Introduction

The normative and conceptual framework for this book identifies a set of provisions in the CRC that protect children's relationships with their parents and recognise and privilege the parental role in children's upbringing and development. These are children's right to be cared for by their parents (Art 7); to have their family life protected from unlawful and arbitrary interference (Art 16); to have direct and regular contact and personal relations with their parents if separated (Art 10(2)); and to receive direction and guidance from their parents (Art 5). Additionally, parents are entitled to State assistance to perform their child-rearing responsibilities as their children's primary caregivers (Art 18), which includes securing conditions necessary for their children's physical, mental, spiritual, moral and social development (Art 27). These CRC provisions are outlined in the first section of this chapter and are used to structure the analysis of how TLM interferes with the child-parent relationship in Part B of this book.

The second section of this chapter focuses on the interconnectedness of the CRC provisions in the framework. It demonstrates that interference with one of the rights protecting the child-parent relationship necessarily causes interference with the other related rights. It argues that States need to justify interferences with each of the rights identified in the framework caused by TLM policies. This is because an interference with one right may be justifiable but can generate (possibly inadvertently) interferences with the other rights that cannot be justified as being reasonable and in pursuit of a legitimate aim.

Importantly, the CRC provisions in the normative and conceptual framework entitle parents to be assisted by the State to fulfil their role as their children's primary caregivers. This reflects the interdependence of children's rights with those of their parents. It also highlights that children cannot be considered in isolation from their parents and family when considering the potential impacts of policies on children's rights. In this regard, the CRC Committee has emphasised that children's rights 'will be especially meaningful in the context of the rights of parents and other members of the family' that are to be recognised, respected and promoted.[1] The interdependence of children's rights with those of their parents is also reflected in the ICRMW, which assumes that a migrant worker is able to move with his or her dependent children and spouse (as a family unit) and protects his or her right to do so.[2] This reflects the reality that a migrant worker's family rights are inextricably linked with their children's family rights and that denying these rights to either the parent or the child will inevitably limit the rights of the other.

2.1.1 Articles 9 and 10(1)

Importantly, Arts 9 and 10(1) of the CRC have been omitted from the normative and conceptual framework even though they also reflect the CRC's presumption that, in ordinary circumstances, it is in children's best interests to be with their parents (unless shown otherwise).[3] Both articles protect a child's right not to be separated from his or her parents and reflect the principles embodied in the rights in the framework. These are that children's family life (including their relationship with their parents) is fundamental to their development and should be protected; and parents should be recognised and supported as their children's primary caregivers. They are discussed in Part B as they provide important context for understanding the rights in the framework, particularly Arts 10(2) and 16.[4]

However, Arts 9 and 10(1) have not been included in the framework because the obligations on States that they evoke in the context of TLM are not strong.[5] Briefly, this is due to the intended purpose of Art 9 to apply to the separation of children and parents *within* a State to achieve child protection measures.[6] Moreover, while Article 10(1) provides for child-parent reunification in the event of transnational separation, State obligations to reunify children and parents in the context of TLM are significantly limited by the general capacity for reunification

1 CRC Committee, *Report on the Seventh Session*, UN Doc CRC/C/34 (8 November 1994) [198].
2 *ICRMW* arts 29, 30, 44, 45.
3 These CRC articles state that:
-Art 9(1): 'States Parties shall ensure that a child shall not be separated from his or her parents against their will, except when competent authorities subject to judicial review determine, in accordance with applicable law and procedures, that such separation is necessary for the best interests of the child…'
-Art 10(1): 'In accordance with the obligation of States Parties under article 9, paragraph 1, applications by a child or his or her parents to enter or leave a State Party for the purpose of family reunification shall be dealt with by States Parties in a positive, humane and expeditious manner…'
4 Articles 9 and 10(1) are discussed in Chapter 5 (see Section 5.2.2) and Chapter 6 (see Section 6.2.2).
5 This is discussed further in Chapter 5 (see Section 5.2.2) and Chapter 6 (see Section 6.2.2).
6 John Tobin and Judy Cashmore, 'Article 9. The Right Not to Be Separated from Parents' in J Tobin (ed), *The UN Convention on the Rights of the Child: A Commentary* (OUP, 2019) 305, 308; Sharon Detrick, *A Commentary on the United Nations Convention on the Rights of the Child* (Martinus Nijhoff, 1999), 170.

to take place in the family's country of nationality.[7] Hence, while Arts 9 and 10(1) are not included in the framework, they inform the rights and obligations in those articles that the framework covers, once again demonstrating the interconnectedness and inseparability of the CRC's provisions.

2.2 Why and how have CRC rights been used in the framework?

The CRC entitles all children to benefit from the unique role that parents play in their upbringing and in enabling them to enjoy their own rights as children. The CRC Committee has emphasised the important role that parents play in their children's capacity to realise their rights, particularly when they are young. This is because of the relationship between children and their parents (or primary caregivers) that is based on 'strong mutual attachments' and provides children with 'physical and emotional security' and 'consistent care and attention'.[8] The Committee has observed that, in ordinary circumstances:

> Through these relationships children construct a personal identity and acquire culturally valued skills, knowledge and behaviours. In these ways, parents (and other caregivers) are normally the major conduit through which young children are able to realise their rights.[9]

For such reasons, the CRC strongly protects the child-parent relationship and requires States to support parents to fulfil their parental role and responsibilities. The six (6) rights protecting this relationship that are directly interfered with by TLM have been identified across a spectrum to form the normative and conceptual framework for this book. This is represented in Figure 2.1. They have been presented in this way to capture the notion that each right relates to the other and together support a child's right to be cared for as far as possible by their parents under Art 7.

Importantly, improved support for each and any right in the framework will to some degree improve children's capacity to be cared for by their parents (Art 7). That is, measures that support parents to continue to meet their children's psychosocial and emotional development needs (Art 27), maintain direct and regular contact with their children (Art 10(2)) and provide direction and guidance to their children (Art 5) can assist migrant workers to continue to fulfil elements of their parenting role even if separated transnationally. Furthermore, measures that reduce the prolonged physical separation of parents and children can decrease the degree of interference by TLM with children's family life (Art 16) and support parents to continue their role as those adults with the primary responsibility for the upbringing and development of their children (Art 18).

7 This is discussed in Chapter 5 (see Section 5.2.2) and Chapter 6 (see Section 6.2.2). See also CRC Committee, *General Comment No 6: Treatment of Unaccompanied and Separated Children Outside their Country of Origin*, 39th sess, UN Doc CRC/GC/2005/6 (1 September 2005) para 83 ('*General Comment No 6*').
8 *General Comment No 7*, UN Doc CRC/C/GC/7/Rev.1, para 16.
9 Ibid.

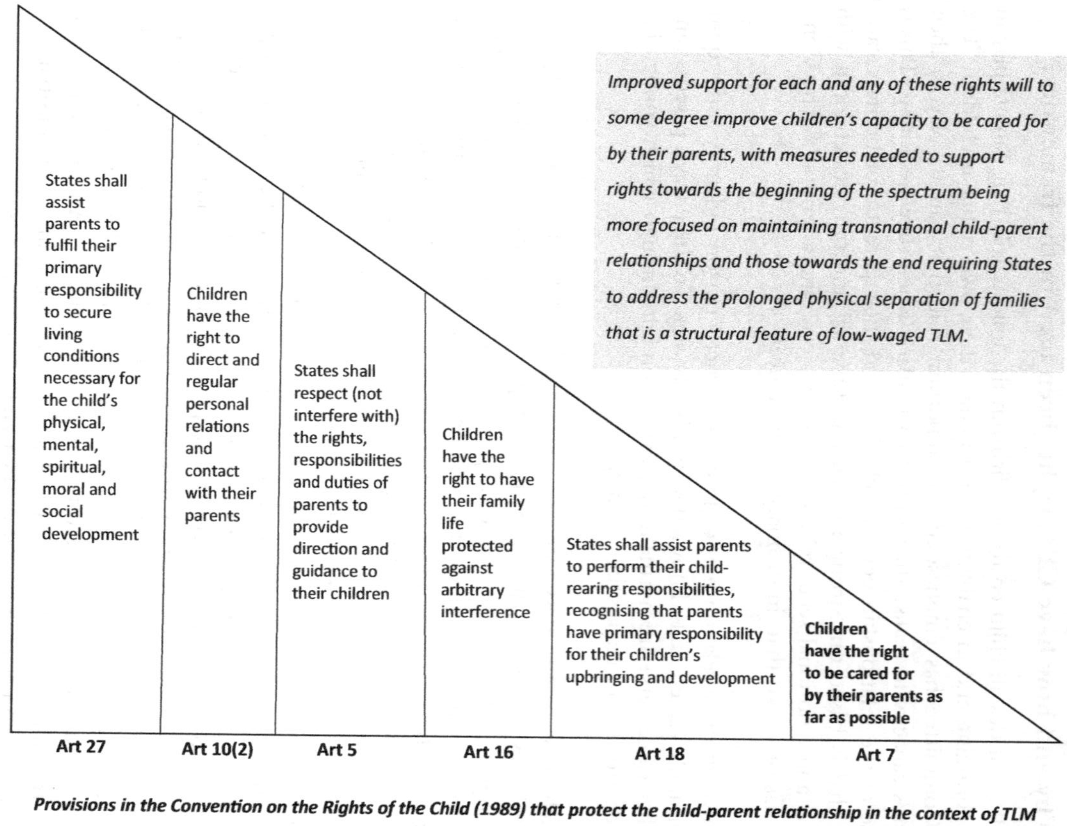

Figure 2.1 Normative and conceptual framework

As measures required to support transnational child-parent relationships in the context of TLM are less challenging for States, the associated rights appear at the beginning of the spectrum. Whereas measures identified in relation to Arts 16, 18 and 7 all require States to consider and address the more complex policy challenges that arise from the prolonged physical separation of children and parents upon which TLM is premised. Hence, these rights have been located towards the end of the spectrum. Using this spectrum of interrelated CRC rights to map issues and measures permits the identification of a range of measures that can reduce interferences with children's rights to different degrees depending upon the will of the labour-receiving country. These measures are identified in Part B of this book. This approach reflects an attempt to navigate what Carens describes as 'the challenges of exploring tensions between what is feasible and what is right'.[10]

The approach to the normative and conceptual framework adopted in this book also allows for the significant variations between TLM regimes to be addressed. This is because some States will require fewer or more measures in relation to each right depending on the nature of their existing policies and practices. This is particularly so in relation to supporting direct and regular communication between children and parents, where the greatest variations between policies and practices in labour-receiving countries are evident. However, *all* low-waged TLM regimes interfere to some degree with those rights towards the end of the spectrum given that they are premised on the physical separation of children and parents. Moreover, the willingness of labour-receiving countries to engage with the challenges that TLM presents for children's rights will also vary across this spectrum depending on the policy environment in which the TLM regime operates, and the cost of the measures required to improve existing practices.[11]

2.2.1 The need for a framework that can account for context

Understanding the impact of TLM across this spectrum of rights allows for the identification of reasonable measures that are relative to the contexts within which TLM regimes operate. The significant variation between TLM regimes is generated by the policy environments in *labour-receiving* countries. As a result, workers from the same or similar labour-sending countries are afforded different rights according to their country of employment *and* the TLM programme under which they migrate. Hence, the degree to which the capacity of migrant workers to fulfil their parenting role is impacted by TLM – and their children's interdependent rights subsequently interfered with – will vary according to the particular TLM regime. This demonstrates the importance of recognising context when applying a normative framework to understand the complex and competing policy issues that arise in different scenarios. However, it should be noted that, to date, the absence

10 Joseph Carens, *The Ethics of Immigration* (Oxford University Press, 2013) 4.

11 The perceived willingness of labour-receiving countries to engage with these issues is addressed in Chapter 7 (see Section 7.3.2).

of any process for considering the impact of TLM on children's rights and best interests is a common feature across TLM regimes.

Importantly, like other labour-receiving countries, TLM policies and practices in liberal, democratic countries like Canada and Australia also create conditions that unnecessarily interfere with the parenting capacity of migrant workers. However, they are less likely to be challenged by workers and the governments of labour-sending countries because the treatment of migrant workers in alternative destinations (such as the Gulf States and Asian labour-receiving countries) is significantly worse. However, infringements on workers' rights in contexts such as the Gulf States and Asian labour-receiving countries are so extreme that conditions that are simply better than these practices do not necessarily meet State obligations under human rights law. Moreover, while conditions that interfere with rights that protect the child-parent relationship may be less restrictive in liberal, democratic countries, they present significantly greater contradictions with the expressed values and commitments made by these countries. These contradictions are explored throughout this book, particularly in Chapter 7 in relation to public recognition by States of the value of the child-parent relationship to children's development and well-being.[12]

2.2.2 Reasons for limiting the framework to CRC rights

i. Labour-receiving countries are parties to the CRC

As discussed in the Introduction to this book, all countries (except the United States) have ratified the CRC and therefore committed to upholding the rights and principles that it protects.[13] Hence, CRC rights form this normative and conceptual framework because they bind both labour-sending *and* labour-receiving countries under international law. By contrast, all major labour-receiving countries have failed to ratify the ICRMW, which clarifies and protects human rights specifically in relation to migrant workers and their families.[14] To illustrate, Canada now admits more temporary foreign workers than permanent residents[15] and, in 2013, its workforce comprised 386,406 temporary migrant workers.[16] In the same year, Canada did not accept the recommendation arising from the UN's review of its implementation of international obligations that it

12 See Chapter 7 (Section 7.2).

13 UN, *Treaty Collection* (13 November 2019) <https://treaties.un.org>.

14 The *ICRMW* currently has only 55 States parties of which none are major labour-receiving countries. See UN, *Treaty Collection* (26 November 2020) <https://treaties.un.org>.

15 Carens, above n 10, 110.

16 This amounts to two percent of Canada's national workforce. See Employment and Social Development Canada, *Overhauling the Temporary Foreign Worker Program: Putting Canadians First* (Government of Canada, 2014) 4–5, cited in Delphine Nakache and Leanne Dixon-Perera, 'Temporary or Transitional? Migrant Workers' Experiences with Permanent Residence in Canada' (IRPP Study No 55, Institute for Research on Public Policy, October 2015) 4.

ratify the ICRMW.[17] The UN Member States making this recommendation were predominantly labour-sending countries that recognise the ICRMW as the primary human rights instrument for the protection of migrant workers and their families.

The reasons provided by Canada for its failure to ratify the ICRMW reflect those of similar countries like Australia and include the argument that the ICRMW protects existing rights that are already protected in other human rights treaties.[18] However, the uniqueness of the ICRMW, as the CMW Committee has explained, is that it stresses the connection between human rights and migration in light of the reality that migrants (including children affected by migration) are less protected than nationals in transit and destination countries and therefore 'require positive action by governments to protect their rights'.[19] Nonetheless, Canada has emphasised that it is party to other 'core international human rights treaties and efforts are focused on the implementation of these treaties'.[20] Significantly, the CRC *is* one of the core human rights treaties to which Canada is a party and, in the same review, Canada reiterated that it 'is committed to the promotion and implementation of the *Convention on the Rights of the Child*'.[21] Similarly, in the Australian context, it is recognised that for the purposes of reviewing domestic legislation against Australia's human rights obligations:

> [H]uman rights are defined as the rights and freedoms contained in the seven core human rights treaties to which Australia is a party, including the Convention on the Rights of the Child.
>
> (CRC)[22]

17 *Report of the Working Group on the Universal Periodic Review: Canada: Addendum: Views on Conclusions and/or Recommendations, Voluntary Commitments and Replies Presented by the State under Review*, UN GAOR, 24th sess, Agenda Item 6, UN Doc A/HRC/24/11/Add.1 (17 September 2013) [6] ('*Universal Periodic Review: Canada, Addendum*'); *Report of the Working Group on the Universal Periodic Review: Canada*, UN GAOR, 24th sess, Agenda Item 6, UN Doc A/HRC/24/11 (28 June 2013) [128.3].

18 Ibid. Reasons provided by the Australian Government for its failure to ratify the ICRMW include that the rights within the ICRMW are already protected under other human rights treaties and international law to which Australia is a party; and migrant workers are protected by Australian domestic employment legislation. See Human Rights Council of Australia (HRCA), 'Australian Ratification of the Migrant Worker Conventions – Responses to Concerns Raised by the Australian Government' (Briefing Paper, HRCA, 2012).

19 CMW Committee, *Contribution to the 2030 Sustainable Development Goals in Response to a Call for Inputs by the High-Level Political Forum on Sustainable Development (HLPF)* (19 April 2018) 1 pt 1.

20 *Universal Periodic Review: Canada: Addendum*, UN Doc A/HRC/24/11/Add.1 [6].

21 Ibid.

22 National Children's Commissioner, *Children's Rights Report 2017* (Australian Human Rights Commission, 2017) 61.

In the context of Asia and the Gulf States, all labour-receiving countries are States parties to the CRC and have also failed to ratify the ICRMW. However, in response to regional concerns, Asian labour-receiving countries (namely Singapore and Malaysia) have recently committed to the non-binding ASEAN *Consensus on the Protection and Promotion of the Rights of Migrant Workers* of March 2018 ('*ASEAN Consensus on the Rights of Migrant Workers*').[23]

ii. Limitations of non-binding instruments

As discussed briefly in the following chapter, while the ASEAN Consensus on the Rights of Migrant Workers attempts to promote shared human rights standards for migrant workers and their families in the Asian region, it remains a non-binding instrument.[24] Moreover, many of its obligations are in effect discretionary as they are subject to domestic regulation in labour-receiving States, including its stipulations related to family visitation rights.[25] Hence, its obligations on labour-receiving States to adopt measures to preserve familial relationships in the context of TLM are weak, which is reflected in the views of the ASEAN Parliamentarians for Human Rights that:

> This Consensus fails to meet the basic criteria that we … have been calling for: a legally-binding document that would provide genuine protections in accordance with international human rights law.[26]

Most recently, at the international level, States have come together to declare a global commitment to 'cooperate to create conditions' that enable people to live in their home countries, recognising that '[m]igration should be a choice, not a necessity'.[27] These statements in the New York Declaration[28] inform the recently adopted Global Compact for Migration,[29] which recognises the need to create viable employment opportunities for workers *in* labour-sending countries. This is an issue addressed in Chapters 4 and 7 in relation to parental migration and sustainable development.[30] Suffice to say here that as the New York Declaration and

23 *ASEAN Consensus on the Protection and Promotion of the Rights of Migrant Workers*, 31st ASEAN Summit (14 November 2017) *('ASEAN Consensus the Rights of Migrant Workers')*.
24 The Consensus is discussed in Chapter 3 (see Section 3.3.4).
25 *ASEAN Consensus on the Rights of Migrant Workers* paras 1(d), 8.
26 Hon Teddy Baguilat, Jr (APHR Board Member and Member of the House of Representatives of the Philippines), quoted in ASEAN Parliamentarians for Human Rights (APHR), *Regional MPs: ASEAN Consensus on Migrant Workers Does Not Provide Adequate Protections* (24 November 2017) <https://aseanmp.org/2017/11/24/regional-mps-asean-consensus-on-migrant-workers-does-not-provide-adequate-protections/>.
27 *New York Declaration*, UN Doc A/RES/71/1, para 43.
28 Ibid.
29 *Global Compact for Migration*, UN Doc A/RES/73/195.
30 See Chapter 4 (Section 4.2.3) and Chapter 7 (Section 7.3.3).

the Global Compact are both non-binding, States are not legally obligated to adopt the measures that they identify, which limits the potential effectiveness of both instruments. This is reflected in the fact that the non-binding *Declaration on the Commitments for Children in ASEAN (2001)* [31] made similar recommendations that ASEAN States should:

> Create employment opportunities for adult family members in ASEAN countries, as stable families are the key to the social, physical and emotional development of children.[32]

However, almost two decades later – and with two additional non-binding regional instruments specific to migrant workers and their families[33] – TLM based on parental migration continues to grow in the Asian region in the face of un- and under-employment.

It is for these reasons that the legally binding, near-universally ratified CRC has been used to develop the normative and conceptual framework for this book. States parties to the CRC, which include labour-receiving countries, are legally bound to implement its provisions and, in doing so, be guided by the CRC Committee. In its instruction to States on implementing the CRC in the context of children affected by migration, the CRC Committee, together with the CMW Committee, has stressed:

> [T]he primacy of the rights of the child in the context of international migration and therefore the need for the Conventions to be integrated by States into migration-related frameworks, policies, practices and/or other measures.[34]

States, including labour-receiving countries with strong commitments to human rights, have yet to integrate any consideration of children's rights and their obligations under the CRC into the development of TLM policies.

2.2.3 Practical measures to guide States

The analysis in Part B identifies measures available to States to support the rights in the normative and conceptual framework. These measures draw on knowledge from fields including the social sciences and child psychology about the value of

31 *Declaration on the Commitments for Children in ASEAN*, 4th Meeting of ASEAN Ministers Responsible for Social Welfare (2 August 2001) ('*Declaration on the Commitments for Children in ASEAN*').

32 Ibid art 8.

33 *ASEAN Consensus on the Rights of Migrant Workers; ASEAN Declaration on the Protection and Promotion of the Rights of Migrant Workers*, 12th ASEAN Summit (13 January 2007).

34 *Joint General Comment on Children in the Context of International Migration*, UN Doc CMW/C/GC/3-CRC/C/GC/22, para 13.

investing in strong child-parent relationships to children's development and well-being; and the potential long-term consequences of child-parent separation if risks to children are not properly mitigated. This approach is necessary because, as Tobin observes, legal and moral arguments alone 'are limited in the extent to which they can guide states' about the *practical* measures needed to implement CRC rights.[35] Given the scale of TLM, States will inevitably have to address the multiple effects of the widespread separation of children and parents if TLM is to be sustainable and of benefit to labour-sending countries. This requires understanding the issues arising for families, communities and countries in the context of TLM from multidisciplinary perspectives (not only rights-based but also social, health, international development and long-term economic). A comprehensive understanding can assist in the identification of practical and effective measures to mitigate the negative effects of TLM.

Analysing these issues within a rights-based framework offers one way to understand the challenges that TLM presents to children and parents from labour-sending countries. Its value lies in its recognition of how the treatment of parents in one State can directly and indirectly limit the rights of their children in another State; and how the limitation of even one of their children's rights will inevitably affect their capacity to realise other related CRC rights. Each of these limitations demands justification by the States responsible for the limitation. In applying the justification test, it is hoped that labour-receiving States will realise the severity of the interferences with children's rights caused by TLM policies *and* the availability of reasonable and practical measures that can reduce the degree of these interferences.

2.3 The interconnectedness of the rights in the framework

The rights identified in the normative and conceptual framework are so heavily interconnected that interference with one will necessarily generate interferences with the others. This represents the reality that, as Freeman explains, the interdependent and indivisible nature of children's rights means that 'denial of one right can impact upon, even totally undermine, other rights'.[36] Similarly, support for one of the rights identified in the framework will enhance the capacity of children to realise their related rights across the spectrum. These rights that protect the child-parent relationship are held equally by children in labour-sending and labour-receiving countries. Moreover, as discussed in the following chapter, the child-parent relationship is considered special and protected regardless of whether a child lives in a nuclear or extended family arrangement.[37]

35 John Tobin, 'Taking Children's Rights Seriously: The Need for a Multilingual Approach' in Alison Diduck, Noam Peleg and Helen Reece (eds), *Law in Society: Reflections on Children, Family, Culture and Philosophy* (Brill, 2015) 125, 131.

36 Michael Freeman, 'The Value and Values of Children's Rights' in Antonella Invernizzi and Jane Williams (eds), *The Human Rights of Children: From Visions to Implementation* (Ashgate, 2011) 21.

37 See Chapter 3 (Section 3.4).

While the formal theory of attachment between children and their primary carer has Western origins,[38] the way that many (albeit not all) children and parents experience separation due to TLM is similar to experiences of children separated from their parents for other reasons. These include post-divorce relocation and military deployment, which are discussed in Chapters 6 and 7. [39] Feelings of loss, abandonment and uncertainty are frequently expressed in social science studies of children of low-waged migrant workers residing in labour-sending countries; and feelings of sadness, longing and loss emerge in studies of migrant workers who are living separately from their children.[40] Hence, while the framework is based on normative standards established in the CRC, rationales from child psychology and child development disciplines underpin *why* these standards have been embodied in the CRC; why it is so important that they are upheld; and how they are interconnected.

2.3.1 The connection between the normative and conceptual framework and child development

Developmental theory is clearly embedded in the CRC in notions such as children's evolving capacities.[41] It is implied in the CRC's rights, responsibilities and principles,[42] including those that recognise the important role that parents and families play in raising and guiding children in ways appropriate to their age and stage of development. Hence, the experiences and interactions that children have from birth shape their developmental trajectories,[43] which include the quality and consistency of their primary attachment relationships. The CRC recognises that in ordinary circumstances, these primary attachment relationships are formed between children and their parents (and possibly other primary caregivers). It therefore protects children's relationships with their parents/primary caregiver *because* (in normal circumstances) strong and healthy child-parent relationships are central to maximising positive development trajectories for children. Under the CRC, States must ensure children's development to the maximum extent possible and protect and assist the family as the natural environment for children's growth, both of which are discussed in the following chapter on general

38 The basic tenets of attachment theory are attributed to John Bowlby and Mary Ainsworth. See John Bowlby, *Attachment and Loss, Vol 1: Attachment* (Basic Books, 1969); John Bowlby, *Attachment and Loss, Vol 2: Separation* (Basic Books, 1973); John Bowlby, *Child Care and the Growth of Love: Abridged and Edited by Margery Fry. With Two New Chapters by Mary D Salter Ainsworth* (Penguin Books, 1965); Inge Bretherton, 'The Origins of Attachment Theory: John Bowlby and Mary Ainsworth' (1992) 28 *Developmental Psychology* 759.

39 See Chapter 6 (Section 6.4.2) and Chapter 7 (Section 7.3.2).

40 These findings from social science studies are discussed in Chapter 4 (see Section 4.3).

41 Colette Daiute, 'The Rights of Children, the Rights of Nations: Developmental Theory and the Politics of Children's Rights' (2008) 64(4) *Journal of Social Issues* 701, 708–10.

42 Ibid 704.

43 Ibid 705–6.

legal principles.[44] This demonstrates the connection between the CRC's provisions and recognition of the centrality of the family to children's development processes. In this sense, the CRC offers a normative framework for understanding child well-being,[45] with family being considered one of the main elements (together with health and education) necessary for children's growth and development.[46]

As Crock and Benson explain, because childhood is transitory and children's capacities evolve, children require particular assistance and protection that accords with their stage of development 'if they are to develop and thrive'.[47] Without this, children and communities face long-term consequences with the reality being that '[d]amaged children too frequently become damaged … adults.'[48] In the context of TLM, this has foreseeable negative long-term social impacts for families and communities in labour-sending countries. However, it also may produce a damaged generation of future workers with implications for both labour-sending and labour-receiving countries.

The rights identified in the normative and conceptual framework mirror the concerns of child psychologists in matters involving the separation of children and parents in other circumstances. In the context of family law, it has been found that the separation of a child from one parent can 'create psychological risks with long-term consequences'.[49] This is particularly so if the child is young and/or age-appropriate strategies are not adopted to reduce potential harms to the child-parent relationship arising from the separation.[50] Hence, as Kelly and Lamb explain, to minimise potential psychological risks to children in relation to post-divorce relocation:

> Steps must be taken to promote continued relationships with both parents by attempting to discourage or delay moves with very young children, and by ensuring that children continue to have regular and meaningful interaction with their … parents.[51]

44 See Chapter 3 (Section 3.2.3 on a child's right to development under Art 12 of the CRC and Section 3.4 on the fundamental role of the family in human rights law).

45 John Bradshaw, Petra Hoelscher and Dominic Richardson, 'Comparing Child Well-being in OECD Countries: Concepts and Methods (Innocenti Working Paper, UNICEF, 2006) 6.

46 Mary Crock and Hannah Martin, 'First Things First: International Law and the Protection of Migrant Children' in Mary Crock and Lenni Benson (eds), *Protecting Migrant Children: In Search of Best Practice* (Elgar, 2018) 75, 88.

47 Mary Crock and Lenni B Benson, 'Central Issues in the Protection of Child Migrants' in Mary Crock and Lenni Benson (eds), *Protecting Migrant Children: In Search of Best Practice* (Elgar, 2018) 1, 10.

48 Ibid.

49 Joan B Kelly and Michael E Lamb, 'Developmental Issues in Relocation Cases Involving Young Children: When, Whether, and How?' (2003) 17(2) *Journal of Family Psychology* 193, 202.

50 Ibid.

51 Ibid.

This reflects an understanding in child psychology about the importance to children's development of continuous and meaningful child-parent relationships that enable parents to fulfil their parenting role. This accords with the rights and entitlements of children and parents protected in the CRC provisions that form this normative and conceptual framework. It is recognised that the *potential* risks to children's development and well-being arising from prolonged or undetermined periods of child-parent separation may not result in actual harms for every child whose parents migrate for low-waged work. However, the foreseeability of these real risks to children means that TLM policies that demand child-parent separation must assess these risks to children and justify the interferences that they cause to children's rights that protect their family life and development, which are inseparable.

i. The extended family cannot be presumed to mitigate risks to children

It is often argued that risks posed to children by parental migration are mitigated if members of their extended family assume their primary care. This argument is addressed in Chapter 5. [52] However, without downplaying the valuable role of the extended family in the raising of a child, the extended family does not *replace* but rather complements the child-parent relationship. Moreover, blind deference to the extended family ignores significant constraints on the capacity of many extended families to effectively take on the primary care of additional children. In fact, contemporary demographic factors, including intra- and inter-country migration and women's increased labour force participation, are causing the breakdown of traditional extended family structures in many communities and subsequent decline in the social protection role that they traditionally played.[53]

In addition, it cannot be assumed that family networks can replace the specialised care that children require and receive (in normal circumstances) from parents.[54] This is particularly so when families are under increasing pressure to provide care for multiple additional children in the face of large-scale parental migration; and when alternative caregivers are aged, with grandmothers commonly becoming children's primary carers, particularly when mothers migrate.[55] The CRC Committee has reiterated concerns about the assumption that extended families will fill the parental role for the children of migrant workers. This is evident in its observations concerning parental migration from the Philippines as follows:

52 See Chapter 5 (Section 5.4.3).

53 ILO and UNDP, *Decent Work in Latin America and the Caribbean: Work and Family: Towards New Forms of Reconciliation with Social Co-Responsibility* (ILO/UNDP, 2009) 70; *Report of the United Nations Expert Group Meeting: Family Policies and 2030 Sustainable Development Agenda* (UN Department of Economic and Social Affairs, New York, 12–13 May 2016) 12.

54 ILO and UNDP, above n 53, 70.

55 See the discussion on the role of the extended family in Chapter 5 (see Section 5.4.3).

> As regards parental responsibilities for the upbringing and development of the child, the Committee is concerned about many Philippine children living with loose family ties due to the fact that at least one parent is working overseas.[56]

Moreover, existing social studies demonstrate that children in labour-sending countries frequently experience a deep sense of loss in the absence of their parent(s) *even when* they are well cared for by alternative caregivers.[57] This highlights that even if a child is well cared for within an extended family environment, their relationship with their parents is special. Hence, in the context of TLM, the child-parent relationship is equally deserving and in need of the protection that is afforded by the CRC irrespective of whether children of migrant workers are cared for by members of the extended family.

Hence, even if States can justify TLM as an opportunity for parents to provide for some of their children's development needs (those that require money), this is only *one* part of *one* right that protects the child-parent relationship. That is, Art 27 requires parents to secure living conditions necessary to meet their children's development needs, *some* of which are economic. However, by requiring parents to leave their children for employment, TLM sets into motion a series of risks to children that can potentially generate interferences across the spectrum of CRC rights identified in the normative and conceptual framework. How interferences with one of these rights can cause interferences with interconnected CRC rights is demonstrated in Figure 2.2. While each of these interferences with CRC rights may not be intended by TLM policies, *they are certainly foreseeable.* This means that they must be justified by those States whose TLM policies mandate (explicitly or implicitly) child-parent separation.

Part B of this book identifies measures to *reduce interference* with each right in the framework and demonstrates that by reducing interference with one right, children's capacity to realise the other interconnected rights will be enhanced.

2.3.2 Recognition of the relationship between familial separation and emotional well-being in the context of migration

Labour-sending countries and multilateral organisations have publicly recognised the disruption that low-waged TLM is causing to families and communities and acknowledged that remittances do not counter this disruption.[58] To illustrate, a former President of the Philippines – one of the world's largest labour-sending countries – stated almost two decades ago that:

56 CRC Committee, *Concluding Observations: Philippines*, 39th sess, UN Doc [44].

57 These findings from social science studies are discussed in Chapter 4 (see Section 4.3).

58 See, eg, IOM, *International Dialogue on Migration (No 24): Migration and Families* (IOM, 2015) 91; ILO, *Report VI: Towards a Fair Deal for Migrant Workers in the Global Economy*, above n 68, [77]; Hon Rajiva Wijesinha MP, 'Preface' in Nirasha Perera and Madhubhashini R Rathnayaka, *Sri Lanka's Missing Mothers: A Working Paper on the Effects of Mother Migration on Children* (Save the Children Sri Lanka, November 2013) 5–6.

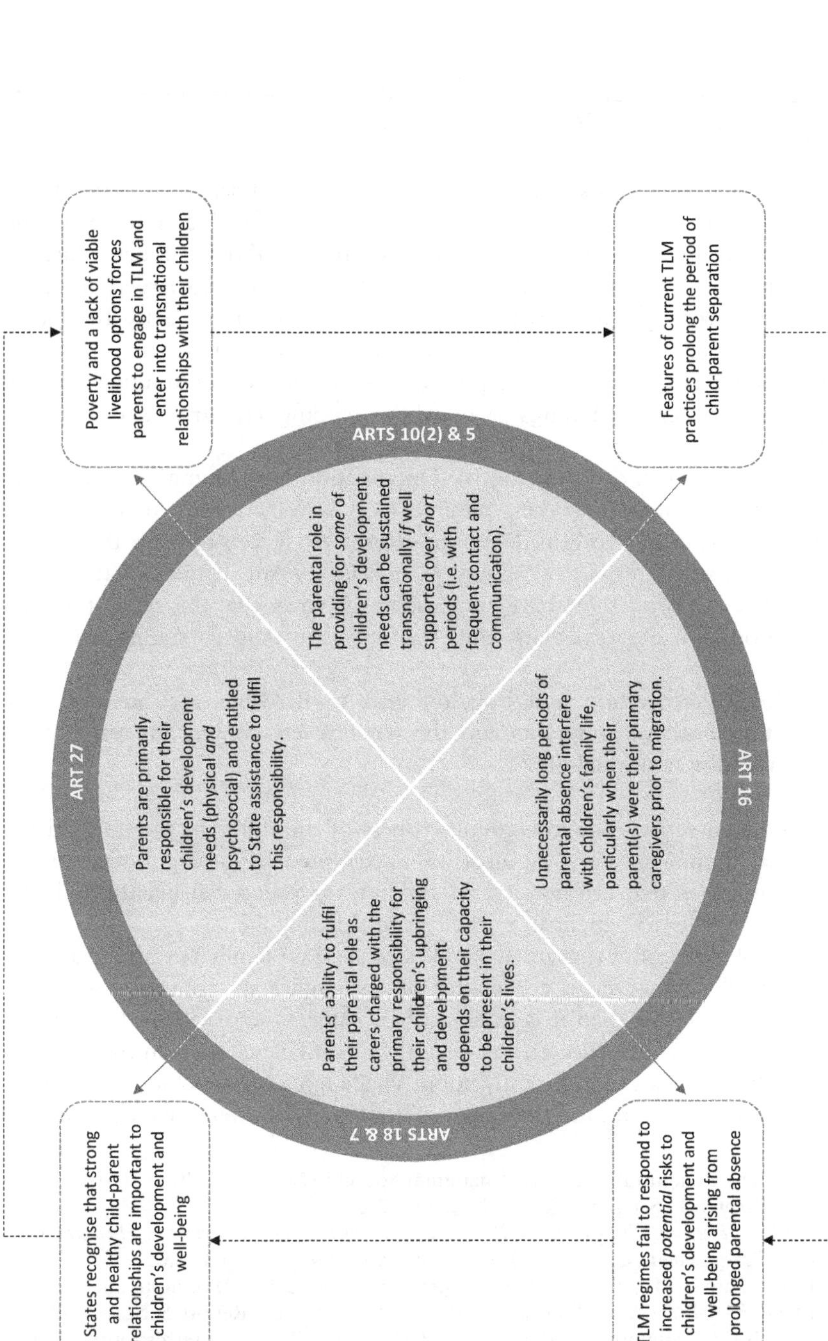

Figure 2.2 Interconnectedness of CRC rights

> Our goal is to create jobs at home so that there will be no need to look for employment abroad.[59]

However, many labour-sending countries are now financially dependent on remittances and are therefore invested in promoting TLM despite their limited negotiating power to determine and enforce the conditions under which their workers migrate.[60] Hence, measures identified in Part B focus largely on the role that labour-receiving countries can play in reducing interferences with children's rights given that labour-receiving countries primarily determine the parameters of TLM policies. These measures are premised on learnings from multiple disciplines that includes research findings from labour-sending countries and multilateral organisations.

The UN, ILO and International Organisation for Migration (IOM) have recognised that migrant workers migrate for low-waged work to improve their family's life chances;[61] and, in doing so, parents are forced to leave their children behind because of restrictive migration policies or the nature of the employment.[62] The ILO and IOM have emphasised the stress that this type of migration is placing on families, particularly child-parent relationships,[63] stating that:

> Prolonged separation and isolation lead to hardship and stress situations affecting both the migrants and the families left behind and prevent them from leading a normal life.[64]

This statement reflects the interconnectedness of the rights in the normative and conceptual framework as it captures how prolonged child-parent separation can create conditions that are harmful to children's psychosocial health; and hinder children's capacity to benefit from their normal family life.

This book recognises that many families can sustain family ties and relationships transnationally. However, it argues that when families are able to achieve this in the context of TLM, then it is done at their *own cost* and with little or no assistance from States.[65] Suffice to say that the maintenance of transnational child-parent relationships is significantly more challenging when children are young; workers' access to communication is restricted; and/or alternative caregivers have

59 President Benigno Aquino III, 'Inaugural Speech' (Manila, 30 June 2010).

60 See Chapter 4 (Sections 4.2.2, 4.2.3 and 4.2.4).

61 UNDP, *Human Development Report 2009: Overcoming Barriers – Human Mobility and Development* (UNDP, 2009), 1; See Chapter 4 (Section 4.2.3).

62 IOM, 'Family Migration' in *World Migration Report 2008: Managing Labour Mobility in the Evolving Global Economy* (IOM World Migration Report Series, 2008) vol 4, 151; IOM, 'Migration and Families: Background Paper' (Intersessional Workshop, International Dialogue on Migration, 7–8 October 2014) 5.

63 IOM, *International Dialogue on Migration (No 24): Migration and Families* (IOM, 2015) 91.

64 ILO, quoted in IOM, 'Section 2.5: Migration and Family' in *Essentials of Migration Management Volume Two: A Guide for Policy Makers and Practitioners* (IOM, 2004) 7.

65 See Chapter 5 (Section 5.4).

limited resources or capacity to assist in maintaining the relationship.[66] It is also widely recognised that the potential impact on children's family life and well-being is compounded when their primary caregiver migrates, as this involves disruption to their primary attachment relationship and their primary care arrangements.[67] While acknowledging that child-rearing patterns vary between and within societies, it remains that in most societies mothers are still expected to perform the primary caregiving role.[68] Hence, the migration of a child's primary caregiver is a frequent occurrence in countries where women's migration for domestic and care work is common.[69]

In response to such concerns, some governments have attempted to ban the migration of women with young children, premising these restrictions on concern for the social well-being and 'safety and protection of the child' in the absence of his or her mother.[70] The controversial nature of these restrictions that limit women's right to freedom of movement, and fail to address the deeper social issues that drive parental migration, are discussed in Chapter 4.[71] However, they do reflect the concern in labour-sending countries about the heightened potential impacts on young children when their primary caregiver migrates. This goes to the pressing need to improve understanding about the connection between child-parent separation and children's health and well-being in the context of TLM.[72] This includes children's psychosocial health and development that is protected in Art 27.

At present, any consideration of children's development needs in relation to parental migration has been limited to 'a few parts of the chain',[73] such as potential improvements to children's physical health and educational outcomes

66 See Chapter 5 (Sections 5.3 and 5.4).

67 See Chapter 4 (Section 4.3.2).

68 Delali Badasu and Sonya Michel, 'On a Collision Course: Millennium Development Goals and Mothers' Migration' in Zahra Meghani (ed), *Women Migrant Workers: Ethical, Political and Legal Problems* (Taylor and Francis, 2015) 75, 75–6.

69 The feminisation of migration is discussed in Chapter 1 (see Section 1.4) and Chapter 4 (see Section 4.3.2). The ILO has highlighted that women account for nearly half (44.3 per cent) of all migrant workers, amounting to an estimated 66.6 million women migrant workers worldwide in 2013. See ILO, *Labour Migration: Facts and Figures* (26 March 2014) <http://www.ilo.org/global/about-the-ilo/media-centre/issue-briefs/WCMS_239651/lang--en/index.htm>; ILO, *Report IV: Addressing Governance Challenges in a Changing Labour Migration Landscape*, International Labour Conference, 106th sess, 2017, [13].

70 See, eg, Sri Lankan Ministry of Foreign Employment, *Ministerial Circular 2015/1: Obtaining a Report on the Family Background of Women Who Expect to Migrate for* Employment, Circular No. MFE/RAD/10/13 (June 2015).

71 See Chapter 4 (Section 4.3.3).

72 Elspeth Graham and Lucy P Jordan, 'Migrant Parents and the Psychological Well-Being of Left-Behind Children in Southeast Asia' (2011) 73 *Journal of Marriage and Family* 763.

73 Kristine M Zentgraf and Norma Stoltz Chinchilla, 'Transnational Family Separation: A Framework for Analysis' (2012) 38(2) *Journal of Ethnic and Migration Studies* 345, 346.

generated by remittances.[74] However, the risk of addressing particular aspects of children's development in isolation is that equally important determinants of children's well-being are overlooked or downplayed. That is, assessments of the potential impacts of TLM on children's development and well-being that are limited to remittance-based measures can only respond to a) a small subset of children's development needs; and b) one aspect of the parental role in children's upbringing.

2.4 Conclusion

This chapter demonstrates the need for a more holistic approach to understanding the impact of TLM on families and specifically the challenges that it poses to children's relationships with their parents. It highlights the need for States to consider and address the spectrum of children's rights that are affected by parental migration and the potential longer-term effects that disruption to child-parent relationships can have on children's well-being. This provides the foundation for Part B of this book, which analyses these potential effects to inform the identification of measures to better protect the child-parent relationship in the context of TLM. It is hoped that a comprehensive understanding of how States can reduce interferences with CRC rights caused by TLM policies will contribute to the global efforts needed 'to mitigate the inherent vulnerabilities of migrant workers and their families'.[75]

Given the sheer scale of TLM, and likelihood that it will remain high on national and international policy agendas,[76] States have an obligation to address the rights and realities of transnational families.[77] Learnings from other disciplines that manage child-parent separation offer guidance to governments in the development of strategies to reduce potential harms to children arising from TLM. Similarly, principles in other agendas – such as the importance of investing in children and strong family units for sustainable development – can also inform effective measures in relation to TLM. This is reflected in the CRC Committee having urged States to recognise and strengthen the connections between migration policies, international development policies and children's rights.[78] To this end, it is important to recognise that not only are the rights in the normative and conceptual framework interconnected, so are the interdisciplinary issues that parental migration presents for children and families; and the policy agendas that intersect in the context of TLM.

74 Ibid.

75 Ryszard Cholewinski, 'Migration for Employment' in Sir Richard Plender (ed), *Issues in International Migration Law* (Brill Nijhoff, 2015) 28, 32.

76 Ibid.

77 Kate Jastram, *Family Unity: The New Geography of Family Life* (1 May 2003) Migration Policy Institute <https://www.migrationpolicy.org/article/family-unity-new-geography-family-life>.

78 CRC Committee, *CRC Committee, Report of the 2012 Day of General Discussion: The Rights of All Children in the Context of International Migration* (28 September 2012) [42].

3 General legal principles

3.1 Introduction

The children's rights identified in the conceptual framework for this book must be understood in light of general legal principles that inform the interpretation of *all* provisions in the CRC. The purpose of this chapter is to establish the main general principles in international human rights law that relate to all children's rights including those that protect the child-parent relationship. A brief examination of each of these principles in this chapter demonstrates how these general principles are inseparable from any consideration of the rights of children impacted by TLM. These principles are subsequently referred to in Part B of this book to inform the analysis of how TLM impacts each right in the conceptual framework that has been outlined.

The first four legal principles discussed in the initial section of this chapter are that: children's best interests must be a primary consideration in all matters affecting them[1]; children should not be arbitrarily discriminated against and any differential treatment must be lawful and justified;[2] States must recognise the right to life, survival and development for all children;[3] and children must be heard in all matters affecting them in a manner appropriate to their age and maturity.[4] These principles are frequently identified by the CRC Committee to be overarching principles established in the CRC that must inform the interpretation of all CRC provisions.[5] Although their status as 'overarching' principles has been contested,[6] for the purposes of this book, these four general principles are adopted as overarching principles given their affirmation by the CRC and CMW Committees.

1 *CRC* art 3; See also Section 3.2.1.
2 *CRC* art 2; See also Section 3.2.2.
3 *CRC* art 6; See also Section 3.2.3.
4 *CRC* art 12; See also Section 3.2.4.
5 *General Comment No 5*, UN Doc CRC/GC/2003/5, para 12; *General Comment No 7*, UN Doc CRC/C/GC/7/Rev.1, para 9; CRC Committee, *General Comment No 14 (2013): The Right of the Child to have His or Her Best Interests Taken as a Primary Consideration (Art 3, Para 1)*, 62nd sess, UN Doc CRC/C/GC/14 (29 May 2013) paras 41–43 ('*General Comment No 14*').
6 See Karl Hanson and Laura Lundy, 'Does Exactly What it Says on the Tin? A Critical Analysis and Alternative Conceptualisation of the So-called "General Principles" of the

The Committees have recently reiterated that these four overarching principles *must* guide all State actions concerning children in the context of migration.[7] The Special Rapporteur on the Human Rights of Migrants has also emphasised that these overarching principles are intended to guide *all* actions concerning children taken by States parties to the CRC.[8]

This chapter then considers two additional legal principles in human rights law that are of particular significance in relation to the impact of TLM on children's rights. These are the principle that States must engage in international cooperation to achieve the realisation of children's rights globally;[9] and that the family must be respected and protected as the fundamental group unit in society.[10] The section on the principle of international cooperation establishes how this principle creates duties for *labour-receiving* States to share responsibility for mitigating the impact of TLM on children who reside in labour-sending countries. The following section on the fundamental role of the family unit in human rights law establishes the duty of States to protect children's family-related rights, including those that pertain to their relationship with their parents.

Together, the principles considered in this chapter form an important part of the interpretative context for each right identified in the conceptual framework.[11] As States parties to the CRC (and other related human rights instruments discussed in this chapter), both labour-receiving and labour-sending States have a duty to uphold these principles. This is because, as directed by the CRC Committee, States assume international legal obligations to implement the CRC upon its ratification.[12] The Committee has further urged that measures supporting the best interests of children in the context of migration should provide 'for the maintenance of family relations and contact to the greatest extent possible'.[13] This, once again, demonstrates the inseparability of the general legal principles

Convention on the Rights of the Child' (2017) 25(2) *The International Journal of Children's Rights* 285.

7 *Joint General Comment on Children in the Context of International Migration*, UN Doc CMW/C/GC/3-CRC/C/GC/22, para 19.

8 Special Rapporteur on the Human Rights of Migrants, *Promotion and Protection of All Human Rights, Civil, Political, Economic, Social and Cultural Rights, including the Right to Development*, 11th sess, UN Doc A/HRC/11/7 (14 May 2009) [32].

9 See Section 3.3. See also *CRC* Preamble para 12, art 4.

10 See Section 3.4. See also *CRC* Preamble para 6; *UDHR* art 16(3); *ICCPR* art 23(1); *ICESCR* art 10(1); *ICRMW* art 44.

11 This accords with the *Vienna Convention on the Law of Treaties 1969*, opened for signature on 23 May 1969, 1155 UNTS 331 (entered into force 27 January 1980) art 31 ('*VCLT*'). Article 31 of the VCLT requires States to interpret treaties 'in good faith in accordance with the ordinary meaning to be given to the terms of the treaty in their *context* and in the light of its object and purpose' (emphasis added). Article 31 defines 'context' to include – in addition to the text of the treaty and its Preamble and annexes – other related instruments, established practices in the interpretation of the treaty by States parties and relevant rules under international law.

12 *General Comment No 5*, UN Doc CRC/GC/2003/5, para 1.

13 *Report on the Forty-sixth Session*, UN Doc, [81].

discussed below and the specific rights in the conceptual framework that protect the maintenance of the child-parent relationship.

3.2 The CRC's overarching principles

3.2.1 Best interests of the child

The principle that the best interests of the child must be a primary consideration in *all* actions concerning children is embodied in Art 3 of the CRC. 'All actions' concerning children defines the scope of Art 3. There are *no* exceptions or, as Eekelaar and Tobin explain, 'no limitations to the application of this principle where children are concerned'.[14] The CRC Committee has clearly identified three purposes served by Art 3. First, it constitutes a substantive right held by children as individual rights-holders – that is, children have the *right* to have their best interests be a primary consideration in actions concerning them. Second, it is an interpretative legal principle that must inform the interpretation of all other children's rights. And third, it is a rule of procedure that requires that *all* decision-making that affects children include 'an evaluation of the possible impact (positive or negative) of the decision on the child or children concerned'.[15] In this way, the CRC demands that children's best interests are considered at each stage and in all decision-making processes.[16] This concept offers, as Crock and Martin explain, a way to identify and promote positive outcomes for children, reducing the gap between children's rights in theory, the actions of States and the actual protection of children.[17]

Hence, States are *required* under Art 3 of the CRC to engage in a process that gives due consideration to the potential impact of State policies on children's best interests. This requirement has a number of elements that have been identified by the CRC Committee and are of particular relevance in the context of TLM. These are that as a rule of procedure, this requirement applies to State actions that affect not only individual children, but also a specific group of children or children in general;[18] that have both a direct *and* indirect impact on children;[19] and even when the affected children are not the intended targets of the action.[20] Therefore, while children are not the direct subject of TLM policies, the foreseeable effects on children arising from

14 John Eekelaar and John Tobin, 'Article 3. The Best Interests of the Child' in J Tobin (ed), *The UN Convention on the Rights of the Child: A Commentary* (OUP, 2019) 73, 74.
15 *General Comment No 14*, UN Doc CRC/C/GC/14, para 6.
16 Mary Crock and Hannah Martin, 'First Things First: International Law and the Protection of Migrant Children' in Mary Crock and Lenni Benson (eds), *Protecting Migrant Children: In Search of Best Practice* (Elgar, 2018) 75, 89.
17 Ibid.
18 *General Comment No 14*, UN Doc CRC/C/GC/14, para 6.
19 *General Comment No 7*, UN Doc CRC/C/GC/7/Rev.1, para 13(b).
20 *General Comment No 14*, UN Doc CRC/C/GC/14, para 19.

policies that separate them from their parents engages the obligation on States to give due consideration to children's best interests in the development of TLM policies.

It is recognised that children's best interests (once properly assessed) need to be balanced with other interests affected by a given action or policy.[21] These include State interests such as immigration control.[22] However, as established by the CRC Committee and the Courts, the exercise of balancing interests is premised on a proper assessment of children's best interests having first been undertaken.[23] Children's best interests must then be given primary consideration in the decision-making process and any interferences with their best interests *must be justified by States*. The CRC Committee has directed that States, in justifying their decisions, must be able to show that the best interests of the child have been *explicitly* considered.[24] This includes demonstrating how children's interests have been determined and weighed against other considerations including broad policy issues.[25]

In the context of TLM, broad policy rationales for the separation of parents and children include immigration control and ensuring that costs associated with TLM for labour-receiving countries remain low.[26] While these may constitute legitimate aims for States, States have not even sought to demonstrate how these rationales have been *weighed against* children's best interests. In part, this is because children's best interests in the context of TLM have, to date, never been *properly* and *holistically* assessed. Moreover, if these policy aims are found to be inconsistent with children's best interests, States maintain a duty to justify the policy as being necessary and reasonable in the circumstances.[27] This goes to the fundamental notion in human rights law that when rights are limited by the State, then the State – as the duty-bearer – must demonstrate that the limitation is for a legitimate aim; it is necessary, reasonable and proportionate to that aim; and it uses the *least restrictive* measures reasonably available to achieve that aim.[28] Hence, interferences with children's best interests, as with limitations on their rights, must be proportionate to a legitimate aim. This involves, as Eekelaar and Tobin explain, establishing whether there is:

21 Ibid para 39; *Joint General Comment on Children in the Context of International Migration*, UN Doc CMW/C/GC/3-CRC/C/GC/22, para 28.

22 *ZH (Tanzania) v Secretary of State for the Home Department* [2011] UKSC 4, 16 [33] (Lady Hale) ('*ZH Tanzania*').

23 *General Comment No 14*, UN Doc CRC/C/GC/14, para 39; *Joint General Comment on Children in the Context of International Migration*, UN Doc CMW/C/GC/3-CRC/C/GC/22, para 28; *ZH (Tanzania)* [2011] UKSC 4, 16 [33] (Lady Hale).

24 *General Comment No 14*, UN Doc CRC/C/GC/14 (29 May 2013), para 6(c).

25 Ibid.

26 These policy rationales are discussed in Chapter 6 (see Section 6.3, which discusses the notion of immigration control as a justification used by States for prolonged child-parent separation under TLM policies).

27 Eekelaar and Tobin, above n 14, 77.

28 *Siracusa Principles*, UN Doc E/CN.4/1985/4, annex pt I A paras 10–12.

(a) a rational connection between the measure taken and the aim sought; and
(b) ***reasonably available alternative measures that would avoid or minimise interference with the right.*** [29]

[emphasis added]

This book focuses on the 'reasonably available alternative measures that would avoid or minimise interference'[30] by TLM policies with children's rights that protect the child-parent relationship. Throughout the book, it is argued that both labour-receiving and labour-sending States: a) completely overlook their legal obligation to give due consideration to children's best interests in the development of TLM policies; b) provide no justification for any interferences with children's best interests caused by TLM, even if they are unintended; and c) fail to consider any reasonably available ***alternative measures***, which could minimise interferences with children's best interests and their specific rights that protect the child-parent relationship. This failure on the part of States to uphold their CRC commitments to children in the context of TLM is understood in light of recent guidance from the CRC and CMW Committees, which directs that:

> States parties shall ensure that the best interests of the child are taken fully into consideration in immigration law, planning, implementation and assessment of migration policies...[31]

The Committees have also directed that a best interests assessment must consider how children's rights could be affected in *both* the short and the long-term;[32] and that best interest determinations must be present in all migration-related procedures, policies and decision-making processes that affect children including decisions by States parties 'that would separate children from their family'.[33] These directions are of utmost significance in the context of children affected by TLM. Not only are these children separated from their parents, prolonged child-parent separation potentially harms children's development by undermining their relationship with their parents in both the short- and long-term.

Recognising the heightened vulnerability of children affected by migration processes, the CRC and CMW Committees have further urged that child welfare agencies be properly involved in the formation of bilateral, regional and international agreements that affect the rights of children.[34] This would enhance the capacity of States to ensure that such arrangements – including agreements that govern TLM – are consistent with children's best interests.[35] In the context of

29 Eekelaar and Tobin, above n 14, 97.
30 Ibid.
31 *Joint General Comment on Children in the Context of International Migration*, UN Doc CMW/C/GC/3-CRC/C/GC/22, para 29.
32 Ibid para 32.
33 Ibid paras 31–2.
34 Ibid para 65.
35 Ibid.

TLM, the inclusion of such agencies in the design and development of policies would also ensure that interferences with the rights identified in the conceptual framework are properly assessed in accordance with State obligations. This approach aligns with the recent affirmation by States, in the New York Declaration, of a global commitment to ensuring that the best interests of children be a primary consideration 'in all relevant policies' concerning the human rights of the children of migrants.[36]

3.2.2 Non-discrimination

Article 2 of the CRC establishes the principle of non-discrimination. It imposes an obligation on States to respect, protect and ensure the rights set out in the CRC 'to each child within their jurisdiction without discrimination of any kind'.[37] The duty to 'respect, protect and ensure' is a tripartite obligation that requires States to a) refrain from interfering with the rights enshrined in the CRC (that is, to *respect* these rights); b) take efforts to prevent interference by non-State actors (that is, to *protect* these rights); and c) take positive measures to give effect to these rights (that is, to *ensure* these rights).[38] The Human Rights Committee has reiterated that the general legal obligation to implement treaty rights requires States to not only refrain from committing rights violations, but also protect against violations by private entities (such as employers) and take necessary steps to give effect to the treaty rights.[39] The CRC and CMW Committees have further directed that in the context of children and migration, '[t]he principle of non-discrimination shall be at the centre of all migration policies and procedures … regardless of the migration status of children or their parents'.[40]

State obligations under Art 2 to respect, protect and ensure the CRC rights of all children without discrimination is limited in scope to those children within a State's jurisdiction.[41] Hence, in the context of TLM, labour-sending countries have a clear obligation to support the children of migrant workers as a group to

36 *New York Declaration*, UN Doc A/RES/71/1, para 59.

37 *CRC* art 2(1).

38 Samantha Besson and Eleonor Kleber, 'Article 2. The Right to Non-discrimination' in J Tobin (ed), *The UN Convention on the Rights of the Child: A Commentary* (OUP, 2019) 41, 50. See also Manfred Nowak, *The UN Covenant on Civil and Political Rights: CCPR Commentary* (Engel, 2nd ed, 2005).

39 Human Rights Committee, *General Comment No 31: The Nature of the General Legal Obligation Imposed on States Parties to the Covenant*, 80th sess, 2187th mtg, UN Doc CCPR/C/21/Rev.1/Add.13 (26 May 2004) paras 6, 8, 13 ('*CCPR General Comment No 31*').

40 *Joint General Comment on Children in the Context of International Migration*, UN Doc CMW/C/GC/3-CRC/C/GC/22, para 22.

41 Jurisdiction is understood to include a State's territory *and* areas under its 'effective control', which are areas over which a State exercises state-like powers. If an area is under a State's effective control then, as Abramson explains, 'it must treat the children and adolescents in that area as CRC right-holders'. See Bruce Abramson, *Article 2: The Right of Non-Discrimination* (Martinus Nijhoff, 2008) 127–8.

realise the full extent of their CRC rights. This is because these children continue to reside within the jurisdiction of their country of nationality when their parents migrate. In fact, the act of not permitting these children to accompany their parents into the jurisdiction of labour-receiving countries can be seen as a deliberate attempt by labour-receiving countries to limit their CRC obligations towards these children.[42] However, when the parents of dependent children reside in labour-receiving countries, it becomes impossible for children in labour-sending countries to enjoy those rights protecting the child-parent relationship without measures being taken by labour-receiving States. To this end, the principle of international cooperation must be engaged if labour-sending States are to be able to give effect to the rights of the children of migrant workers without discrimination based on their parents' status as low-waged migrant workers. The principle of international cooperation is discussed in Section 3.3.

While TLM policies may not overtly or *directly* discriminate against the children of migrant workers,[43] low-waged TLM policies interfere with children's rights in ways not experienced by the children of other migrant groups. For example, labour-receiving countries permit the children of *other* temporary migrants, including skilled migrants and international students, to accompany their parents into their jurisdiction.[44] While differential treatment alone is not unlawful, States are required in human rights law to provide a justification for such distinction. This requirement has been reiterated by the CRC and CMW Committees as follows:

> Any differential treatment of migrants shall be lawful and proportionate, in pursuit of a legitimate aim and in line with the child's best interests and international human rights norms and standards.[45]

To date, States have not provided an explicit and transparent justification for the differential restrictions to the family rights of the children of low-waged migrant workers. Rather, the restrictions appear to be based on their parents' migration status and their family's socio-economic status. Hence, such practices are discriminatory, with the CRC defining discrimination as a distinction based on a characteristic of the child *or his or her parents* such as 'national, ethnic or social origin'.[46] Moreover, without justification by States responsible for these discriminatory policies, they amount to forms of arbitrary discrimination, which is unlawful under the CRC. The ICRMW reinforces the duty of States to not discriminate against migrant workers and their families in its general non-

42 This is discussed in Chapter 6 (see Section 6.3.1).

43 Overt (or 'de jure') discrimination involves discrimination that is legally imposed. See Abramson, above n 41, 51.

44 The differential treatment of the children of 'skilled' temporary workers is discussed in Chapter 6 (see Section 6.5).

45 *Joint General Comment on Children in the Context of International Migration*, UN Doc CMW/C/GC/3-CRC/C/GC/22, para 22.

46 *CRC* art 2(1).

discrimination provision.[47] This provision requires States parties to respect and ensure the rights of all migrant workers and their families in accordance with international human rights instruments 'without distinction of any kind', including social and economic position.[48]

Importantly, discrimination can have either the purpose or *effect* of impairing a child's enjoyment of his or her rights.[49] That is, discrimination can involve harm that is intended but does not materialise *or* harm that is unintended but injury is caused to members of a group because of differential treatment.[50] The latter is the predominant form of discrimination experienced by the children of migrant workers in labour-sending countries, whose rights are impaired because of discrimination intended towards their parents and not directly towards them. The discriminatory effect of TLM policies on the children of migrant workers must be understood in light of the CRC and CMW Committees having reaffirmed to States that:

> The non-discrimination principle of the Convention on the Rights of the Child obliges States parties to respect and ensure the rights set forth in the Convention to all children … irrespective of the child's or the parents' … migration status…[51]

The Committees have highlighted that children in the context of international migration are particularly vulnerable to 'de facto' discrimination.[52] For this reason, they have emphasised that for these children's CRC rights to be fulfilled, States must adopt 'positive measures to prevent, diminish and eliminate the conditions and attitudes that cause or perpetuate de facto discrimination' against these children.[53]

The CRC Committee has also highlighted that the non-discrimination obligation on States under the CRC requires States to identify those groups of children who require special measures to realise their rights.[54] This means that children with particular vulnerabilities – such as the children of migrant workers – may need additional assistance to enjoy their CRC rights and this type of differential treatment accords with Art 2. That is, the non-discrimination principle does not

47 *ICRMW* art 7.
48 *ICRMW* art 7.
49 Samantha Besson and Eleonor Kleber, above n 38, 59–60; Abramson, above n 41, 71.
50 Abramson, above n 41, 71.
51 *Joint General Comment on Children in the Context of International Migration*, UN Doc CMW/C/GC/3-CRC/C/GC/22, para 9.
52 Ibid para 26. 'De facto' discrimination involves patterns of discrimination that are not legally sanctioned but are sufficient to create disparities between groups that reflect those created by legally sanctioned (de jure) discrimination. See Abramson, above n 41, 51.
53 *Joint General Comment on Children in the Context of International Migration*, UN Doc CMW/C/GC/3-CRC/C/GC/22, para 26.
54 *General Comment No 5*, UN Doc CRC/GC/2003/5, para 12.

demand the identical treatment of children but rather that children have equal access to their rights.[55]

3.2.3 Right to life, survival and development

Article 6 of the CRC recognises every child's right to life and requires States to 'ensure to the maximum extent possible the survival and development of the child'.[56] This requires States to take all reasonable measures within their capacity to ensure that children live *and* have the greatest possible opportunity to develop in a 'healthy' manner.[57] This obligation is interconnected with children's discrete right to an adequate standard of living to ensure their physical, mental, spiritual, moral and social development under Art 27 of the CRC.[58] Article 27 mandates that States shall assist parents to achieve the conditions necessary for their children's development, and is one of the specific rights identified in the conceptual framework.

As an overarching principle, the duty of States to recognise children's inherent right to life, survival and development not only informs Art 27 because of their direct relationship. It informs all provisions in the CRC, including those that are inextricably linked with Art 27. Article 18, which is also included in the conceptual framework, charges parents with the primary responsibility for their children's upbringing and development. A part of this role is to secure the living conditions necessary to meet their overall development needs, as specified in Art 27, and only some of these conditions are economic. Other aspects of the parental role in children's 'healthy' development relate to the provision of emotional and psychosocial support, as well as guidance and direction (which is recognised in Art 5). These aspects are impeded by TLM policies that physically separate children and parents and create conditions that limit the capacity of migrant workers to continue parenting while separated.

The CRC and CMW Committees have expressed concerns that policies restricting the basic rights of adult migrants based on their migration status can have a direct or indirect impact on a child's right to life, survival and development.[59] In this vein, they have emphasised that in accordance with Art 18:

> States parties should ensure that children's development, and their best interests, are taken fully into account when it comes to policies and decisions aimed at regulating their parents' access to social rights, regardless of their migration status.[60]

55 Ibid.
56 *CRC* art 6.
57 Manfred explains that the notion of 'healthy development' is discussed in the CRC's *Travaux Preparatoires* and was first proposed by the Indian delegation as a way of enhancing a child's right to simply survive. See Nowak, above n 38, 12.
58 Ibid 14.
59 *Joint General Comment on Children in the Context of International Migration*, UN Doc CMW/C/GC/3-CRC/C/GC/22, para 44.
60 Ibid.

This is because Art 18 obligates States to assist parents to fulfil their child-rearing responsibilities, which arise from having the primary responsibility for their children's development.[61] Importantly, the CRC defines children's development in significantly broader terms than their economic and material needs, which can potentially (but not necessarily) be met with remittances. It includes children's psychosocial development needs, risks to which are posed by parental migration. These risks are heightened if the period of child-parent separation is prolonged and if it is the child's primary caregiver who migrates.[62] The tendency to justify TLM as increasing parental capacity to provide for children's physical and material needs, and the potential psychosocial impacts of parental migration on children's development and well-being, are discussed in Chapter 4. [63]

The CRC adopts a comprehensive understanding of children's development needs and recognises that they will vary according to a child's age and stage of development.[64] As Nowak explains, the drafting of the CRC saw references to a child's right to living standards 'adequate for his healthy and normal physical, mental and moral development in every phase of the child's development'.[65] Moreover, and of particular relevance in relation to TLM, the drafters of the CRC recognised the obligation of States to:

> ensure the child such protection and care as his status requires, taking due account of the various stages of his development in family environment and in social relations.[66]

This accounts for the significant role that the family environment (which includes the child-parent relationship) plays in children's development. In this regard, the CRC and CMW Committees have urged States to recognise that although 'migration can provide opportunities to improve living conditions', aspects of migration processes pose risks to children including family separation and psychological trauma.[67] At present, States are focused solely on the potential economic benefits that TLM can generate for families and economies *without* considering the aspects of TLM policies that pose significant risks to children. However, it is

61 John Tobin and Florence Seow, 'Article 18. Parental Responsibilities and State Assistance' in J Tobin (ed), *The UN Convention on the Rights of the Child: A Commentary* (OUP, 2019) 646, 651.

62 Risks to children's psychosocial development are discussed in Chapter 4 (see Section 4.3).

63 See Chapter 4 (Sections 4.2.5 and 4.3).

64 Nowak, above n 38, 12; *Question of a Convention on the Rights of the Child*, UN ESCOR, 36th sess, Agenda Item 13, UN Doc E/CN.4/1349 (17 January 1980) ('*Travaux Préparatoires*'). See also Sharon Detrick (ed), *The United Nations Convention on the Rights of the Child: A Guide to the 'Travaux Préparatoires'* (Martinus Nijhoff Publishers, 1992) 96–8.

65 Ibid; *Travaux Préparatoires*, UN Doc E/CN.4/1349, 5.

66 Ibid; *Travaux Préparatoires*, UN Doc E/CN.4/1349, 3.

67 *Joint General Comment on Children in the Context of International Migration*, UN Doc CMW/C/GC/3-CRC/C/GC/22, para 40.

because of the central role of the family in children's development that the CRC protects the family unit and child-parent relationship in multiple provisions including those in the conceptual framework. The protected role of the family in human rights law is discussed further in Section 3.4.

3.2.4 Right to be heard

Article 12 of the CRC establishes the principle that children's views must be heard in all matters affecting them, with their views to be 'given due weight in accordance with the age and maturity of the child'.[68] As Hart explains, this right of the child to participate in decisions affecting them is 'not only a right in itself but also a vital means to the realisation of children's other rights'.[69] This includes their right to have their best interests be a primary consideration in all matters affecting them under Art 3 (discussed in Section 3.2.1), an assessment of which must include children's views. The CRC and CMW Committees have highlighted this interconnectedness between children's right to be heard and to have their best interests be a primary consideration, stating that:

> [T]here can be no correct application of article 3 if the components of article 12 are not respected. Likewise, article 3 reinforces the functionality of article 12, facilitating the essential role of children in all decisions affecting their lives.[70]

In the context of TLM, however, there are existing studies that capture the views of children of migrant workers that are currently not used by decision-makers to inform TLM policies. This is despite TLM policies that separate parents and children being a matter that has a direct and significant impact on children. These studies are referred to throughout this book and include studies that indicate potential psychosocial impacts of parental migration on children.[71] Failure to consider the views of children in the design of TLM policies occurs despite clear guidance from the CRC and CMW Committees that:

> States parties should adopt measures directed at facilitating the participation of all children in the context of international migration in the design, implementation, monitoring and evaluation of policies that could directly or indirectly affect them, as individuals or a group, including in the fields of social policies and social services.[72]

68 *CRC* art 12.

69 Jason Hart, 'Children's Participation and International Development: Attending to the Political' (2008) 16 *International Journal of Children's Rights* 407, 408.

70 *Joint General Comment on Children in the Context of International Migration*, UN Doc CMW/C/GC/3-CRC/C/GC/22, para 37.

71 For examples of these studies, see Chapter 4 (Sections 4.3.1 and 4.4) and Chapter 5 (Section 5.4.4).

72 *Joint General Comment on Children in the Context of International Migration*, UN Doc CMW/C/GC/3-CRC/C/GC/22, para 39.

Article 12 both reinforces children's agency[73] and recognises that children's capacity to form their own views develops as they mature. The CRC Committee has described this notion of children's evolving capacity as 'processes of maturation and learning whereby children progressively acquire knowledge, competencies and understanding'.[74] It reflects the notion that a child's capacity to form and express their own views – and understand and exercise their own rights – will develop as they mature. As children across the age spectrum are separated from their parents in the context of TLM, there will be significant variation in their capacity to understand the reasons for their parents' migration; form and express their own views about their parents' migration; and maintain transnational relationships with their parents. This can affect both their preparedness for and experience of the period for which they are separated from their parent(s).

Existing studies also highlight failures to involve children in decisions concerning parental migration.[75] This is not only by States but also by parents and families, particularly where involving children in what are traditionally 'adult' decision-making processes is at odds with cultural practices.[76] These issues are discussed in Chapter 5 in relation to Art 5, which reflects the CRC's presumption that children's rights are realised within a family environment in ways that account for children's age and maturity.[77] Article 5, which is included in the conceptual framework, recognises the role of parents and family members in providing direction and guidance to children in relation to the exercise of their rights and requires this to be done 'in a manner consistent with the evolving capacities of the child'.[78] Hence, it recognises that a child's parents and extended family have a responsibility to create an environment that supports a child to realise his or her rights.[79]

As discussed throughout this book, States have a duty to assist parents and families to fulfil their responsibilities towards children, which includes creating a family environment where children can receive guidance and have their views heard and considered commensurate to their age and maturity. States also have a duty to consider the views of children in policies and actions that concern them. In the context of TLM, the CRC and CMW Committees have stressed – for labour-sending countries in particular – the paramountcy of children's participation in developing policies to address the *drivers* of the parental migration.[80]

73 *OHCHR Study on the Protection of the Rights of the Child in the Context of Migration*, UN Doc A/HRC/15/29, [28].

74 *General Comment No 7*, UN Doc CRC/C/GC/7/Rev.1, para 17.

75 For examples of these studies, see Chapter 5 (Section 5.4.4).

76 Ibid.

77 John Tobin, 'Understanding a Human Rights Based Approach to Matters Involving Children: Conceptual Foundations and Strategic Considerations' in Antonella Invernizzi and Jane Williams (eds), *The Human Rights of Children: From Visions to Implementation* (Ashgate, 2011) 61, 72 n 7.

78 *CRC* art 5.

79 Savitri Goonesekere, 'Human Rights as a Foundation for Family Law Reform' (2000) 8 *The International Journal of Children's Rights* 83, 89.

80 *Joint General Comment on Children in the Context of International Migration*, UN Doc CMW/C/GC/3-CRC/C/GC/22, para 39.

These drivers are discussed in Chapter 4 and frequently relate to matters that concern children including inadequate parental assistance to meet children's economic and material needs.[81]

3.3 The principle of international cooperation

3.3.1 International cooperation and the CRC

The Preamble to the CRC acknowledges 'the importance of international cooperation for improving the living conditions of children in every country'.[82] This forms part of the context in which the CRC as a whole should be interpreted.[83] The need for international cooperation between States has been reiterated by the CRC Committee in its view that developed and developing countries share responsibility for children's rights.[84] The Committee has clearly stated that:

> Upon ratification of the Convention, States bear upon themselves the obligation not only to implement the Convention within their respective territorial jurisdiction, but also to contribute, through international cooperation, to global implementation.[85]

It has also directed that in relation to public budgeting for the realisation of children's rights, States parties are obliged to seek international cooperation if they lack the resources to implement CRC rights and:

> States parties with resources for international cooperation have an obligation to provide such cooperation with the aim of facilitating the implementation of children's rights in the recipient State.[86]

This is of particular relevance in the context of TLM, where labour-sending States have significantly *fewer resources* than labour-receiving States but carry the burden of managing the social impacts arising from parental migration.

i. The principle of international cooperation applies to all CRC rights

States have recently reaffirmed their commitment to comply with their CRC obligations in the New York Declaration, including their obligation to provide for

81 See Chapter 4 (Sections 4.2.2 and 4.2.3).
82 *CRC* Preamble para 12. See also *CRC* art 4.
83 *VCLT* art 31.
84 *Report on the Forty-sixth Session*, UN Doc, [92].
85 *General Comment No 5*, UN Doc CRC/GC/2003/5, para 7. See also *Maastricht Principles on Extraterritorial Obligations of States in the Area of Economic, Social and Cultural Rights* (ETO Consortium, January 2013) [31] ('*Maastricht Principles*').
86 *General Comment No 19*, UN Doc CRC/C/GC/19, para 35.

children's 'basic health, education and psychosocial development'.[87] Although it is non-binding, the Declaration is one of the most recent international human rights instruments that goes to the context for interpreting provisions in the CRC. These include the CRC's general obligation on States to take all appropriate measures to implement all CRC rights under Art 4. Importantly, Art 4 mandates that:

> With regard to economic, social and cultural rights, States Parties shall undertake such measures to the maximum extent of their available resources and, where needed, within the framework of international co-operation.[88]

While Art 4 explicitly identifies children's economic, social and cultural (ESC) rights as those to be realised within a framework of international cooperation, this does not mean that the realisation of non-ESC rights does not require cooperation between States. As explained by the CRC Committee:

> There is no simple or authoritative division of human rights in general or of Convention rights into the two categories … Enjoyment of economic, social and cultural rights is inextricably intertwined with enjoyment of civil and political rights.[89]

The inextricable link between children's ESC and civil and political rights is demonstrated in relation to a child's right to family unity. The right to family unity, which is discussed in Section 3.4, has traditionally been classified as a civil and political right. However, as reflected in the conceptual framework for this book, a child's right to have their family life (which includes their relationship with their parents) protected is inextricably linked with other rights that have traditionally been classified as ESC rights, such as the right of adults to earn a decent living to provide for their families.[90] This latter right is established in the *International Covenant on Economic, Social and Cultural Rights (1966)* ('*ICESCR*') and relates directly to the role of parents in securing living conditions necessary for their children's overall development as recognised in Art 27 of the CRC, which is one of the interrelated rights in the conceptual framework that protect the child-parent relationship.

States are increasingly accepting that the historical dichotomy between ESC and civil and political rights is flawed, with newer constitutions integrating these two groups of rights.[91] Moreover, by incorporating both sets of rights into single instruments, the CRC and other human rights treaties themselves represent a form of consensus about the indivisibility of human rights.[92] Hence, the distinction

87 *New York Declaration*, UN Doc A/RES/71/1, para 32.
88 *CRC* art 4.
89 *General Comment No 5*, UN Doc CRC/GC/2003/5, para 6.
90 *ICESCR* art 7(a).
91 See, eg, *Constitution of the Republic of South Africa Act 1996* (South Africa). See also Goonesekere, above n 79, 84–5.
92 Goonesekere, above n 79, 85. See, eg, *ICRMW; Convention on the Elimination of All Forms of Discrimination Against Women*, opened for signature 18 December 1979, 1249 UNTS 13 (entered into force 3 September 1981) ('*CEDAW*').

between ESC and civil and political rights remains an artificial one,[93] which is reflected in the conceptual framework for this book that highlights the interdependence of CRC rights in the context of protecting the child-parent relationship.

3.3.2 States should not cause harm to children outside their jurisdiction

In the context of TLM, States should also be guided by the CRC Committee's view that agreements between States should not have a negative impact on children, especially children with heightened vulnerabilities.[94] Given that poverty and unemployment are consistent drivers of parental migration, it is foreseeable that the children of migrant workers already experience conditions that increase their vulnerability as children. While arguments in favour of remittance-based development frame TLM as a form of development assistance, child-parent separation can have potentially harmful effects for children's development and well-being, which are discussed in Chapter 4. [95] Hence, in the design of TLM policies – particularly those pursuing an international development objective – labour-receiving countries should heed guidance from the CRC Committee that:

> [B]ilateral and multilateral international aid should not depend on any conditions which may have negative or harmful impact on the rights of children and other marginalised and disadvantaged groups.[96]

Moreover, the CRC and CMW Committees have jointly reaffirmed the need for States to engage in international cooperation to address issues concerning children affected by migration in ways that respect their human rights and do not aggravate their vulnerability.[97] The need to prioritise the rights of vulnerable groups of

93 See John Tobin, 'Article 4. A State's General Obligation of Implementation' in J Tobin (ed), *The UN Convention on the Rights of the Child: A Commentary* (OUP, 2019) 108, 128–30, 144–5; Tobin, above n 76, 74.

94 *General Comment 19*, UN Doc CRC/C/GC/19, para 38. The Committee on Economic, Social and Cultural Rights (CESCR) has also urged that international agreements should not impact adversely on the rights of people in other countries. See CESCR, *General Comment No 14: The Right to the Highest Attainable Standard of Health (Art 12 of the Covenant)*, 22nd sess, UN Doc E/C.12/2000/4 (11 August 2000) para 39 ('*CESCR General Comment No 14*').

95 See Chapter 4 (Section 4.3).

96 *Report on the Forty-sixth Session*, UN Doc, [93.f]. This also goes to directions from the CESCR that States that are members of international institutions such as the World Bank (which heavily promotes TLM) should give greater attention to the protection of rights in their policies and practices. See *CESCR General Comment No 14*, UN Doc E/C.12/2000/4, para 39.

97 CMW and CRC Committees, *Joint General Comment No 4 (2017) of the Committee on the Protection of the Rights of All Migrant Workers and Members of Their Families and No 23 (2017) of the Committee on the Rights of the Child on State Obligations Regarding the Human Rights of Children in the Context of International Migration in Countries of Origin, Transit, Destination and Return*, UN Doc CMW/C/GC/4-CRC/C/GC/23 (16 November 2017) para 64 ('*Joint General Comment on State*

children in international cooperation between States to achieve the fulfilment of children's rights is also supported by the Maastricht Principles on Extraterritorial Obligations of States in the Area of ESC Rights ('Maastricht Principles').[98] These principles inform the obligations of labour-receiving States to take measures to limit the harms to children in labour-sending countries arising from TLM policies that they predominantly dictate and govern. Children's ESC rights directly include rights pertaining to their development needs, such as those under Art 27. However, as discussed, these rights are interdependent and inextricably linked with all of their rights under the CRC including their family rights. As children's family life and relationship with their parents are central to their psychosocial development and well-being, interferences with rights protecting both of these will necessarily impact their ESC rights.

i. Maastricht Principles on Extraterritorial Obligations of States

The Maastricht Principles of 2011 were developed by a group of international law and human rights experts from all global regions to clarify the extraterritorial obligations of States in relation to ESC rights under existing international law.[99] The Principles do not create new law but reiterate existing extraterritorial obligations under standing international law in response to attempts by States to 'interpret their human rights obligations as being applicable only within their own borders'.[100] They recognise the general obligation of States to act jointly through international cooperation to respect people's ESC rights both 'within their territories and extraterritorially'.[101] This includes an obligation on States to refrain from conduct that directly and indirectly interferes with the ESC rights of people outside their territories.[102]

A direct interference is understood under the Maastricht Principles as conduct by States that 'nullifies or impairs the enjoyment and exercise of economic, social and cultural rights'.[103] An indirect interference, on the other hand, includes conduct by States that 'impairs the ability of another State … to comply with that State's … obligations as regards economic, social and cultural rights'.[104] Both are

Obligations Regarding the Human Rights of Children in Countries of Origin, Transit, Destination and Return'). See also *Resolution on International Migration and Development*, UN Doc A/RES/71/237, para 5.

98 *Maastricht Principles*, above n 85, [32.a]. For discussion on the prioritisation of the rights of marginalised and disadvantaged children, see Tobin, above n 93, 142–3.

99 The Maastricht Principles restate human rights law on extraterritorial obligations and were developed by 40 international law experts 'including current and former members of international human rights treaty bodies, regional human rights bodies, as well as former and current Special Rapporteurs of the United Nations Human Rights Council'. See *Maastricht Principles*, above n 85, 3.

100 Ibid.

101 Ibid [19].

102 Ibid [20]–[21].

103 Ibid [20].

104 Ibid [21].

of immediate relevance in the context of TLM. This is because, as discussed throughout this book, the capacity of children in labour-sending countries to enjoy multiple CRC rights is directly impeded by the TLM policies of labour-receiving States that create prolonged periods of parental absence. Moreover, the capacity of labour-sending States to support children to realise those rights impaired by TLM is significantly constrained by the policies of labour-receiving countries and compounded by the limited resources of labour-sending States.

The Maastricht Principles reiterate the duty of States to jointly contribute to the universal fulfilment of ESC rights in Principle 31. It recognises that States have an obligation to contribute to the fulfilment of ESC rights extraterritorially, relative to their economic capacity, available resources and 'influence in international decision-making processes'.[105] This is of utmost importance in the context of TLM, where labour-receiving States have vastly greater capacity, resources and influence to improve conditions that are currently causing significant and unjustified interferences with children's rights. The Principles also state that in cooperating to fulfil ESC rights extraterritorially, States must avoid retrogressive measures or:

> else discharge their burden to demonstrate that such measures are duly justified by reference to the full range of human rights obligations, and are only taken after a comprehensive examination of alternatives.[106]

This returns to the undeniable and unfulfilled duty of States to justify measures in TLM policies that require the prolonged separation of children and parents, which includes the duty to demonstrate that *no other reasonable alternatives are available.*

The principles and priorities under the Maastricht Principles also inform the obligation on States that 'are in a position to do so' to 'provide international assistance to contribute to the fulfilment of economic, social and cultural rights in other States'.[107] Hence, together, these Principles inform the duty of States under Art 4 of the CRC to refrain from acts that cause harm to children extraterritorially and to engage in international cooperation to assist lesser-resourced States to fulfil children's CRC rights. This reflects, as Tobin explains, that the international obligation to respect children's rights demands that States be cognisant of 'the consequences of their actions beyond the sphere of their own jurisdiction'.[108] The CRC Committee has affirmed this understanding, reflecting in its discussions that:

> State parties must respect and protect economic, social and cultural rights of children in all countries with no exceptions, and take all possible measures to fulfil these rights – whenever they are in a position to do so – through development cooperation.[109]

105 Ibid [31].
106 Ibid [32.d].
107 Ibid [33], [35].
108 Tobin, above n 93, 147.
109 *Report on the Forty-sixth Session*, UN Doc, [92].

This highlights an expectation that international development cooperation between States will advance, rather than impede, children's CRC rights.

3.3.3 International cooperation in migration and development

In the recent New York Declaration, States have collectively recognised that 'poverty, underdevelopment, lack of opportunities' and global economic imbalances are all factors driving migration.[110] In this Declaration, they have committed to addressing the root causes of large movements of migrants[111] and acknowledged that management of these movements is a 'shared responsibility' between States.[112] In sharing responsibility, States have recognised in the Declaration that the capacity and resources of countries will vary and that cooperation is required at bilateral, regional and multilateral levels.[113] The Declaration, which includes and promotes TLM,[114] emphasises that:

> International cooperation and, in particular, cooperation among countries of origin or nationality, transit and destination, has never been more important.[115]

The Declaration is the foundation for the recently adopted Global Compact for Migration,[116] which is an effort by States to respond to the lack of existing global governance structures in international migration. The Global Compact, which is also non-binding, is discussed in the context of TLM and an emerging global governance framework in Chapter 7. [117] Importantly, the Global Compact is premised heavily on the Sustainable Development Agenda and the UN Declaration of the High-level Dialogue on International Migration and Development (2013).[118] These instruments are discussed in Chapter 7 in relation to the implications that a migration-for-development approach has on children's family rights.[119] Suffice to note here that the Sustainable Development Agenda recognises that developed countries need to instigate changes to address factors contributing to poverty and inequality in developing countries if 'just and equitable global development' is to be achieved.[120]

110 *New York Declaration*, UN Doc A/RES/71/1, para 12, annex II para 7.
111 Ibid.
112 Ibid para 11.
113 Ibid paras 11, 38.
114 Ibid para 46, 57, annex II para 8(q).
115 Ibid para 11.
116 *Global Compact for Migration*, UN Doc A/RES/73/195.
117 See Chapter 7 (Section 7.3.4).
118 *New York Declaration*, UN Doc A/RES/71/1, annex II para 2.
119 See Chapter 7 (Section 7.3.3).
120 Migration and Development Civil Society Network (MADE), 'Migration and SDG Implementation: The Real Challenge Starts Now' (Briefing Paper, MADE, 18 December 2015) 2. The Sustainable Development Agenda is discussed in Chapter 7 (see Section 7.3.3).

Moreover, States have acknowledged in the UN Resolution on Migration and International Development that because 'international migration is a cross-cutting phenomenon', the challenges that it presents and solutions that it requires cannot be addressed by one State alone.[121] Rather, the Resolution calls for 'global approaches and global solutions'[122] that recognise the roles and responsibilities of origin, transit and destination countries in protecting and promoting the human rights of migrants.[123] To this end, it urges States to avoid approaches that could aggravate the vulnerability of migrants, and in particular women and children.[124] In this Resolution, States have also expressed concerns about domestic legislation being used to permit measures and practices that restrict the fundamental human rights of migrants.[125] In this regard, the Resolution reaffirms that:

> [W]hen exercising their sovereign right to enact and implement migratory and border security measures ... States have the duty to comply with their obligations under international law.[126]

This reiterates the duty of labour-receiving States to uphold their obligations under human rights law, which includes justifying interferences with CRC rights, in the design and development of migration policies that govern TLM.

The ILO has also developed a multilateral framework that provides States with principles for a rights-based approach to labour migration in line with their international legal obligations.[127] While non-binding, it reiterates the notion that *because* migrant workers move across national borders, issues generated by labour migration cannot be effectively managed by countries acting in isolation.[128] Hence, the ILO urges that if the 'beneficial elements' of labour migration are to be realised, then international cooperation is essential.[129] These include benefits to countries in terms of economic growth and benefits for migrant workers and their families.[130] At present, while TLM may contribute to the economies of both labour-sending and labour-receiving countries, the bilateral agreements that govern it fail to mitigate the social costs of these economic gains. Rather, these costs are borne by the workers and their families and include those arising from conditions that cause prolonged child-parent separation.

121 *Resolution on International Migration and Development*, UN Doc A/RES/71/237, para 2.
122 Ibid.
123 Ibid para 5.
124 Ibid.
125 Ibid para 7.
126 Ibid.
127 ILO, *ILO Multilateral Framework on Labour Migration: Non-binding Principles and Guidelines for a Rights-Based Approach to Labour Migration* (ILO, 2006).
128 Ibid [3].
129 Ibid [2]; ILO, *Report IV: Addressing Governance Challenges in a Changing Labour Migration Landscape*, International Labour Conference, 106th sess, 2017 [61].
130 ILO, above n 127, [2].

3.3.4 International cooperation in regional human rights instruments

i. ASEAN instruments

Regional human rights instruments have sought to complement international human rights law by imposing additional duties on States in high labour migration regions to engage in international cooperation to better protect migrant workers and their families. This includes, for example, the ASEAN *Declaration on the Protection and Promotion of the Rights of Migrant Workers* ('*ASEAN Declaration on the Rights of Migrant Workers*'), which was adopted in 2007.[131] While this Declaration is non-binding, it includes a political commitment to finalise a legally binding human rights instrument to assist in the effective protection of migrant workers and their families in the Asian region.[132] This is significant given that the Asian region has a number of major labour-sending and labour-receiving countries. However, over a decade later, the adoption of a legally binding instrument is yet to be achieved. Rather, the most recent initiative – the *ASEAN Consensus on the Rights of Migrant Workers* of March 2018[133] – also has a non-binding status. Nonetheless, its Preamble confirms:

> [T]he shared and balanced responsibilities of the Receiving and Sending ASEAN Member States to protect and promote the rights of migrant workers and members of their families in the entire migration process.[134]

However, the Preamble simultaneously recognises 'the sovereignty of ASEAN Member States in determining their own migration policies relating to migrant workers'.[135] Moreover, its General Principles include upholding 'the fundamental rights and dignity of migrant workers without undermining the application by the Receiving States of their laws, regulations and policies'.[136] Hence, the Consensus permits the duty of labour-receiving States to support the protection of the rights of migrant workers and their families to be limited by their domestic laws. The Consensus also clearly differentiates between the obligations of labour-sending States and labour-receiving States, much like the preceding ASEAN Declaration on the Rights of Migrant Workers. This approach, as Kneebone explains, 'juxtaposes the obligations of sending and receiving states, rather than stressing the shared obligations of states in the

131 *ASEAN Declaration on the Protection and Promotion of the Rights of Migrant Workers*, 12th ASEAN Summit (13 January 2007) ('*ASEAN Declaration on the Rights of Migrant Workers*').

132 Ryszard Cholewinski, 'Migration for Employment' in Sir Richard Plender (ed), *Issues in International Migration Law* (Brill Nijhoff, 2015) 27, 71.

133 *ASEAN Consensus on the Protection and Promotion of the Rights of Migrant Workers, 31st ASEAN Summit (14 November 2017) ('ASEAN Consensus the Rights of Migrant Workers').*

134 Ibid Preamble para 8.

135 Ibid Preamble para 10.

136 Ibid para 1(d).

region'.[137] As a result, the rights of migrant workers and their families remain unprotected in numerous circumstances where effective protection requires action by *both* States. Furthermore, it is often difficult for a labour-sending State to effectively implement the protective measures required of them in these instruments *without* cooperation from the labour-receiving State, which has significantly greater power in the bilateral relationship.[138]

ii. European instruments

While legally binding regional human rights instruments are not specifically directed at the protection of migrant workers and their families, they represent joint agreements by States about the need to collectively protect the family unit. Perhaps the strongest is the legally binding *European Convention on Human Rights* ('*ECHR*'), which represents an effort by European States towards 'the collective enforcement of certain of the rights stated in the Universal Declaration'.[139] Importantly, Art 8 of the ECHR obliges States parties to not arbitrarily interfere with people's right to family life.[140] The right to family life is discussed in Chapter 6 in relation to Art 16 of the CRC.[141] However, in relation to European labour-receiving countries, the duty of States to cooperate in the protection of children's right to family life is strengthened by provisions in the ECHR.

European courts have adopted a view of 'family life' as a broad, overarching concept that offers a way of identifying whether a family is existing and functioning as a unit. This, in turn, enables the identification of whether the right to family unity has been violated. Article 8 of the ECHR provides the basis for interpretations of the concept of 'family life' by European courts and, subsequently, a strong body of case law regarding the notions of family unity and family life has developed in Europe. While this body of law does not bind non-European States, it does offer guidance for non-European labour-sending and labour-receiving countries. It includes, for example, the landmark case of *Marckx v Belgium*, [142] in which the European Court of Human Rights held that critical to the State ensuring *respect* for family life is the right of family members to live together to enable family relationships to 'develop normally'.[143] Additionally, in his dissenting judgement in *Gul v Switzerland*, Judge Martens stated that 'the mutual enjoyment by parent and child of each other's company constitutes a fundamental element of

137 Susan Kneebone, 'Migrant Workers Between States: In Search of Exit and Integration Strategies in South East Asia' (2012) 40 *Asian Journal of Social Science* 367, 369.

138 Ibid 376.

139 *Convention for the Protection of Human Rights and Fundamental Freedoms*, opened for signature 4 November 1950, 213 UNTS 221 (entered into force 3 September 1953) Preamble ('*ECHR*').

140 *ECHR* art 8.

141 See Chapter 6 (Section 6.2).

142 *Marckx v Belgium* [1979] Eur Court HR 2.

143 Ibid [31], [45]; Ben Saul, 'Indefinite Security Detention and Refugee Children and Families in Australia: International Human Rights Law Dimensions' (2013) 20 *Australian International Law Journal* 55, 58.

family life'.[144] This idea has since become a central feature in European case law interpreting 'family life' under Art 8 and European courts have held that '(t)he ***mutual enjoyment*** of each other's company constitutes a fundamental element of family life'.[145]

European courts also consider the interests of a child as integral to the right to respect for family life.[146] The overriding nature of the best interests principle in the decisions of European courts is reflected in the following words of Lady Hale of the UK Supreme Court:

> The family rights of children are of a different order from those of adults … Children need a family life in a way that adults do not … their emotional needs can only be fully met within a functioning family. Depriving a child of her family life is altogether more serious than depriving an adult of his … the effect upon the child's interests is always likely to be more severe than the effect upon an adult's.[147]

Additionally, the EU Directive on the Right to Family Reunification identifies family reunification as a ***right*** that is necessary for a migrant's right to family life to be protected and preserved in host States.[148] However, in reality, the conditions that migrants are required to meet under the Directive in order to exercise their right to family unity are such that they render the right inaccessible to low-waged migrant workers.[149] Moreover, in September 2020, the European Commission launched the EU Pact on Migration and Asylum, which outlines a series of proposals to strengthen migration management in the EU, recognising that 'no Member State should shoulder a disproportionate responsibility'.[150] The Pact reiterates the importance of family reunification, and ensuring that the best

144 Ibid.

145 Helene Lambert, 'Family Unity in Migration Law: The Evolution of a More Unified Approach in Europe' in Vincent Chetail and Céline Bauloz (eds), *Research Handbook on International Law and Migration* (Edward Elgar Publishing Ltd, 2014) 194, 203. See, for example, *Mehemi v France (No.2)* (European Court of Human Rights, Third Section, Application No 53470/99, 10 April 2003) [45].

146 Giovanna I Wolf, 'Preserving Family Unity: The Rights of Children to Maintain the Companionship of Their Parents and Remain in Their Country of Birth' (1996) 4(1) *Indiana Journal of Global Legal Studies*, 207, 211.

147 *HH v Deputy Prosecutor of the Italian Republic, Genoa* [2012] UKSC 25, [33] (Hale LJ).

148 *Council Directive 2003/86/EC of 22 September 2003 on the Right to Family Reunification* [2003] OJ L 251/12, art 1, Preamble para 6.

149 These conditions are outlined in Art 7 of the Directive and include that the principal migrant must meet an income threshold to support their family without accessing social assistance; have accommodation that is considered of a normal standard for a comparable family in the same region; and have health insurance for the whole family.

150 European Commission, 'Communication from the Commission to the European Parliament, the Council, the European Economic and Social Committee and the Committee of the Regions on a New Pact on Migration and Asylum' (Brussels, 23 September 2020) 2.

interests of the child are the primary consideration in decision-making, in the migration contexts that it covers. It also offers a number of models for burden-sharing that could be drawn on to inform measures for the sharing of responsibility between States in the context of labour migration.

iii. Other regional instruments

Similarly, legally binding human rights treaties operate in other regions that are highly impacted by labour migration having both labour-sending and labour-receiving countries. For example, the *American Convention on Human Rights* recognises the rights of the family and reiterates that '[t]he family is the natural and fundamental group unit of society and is entitled to protection by society and the state'.[151] The Convention's *Additional Protocol of San Salvador* also provides that '[e]very child has the right to grow under the protection and responsibility of his parents ... a child of young age ought not to be separated from his mother'.[152] Similarly, the *African (Banjul) Charter on Human and Peoples' Rights* guarantees State protection for the family.[153] Provisions in these regional instruments reinforce the general notion in human rights law that the family is the most fundamental group unit in society and central to children's growth and development. This is the focus of the following section.

3.4 The fundamental role of the family in human rights law

The CRC defines 'children' as persons under the age of 18 years,[154] but it does not offer a definition of the term 'family'. This is because human rights law recognises that it is not possible to provide a standard definition of 'the family'.[155] Rather, as explained by the Human Rights Committee, the notion of 'family' can vary not only between but even within States.[156] Likewise, the CRC does not adopt a single definition of the term 'parents', also because an understanding about who constitutes a 'parent' can also vary between States and cultures.[157]

151 *American Convention on Human Rights*, opened for signature 22 November 1969, 1144 UNTS 123 (entered into force 18 July 1978) art 17.

152 *Additional Protocol to the American Convention on Human Rights in the Area of Economic, Social and Cultural Rights*, opened for signature 17 November 1988, OAS Doc OAS/Ser.L/V/I.4 rev.13 (entered into force 16 November 1999) art 16 ('*Additional Protocol of San Salvador*').

153 *African (Banjul) Charter on Human and Peoples' Rights*, opened for signature 27 June 1981, OAU Doc CAB/LEG/67/3 rev.5 (entered into force 21 October 1986) art 18.

154 *CRC* art 1. This is the definition of 'children' adopted for the purposes of this book.

155 Human Rights Committee, *General Comment No 19: Article 23 (The Family) Protection of the Family, the Right to Marriage and Equality of the Spouses*, 39th sess, UN Doc HRI/GEN/1/Rev.1 (27 July 1990) para 2 ('*CCPR General Comment No 19*').

156 Ibid.

157 States vary in their recognition of parental status in contexts such as polygamy, adoption and same-gender parenting as well as in relation to assisted reproduction such as

However, the ordinary meaning of the term 'parents' is generally understood as 'the two individuals with a direct biological, gestational *and* social nexus with the child'.[158] This covers the group of parents being considered in this book. Nonetheless, a broader definition of 'parents' that goes beyond a child's biological or legal parents to refer to a child's *primary* caregiver(s)[159] does not conflict with the group of parents being considered in this book. This is because of its focus on implications for children arising from the migration of their primary caregivers who are generally their parents prior to their migration. However, for the purposes of this book, how the term 'family' is understood in human rights law requires greater attention. Hence, this section focuses on defining 'the family' and State obligations to protect family life and family unity.

3.4.1 Defining 'the family' to include the child-parent relationship

The CRC Committee has affirmed the position in the CRC that the family environment can comprise different family structures based on cultural practices and changing familial relationships.[160] In this regard, the Committee has explained that:

> [T]he Convention refers to the extended family and the community and applies to situations of nuclear family, separated parents, single parent family, common law family and adoptive family.[161]

The Committee has urged that efforts to preserve the family environment in pursuit of realising children's best interests must be based on a broad interpretation of family.[162] It explains that this includes, 'where applicable, the members of the extended family or community as provided for by local custom' in accordance with Art 5 of the CRC.[163]

In the context of TLM, extended families play a significant role in the care of the children of migrant workers following parental migration.[164] This has led to cultural relativism being frequently employed to argue that the traditional role of

IVF and surrogacy. See John Tobin, 'To Prohibit or Permit: What is the (Human) Rights Response to the Practice of International Commercial Surrogacy?' (2014) 63 (2) *International and Comparative Law Quarterly* 317.

158 Ibid 326. See also John Tobin and Florence Seow, 'Article 7. The Rights to Birth Registration, a Name, Nationality, and to Know and Be Cared for By Parents' in J Tobin (ed), *The UN Convention on the Rights of the Child: A Commentary* (OUP, 2019) 236, 256.

159 UNICEF Office of Research (Innocenti), *Family and Parenting Support: Policy and Provision in a Global Context* (UNICEF, 2015) 11.

160 CRC Committee, *Report on the Fifth Session*, 5th sess, 130th mtg, UN Doc CRC/C/24 (8 March 1994) annex V [2.1].

161 Ibid.

162 *General Comment No 14*, UN Doc CRC/C/GC/14, para 59.

163 Ibid.

164 The role of the extended family is discussed in Chapter 5 (see Section 5.4.3).

the extended family in many labour-sending countries lessens the impact of child-parent separation on the children of migrant workers.[165] However, this approach is problematic for a number of reasons that are discussed in Chapter 5 in relation to the role of the extended family as children's alternative caregivers in the context of TLM.[166] Briefly, these reasons include the diminishing capacity of extended families to perform primary child-rearing responsibilities and provide their traditional protective function for children in many communities due to increasing social and economic pressures on families.[167] Moreover, it ignores the CRC's deliberate framing of family rights – including those that protect the child-parent relationship – as applying equally to all children irrespective of family formation. As Goonesekere observes:

> [T]he concept of a nuclear family … can be accommodated within other family structures … Human rights concepts … can accommodate pluralism in family structures. They can be integrated into a pluralistic concept of family.[168]

Hence, the notion in human rights law that the child-parent relationship is protected because of its unique and significant role in children's lives and development stands *even if* children live in an extended family arrangement. That is, under the CRC, a child's family structure has no bearing on the duty of States to support children's access to those rights that protect their relationship with their parents.

Moreover, the Human Rights Committee has reiterated that the term 'family' includes 'relations in general between parents and the child'.[169] Again, this relational tie between children and parents exists irrespective of the family structure and is significant in both nuclear and extended family arrangements. As a result, attempts to define the family in human rights and immigration law – be they broad or narrow – always include parents (as understood in the ordinary sense) and their dependent children.[170] For example, the ICRMW defines a migrant worker's family to include his or her dependent children for the purposes of identifying who this Convention covers, including its provisions protecting family unity.[171] Thus, while the outer boundaries of who constitutes 'family' for the

165 This is discussed in Chapter 5 (see Section 5.4.3).
166 See Chapter 5 (see Section 5.4.3).
167 The role of the extended family is discussed further in Chapter 5 (see Section 5.4.3).
168 Goonesekere, above n 79, 84.
169 Human Rights Committee, *Views: Communication No 1052/2002*, 89th sess, UN Doc A/62/40 (Vol.II) (20 March 2007) 44 [8.2] ('*J.T. v Canada*').
170 In a comparative study of the immigration laws of thirty-one countries, every legal system offered protections to the migrant's immediate family members and 'privileges to the nucleus of the family, comprising spouses and minor children'. See Sabine Thomsen, 'The Legal Position of the Spouse and Family Members' in Jochen Frowein and Torsten Stein (eds), *The Legal Position of Aliens in National and International Law* (Springer-Verlag, 1987) cited in Eliahu Frank Abram, 'The Child's Right to Family Unity in International Immigration Law' (1995) 17(4) *Law and Policy* 397, 404.
171 *ICRMW* arts 4, 44; CMW Committee, *Working Paper: Terminology in the International Convention on Migrant Workers: A Comparison with Other International and*

purposes of family rights are not strictly defined in international law, a child's family rights will necessarily extend to their relationship with their parents irrespective of their family structure.

3.4.2 Protecting the family unit and family life

i. The family unit is protected in general and specialised human rights instruments

The CRC casts the family as 'the fundamental group of society and the natural environment for the growth and well-being of all its members and particularly children'.[172] Because of this status assigned to the family, the CRC's Preamble further declares that States should afford the necessary protection and assistance to the family 'so that it can fully assume its responsibilities within the community'.[173] This preambular text goes to the context for interpreting a child's family rights, including those that relate to the child-parent relationship. It recognises the role that families play in children's development and requires States to assist families to fulfil their responsibilities towards children. This informs State obligations to assist parents to fulfil their role as those family members charged by the CRC with the primary responsibility for children's upbringing and development.[174] It also reflects the crucial role of the family (which includes but is not limited to a child's parents) in the ability of children to realise their rights.[175]

The principle in the CRC that the family is the most fundamental group unit in society is supported by general, legally binding human rights instruments, including the *International Covenant on Civil and Political Rights (1966)* ('*ICCPR*')[176] and the ICESCR.[177] The ICESCR emphasises the need for States to protect and assist the family particularly 'while it is responsible for the care and education of dependent children'.[178] These Covenants uphold the principle established in the non-binding Universal Declaration on Human Rights that:

> The family is the natural and fundamental group unit of society and is entitled to protection by society and the State.[179]

Binding specialised human rights treaties, including the ICRMW, also oblige States parties to recognise the natural and fundamental role of the family *as a unit.*

Regional Instruments, 2nd sess, UN Doc CMW/C/2/L.1 (22 March 2005) [5]. Article 44(2) of the ICRMW provides a narrow definition of who comprises the family of a migrant worker for the purposes of family reunification, which includes his or her spouse, de facto partner and any minor dependent unmarried children.

172 *CRC* Preamble para 6.
173 Ibid.
174 *CRC* arts 27, 18.
175 *General Comment No 7*, UN Doc CRC/C/GC/7/Rev.1, para 15.
176 *ICCPR* art 23(1).
177 *ICESCR* art 10(1).
178 *ICESCR* art 10(1).
179 *UDHR* art 16(3).

For example, Art 44 of the ICRMW requires States to take 'appropriate measures to ensure the protection of the unity of the families of migrant workers'.[180] While the ICRMW has had a remarkably low rate of ratification,[181] its adoption alone reinforces a recognition that, as Cholewinski argues:

> [M]igrant workers are more than just a factor of production; they are social entities with families and accordingly are entitled to protection of their basic economic, social, cultural and civil rights.[182]

Nonetheless, those States that have failed to ratify the ICRMW – which includes all major labour-receiving States – remain bound to protect the family unit by virtue of being a party to one or all of the widely ratified CRC, ICCPR and/or ICESCR.[183] The UN Human Rights Council has reiterated the particularly important protective function that the preservation of the family unit has for children affected by migration. In this context, it has emphasised the importance of the principle of family unity when assessing the best interests of children whose relations with their parents have been interrupted by migration processes.[184]

Hence, the duty for States to justify the interference caused by TLM policies with children's right to have their family unit protected and assisted is established in both general and specialised human rights law. Once again, this goes to the *failure by States to justify* the need for measures that cause significant disruptions to family unity in the context of TLM. This reflects the direction by the Human Rights Committee that if any right under the ICCPR is restricted, then States must demonstrate the necessity of the restriction and ensure that measures are 'proportionate to the pursuance of legitimate aims'.[185] Additionally, the CRC and CMW Committees have urged that protecting a child's right to family life in the context of migration requires:

> that States not only refrain from actions which could result in family separation or other arbitrary interference in the right to family life, but also take positive measures to maintain the family unit, including the reunion of separated family members.[186]

180 *ICRMW* art 44.

181 The ICRMW currently has 55 States parties. See UN, *Treaty Collection* (1 November 2020) <https://treaties.un.org>.

182 Cholewinski, above n 132, 51–2.

183 To date, the ICCPR has 173 State Parties and the ICESCR has 171 State Parties. The only State not a party to the CRC – the United States – is a State Party to the ICCPR and a signatory to the ICESCR. See UN, *Treaty Collection* (1 November 2020) <https://treaties.un.org>.

184 *OHCHR Study on the Protection of the Rights of the Child in the Context of Migration*, UN Doc A/HRC/15/29, [60], [66].

185 *CCPR General Comment No 31*, UN Doc CCPR/C/21/Rev.1/Add.13, para 6.

186 *Joint General Comment on State Obligations Regarding the Human Rights of Children in Countries of Origin, Transit, Destination and Return*, UN Doc CMW/C/GC/4-CRC/C/GC/23, para 27.

This goes to the obligation on States to not only respect (or not interfere with) a child's family life, but to also actively assist children and their families affected by migration to enjoy their right to family unity and family life. The CRC Committee has acknowledged that the right to family unity in the context of migration 'may intersect with States' legitimate interests in making decisions on the entry or stay of non-nationals'.[187] This, again, requires States to demonstrate the legitimacy of migration policies that interfere with the family unit to ensure that they do not 'amount to arbitrary or unlawful interference with family life'.[188] Moreover, the CRC and CMW Committees have emphasised that because the right to protection of family life is covered by multiple human rights instruments, this right 'should be fully respected, protected and fulfilled in relation to every child without any kind of discrimination'.[189]

ii. Specific CRC provisions support children's right to family life

A child's right to have their family life protected from arbitrary interference is embodied in Art 16 of the CRC. This right is included in the conceptual framework for this book and is the focus of Chapter 6. [190] Hence, the principle that the family is the fundamental unit in society entitled to protection by the State is central to understanding Art 16, which entitles children to protection from arbitrary interference with their family life.[191] In this sense, Art 16, as Tobin and Field explain, 'represents another illustration of the special protection accorded to the family under international law'.[192] It reflects the obligation on States to support family life and take positive measures to ensure that children can enjoy their right to family life without arbitrary interference.

Measures to support family life include assistance to parents so that they can provide for their children without being forced to compromise their children's right to family life. As Goonesekere explains, the protection of the family unit in human rights law reinforces State obligations in binding human rights instruments to 'support individuals as they seek to fulfil their family responsibilities and provide for the well-being of family members'.[193] This reflects the interconnectedness of Art 16 with other CRC articles that require States to assist parents to fulfil their parenting role. This includes Arts 27 and 18, both of which are also identified in the conceptual framework for this book.

187 Ibid para 28.
188 Ibid.
189 Ibid para 27.
190 See Chapter 6 for discussion on how restrictive aspects of TLM policies that unnecessarily and unreasonably disrupt the child-parent relationship constitute arbitrary interferences with children's family life.
191 *CRC* art 16.
192 John Tobin and Sarah M Field, 'Article 16. The Right to Protection of Privacy, Family, Home, Correspondence, Honour, and Reputation' in J Tobin (ed), *The UN Convention on the Rights of the Child: A Commentary* (OUP, 2019) 550, 576.
193 Goonesekere, above n 79, 86–7.

In this vein, the principle that the family is the fundamental unit in society to be protected and supported by the State informs each of the rights in the conceptual framework. These include children's rights to be cared for by their parents under Art 7; to receive direction and guidance from their parents under Art 5; to maintain direct and regular contact with their parents if separated under Art 10(2); and to have their parents assisted to fulfil their parental responsibilities under Arts 18 and 27. Positive measures to support each of these CRC rights in the context of TLM will necessarily reduce the degree of interference by TLM policies with a child's family life. In developing measures to protect the family, the CRC Committee has urged States to give 'particular attention to children and families in migration situations and including children left behind'.[194] This reflects the growing concern about the need for States to mitigate the effects of familial separation on children of migrant workers who are growing up in the absence of their parents.

3.5 Conclusion

The children of migrant workers are first and foremost protected under international human rights law by virtue of being children and irrespective of their parents' migration or employment status.[195] In other words:

> Children in the context of migration, including children left behind … appear in the universal protected group of 'children'.[196]

Hence, States parties to the CRC have an obligation to consider the best interests of this group of children in the development of TLM policies, just as they do in all policies and actions that affect children. This requires that policy development processes include an evaluation of the possible negative and positive impacts of the policy on the children concerned.[197] As TLM policies are premised on the separation of children and parents, they have significant and foreseeable implications for children. By engaging in a best interests assessment as required under the CRC, States would be forced to turn their attention to understanding how children's interests may be impacted by TLM. This understanding must be informed by the general principles identified in this chapter. Moreover, any interferences with children's best interests arising from TLM policies must be justified as being necessary, proportionate and in pursuit of a legitimate aim.[198] As a binding treaty,

194 CRC Committee, *Report of the 2012 Day of General Discussion: The Rights of All Children in the Context of International Migration* (28 September 2012) [85] ('*Report of the 2012 Day of General Discussion*').

195 *OHCHR Study on the Protection of the Rights of the Child in the Context of Migration*, UN Doc A/HRC/15/29, [9].

196 Ibid [4].

197 *General Comment No 14*, UN Doc CRC/C/GC/14, para 6.

198 *Joint General Comment on Children in the Context of International Migration*, UN Doc CMW/C/GC/3-CRC/C/GC/22, para 22; *CCPR General Comment No 31*, UN Doc CCPR/C/21/Rev.1/Add.13, para 6.

the CRC legally commits States to adopting this process of giving primary consideration to, and justifying interferences with, children's best interests. In fulfilling this obligation, the CRC Committee has directed that:

> If the solution chosen is not in the best interests of the child the grounds for this must be set out in order to show that the child's best interests were [treated] as a primary consideration, despite the result.[199]

To date, States *have failed to engage* in a process that gives due consideration to the impact of TLM on children's best interests *and* their specific rights pertaining to the child-parent relationship. This is demonstrated throughout this book, which also argues that there are measures reasonably available to States that would reduce interferences with children's rights. The impact of TLM on specific CRC rights identified in the conceptual framework is analysed in Part B of this book in light of the general legal principles outlined in this chapter. That is, the CRC's overarching principles; the principle of international cooperation embedded in the CRC; and the principle in human rights law that the family is the fundamental group unit in society entitled to protection by the State.

Each right in the conceptual framework, which has been outlined in the previous chapter, is informed by and interconnected with these general principles. This highlights that children's best interests and right to development are inevitably affected by policies that separate families, especially dependent children from their parents. The CRC Committee has expressed its concern about children who are left behind when their parents migrate for employment, stressing the potential negative implications that this can have on a child's upbringing and well-being.[200] This concern is reiterated throughout this book and goes to the urgency for States to adopt measures to mitigate the harms being caused to children by TLM policies that fundamentally disrupt the child-parent relationship.

199 *General Comment No 14*, UN Doc CRC/C/GC/14, para 97.
200 CRC Committee, *Report of the 2012 Day of General Discussion*, above n 185, [42].

Part B

4 Article 27

Is TLM an appropriate form of assistance to parents to meet their children's development needs?

> ***Article 27***
>
> *1. States Parties recognize the right of every child to a standard of living adequate for the child's physical, mental, spiritual, moral and social development.*
> *2. The parent(s) or others responsible for the child have the primary responsibility to secure, within their abilities and financial capacities, the conditions of living necessary for the child's development.*
> *3. States Parties, in accordance with national conditions and within their means, shall take appropriate measures to assist parents and others responsible for the child to implement this right and shall in case of need provide material assistance and support programmes, particularly with regard to nutrition, clothing and housing.*

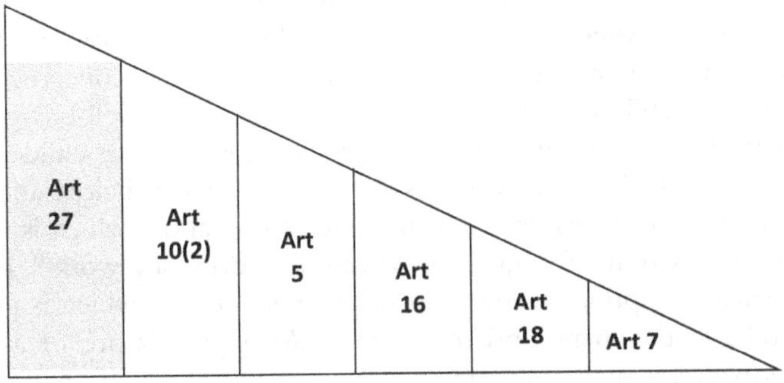

4.1 Introduction

Article 27 is the first CRC article identified in the normative and conceptual framework outlined in Part A. Its immediate relevance to TLM is twofold. First, it protects children's right to a standard of living that is adequate not only for their physical development, but also for their mental, spiritual, moral and social development.[1] (For the purposes of brevity, these non-physical aspects will be referred to hereafter as a child's psychosocial development.) Second, it entitles parents to appropriate measures of assistance from States to meet their primary responsibility to secure the necessary living conditions to fulfil this right of children.[2] This chapter examines these separate but connected prongs of Art 27 in light of both labour-sending and labour-receiving States encouraging parental migration as a measure to enable parents to provide for their children's development needs.

The chapter argues that the promotion of parental migration for employment by States has two consequences. The first is that it inappropriately shifts the entire burden of providing for children's material needs to parents who have limited alternatives to migration in the face of poverty and un- or under-employment. This is despite the duty of labour-sending States to assist parents in need (subject to available national means) to provide for children's basic material requirements.[3] The second is that TLM completely ignores the potential impact of prolonged parental absence on children's psychosocial development and well-being. This is despite labour-sending States having the duty to assist parents to secure the living conditions necessary for their children's psychosocial development needs *as well as* their material needs; and labour-receiving States having a duty to not cause harm to children outside their jurisdiction in line with the principle of international cooperation.[4] These arguments comprise the first two parts of this chapter. Together, they demonstrate that it is misleading to conceive of TLM in its current forms as an 'appropriate' measure of assistance to parents by States in fulfilment of their obligations under Art 27(3). The notion of 'appropriate' assistance is defined in Section 4.2.1.

On the contrary, while TLM *may* create an opportunity for parents to provide for their children economically, this chapter demonstrates that the provision of parental assistance is by no means an *intended* purpose of TLM. Rather, is shows that findings as to whether TLM improves children's education, health and material outcomes are mixed and there are considerable concerns about the impact of TLM on children's psychosocial development and well-being. The latter is largely attributed to the disruption that TLM causes to the child-parent relationship. It highlights the heightened risks to children when their relationship with their primary caregiver is disrupted at the time of migration, which is increasingly so with the feminisation of migration for care and domestic work.[5] The chapter argues that such disruption to the child-parent relationship, which is protected in the CRC, reflects the inappropriateness of TLM as a measure of assistance to parents to provide for their children.

1 *CRC* art 27(1).
2 *CRC* art 27(3).
3 *CRC* art 27(3).
4 The principle of international cooperation is discussed in Chapter 3 (see Section 3.3).
5 The feminisation of migration is discussed in Section 4.3.2(i) below.

The final part of this chapter considers the significance of a child's age and capacity in relation to understanding their development needs and how they may be impacted by parental migration. It argues that appropriate measures of assistance to parents cannot be determined without due consideration of the age of their children at the time of separation. It emphasises that if TLM is to genuinely assist parents to provide for their children's development needs, then it must incorporate measures that actively support children and parents to sustain their relationship in the event of migration. To be effective, these measures must be age-appropriate and respond to children's changing development needs. Moreover, their implementation must be supported by both labour-sending and labour-receiving countries. This is because children's capacity to enjoy and benefit from their relationship with their parents in the context of TLM is determined by transnational arrangements between States.

4.2 The framing of TLM as a form of assistance to parents to provide for their children's needs

4.2.1 Defining appropriate measures of assistance

The CRC Committee has explained that when States ratify the Convention, they assume 'obligations under international law to implement it'.[6] Furthermore, Art 4 of the CRC obliges States to 'undertake all appropriate legislative, administrative, and other measures' necessary for the implementation of all CRC rights. The CRC does not define what these appropriate measures are in either the general measures of implementation identified in Art 4 or in relation to parental assistance in Art 27. Rather, States maintain discretion in deciding those measures they deem appropriate to ensure the realisation of CRC rights.[7] This approach is reflected in the ICRMW, which also affords States significant discretion in determining what measures they deem appropriate to facilitate the unity of migrant workers and their families.[8] However, as Tobin explains:

> [T]he ordinary meaning of the word 'appropriate' demands that there must be a nexus between the measures undertaken and the end sought, namely, the effective implementation of the right in question.[9]

Hence, State discretion is limited by the need for measures to 'actually contribute to the realisation of children's rights', as well as for their implementation to be consistent with all other CRC articles.[10] Respectively, these reflect 'the principle of

6 *General Comment No 5*, UN Doc CRC/GC/2003/5, para 1.

7 John Tobin, 'Article 4. A State's General Obligation of Implementation' in J Tobin (ed), *The UN Convention on the Rights of the Child: A Commentary* (OUP, 2019) 108, 111–12; *Maastricht Principles on Extraterritorial Obligations of States in the Area of Economic, Social and Cultural Rights* (ETO Consortium, January 2013) [8].

8 *ICRMW* art 44.

9 Tobin, above n 7, 112.

10 Ibid 111.

effectiveness' and 'the consistency principle',[11] which assist in understanding whether a measure can be considered appropriate.

i. Measures must be effective

The requirement for measures to be effective requires States to develop measures that are evidence-based rather than based on assumptions about their likely effect.[12] This presents a significant challenge to arguments in favour of parental migration as a form of assistance to parents given that the evidence about the impacts of TLM on children's development outcomes are heavily mixed. Examples of this mixed evidence are presented in Sections 4.2.5 and 4.3. Furthermore, when sufficient evidence is not available, then States must ensure that any measures that they do adopt are properly monitored, reviewed and evaluated to determine if they are effective.[13] This is necessary because States carry the burden of demonstrating the appropriateness of the measures that they adopt to implement children's rights.[14] To date, labour-sending and labour-receiving States have not demonstrated that TLM effectively assists parents to meet their children's *overall* development needs, despite State duties under Art 27 to assist parents to secure the conditions necessary for their children's physical *and* psychosocial growth and development.

The CRC Committee has held that effective implementation of CRC rights requires – in addition to both government and independent monitoring mechanisms – domestic legislation that is compatible with the CRC's provisions and principles, training and awareness-raising and comprehensive data collection.[15] Moreover, the Committee has stressed that in implementing children's rights, States are required to not only engage with all sectors but also with children themselves.[16] At present, both labour-sending and labour-receiving States have failed to undertake any of these requirements to inform the design or assess the effectiveness of TLM policies as a measure of assistance to parents.

It is recognised that the general implementation obligation under Art 4 and the obligation to provide appropriate assistance to parents under Art 27 apply to the State within which the child resides. However, Art 4 recognises that the realisation of certain CRC rights will need to be achieved 'within the framework of international co-operation'.[17] Existing TLM policies, which are largely dictated by labour-receiving countries, force the child-parent relationship into a transnational

11 Ibid.
12 Ibid 113.
13 Ibid 113.
14 Ibid 112; Committee on Economic, Social and Cultural Rights Committee (CESCR), *General Comment No 3: The Nature of States Parties' Obligations (Art. 2, Para. 1, of the Covenant)*, 5th sess, UN Doc E/1991/23 (14 December 1990) para 4; *Siracusa Principles*, UN Doc E/CN.4/1985/4, annex pt I A para 12.
15 *General Comment No 5*, UN Doc CRC/GC/2003/5, paras 1, 9.
16 Ibid para 1.
17 *CRC* art 4.

arrangement. This means that international cooperation becomes an absolute necessity if those CRC rights protecting the child-parent relationship are to be realised. That is, these rights cannot be effectively implemented through unilateral measures taken by labour-sending countries when a parent's capacity to fulfil their parenting role is determined by policies in labour-receiving countries.

ii. Measures must be consistent with other CRC provisions

The CRC Committee has reiterated that State actions to implement CRC rights must be consistent with all CRC provisions including the CRC's overarching principles.[18] These principles are outlined in Chapter 3.[19] As Tobin highlights, any measures taken by States to implement children's rights will necessarily affect children.[20] Hence, the development of 'appropriate' measures *must* have given due consideration to children's best interests (as required under Art 3) and incorporated processes for hearing children's views (as required under Art 12), whether or not these determine the nature of the measure.[21] TLM policies have met neither of these requirements, both of which are essential if implementation measures are to be considered appropriate. Furthermore, as demonstrated in Section 4.3, TLM increases risks to children's psychosocial development, which is inconsistent with the general principle in Art 6 that States shall ensure children's development to the 'maximum extent possible'.[22]

Importantly, Art 27(1) makes it clear that the CRC adopts a holistic conception of children's development, referring explicitly to physical and non-physical aspects of human development. This approach finds its foundation in the earlier non-binding Declarations of the Rights of the Child of 1924 and 1959, which provide context for understanding Art 27. The earlier Declaration (1924) directs States to provide the child with 'the means requisite for its normal development, both materially and spiritually'.[23] The latter Declaration (1959) directs States to provide protection and opportunities to enable the child 'to develop physically, mentally, morally, spiritually and socially in a healthy and normal manner'.[24] Numerous CRC provisions, including those identified in the conceptual framework, reflect the CRC's presumption that in ordinary circumstances, the family unit is the 'healthy and normal' environment for children's growth and development.[25] Moreover, specific CRC articles – namely Art 18 – protect the primary role of

18 *General Comment No 5*, UN Doc CRC/GC/2003/5, para 12.
19 See Chapter 3 (Section 3.2).
20 Tobin, above n 7, 113.
21 Ibid.
22 *CRC* art 6.
23 *Declaration of the Rights of the Child*, League of Nations Res (adopted on 26 September 1924), League of Nations Official Journal, Special Supp No 21, 43 para 1.
24 *The Declaration of the Rights of the Child*, GA Res 1386(XIV), UN GAOR, 14th sess, 841st plen mtg, Agenda Item 64, UN Doc A/RES/14/1386 (20 November 1959) principle 2 ('*Declaration of the Rights of the Child*').
25 These CRC provisions are discussed in Chapter 3 in relation to the protection of the family in human rights law (See Section 3.4.2).

parents in children's upbringing and development. Like Art 27, Art 18 also requires States to provide appropriate assistance to parents to perform their child-rearing responsibilities as primary carers.[26] Importantly, the parental role, the child-parent relationship and children's family life are all protected in the CRC *because* they are considered central to children's development and well-being.[27] Hence, TLM policies that interfere with each of these protected interests cannot be considered appropriate measures of assistance to parents on the part of States.

Importantly, the CRC Committee has explained that for measures to be considered appropriate, they must be 'relevant to directly or indirectly advancing children's rights in a given context'.[28] However, TLM policies currently undermine rather than advance most CRC rights that protect the child-parent relationship and parental role in providing for children's non-economic development needs. This is despite States having a duty to assist parents to meet their primary responsibility to provide the necessary living conditions for their children's *overall* development if needed.[29]

The use of the term 'shall' in Art 27(3) reflects the mandatory nature of the obligation on States to provide appropriate assistance to parents. Moreover, the CRC Committee has emphasised that the implementation of children's rights is a clear legal obligation held by States and 'must not be seen as a charitable process, bestowing favours on children'.[30] Similarly, the duty for States to appropriately assist parents to fulfil their responsibility to provide for their children's development needs is a legal one under Art 27(3). Too often is TLM framed as a coveted employment opportunity for which parents should be grateful in the face of poverty and unemployment in labour-sending countries. However, in reality, parents are being encouraged to migrate to meet their family's financial needs rather than States being required to fulfil their duty under Art 27(3) to provide appropriate assistance to parents in need. This is discussed in Section 4.2.2(ii) in relation to remittances being used by States to replace welfare assistance and in Section 4.2.3 concerning the failure by States to invest in creating local employment options for parents.

4.2.2 Challenges with addressing poverty through parental migration

It is acknowledged that TLM is not a form of emergency migration and hence there remains an element of agency in the decision of migrant workers to migrate.[31] That is, parents are not forced by States or natural disasters to migrate

26 Article 18 is discussed in detail in Chapter 7.

27 The connection between the child-parent relationship and children's development and well-being is discussed in Chapter 2 (see Section 2.3.1) and Chapter 7 (see Section 7.2.3).

28 *General Comment No 19*, UN Doc CRC/C/GC/19, para 22.

29 *CRC* art 27(2).

30 *General Comment No 5*, UN Doc CRC/GC/2003/5, para 11.

31 Stephen Castles, 'The Forces Driving Global Migration' (2013) 34(2) *Journal of Intercultural Studies* 122, 124.

for TLM, and it is frequently argued that parents 'choose' to engage in this form of migration. The notion of parental 'choice' in relation to TLM is discussed in Chapter 6.[32] However, parents who leave dependent children for low-waged work migrate in response to a variety of push and pull factors that are created and perpetuated by both labour-sending and labour-receiving States.[33] These include poverty and failure to create employment opportunities in labour-sending countries that would enable parents to remain with their children while providing for them financially,[34] which is discussed in Section 4.2.3. Hence, without denying the agency of migrant workers, it is important to recognise that parental migration for low-waged employment generally occurs in the face of very limited alternatives for parents. Studies reveal that parents are frequently motivated to migrate to meet financial challenges including debt payments, housing needs and costs associated with their children's education.[35] As observed by a key informant in reference to TLM from Asia to the Gulf States:

> 'The problem is poverty, isn't it? These children come from poverty-ridden families, and the only way that these families think that they can get out of it is through migrating ... So I would imagine that the poverty has to be addressed first'. *(Key Informant – Government 6)*

This observation captures the reality that if labour-sending States are unable or unwilling to provide the necessary welfare assistance to parents in need to enable them to meet their children's basic development requirements as required under Art 27(3), then parents will have few options but to migrate. This situation encourages parents to assume private responsibility for providing for their children in the face of poverty and unemployment, without requiring labour-sending States to deliver more effective measures of parental assistance that would prevent migration. This is because neither labour-sending nor labour-receiving States wish to prevent parental migration. Rather, labour-sending countries depend on remittances from TLM to support their national economies; and labour-receiving countries rely on TLM not only for cheap labour but also as a justification for reducing official development assistance[36].

32 See Chapter 6 (Section 6.3.4).

33 See, eg, Castles, above n 31, 128–9. See also Daphna Hacker, *Legalized Families in the Era of Bordered Globalization* (Cambridge University Press, 2017) 197–244.

34 Ibid.

35 See, eg, Lalana Kanti Yapa, *The Decision Making Process of International Labour Migration with Special Reference to the Sri Lankan Housemaid* (1995) cited in Malsiri Dias and Ramani Jayasundere, 'Sri Lanka: Good Practices to Prevent Women Migrant Workers From Going into Expolitative Forms of Labour' (GENPROM Working Paper No 9, Series on Women and Migration, Gender Promotion Program, ILO, 1 December 2002) 4.

36 Official development assistance (ODA) is understood in line with the Organisation for Economic Cooperation and Development's (OECD) definition that it involves

i. Favouring remittance-based development over official development assistance

In recent years, remittances to labour-sending countries have far surpassed official development assistance from labour-receiving countries.[37] The relationship between remittances and international development is discussed further in Chapters 1 and 7, including the challenges that development outcomes based on remittance-based measures alone present to sustainable development outcomes in communities.[38] Suffice to say that the shift towards 'remittance-based development' has contributed to an economic dependence on remittances in labour-sending countries. For example, in 2015, migrant workers generated roughly $601 billion in remittances (of which developing countries received approximately $441 billion).[39] This equates to almost triple the amount of assistance in the same year.[40] This leaves labour-sending countries little choice but to continue encouraging the migration of their workers. As observed by a key informant:

> 'For a sending country, it's about money, because it is the highest income earner ... It's *not about* building people's capacity or addressing unemployment. It is primarily *about revenue*'. *(Key Informant – MLO-NGO 2)*

This observation reflects that labour-sending countries are driven to promote TLM because of their economic dependence on remittances, regardless of social impacts and unfavourable conditions for workers. However, numerous studies have questioned the potential of remittances to generate long-term economic growth in labour-sending countries.[41] Moreover, as Cortes notes in her study on remittances and children in the Philippines, there 'is no consensus on their impact

government aid that has as its main objective 'the promotion of the economic development and welfare of developing countries' and 'is concessional in character'. See OECD, *Official Development Assistance: Definition and Coverage* (2018) <http://www.oecd.org/dac/stats/officialdevelopmentassistancedefinitionandcoverage.htm>; OECD, *Geographical Distribution of Financial Flows to Developing Countries 2018: Disbursements, Commitments, Country Indicators* (OECD Publishing, 2018).

37 In 2013, remittances nearly tripled official development assistance globally. See Dilip Ratha et al, 'Migration and Remittance Flows: Recent Trends and Outlook, 2013–2016' (Migration and Development Brief No 21, Migration and Remittances Team, Development Prospects Group, The World Bank, 2 October 2013) 2.

38 See Chapter 7 for discussion on TLM and the Sustainable Development Agenda (Section 7.3.3) and the need to measure social impacts in addition to economic to fully understand international development outcomes (Section 7.3.5). See also Chapter 1 (Section 1.2) on remittances and development.

39 Global Knowledge Partnership on Migration and Development (KNOMAD), *Migration and Remittances Factbook 2016* (World Bank Group, 3rd ed, 2016) v.

40 Ibid iv–v.

41 Hacker, above n 33, 200. See also Waoma G Nwaogu and Michael J Ryan, 'FDI, Foreign Aid, Remittance and Economic Growth in Developing Countries' (2015) 19 (2) *Review of Development Economics*, 19(1) (2015) 100.

on poverty eradication, equity or children's rights'.[42] Rather, studies have found that the economic situation of the families of migrant workers frequently do not improve for reasons including debt to recruiters, exploitative employment conditions, costs of living in labour-receiving countries and financial demands on the worker by extended family members.[43] In many instances, this prevents parents from being able to improve their children's economic conditions despite their migration.[44] It has also been widely argued that if economic gains are generated for families, they are relatively short-term. As Hacker highlights:

> [T]he long-term impact of the economic mobilization created by remittances is doubtful, as very little is saved or invested in projects that might protect the current or next generation from poverty.[45]

Remittances are instead frequently used for immediate consumption to meet a family's basic needs including food, housing and access to education and health services.[46] Again, this is in spite of State obligations under Art 27(3) to assist parents to meet these basic needs for their children if they cannot.

Hence, States have yet to demonstrate the role of remittances in enhancing parental ability to create sustainable improvements to children's living conditions in ways that advance their overall development. This has been reiterated by the Department of Labor and Employment in the Philippines in its observation that 'there is a dearth of studies that explore the relationship between labor migration and poverty alleviation in the Philippines'.[47] Moreover, the UN General Assembly has held that while remittances may be an important source of private capital, they 'cannot be equated to other international financial flows' including official development assistance and public funding for development.[48] This is in part because excessive dependency on remittances can thwart the types of public funding

42 Rosalia Cortes, 'Remittances and Children's Rights: An Overview of Academic and Policy Literature' (Division of Policy and Practice Working Paper, UNICEF, January 2007) 6.

43 Hacker, above n 33, 202; Catalina Amuedo-Dorantes, 'The Good and the Bad in Remittance Flows: Remittances Have the Potential to Lift up Developing Economies' (2014) 97 *IZA World of Labor* 1.

44 Hacker, above n 33, 202.

45 Ibid 200–1. See Jeffrey H Cohen, 'Remittance Outcomes and Migration: Theoretical Contests, Real Opportunities' (2005) 40(1) *Studies in Comparative International Development* 88, 93–9; Ernesto Castañeda, 'Living in Limbo: Transnational Households, Remittances and Development' (2012) (51) *International Migration* 13.

46 Ibid. See also Jonathan Crush et al, *Migration, Remittances and 'Development' in Lesotho* (Southern African Migration Programme, 2010).

47 Rebecca J Calzado, Department of Labor and Employment Philippines, 'Labour Migration and Development Goals: The Philippine Experience' (Paper presented at International Dialogue on Migration, Geneva, 8 October 2007) 5–6.

48 *Resolution on International Migration and Development*, UN Doc A/RES/71/237, para 16.

needed to achieve the structural reforms necessary to achieve sustainable development outcomes.[49]

ii. Replacing welfare assistance with remittances

Labour-sending countries frequently encourage families to assume private responsibility for improving their children's circumstances through remittances, including in areas of State responsibility such as education and healthcare. For example, the National Labour Migration Policy of Sri Lanka – a major labour-sending country – states that:

> Migrant remittances are private household transfers that enable education and healthcare for children…[50]

As raised above, remittances then become a substitute for welfare assistance that should be government-provided.[51] This conflicts with the very purpose of Art 27 (3), which is to ensure that States provide appropriate assistance to parents to meet their children's basic development needs. Instead, parents are being encouraged by States to meet these needs themselves (not always successfully) through migration. As Piper explains:

> [I]nadequate social policy and social welfare provisioning is an important source of insecurity which easily translates into a push to migrate.[52]

Hence, TLM, rather than being a form of parental assistance, is largely driven by parental endeavours to improve the living standards and welfare of their children in the *absence* of appropriate parental assistance. Without adequate assistance from States, parents are left with few options but to migrate to improve their children's access to education, healthcare, nutrition and housing.[53] For example, an

49 Bimal Ghosh, *Migrants' Remittances and Development: Myths, Rhetoric and Realities* (IOM, 2006), 60.

50 Sri Lankan Ministry for Foreign Employment Promotion and Welfare, *National Labour Migration Policy for Sri Lanka* (Government of Sri Lanka, October 2008) vi.

51 Julia O'Connell Davidson and Caitlin Farrow, *Child Migration and the Construction of Vulnerability* (Save the Children, 2007) 14.

52 Nicola Piper, 'Gender and Migration: A Paper Prepared for the Policy Analysis and Research Programme of the Global Commission on International Migration' (GCIM, September 2005) 20.

53 Maruja M B Asis, 'Living with Migration: Experiences of Left Behind Children in the Philippines' (2006) 2(1) *Asian Population Studies* 45, 60; Gabrielle Marcelletti Rocha de Oliveira, *Transnational Care Constellations: Mexican Immigrant Mothers and their Children in Mexico and in New York City* (PhD Thesis, Columbia University, 2015) 2; IOM, 'Migration and Families: Background Paper' (Intersessional Workshop, International Dialogue on Migration, 7–8 October 2014) 2; UN Population Fund, *State of World Population 2006: A Passage to Hope: Women and International Migration* (UNFPA, 2006) 1; IOM, *Labour Migration from Indonesia: An Overview of*

evaluation of New Zealand's seasonal labour migration programme found that one of the most important motivations behind migrant worker participation 'was the chance to raise money to pay for school fees'.[54] Thus, rather than providing parents with assistance to meet school fees or reducing school fees, as required under international law,[55] TLM requires them to leave their children for significant periods to pursue the means to provide for *some* of their children's development needs such as school fees. However, as discussed in Section 4.2.5, improved educational and health outcomes for children do not always eventuate. Moreover, even if they do, this approach fails to account for children's broader psychosocial development needs, which are equally recognised and protected in Art 27.

The dilemma that TLM presents for parents is captured in the following statement by a key informant from the government sector:

> 'There is the whole balancing issue between the needs of the child and the argument that in a poor country the best thing a parent can do for their kids is to travel overseas and provide for their physical and educational needs through remittances ... But whose responsibility is it? Is it the responsibility of the State to make the choices easier so parents don't have to leave?'.
> *(Key Informant – Government 4)*

This statement reflects the reality that parental migration is typically framed as a parent taking a 'necessary and responsible act' for the sake of their children.[56] However, while parents do have the primary responsibility for securing the living conditions necessary for their children's development under Art 27(2), Art 27(3) recognises that not all parents will be able to do this. It therefore entitles them to State assistance to meet this responsibility, which is only part of their parental role.

TLM, however, impedes parental capacity to fulfil other equally important aspects of a parent's role in a child's life. This includes being physically present to provide for their children's psychosocial needs. Hence, while TLM does create employment opportunities for parents, it is far from an 'appropriate' measure of parental assistance. Rather, it shifts the burden of providing for children's basic development needs entirely on to parents who have limited resources and options. For the creation of employment opportunities to be considered an appropriate form of assistance to parents, this measure would have to be consistent with other CRC rights and not interfere with parental capacity to meet children's broad

Indonesian Migration to Selected Destinations in Asia and the Middle East (IOM, 2010) 36.

54 John Gibson and David McKenzie, 'The Development Impact of a Best Practice Seasonal Worker Policy' (2014) 96(2) *The Review of Economics and Statistics* 229, 240. See also Crush et al, above n 46.

55 Article 28 of the CRC requires States to make education accessible to all children in support of their right to education.

56 Hacker, above n 33, 202–3.

development needs. Hence, this would require the creation of viable employment opportunities *within* labour-sending countries, which is discussed in the following section, or TLM policies that did not mandate prolonged child-parent separation. The latter is discussed in Chapter 6.[57]

4.2.3 The need for viable employment opportunities in labour-sending countries

Under Art 27, the principle of effectiveness means that appropriate measures must assist parents in need to secure the living conditions necessary to meet their children's broad development needs. Moreover, the principle of consistency demands that appropriate measures will not be inconsistent with other CRC rights, including those identified in the conceptual framework that protect the child-parent relationship. In contrast, TLM generates prolonged periods of child-parent separation and removes parents from their role as a child's primary carer during the period of migration. Moreover, the undermining of the parental role as primary caregiver frequently continues after reunification if the child-parent relationship has broken down during the period of separation. This is discussed in Chapter 5.[58] Hence, by focusing on creating employment opportunities overseas without simultaneously creating viable employment alternatives *in* labour-sending countries, parents are being stripped of any real choice as to whether to migrate to provide for their children financially.

At present, States are failing to invest in creating viable employment opportunities that would allow parents to provide for their children *while* continuing to reside with or nearer to them.[59] This is despite the CRC Committee having urged States to facilitate family cohesion by creating economic opportunities for workers at a local level and developing rights-based initiatives that incentivise parents to remain in local communities.[60] This view is supported by the ILO's non-binding principles for a rights-based approach to labour migration, which encourage States to promote development assistance aimed at 'generating or increasing opportunities for decent work for women and men in developing countries'.[61]

Labour-sending countries have explicitly recognised the need for States to 'ensure access to employment and livelihood opportunities for their citizens as sustainable alternatives to migration of workers'.[62] This provision in the non-binding ASEAN Declaration on the Rights of Migrant Workers reflects a recognition on the part of labour-sending countries that a lack of viable employment

57 See Chapter 6 (Section 6.4).
58 See Chapter 5 (Section 5.4.4).
59 See, eg, Castles, above n 31, 128–9.
60 CRC Committee, *Report of the 2012 Day of General Discussion: The Rights of All Children in the Context of International Migration* (28 September 2012) [42] ('*Report of the 2012 Day of General Discussion*').
61 ILO, *ILO Multilateral Framework on Labour Migration: Non-binding Principles and Guidelines for a Rights-Based Approach to Labour Migration* (ILO, 2006) [2.4].
62 *ASEAN Declaration on the Rights of Migrant Workers* para 12.

opportunities is one of the main push factors for migrant workers.[63] Key informants from the multilateral/non-government and research and policy sectors emphasised the need for States to invest in creating *real* employment alternatives for parents in labour-sending countries. This included the following observation that was made in relation to the migration of women for domestic work:

> 'You have to give them *viable* alternatives, not 2000 rupee handicraft making things where women can sit at home and carry this triple burden of work, child care, the home ... It has to be a proper, viable livelihood'. *(Key Informant – MLO-NGO 2)*

This observation emphasises the creation of 'viable alternatives' for parents in labour-sending countries, which means that there is nothing preventing investment in local livelihood options from occurring in parallel with the operation of TLM. The availability of these options would result in a more genuine choice for parents in their decision to migrate, serving to disincentivise rather than incentivise parental migration. It would also better fulfil State obligations to provide 'appropriate' measures of assistance to parents in need under Art 27(3). This is because local employment opportunities would assist parents to secure living conditions necessary for their children's material well-being while remaining physically present to provide for their psychosocial development needs.

i. Incentivising TLM and encouraging misinformed decision-making

At present, the desire by States to encourage participation in TLM has led to people's migration decisions being based on 'limited and positively biased information' and with limited knowledge about the consequences of migration.[64] This concern was stressed by key informants in views such as:

> 'Incentives are given to domestic workers – they get paid upfront a huge amount of money to go. If we can scrap that, then uninformed or hasty decisions will reduce ... You need to make the migration process, at every step, depend on very well-informed decisions that make it difficult to migrate, like in other areas of migration'. *(Key Informant – MLO-NGO 2)*

63 See, eg, H.E. Ravinatha P Aryasinha, 'Introductory Statement at the Presentation of Sri Lanka's 2nd Periodic Report (CMW/C/LKA/2) Submitted under the ICRMW' (Presented at the 25th Session of the CMW Committee, Geneva, 1 September 2016) 6.

64 John F Helliwell, Richard Layard and Jeffrey D Sachs (eds), *World Happiness Report 2018* (Sustainable Development Solutions Network, 2018) 46–7.

This view highlights the way that low-waged migrant workers in particular are encouraged to migrate with limited information about and preparedness for the potential risks and consequences that could arise from their migration. The recent World Happiness Report has raised similar concerns about the misinformation on which people's decisions to migrate are frequently made. It found that:

> [P]eople are believed to put excessive weight on satisfying salient desires, most notably economic gain, at a cost to more basic needs such as social needs. These beliefs are inspired by the weak correlation between economic welfare and happiness for people who have sufficient money to make ends meet.[65]

Hence, while people may be able to earn *more* overseas, if they had viable opportunities to earn the salary needed to support their families in their home country, parents would be incentivised to remain with their children. Moreover, findings that increased income from a family member's migration does not correlate with improvements to psychosocial well-being – and that the migration itself can negatively impact psychosocial well-being – have been reiterated in non-TLM contexts. For example, the above-mentioned World Happiness Report points to findings from the migration lottery that allows selected Tongan residents to migrate to New Zealand that:

> Four years after migration, the 'lucky' Tongans who were allowed to migrate were less happy than the 'unlucky' Tongans who were forced to stay, even though the voluntary migrants enjoyed substantially better objective well-being, such as nearly triple their pre-migration income.[66]

This demonstrates that even when migration does generate increased income, this alone does not improve outcomes in relation to non-material aspects of human development. The inability of money alone to enhance broader aspects of human development is why the CRC considers all aspects of a child's development together and protects them equally in Art 27.

Research in the context of TLM has shown that remittances alone do not generate improved outcomes for children even in relation to the physical and material aspects of child development. Rather, a number of familial and social variables determine whether a family is able to utilise remittances to effectively improve a child's education, health and material outcomes. This is discussed at Section 4.2.5. Nonetheless, just like labour-sending countries, labour-receiving countries emphasise the *potential* of remittances to improve selective aspects of children's development to justify their TLM policies that demand child-parent separation.

65 Ibid 47.
66 Ibid.

4.2.4 Labour-receiving States promote selective aspects of TLM to their advantage

Rather than improving employment options and conditions for parents in labour-sending countries, the growth of TLM is rooted in 'the widening gap in wages and living standards between nations'.[67] In fact, high unemployment rates and remittance-dependent economies have created the ideal conditions for labour-receiving countries to source low-wage workers on their terms. This enables labour-receiving countries to maintain low wages for particular jobs[68] with, as Castles explains, their 'need' for migrant workers being 'socially constructed by the poor wages, conditions and social status in certain sectors'.[69] This view was reiterated by key informants from the multilateral/non-government and research and policy sectors in comments such as:

> 'Increasingly, I see migration policy in countries like Australia as very *self-interested* policy on the part of the receiving country. I see it as being over-whelmingly about the needs of business and industry. It's about *our* labour shortages, *our* care needs. In the care space, it's a quick fix for our care needs'. *(Key Informant – R & P 7)*

The 'self-interested' nature of TLM policies on the part of labour-receiving countries is highlighted by the fact that they explicitly restrict the family rights of migrant workers with *no consideration* of how this foreseeably impacts children's rights and best interests. Instead, labour-receiving countries and international organisations conflate TLM with assistance from States to parents to provide for their children's financial needs. Both frequently purport that TLM increases the capacity of parents to provide for their children's basic physical, material and educational needs, as discussed in Section 4.2.5. For example, IOM has highlighted the 'success' of its 'Temporary Agricultural Workers to Canada' project – which brings workers from Guatemala to Canada for four to six months a year – by highlighting the experience of individual parents in quotes such as:

> Going to work in Canada has changed many things in my life. Now my children have corn flakes and milk before they go to school in the morning. We can afford to eat meat every day, while before we did not have money for bread, let alone corn flakes.[70]

67 IOM (2013) cited in Zahra Meghani, 'Women on the Move' in Zahra Meghani (ed), *Women Migrant Workers: Ethical, Political and Legal Problems* (Taylor and Francis, 2015) 5.

68 Meghani, above n 67, 7.

69 Munz et al (2007) cited in Castles, above n 31, 128.

70 Sonia Pellecer (IOM Guatemala), 'Short-term Temporary Labour Migration Yields Long-Term Results' (July 2007) *Migration* 19, 20.

This demonstrates that TLM is considered a 'success' if it enables individual parents to meet their children's basic physical and material needs, such as the provision of food. This is despite parents being entitled to State assistance under Art 27 (3) to meet such basic needs without having to leave their children. Moreover, the father quoted above participated in IOM's programme for over three years, allowing him to send his children to school, build a house and purchase land.[71] While the benefits for this individual family are very real, this presents two further difficulties with this form of migration being considered a measure of parental assistance.

First, it highlights that migrant workers often initially migrate for a short period of time, which becomes protracted if longer-term financial endeavours are undertaken, such as building a house. These endeavours go beyond meeting children's immediate basic needs and depend upon a parent's remigration. This extends the cumulative period of parental absence over their children's childhood, which further diminishes the capacity of parents to fulfil other aspects of the parenting role. Second, TLM programmes frequently restrict participation in TLM to a favoured pool of workers and encourage their remigration over years or even decades.[72] This means that any economic opportunity that TLM does bestow on parents to provide for their children financially is not available to all parents nor evenly distributed across communities. Nonetheless, because TLM is not designed to be a measure of parental assistance, the remigration of migrant workers is actively encouraged by labour-receiving States because it reduces training costs for employers.[73] The causes of remigration and challenges that it presents to the child-relationship are discussed in Chapter 6.[74]

i. Parental assistance is not an intended or legitimate aim of TLM

Attempts to justify TLM as a measure by States to assist parents to improve their children's living conditions by providing employment opportunities overseas are misleading because, as discussed in Section 4.2.1, such measures need to be effective in implementing the CRC right in question and consistent with other CRC provisions. Multiple CRC provisions protect the unity of children and parents and parents' broad role as their children's primary caregivers. Hence, measures that require a parent to be absent to provide for their children's economic and material needs are not an effective way of ensuring that parents are assisted to create living conditions to enhance their children's psychosocial development, which is protected equally in Art 27.

Moreover, measures legitimately aiming to assist parents to fulfil the parenting role would not simultaneously remove them from their protected role as the children's primary caregivers, unless it was explicitly shown to be in a child's best

71 Ibid.
72 Remigration is discussed in Chapter 6 (see Section 6.4.2).
73 See Chapter 6 (Section 6.4.2).
74 See Chapter 6 (Section 6.4.2).

interests. To date, States have not shown parental migration to be in children's best interests nor incorporated any process for assessing children's best interests in the development of TLM policies. The requirement under the CRC to give due consideration to children's best interests is discussed in Chapter 3 and in Section 4.4.1.[75]

The challenge for States in reconciling economic arguments in favour of TLM with the inherent difficulties presented by policies that separate parents from dependent children are reflected in the following observation made by a key informant from the government sector in the Canadian context:

> 'The opportunity to come to Canada and work on a seasonal basis and return home for a good portion of the year enables them to bring a degree of economic stability or progress to their family ... But that by itself doesn't answer all the questions. Because there is the question about family unity and the children's need to have both of their parents, to the extent possible, available to them as they go through their younger years'. *(Key Informant – Government 3)*

This observation demonstrates that governments are aware of the benefits to children that flow from having their parents physically present to raise them, particularly when they are young. Recognition by labour-receiving countries about the importance of strong child-parent relationships to children's psychosocial development is discussed in Chapter 7.[76] Nonetheless, labour-receiving countries continue to design TLM policies that disrupt this relationship, despite the duty to assist less-resourced countries to implement (not undermine) CRC rights in line with the principle of international cooperation.[77]

Importantly, labour-receiving countries such as Canada do not frame their Temporary Foreign Worker Program (TFWP) as an international development programme. Hence, the TFWP is intended to operate to Canada's benefit and does *not* have an *explicit* goal of contributing to development in its labour-sending countries. Australia, on the other hand, has framed its temporary labour migration programmes as having both labour market and international development objectives.[78] Hence, its TLM policies that separate children and parents not only affect

75 See Chapter 3 (Section 3.2.1).
76 See Chapter 7 (Section 7.2.3).
77 The principle of international cooperation is outlined in Chapter 3 (see Section 3.3).
78 Explicit development objectives of Australia's TLM programmes with the Pacific comprise of economic based outcomes that are measured by remittances. However, the Australian Government has drawn an explicit link between remittances from its Pacific Labour Scheme and development benefits in terms of housing, education and support for communities in the Pacific. See Australian Government Department of Foreign Affairs and Trade (DFAT), *Pacific Labour Mobility* (November 2018) <https://dfat.gov.au/geo/pacific/engagement/pacific-labour-mobility/Pages/default.asp

the capacity of labour-sending countries to implement CRC rights that protect the child-parent relationship, but also pose challenges to its stated international development goals that include supporting communities in Pacific Island countries.[79] The challenges that TLM presents to sustainable development goals are discussed in Chapter 7.[80]

ii. International development as an explicit aim of Australia's TLM policies

The Australian Seasonal Workers Program (SWP) is one the few TLM schemes that has an explicit objective of contributing to economic development in labour-sending countries.[81] It is recognised that the Pacific region faces different challenges from other labour-sending regions in terms of the capacity of its smaller countries to generate local employment opportunities. This is because of their size, remoteness, limited formal economies and forced internal migration due to climate change.[82] Moreover, as highlighted by the Lowy Institute, these challenges will be compounded by the region's youth bulge and expected population growth of 49 per cent over the next two and a half decades.[83] However, as observed by UN bodies and the ILO, those countries in the Pacific facing the greatest potential migration pressures – such as Tuvalu, Kiribati and Nauru – are also the countries with the fewest options for international migration.[84] Hence, migration programmes targeting workers from these smaller Pacific Island countries do operate in a different context where alternatives to migration are not necessarily viable, particularly in the face of climate change. This was reiterated by a key informant from the government sector in the following observation:

> 'In the Pacific, domestic economies are not of the size that allows for formal sector jobs or sustainable economies that are going to hold a private sector ... whereas somewhere like Sri Lanka, it should be a sustainable economy. So, I think we do have to think slightly differently with the Pacific from the rest of the world'. *(Key Informant – Government 4)*

x>. See also Rochelle Bailey, 'Using Material Remittances from Labour Schemes for Social and Economic Development: Case Study Vanuatu' (In Brief 2015/15, State, Society and Governance in Melanesia Program (SSGM), ANU, 2015).

79 Ibid.

80 See Chapter 7 (Section 7.3.3).

81 World Bank Group, *Maximizing the Development Impacts from Temporary Migration: Recommendations for Australia's Seasonal Worker Programme* (International Bank for Reconstruction and Development/The World Bank, 2017) x.

82 Leon Berkelmans and Jonathan Pryke, 'The Development Benefits of Expanding Pacific Access to Australia's Labour Market' (Lowy Institute Analyses Paper, December 2016), 2; John Campbell and Olivia Warrick, *Climate Change and Migration Issues in the Pacific* (UN Economic and Social Commission for Asia and the Pacific, 2014) 2–3.

83 Berkelmans and Pryke, above n 82, 2.

84 Campbell and Warrick, above n 82, 3.

This observation points to the need to consider factors unique to the Pacific region in the development of TLM policies, particularly in relation to the smaller Pacific Island countries, which may enhance the legitimacy of policy aims that target these specific countries. However, even if Australia can demonstrate the legitimacy of the development aims behind specific TLM programmes targeting countries that are unable to sustain local employment opportunities, States involved in these programmes are still required to assess how children's rights and best interests may be affected by their parents' migration. Given that parental migration will inevitably interfere with CRC rights protecting the child-parent relationship, States must also demonstrate that the nature of the child-parent separation (such as the duration) is necessary to achieve the development aim; and identify whether there are other reasonably available measures that would reduce any interferences with children's rights and best interests.

To date, the Australian government has only attempted to justify the legitimacy of the development aim of its TLM policies based on economic indicators. In relation to the SWP, it has expressly committed to ensure that it contributes to economic development in labour-sending countries through remittances.[85] In this vein, a recent evaluation of the SWP found that since 2012, it had generated roughly A$144 million in net income gains to the Pacific region.[86] The evaluation therefore held that:

> The programme is clearly delivering on its core objective of contributing to the economic development of participating countries, as measured in terms of income.[87]

Earlier reporting on the SWP also found that workers remitted approximately $5,000 per person per year.[88] This was found to represent 'a gain of $2,600 once opportunity costs of staying in Pacific is discounted',[89] which amounts to 'a 39% increase in per-capita annual income for each household'.[90] While this is undoubtedly a significant economic gain to individual families, it is important that the notion of 'development' in labour-sending countries is not restricted to economic measures alone. This is because measures that only assess economic indicators mask the social impacts of TLM, many of which relate to people's broader human development needs. As De la Garza explains, the conventional analyses of TLM that measure outcomes predominantly based on economic factors significantly overestimate its gains 'and undervalue the costs immigration imposes on

85 Commonwealth, *Australian Government Response to the Joint Standing Committee on Migration Report: Seasonal Change – Inquiry into the Seasonal Worker Programme* (February 2017) 1.
86 World Bank Group, above n 81, xi.
87 Ibid.
88 Australian Agency for International Development (AusAID), 'Labour Mobility Initiative: Independent Progress Report' (AusAID, March 2013) 8.
89 Ibid.
90 Gibson and McKenzie (2011) cited in AusAID, above n 88, 35.

the overall well-being of families left behind'.[91] Article 27 reiterates the importance of adopting a holistic approach to development in the context of children, recognising that their psychosocial development needs are as important as their economic and material needs. For this reason, it protects them equally.

The World Bank's recent evaluation of the SWP did attempt to broaden measures beyond income to examine human development outcomes in relation to school attendance and health outcomes.[92] While this broader approach is welcome, it is again restricted to examining children's health and education outcomes without addressing impacts on their psychosocial development and child-parent relationships. The study identifies 11 recommendations to 'further the development impacts of the scheme',[93] which are again welcomed but do not include longitudinal monitoring of the impact of TLM on familial relationships. This is particularly important in view of the recommendations encouraging increased female participation, which in turn, increases the potential for the worker to be the child's primary caregiver at the time of migration. The increased risks that this poses for children's psychosocial well-being is discussed in Section 4.3.2.

4.2.5 TLM may enhance children's education, health and material development outcomes

i. Educational and health outcomes

In a similar vein to other studies on the impact of remittances on children's health and education outcomes, the World Bank's evaluation of Australia's SWP presented mixed findings. Positively, regarding children's educational development, it found that school enrolment and attendance increased by 7.7 per cent in Tonga.[94] However, there were *no significant impacts* on education outcomes in Vanuatu.[95] Furthermore, in relation to health outcomes, it found that:

> The programme did not have statistically significant impacts on health outcomes in either Tonga or Vanuatu. This is consistent with the existing literature, which does not provide strong evidence that migration significantly impacts health outcomes.[96]

As discussed above, parents are often motivated to participate in TLM by the narrative that remittances will improve their children's education, health and

91 Rodolfo de la Garza, De la Garza, 'Migration, Development and Children Left Behind: A Multidimensional Perspective' (Social and Economic Policy Working Paper, UNICEF, May 2010) i.
92 World Bank Group, above n 81, xi, 47.
93 Ibid xii.
94 World Bank Group, above n 81, 47.
95 Ibid.
96 Ibid.

material living conditions. This motivation, particularly in relation to women's migration, has been explained as follows:

> [T]he spread of globalized images of idealized childhood motivate women to migrate in order to give their children these childhoods, marked by the substitution of material goods and increased access to education for the presence of their mother.[97]

However, studies to date demonstrate conflicting findings in relation to *actual* improvements to children's education and health outcomes, showing positive *and* negative impacts that are influenced by factors such as the gender and age of the child; the level of commitment to the child's health and education shown by the alternative caregiver; and parental (particularly maternal) education levels.[98] To illustrate, a study on Moldova (a labour-sending country) has shown that 'school performance of children left behind is often compromised by increased household responsibilities and obligations to care for their younger siblings';[99] while a review of New Zealand's seasonal labour migration programme found that children of Tongan seasonal workers are 'more likely to be attending school than children from other Tongan households'.[100] Some researchers have attributed these mixed empirical findings to the effects of the child-parent separation on children's psychosocial well-being, which in turn can impact their engagement and motivation at school.[101]

Similarly, studies show mixed findings regarding the benefits of parental migration on children's physical health. As noted above, Australia's SWP has not generated any notable health outcomes for the families of seasonal workers in Tonga or Vanuatu.[102] However, a study conducted in Mexico (a major labour-sending

97 Julia Meredith Hess and Diana Shandy, 'Kids at the Crossroads: Global Childhood and the State' in (2008) 81(4) *Anthropological Quarterly* 765, 772; Sarah Horton, 'Consuming Childhood: "Lost" and "Ideal" Childhoods as a Motivation for Migration' (2008) 81(4) *Anthropological Quarterly* 925.

98 Rasika Jayasuriya and Brian Opeskin, 'The Migration of Women Domestic Workers from Sri Lanka: Protecting the Rights of Children Left Behind' (2015) 48 *Cornell International Law Journal* 579, 608–11. See also Cortes, above n 42; Kolitha Wickramage, Chesmal Siriwardhana and Sharika Peiris, 'Promoting the Health of Left-Behind Children of Asian Labour Migrants: Evidence for Policy and Action' (Issue in Brief, IOM / Migration Policy Institute, Issue No 14, September 2015); Adam Sawyer, 'Is Money Enough?: The Effect of Migrant Remittances on Parental Aspirations and Youth Educational Attainment in Rural Mexico' (2016) 50(1) *International Migration Review* 231, 259.

99 UNICEF Moldova (2006) cited in UNICEF, *Children and Migration* (2007) Global Forum on Migration and Development <https://www.gfmd.org/unicef-children-and-migration>.

100 Gibson and McKenzie (2010) cited in Richard Curtain, Matthew Dornan, Jesse Doyle and Stephen Howes, *Pacific Possible: Labour Mobility: The Ten Billion Dollar Prize* (Pacific Possible Series, World Bank, July 2016) 6.

101 Menjivar and Abrego (2009), Sawyer et al (2009), Dreby (2010) cited Sawyer, above n 98, 241–2.

102 World Bank Group, above n 81, 47.

country) suggested that 'remittances contribute to improvements in infant health' by reducing rates of post-partum malnutrition and infant mortality.[103] On the other hand, a study from the Philippines concluded that economic gains from having a parent working abroad 'does not seem to have altered health-seeking behaviour, which remains poor'.[104]

Such mixed findings reflect the need for a contextualised understanding of the conditions affecting a particular child and his or her family in order to fully understand the potential for a child to benefit from his or her parent's migration.[105] This relates directly to the overarching legal principle of the best interests of the child embodied in Art 3 of the CRC.[106] Article 3 holds that States *must* give primary consideration to a child's best interests in all matters affecting them, which necessitates an assessment of the child's best interests. This, in turn, cannot be achieved without knowledge of the child's specific circumstances including, among other things, the child's age and capacity, family situation, suitability of alternative caregivers and support available to them.

ii. Material outcomes

As noted in Section 4.2.2, there is no definitive evidence as to whether remittances generate material outcomes that are beneficial for families relative to the costs associated with family separation. For example, some economists argue that rather than investing remittances in long-term initiatives such as new businesses, they are frequently spent on consumable items such as TVs and building bigger houses.[107] Moreover, as Piper argues, although the standard of living may be raised for individual families, 'most overseas workers have no substantial savings despite years of working abroad and are often caught in the debt trap'.[108] It was also found in Cortes' study of the risks facing women and children who remain behind in labour-sending countries that:

103 UNICEF Mexico (2006) cited in UNICEF, *Children and Migration* (2007) Global Forum on Migration and Development <https://www.gfmd.org/unicef-children-and-migration>.

104 Rosemarie Edillon, *The Effects of Parent's Migration on the Rights of Children Left Behind in the Philippines* (Division of Policy and Practice Working Paper, UNICEF, August 2008) 71–2.

105 Yao Lu, 'Parental Migration and Education of Left-Behind Children: A Comparison of Two Settings' (2014) 76(5) *Journal of Marriage and Family* 1082, 1083.

106 See Chapter 3 (Section 3.2.1).

107 Frank (2001), Wheatley (2003) cited in Lise Widding Isaksen, Sambasivan Uma Devi and Arlie Russell Hochschild, 'Global Care Crisis: A Problem of Capital, Care Chains, or Commons?' (2008) 52(3) *American Behavioral Scientist* 405 Lise Widding Isaksen, Sambasivan Uma Devi and Arlie Russell Hochschild, 'Global Care Crisis: A Problem of Capital, Care Chains, or Commons?' (2008) 52(3) *American Behavioral Scientist* 405, 420 n 2.

108 Piper, above n 52, 11.

> [E]mpirical research and case studies [suggest] that parents' migration entailed risks for children affecting their rights, which could not be offset by remittances alone.[109]

Governments in labour-sending countries have themselves acknowledged a lack of evidence demonstrating a link between remittances and improved living conditions for those families most in need of assistance. For example, the Department of Labor and Employment in the Philippines has recognised that while remittances have made a significant contribution to the economy of the Philippines, there is no evidence as to whether 'these gains have accrued down to the lower levels of Philippine society'.[110] It has also raised the incidental nature of any improvements to children's health and education that may occur in individual circumstances, recognising that this is not the intended purpose of TLM. Rather, the Department has recognised that TLM is primarily economically and employer driven with a focus on keeping wages and long-term welfare costs low in labour-receiving countries.[111]

Hence, TLM in its current forms operates primarily in the interests of labour-receiving countries, with an overwhelming silence about its impact on the best interests of children. While the operation of TLM to the advantage of labour-receiving countries is unsurprising given that they dictate the terms of TLM policies, States have completely overlooked their duty to consider and assess children's best interests in policies that so obviously affect them. Thus, while remittances *may* improve material conditions and enhance access to education and healthcare for children, TLM is by no means an *intended*, informed and evidence-based 'appropriate' measure of State assistance to parents to provide for their children's development. Rather, arguments that TLM is a measure of assistance to parents appear to be an attempt to retrofit State obligations under the CRC with existing TLM policies, which have not been informed by any consideration of the CRC. Appropriate measures of assistance *at least* demand *an assessment* of children's best interests *and* justification of any inconsistencies with other CRC rights that may be interfered with by that measure. In the context of TLM, this includes those rights that protect the parental role in providing for children's broad development needs that cannot be with money alone.

4.3 Potential impacts of parental migration on children's psychosocial development needs

4.3.1 Evidence from labour-sending countries

Labour-sending countries have publicly recognised the potential risks to children's psychosocial well-being arising from their parents' migration for TLM. For

109 Rosalia Cortes, 'Children and Women Left Behind in Labor Sending Countries: An Appraisal of Social Risks' (Division of Policy and Practice Working Paper, UNICEF, August 2008) 1.

110 Calzado, above n 47, 5–6.

111 Ibid.

example, the Government of the Philippines, over a decade and a half ago, acknowledged that:

> The country faces huge social costs to migrant families as a result of prolonged separation, the breakdown of families and the deterioration and underdevelopment of the psycho-social growth of their children.[112]

During the same period, numerous published studies have raised similar concerns about the disruption to family life, children's psychosocial development and the communities in which children are raised caused by migration.[113] For example, Davidson and Farrow highlight in their study on children and migration that 'researchers have detailed the sense of abandonment, loss and grief experienced by children who have endured lengthy separation from their parents'.[114] This is supported by more recent empirical studies including the World Happiness Report of 2018. This report found that while the migration of a family member generally improved the perceived quality of life for family members in the home country in an economic sense, these members also experienced negative consequences including 'impaired emotional support, psychological disconnection from the migrant, and a greater burden of responsibility for household chores and child nurturing'.[115]

Similarly, IOM – to which many labour-receiving countries are Member States including Canada and Australia – has recognised that:

> [T]he separation of children from their parents has been found to have profoundly negative emotional effects, generating significant behavioural change, and feelings of loss, sadness, abandonment, anger and rejection.[116]

Not all children and families of migrant workers will be affected in this manner. Children's individual circumstances and the protective factors present in their lives will affect the degree to which parental migration impacts their psychosocial development (much like their health and education outcomes). Hence, existing studies on psychosocial impacts also present mixed findings. However, they demonstrate existing knowledge about the heightened *risks* of harm to children's psychosocial well-being posed by parental migration and lengthy periods of child-

112 Erista et al (2003) quoted in Isaksen, Devi and Hochschild, above n 107, 409.

113 See, eg, UNICEF Moldova, 'The Situation of Children Left Behind by Migrating Parents' (Study Report, UNICEF, 2006); Asis, above n 53; Audrey M Pottinger and Sharon Williams Brown, 'Understanding the Impact of Parental Migration on Children: Implications for Counselling Families from the Caribbean' (2006) *American Counselling Association: Vistas Online* <https://www.counseling.org/resources/library/vistas/vistas06_online-only/pottinger.pdf>; S T Hettige et al, *Understanding Psychosocial Issues Faced by Migrant Workers and their Families* (Sri Lankan Ministry of Foreign Employment Promotion and Welfare, 2012).

114 Davidson and Farrow, above n 51, 51.

115 Helliwell, Layard and Sachs (eds), above n 64, 48.

116 IOM, 'Migration and Families: Background Paper', above n 53, 5.

parent separation. To illustrate, some studies show that depression rates are higher among children who were separated from their parents before being able to join them than children who migrated with their parents;[117] the migration of a child's caregiver can be associated with subsequent academic, behavioural and emotional difficulties experienced by the child;[118] and that children often describe themselves as having feelings of insecurity and being 'lonely, isolated, and deprived of support' following their parents' migration.[119] However, other studies have found that:

> As long as the migrant parents communicated regularly and the family was stable … it is suggested that the strains imposed by migration could be withstood.[120]

The issue of regular communication is discussed in the following chapter in relation to children's right to maintain direct and regular contact with their parents under Art 10(2).[121] Significantly, this latter study, conducted in the Philippines, also found that children with migrant mothers or both parents working overseas were less happy than children in general.[122]

The heightened potential risks and negative impacts that eventuate for children when their mothers (who are also their primary caregivers) migrate is a recurring finding in existing studies across labour-sending countries. For example, a study from Trinidad and Tobago found that even if children of migrant workers felt well supported within temporary family arrangements, they still 'bear marks of abandonment to varying degrees, particularly related to the loss of a mother to a foreign country'.[123] Similarly, a study on the impact of parental migration on the psychological well-being of children in Ghana, Nigeria, and Angola found that for children in each of these countries, poorer well-being is associated with the

117 Oliveira, above n 53, 17–18; Carola Suárez-Orozco and Marcelo M Suarez-Orozco, *Children of Immigration* (Harvard University Press, 2001).

118 See, eg, Jørgen Carling, Cecilia Menjivar and Leah Schmalzbauer, 'Central Themes in the Study of Transnational Parenthood' (2012) 38(2) *Journal of Ethnic and Migration Studies* 191; Jody Heymann et al, 'The Impact of Migration on the Well-being of Transnational Families: New Data from Sending Communities in Mexico' (2009) 12 (1) *Community, Work and Family* 91; UNICEF Moldova, above n 113.

119 UNICEF Moldova, above n 113, 7–8, 33.

120 Piper, above n 52, 34 citing Scalabrini Migration Center et al, *Hearts Apart – Migration in the Eyes of Filipino Children* (SMC, 2004).

121 See Chapter 5 (Section 5.3.2).

122 Piper, above n 52, 34 citing Scalabrini Migration Center et al, *Hearts Apart – Migration in the Eyes of Filipino Children* (SMC, 2004).

123 Rhoda Reddock and Yvonne Bobb-Smith, 'Reconciling Work and Family: Issues and Policies in Trinidad and Tobago' (Conditions of Work and Employment Series, No 18, ILO, 2008) 28–29 quoted in Rianne Mahon and Sonya Michel, 'Not In Focus: Migrant Women Caregivers As Seen by the ILO and the OECD' in Sonya Michel and Ito Peng (eds), *Gender, Migration, and the Work of Care: A Multi-Scalar Approach to the Pacific Rim*' (Palgrave Macmillan, 2017) 269, 277.

changing of caregivers.[124] Moreover, a study commissioned by the Sri Lankan Government found that a mother's migration for two or more years can seriously affect a child in the development of his or her personality;[125] a study from Thailand found that 'the mother's role is not easily filled by other family members';[126] and another study from the Philippines found that 'children of non-migrants reported being happier, less anxious and less lonely than children of migrant mothers'.[127] These issues are captured in Isaksen et al's findings in relation to the children of migrant workers in Kerala that:

> The children … faced a number of emotional issues related to the departure of their mothers: the management of sadness at the lost company of one whose emotional centrality remained in absentia, envy of children with resident mothers … doubt about why a mother had to leave, and an aversion to being a burden to surrogate caregivers.[128]

This study found that separation from their children forced mothers to 'commodify' their love, having 'to express through money and material gifts that which she could not express through talk and hugs'.[129] It clearly demonstrates the dilemma that TLM creates for parents where they must choose between providing for their children's physical and material needs and being present to provide for their psychosocial needs. As Oliviera describes:

> [T]ransnational mothers struggle with the paradox of having to leave their children in order to care for them.[130]

TLM policies create this situation despite Art 27 clearly protecting a parent's role as primary provider for their children's *overall* needs, in conjunction with Art 18 protecting the role of parents as their children's primary caregivers. Both of these articles mandate that States shall assist parents to fulfil their parenting role and responsibilities and do not assign greater importance to any one aspect of the parental role in meeting children's development needs.

4.3.2 Heightened risks associated with the migration of the primary caregiver

Together with Arts 18 and 7, Art 27 protects the role of parents as children's primary caregivers and the right of children to be cared for by their parents.

124 Valentina Mazzucato et al, 'International Parental Migration and the Psychological Well-being of Children in Ghana, Nigeria, and Angola' (2015) 132 *Social Science and Medicine* 215, 222–3.
125 Hettige et al, above n 113, 20.
126 Jampaklay, above n 136, 108.
127 Asis, above n 53, 56.
128 Isaksen, Devi and Hochschild, above n 107, 414.
129 Ibid 414–15.
130 Oliveira, above n 53, 17.

Articles 18 and 7 are discussed further in Chapter 7. These articles represent the presumption in the CRC that, wherever possible, it is in children's best interests to be cared for by their parents. While Art 18 encourages shared responsibility between both parents for the upbringing of a child, it remains the case globally that the primary caregiving role continues to be largely assumed by mothers (and other women in the absence of mothers).[131] This is particularly so in most labour-sending countries where traditional family structures are still predominant[132] and sociocultural values deem mothers to be the 'light of the home' or the provider of nurture and care.[133] These gendered roles – which have contributed to the maintenance of women as primary caregivers globally – have resulted in transnational motherhood having implications for children that are distinct from transnational fatherhood.[134]

When a child's mother migrates, she is often the primary caregiver at the time of migration, which exacerbates the potential adverse consequences for the child.[135] As maternal migration removes from the child the caregiver who has been most central in his or her care, the child then undergoes a marked reorganisation in his or her care arrangements in a way that they do not when fathers migrate.[136] Hence, while studies

131 See ILO, *Care Work and Care Jobs for the Future of Decent Work* (ILO, 2018); Catherine Hein, *Reconciling Work and Family Responsibilities: Practical Ideas from Global Experience* (ILO, 2005).

132 Kusala Wettasinghe, Gethsie Shanmugam and Sarala Emmanuel, *Alternative Care Giving of Migrant Workers' Children* (Terre des Hommes, 2012) 32; Oliveira, above n 53, 16.

133 Rhacel Salazar Parrenas, 'Transnational Fathering: Gendered Conflicts, Distant Disciplining and Emotional Gaps' (2008) 34(7) *Journal of Ethnic and Migration Studies* 1057, 1062; Rhacel Salazar Parrenas, 'Transnational Mothering: A Source of Gender Conflicts in the Family' (2010) 88 *North Carolina Law Review* 1825, 1828; Hondagneu-Sotelo and Avila (1997), Ehrenreich and Hochschild (2002) cited in Oliveira, above n 53, 16; M M B Asis, S Huang and B S A Yeoh, 'When the Light of the Home is Abroad: Unskilled Female Migration and the Filipino Family' (2004) 25(2) *Singapore Journal of Tropical Geography* 198; Swarna Ukwatta, 'Sri Lankan Female Domestic Workers Overseas: Mothering their Children from a Distance' 27 *Journal of Population Research* 107, 128.

134 Carling, Menjivar and Schmalzbauer, above n 118, 192.

135 Graziano Battistella and Cecilia Conaco, 'The Impact of Labour Migration on the Children Left Behind: A Study of Elementary School Children in the Philippines' (1998) 13(2) *Sojourn: Journal of Social Issues in Southeast Asia* 220; David Cox, 'Children of Migrant Workers: A Family Relationship Issue' in Graziano Battistella and Cecilia Conaco (eds), *Children and Migration: A New Challenge for World-Wide Social Services* (International Social Service Hong Kong Branch, 1990); Save the Children Sri Lanka and Kishali Pinto-Jayawardena, *Left Behind, Left Out: The Impact on Children and Families of Mothers Migrating for Work Abroad* (Save the Children Sri Lanka, 2006); Jampaklay, above n 136; Liza Yanovich, *Children Left Behind: The Impact of Labor Migration in Moldova and Ukraine* (23 January 2015) Migration Policy Institute <http://www.migrationpolicy.org/article/children-left-behind-impact-labor-migration-moldova-and-ukraine>.

136 Isaksen, Devi and Hochschild, above n 107, 415; Carling, Menjivar and Schmalzbauer, above n 118, 196; Asis, above n 53; Rhacel Salazar Parrenas, *Children of Global Migration: Transnational Families and Gendered Woes* (Stanford University Press, 2005).

show that children miss their fathers and experience 'emotional displacement' when their fathers migrate, the migration of mothers – or primary caregivers – carries different psychosocial and emotional implications for children.[137] This is demonstrated in recent findings from the United States that children separated from their migrant parents for prolonged periods prior to reunification were not only 'three times as likely to experience serious emotional or behavioral problems' than children who migrated with their parents; but their psychosocial difficulties were most severe when separated from both parents followed by separation from their mothers.[138] On the other hand, this study found that 'separating from fathers alone did not significantly undermine children's psychosocial development'.[139]

i. The feminisation of migration[140]

Nonetheless, women's migration is being actively encouraged by labour-sending and labour-receiving countries, particularly to fill demands for low-waged labour in the care and domestic sectors.[141] In 2013, 42 per cent of migrants from the Asia-Pacific region were women;[142] and, globally, the ILO estimated that of the roughly 67.1 million domestic workers worldwide, 11.5 million were migrant workers of which 8.45 million (73.4 per cent) were women.[143] By way of example, in Singapore alone, roughly 16 per cent of the total foreign workforce is now comprised of women migrant domestic workers, predominantly from Indonesia and the Philippines;[144] and it has been found that Filipino migrant workers typically have an average of 2.74 children who remain in the Philippines.[145]

For labour-sending countries, remittances from women are one of the most significant sources of revenue, with women remitting a higher proportion of their wages more frequently than men.[146] Moreover, in labour-receiving countries, it is

137 Ibid; Parrenas, above n 133; Oliveira, above n 53, 16.

138 Yao Lu, Qian He and Jeanne Brooks-Gunn, 'Diverse Experience of Immigrant Children: How Do Separation and Reunification Shape Their Development?' (2018) *Child Development* (advance).

139 Ibid.

140 The feminisation of migration is further discussed in Chapter 1 (see Section 1.4).

141 See also UN-INSTRAW, *Gender, Migration, Remittances and Development*, UN Doc UN/POP/MIG-5CM/2006/02 (9 November 2006).

142 UN Department of Economic and Social Affairs, *International Migration Report 2013* (UN, 2013) 8.

143 ILO, *ILO Global Estimates on Migrant Workers: Results and Methodology* (ILO, 2015) 6–7, 10–11; ILO, *Report IV: Addressing Governance Challenges in a Changing Labour Migration Landscape*, International Labour Conference, 106th sess, 2017 [19].

144 Anja Wessels, 'Home Sweet Home?: Work, Life and Well-being of Foreign Domestic Workers in Singapore' (Research Report, HOME, March 2015) 10.

145 Erista et al (2003), Morales (2001), Parrenas (2001), Parrenas (2003) cited in Isaksen, Devi and Hochschild, above n 107, 406.

146 Bandita Sijapati, 'Women's Labour Migration from Asia and the Pacific: Opportunities and Challenges' (Issue in Brief, Issue No 12, IOM / Migration Policy Institute, March 2015) 5; Gender, Poverty Reduction and Migration (Irena Omelaniuk, World

seen as an advantage if women have dependent children at home to ensure that they return at the end of their contracts. This is illustrated in Spain's criteria for recruiting Moroccan migrant workers in their strawberry industry, which includes that workers *must be* female, aged 18–40 and have dependent children in Morocco. The policy explicitly deems that these criteria reduce the non-return rates of migrant workers.[147]

The scale of the migration of women who were their children's primary caregivers at the time of migration has been made possible by the provision of unpaid care to their children largely by other female relatives.[148] This 'global care chain' has seen women migrant workers leave their own children to provide care for children and the aged in labour-receiving countries.[149] This has facilitated the increased participation of women from labour-receiving countries in the paid workforce while reducing State-borne costs associated with childcare and eldercare.[150] As Setien and Acosta observe, a mother's decision to migrate is most often an 'economic survival strategy' for the family as a whole.[151] The cost to mothers themselves is captured in Ukwatta's study on women migrant workers from Sri Lanka, in which the main reasons given by participants for advising other mothers not to migrate for work included:

> [T]he social costs outweigh the economic benefits, children need their mothers, the family disruption is a big cost and so is the suffering experienced abroad because of separation from children.[152]

Bank), 2005, 11; UN-INSTRAW, *Gender, Migration, Remittances and Development*, UN Doc UN/POP/MIG-5CM/2006/02 (9 November 2006).

147 Carmen González Enríquez and Miquel Reynés Ramón, 'Circular Migration Between Spain and Morocco: Something More than Agricultural Work?' (METOIKOS Project, European University Institute, 2011), 8, 10; Jörg Gertel, Sarah Ruth Sippel (eds), *Seasonal Workers in Mediterranean Agriculture: The Social Costs of Eating Fresh* (Routledge, 2014); Global Alliance Against Traffic in Women (GAATW), 'Female Temporary Labour Migration and Rights Protection in the Strawberry Sector in Huelva, Spain' (Research Report, GAATW, 2009) 16.

148 Eleonore Kofman, 'Gendered Global Migrations' (2004) 6(4) *International Feminist Journal of Politics* 643, 651; Fiona Williams, 'Markets and Migrants in the Care Economy' (2011) 47 *Soundings* 22, 22; Arlie Russell Hochschild, 'Global Care Chains and Emotional Surplus Value' in Will Hutton and Anthony Giddens (eds), *On the Edge: Living with Global Capitalism* (Jonathan Cape, 2000) 130; Barbara Ehrenreich and Arlie Russell Hochschild(eds), *Global Woman: Nannies, Maids and Sex Workers in the New Economy* (Metropolitan Books, 2003).

149 Ibid.

150 Ibid; Deborah Brennan and Elizabeth Adamson, 'Care and Migration' in Sheila Shaver (ed), *Handbook on Gender and Social Policy* (Elgar, 2018) 253, 253.

151 Maria Luisa Setien and Elaine Acosta, 'Care and Feminized North-South and South-South Migration Flows: Denial of Rights and Limited Citizenship' in Laura Oso and Natalia Ribas-Mateos (eds), *The International Handbook on Gender, Migration and Transnationalism: Global and Development Perspectives* (Edward Elgar, 2013) 397.

152 Ukwatta, above n 133, 122.

Key informants across the multilateral/non-government and research and policy sectors emphasised the challenges that the 'global care chain' presents for women migrant workers who are also mothers. Their reflections included:

> 'There is the irony about taking care of someone else's babies and toddlers whilst you can't see your own children and might not be able to see them for two, three or four years. And then on top of that comes this discourse about blaming women for anything that might happen with the family left behind'. *(Key Informant – R & P 3)*

This highlights the reality that while mothers are removed from their physical role as primary caregivers when they migrate, there is a continued social expectation that they will remain the adult who bears the responsibility for whatever eventuates for their children *regardless* of the extent of their capacity to continue parenting from a distance.

It is recognised that fathers also experience loss when they migrate for low-waged work. This is captured in Becceril's study of Mexican migrant workers in Canada, where fathers spoke about the emotional costs and loss of parental authority arising from their absence.[153] This study found that participants who had been seasonal agricultural workers in Canada for over five seasons had:

> … missed not only the births of their children, but also watching them grow up. Some added that upon their return they find that their children no longer see them as fathers nor do they see the youngsters as their children.[154]

Nonetheless, for *children* the experience differs when the mother migrates and their primary care arrangements are significantly disrupted. Hence, TLM policies need to adopt appropriate measures that respond to gender variables and the compounded challenges that the migration of a child's primary caregiver present for a child's psychosocial development. That is, as IOM has recognised, 'migration policy and research can no longer afford to be gender neutral'.[155] Rather, States and multilateral organisations must invest in understanding the different (non-economic) factors associated with child-parent separation that increase risks to children's well-being. Without this comprehensive understanding, effective measures to minimise the harms to children posed by TLM cannot be developed.

153 Ofelia Becerril, 'Gendered Policies, Single Mothers and Transnational Motherhood: Mexican Female Migrant Farmworkers in Canada' in Zahra Meghani (ed), *Women Migrant Workers: Ethical, Political and Legal Problems* (Taylor and Francis, 2015) 154, 167–8.

154 Ibid.

155 IOM, 'Migration and Families: Background Paper', above n 53, 3.

4.3.3 The need for evidence-based policy responses to manage risks to children

In addition to studies previously mentioned, there is a wealth of evidence from labour-sending countries about the *potential* negative impacts on children's psychosocial well-being arising from prolonged periods of child-parent separation due to TLM.[156] This is supported by existing knowledge from other disciplines about the potential harms to children caused by child-parent separation.[157] As discussed in Chapter 3, the principle of international cooperation in human rights law includes the notion that agreements should not be formed between States that result in harm to children.[158] Moreover, in their guidance on State obligations concerning international cooperation in the context of migration, the CRC and CMW Committees have reiterated that both origin and destination countries have roles and responsibilities to promote and protect children's rights.[159] This involves not only respecting their human rights, but also 'avoiding approaches that might aggravate their vulnerability'.[160]

However, the current response by governments to existing evidence about the potential psychosocial impacts of parental migration on children has been twofold: labour-sending countries have adopted reactionary approaches, such as banning women's migration or requiring their husband's approval to migrate; and labour-receiving countries have completely omitted these concerns in the design of their TLM policies despite being parties to the CRC. These responses, as well as the benefits of developing evidenced-based measures, are discussed below.

i. Inappropriate measures by labour-sending countries enhance the vulnerability of children and mothers

Practices by labour-sending countries are based on the assumption that the wife will be the children's caregiver if the husband migrates.[161] However, they are highly problematic for a number of reasons, including that they infringe on women's rights to freedom of movement and employment;[162] are discriminatory in that they only apply to women; and increase risks to women and their families when overregulation forces women into irregular migration channels.[163] Hence,

156 See Section 4.3.1.

157 See Chapter 2 (Section 2.3.1) and Chapter 7 (Section 7.2.3) on the connection between the child-parent relationship and children's development and well-being.

158 The principle of international cooperation is discussed in Chapter 3 (see Section 3.3).

159 *Joint General Comment on Children in the Context of International Migration*, UN Doc CMW/C/GC/4-CRC/C/GC/23, para 64.

160 Ibid.

161 Becerril, above n 153, 162.

162 For example, these measures restrict women's right to freedom of movement under Art 12(2) of the ICCPR and right to work (which includes the right to the same employment opportunities as men and free choice of employment) under Art 11(1) of CEDAW.

163 Nicola Piper, 'Contributions of Migrant Domestic Workers to Sustainable Development' (Policy Paper for the Pre-GFMD VI High-Level Regional Meeting on Migrant

formally restricting women's migration has not been shown to reduce the risks of TLM for children, particularly when demand for low-waged labour provided by women is being simultaneously encouraged. This was emphasised by key informants, particularly in relation to migration from Asia, in comments such as:

> 'It's all about pointing fingers at women and saying 'bad mother for leaving your child behind', and then pushing women to go irregularly without that support'. *(Key Informant – MLO-NGO 2)*

The Special Rapporteur on the Human Rights of Migrants has recently condemned Nepal's ban on women with children under two years of age from migrating for domestic work. Again, this is because it discriminates against women, violates their right to freedom of movement and forces them into irregular migration channels, which increases not only their vulnerability but also that of their family and children.[164] Similarly, the Special Rapporteur observed that in the context of Sri Lanka, where women's migration is banned if their children are younger than five years of age:[165]

> While the intentions of the Government of Sri Lanka that lie behind those restrictions seem to be good, aiming to protect those women and their children, restrictions on women's right to leave their country are not the right way to achieve such objectives.[166]

This is because restrictions do not address the root causes for women's migration, including that they often have no alternative source of income by which to support their children and families.[167] In this vein, the Special Rapporteur reiterated the need to, among other things, approach the drivers of women's migration including by generating employment opportunities in home countries (as discussed in Section 4.2.3); diversifying measures for childcare support; and

Domestic Workers at the Interface of Migration and Development, UN Women, 2013) 20–21; Sijapati, above n 146, 6.

164 *Report of the Special Rapporteur on the Human Rights of Migrants on His Mission to Nepal*, UN GAOR, 38th sess, Agenda Item 3, UN Doc A/HRC/38/41/Add.1 (30 April 2018) [77]–[79].

165 *Shadow Report – Sri Lanka: To the UN Committee on the Protection of the Rights of All Migrant Workers and Members of their Families (CMW) for Consideration During the 25th Session* (presented by 20 Civil Society Organisations, August 2016) 14–16.

166 *Report of the Special Rapporteur on the Human Rights of Migrants, François Crépeau: Addendum – Mission to Sri Lanka*, UN GAOR, 29th sess, Agenda Item 3, UN Doc A/HRC/29/36/Add.1 (2 April 2015) [66] ('*Special Rapporteur on the Human Rights of Migrants – Mission to Sri Lanka*').

167 *Shadow Report – Sri Lanka: To the UN Committee on the Protection of the Rights of All Migrant Workers and Members of their Families (CMW) for Consideration During the 25th Session* (presented by 20 Civil Society Organisations, August 2016) 14–16.

supporting fathers to undertake a more active role in their children's upbringing.[168] Key informants across the research and policy and multilateral/non-government sectors shared these views in observations such as:

> 'Public debate often sees women's migration as the problem ... It's not about addressing the current gender regime or supporting fathers and families left behind, or trying to advocate for better policies in countries of destination. The knee-jerk reaction is to blame women's migration rather than reduce the necessity for women to migrate'. *(Key Informant – R & P 3)*

Importantly, this observation recognises that labour-sending countries cannot alone address conditions associated with TLM that impact children. Rather, it also requires labour-receiving countries to address their policies that govern TLM given the interconnectedness of children's rights with those of their parents.

ii. Omission of measures to mitigate risks to children by labour-receiving countries

Labour-receiving countries have completely failed to consider children's psychosocial development needs in their TLM policies. Key informants were of the view that, in some instances, this was because of a lack of awareness by labour-receiving governments about the potential impacts on children, with comments including:

> 'I don't know of any governments that are taking into account the psycho-social implications of transnational workers in terms of children and families left behind, partly because I think research and data about this has not been available until recently'. *(Key Informant – R & P 5)*

However, key informants were also of the view that governments in labour-receiving countries feel that they do not have a duty towards these children *even if* they are aware of existing studies on the potential risks to children caused by parental migration. This was reflected in observations such as:

> 'I think primarily, they don't consider this their responsibility ... I think it's mostly the sense that there are limits to a State's responsibilities to non-citizens'. *(Key Informant – R & P 2)*

168 *Special Rapporteur on the Human Rights of Migrants – Mission to Sri Lanka*, UN Doc A/HRC/29/36/Add.1, [66].

This observation goes to the commonly held notion that State sovereignty limits State obligations to uphold the rights of non-citizens and children outside a State's jurisdiction. The relationship between rights, State sovereignty and citizenship in the context of TLM is discussed further in Chapter 6.[169] However, in relation to a lack of awareness of existing studies, labour-receiving countries have their own evidence base – from numerous other disciplines such as family law and military studies – on the potential impacts of child-parent separation. Learnings from these disciplines are discussed further in Chapters 6 and 7.[170] They demonstrate existing knowledge among decision-makers in labour-sending countries about the legal duty for States to give primary consideration to children's best interests in policies affecting children; and the need to employ age-appropriate strategies to mitigate potential harms to children caused by disruption to the child-parent relationship during children's developmental years.

iii. The benefits of longitudinal studies and broader measures

The Deployment Life Study (DLS) conducted by RAND in the USA, a major labour-receiving country, offers a model for the type of longitudinal study needed to examine the impact of parental migration on familial relationships in the context of TLM. As a first of its kind longitudinal study, the DLS examined causal effects between military deployment and family functioning and well-being. This large-scale study achieved this by comparing outcomes over time of well-matched families that both did and did not experience deployment.[171] Of relevance, it found that for children younger than eleven, more difficulties concerning emotional conduct and problems with peers were reported if a parent had deployed;[172] and teenagers reported worse family cohesion in families experiencing deployment.[173] Hence, this study grounds concerns about how parental deployment can impact children in a solid evidence base, enabling the identification of appropriate measures to address these concerns.

Presently, studies examining the social impacts of TLM on children and families have been relatively small and limited in scope. This is because governments and multilateral organisations have invested in researching the more easily measurable economic outcomes. This is reiterated in the recent World Happiness Report, which states that:

> Given that the current literature has predominantly focused on specific countries or communities, a global picture is missing of how migration affects the happiness of those staying behind.[174]

169 See Chapter 6 (Section 6.3.2).
170 See Chapter 6 (Section 6.4.1) and Chapter 7 (Section 7.2.3).
171 RAND Arroyo Center and the National Defense Research Institute, 'Brief: How Military Families Function Before, During, and After Deployment – Findings from the RAND Deployment Life Study' (RAND Corporation, 2016) 2.
172 Ibid.
173 Ibid.
174 Helliwell, Layard and Sachs (eds), above n 64, 48.

In the context of TLM, there is a significant need for comprehensive and longitudinal studies that, among other things, compare the experiences of children of women migrant workers to children of non-migrant mothers; children of fathers who are migrant workers; and children who experience other forms of non-parental care.[175] There is also a pressing need for broader measures of child well-being to be incorporated into future studies to reflect the holistic conception of children's development embodied in Art 27. The holistic approach in Art 27 represents an understanding of health, as defined by the World Health Organization, as 'a state of complete physical, mental, and social well-being'.[176] In relation to the CRC, the use of positive indicators around children's psychosocial health and development enable children's well-being to be understood and measured more broadly than in a traditional welfare sense.[177] In relation to understanding the impact of TLM on children's well-being, this involves the use of indicators that relate to familial relationships and not only those that can be measured in terms of material and physical outcomes. Such evidence can support informed policy measures that are not incongruous with the continuation of TLM but would improve outcomes for children, particularly in the event of primary caregiver migration.

iv. Mainstreaming support for children during periods of parental absence

Military studies also offer insights into the benefits of mainstreaming support for children whose parents deploy for military service. For example, researchers have emphasised the need for school-based support for children with a parent on military deployment given the significant role of the school environment in children's lives.[178] As Macdonald observes, existing research suggests 'that children's academic progress and health outcomes decline during parental deployment, along with an increase in behavioural difficulties'.[179] However, researchers have found that initiatives such as school-based support for the non-deployed parent, the facilitation of family referrals, resilience building programmes and access to counselling assist children in their management of stresses associated with parental deployment.[180] They have also found that students benefit from school staff understanding the deployment

175 Isaksen, Devi and Hochschild, above n 107, 421 n 8.

176 World Health Organisation (1964) cited in Asher Ben-Arieh and Noam Tarshish, 'Children's Rights and Well-being' in Martin D Ruck, Michele Peterson-Badali and Michael Freeman (eds), *Handbook of Children's Rights Global and Multidisciplinary Perspectives* (Routledge, 2017) 68, 73.

177 Ben-Arieh and Tarshish, above n 176, 73.

178 Gail Macdonald, 'School-based Support for Students with a Parent on Military Deployment' (2016) 42(1) *Children Australia* 57; Australian Defence Force, Joint Health Command, *Deployment Guide: A Guide to Assist Your Preparation* <www.defence.gov.au/Health/HealthPortal/docs/JHC%20Deployment%20Guide.pdf> 44.

179 Macdonald, above n 178, 58; See also Australian Defence Force, above n 178, 46–7.

180 Fitzsimons and Krause-Parello (2009), Garcia et al (2015), Waliski et al (2012) cited in Macdonald, above n 178, 59.

experience;[181] and from children being supported to have a meaningful relationship with one adult at least during their parent's deployment.[182] Key informants stressed the need for this type of mainstreamed support for children of migrant workers in labour-sending countries in comments including:

> 'Labour migration is huge ... but it is still not mainstreamed in the education sector, in the justice sector, in the health sector. These are places that can create protective environments for children without banning mothers from migrating and without finding fault with mothers who go. These are areas that can actually support children's well-being while their mother is away'. *(Key Informant – MLO-NGO 2)*

This goes to the need for States to develop appropriate measures to assist parents to continue providing for their children's psychosocial development needs in the event of migration under State-designed TLM programmes. These measures should be developed in consultation with those sectors that have significant engagement with children, including the education, health and justice sectors. The mainstreaming of children's rights in services engaged with the children of migrant workers will help to establish an institutional framework[183] to reduce the child protection risks and social insecurities associated with parental absence. It will also help in reducing structural constraints on the capacity of these children to access and benefit from social services in their parent's absence. Structural approaches to addressing such constraints are essential for children, and particularly those groups with heightened vulnerabilities, given their limited ability to act on their own accord and participate in decision-making processes.[184]

4.4 Significance of a child's age to measures of appropriate parental assistance

Appropriate measures of assistance to parents to provide for children's development needs cannot be determined without due consideration of their children's age and stage of development. In the context of TLM, the support needed by children to maintain transnational child-parent relationships and minimise potential harms caused by their parent's absence will vary according to their age and capacity. As the CRC defines a child as anyone below 18 years of age, childhood spans multiple stages in a person's development.[185] These range from complete

181 Easterbrooks et al (2013) cited in Macdonald, above n 178, 58; Australian Defence Force, above n 178, 44.
182 Macdonald, above n 178, 59.
183 Piper, above n 52, 45.
184 UNICEF, 'The Structural Determinants of Child Well-being' (Expert Consultation Hosted by the UNICEF Office of Research, Florence, 22–23 June 2012) 3.
185 *CRC* art 1.

dependence on caregivers through to partial or total independence from caregivers.[186] For the children of migrant workers, variables affecting the impact of child-parent separation relate not only to the stage in their life course, but also the stage in their parent's migration process.[187] This is discussed further in Chapter 5[188] and is reiterated by Carling et al in their study on transnational parenthood, as follows:

> During the migrant parents' absence, children's lives change rapidly as they go through different developmental stages. Their psychological development and exposure to different experiences in their social environments at different points in time inform the relationships they maintain with their absent parents.[189]

Importantly, a child's age at the time of their parent's migration affects their ability to develop and maintain a transnational child-parent relationship.[190] For young children, maintenance of the child-parent relationship is heavily dependent on other adults maintaining regular communication between children and parents.[191] Without this, the child loses memories of his or her parents over time.[192] The CRC Committee has expressed its heightened concerns for young children affected by parental migration as follows:

> Young children are especially vulnerable to adverse consequences of separations because of their physical dependence on and emotional attachment to their parents [and] primary caregivers. They are also less able to comprehend the circumstances of any separation.[193]

The inability of young children to understand why their parents have migrated was reiterated by key informants in statements such as:

> 'Workers are grown-ups and know what they are doing, but young kids do not understand what is going on. They don't understand why their mum is leaving them behind to raise a foreign kid'. *(Key Informant – MLO-NGO 5)*

186 Davidson and Farrow, above n 51, 23.
187 Elspeth Graham and Lucy P Jordan, 'Migrant Parents and the Psychological Well-Being of Left-Behind Children in Southeast Asia' (2011) 73 *Journal of Marriage and Family* 763, 765.
188 See Chapter 5 (Section 5.4.4) on the relevance of stages in the life cycle and migration cycle.
189 Carling, Menjivar and Schmalzbauer, above n 118, 206.
190 Artico (2003) cited in Carling, Menjivar and Schmalzbauer, above n 118, 206.
191 Carling, Menjivar and Schmalzbauer, above n 118, 207.
192 Ibid.
193 *General Comment No 7*, UN Doc CRC/C/GC/7/Rev.1, para 18.

The limited capacity that young children have to comprehend the reasons for their parent's migration as captured in this statement, relates directly to the CRC Committee's emphasis on the need for States to take measures that respond to the different capacities and vulnerabilities of children in 'early childhood'.[194] This is essential because, as highlighted by the Committee:

> [C]hildren's earliest years are the foundation for their physical and mental health, emotional security, cultural and personal identity, and developing competencies.[195]

As discussed in Chapter 3, the CRC – and in particular Art 12 – recognises that children's capacity to comprehend and shape matters that affect them develops as they age and mature.[196] In the context of TLM, older children generally have a better understand of the reasons for their parent's migration and are often able to continue receiving emotional support from their parents transnationally. However, studies have found that even when older children and adolescents understand the reasons for their parent's migration, they are frequently negatively impacted at an emotional level. This because they are often acutely aware of the (possibly traumatic) separation and remember when they lived together with their parents.[197] The experiences of older children are captured in the following comments by a college student in Devi's study on the migration of women migrant workers from Kerala:

> I want you to write about the human cost for people like us, to be apart for year after year. I'm living here in this hostel, and my classes are fine, but I can't talk to my mother. I can't tell her things. I can't see her face. I can't hug her. I can't help her. My mother misses me too. My mother will retire at some point, but how old will I be then?[198]

Similarly, a UNICEF study on children of migrant workers in Moldova found that younger children's tendency to express their emotions more easily created the impression that they were more affected by the absence of their parents.[199] However, it held that:

> In reality, all children, regardless of their age, suffered painfully from the separation from their parents. Some of them simply do not express their feelings so openly.[200]

194 Ibid para 4. The CRC Committee has roughly defined 'early childhood' as birth to eight years of age to incorporate children's transition to school, which occurs at age 7 in some countries.
195 Ibid [6].
196 See Chapter 3 (Section 3.2.4).
197 Carling, Menjivar and Schmalzbauer, above n 118, 207.
198 Isaksen, Devi and Hochschild, above n 107, 412.
199 UNICEF Moldova, above n 113, 25.
200 Ibid.

The reality that children of all ages are potentially harmed by the absence of their parents was reiterated by key informants in views such as:

> 'There are different problems and obstacles that children have to face at different times in their lives. Five years of age is only the beginning of primary school, so just imagine having to leave a child then'. *(Key Informant – Government 6)*

This observation points to the fact that the guidance and support that children need from their parents varies according to their age. Therefore, effective measures to mitigate harms to children arising from their parents' absence will also vary according to the types of support that children need from the child-parent relationship at each developmental stage.

4.4.1 Need for responses appropriate to children's developmental stages

Hence, it is recognised that parental migration poses risks to children of all ages. This undermines the purpose of Art 27(1), which is to protect children's right to conditions necessary for their overall development and well-being. However, the incorporation of measures to mitigate the risks that TLM creates for children would reduce the degree of interference that TLM causes to children's right to enjoy living conditions necessary for their psychosocial and physical development; and the entitlement of parents to be assisted by the State to secure these living conditions. The identification of effective measures that address child well-being at different developmental stages must be informed by an understanding of children's changing emotional and cognitive development needs.[201] This reflects the approach taken in the drafting of the CRC, which referred to a child's right to healthcare and a standard of living 'adequate for his healthy and normal physical, mental and moral development in every phase of the child's development'.[202] Moreover, during the drafting of Art 6, State obligations were expressed as a duty:

> to ensure the child such protection and care as his status requires, taking due account of the various stages of his development in family environment and in social relations.[203]

201 UNICEF, above n 184, 1.

202 Sharon Detrick (ed), *The United Nations Convention on the Rights of the Child: A Guide to the 'Travaux Préparatoires'* (Martinus Nijhoff Publishers, 1992) 98. See also Manfred Nowak, *The UN Covenant on Civil and Political Rights: CCPR Commentary* (Engel, 2nd ed, 2005) 12.

203 Ibid.

This reiterates that the duty of States to ensure a child's development to the maximum extent possible under Art 6 of the CRC, which is outlined in Chapter 3[204], must be understood in terms of a child's changing developmental needs.

i. Using best interests assessments to inform appropriate measures of support

Best interests assessments involve the consideration of a wide range of variables, including age and capacity, to determine what constitutes children's best interests in a particular context.[205] As required under Art 3 of the CRC, once children's best interests are determined, they must be given primary consideration in matters affecting and in the exercise of balancing children's best interests with competing interests.[206] Assessing children's best interests will necessarily involve an assessment of foreseeable potential interferences that a State policy or action could cause to children's specific rights. In relation to TLM, it is foreseeable that child-parent separation will interfere with a number of CRC rights that protect the child-parent relationship because of its importance to children's development at all ages and stages (albeit in different ways).

The critical role of parental presence in children's development outcomes is supported by a significant body of evidence, particularly from family law and child development fields. While parental migration differs from other forms of family disruption (as it is not typically marked by conflict or declines in economic resources[207]), there is certainly an overlap in experiences of loss, physical and emotional distance, uncertainty and often subsequent relationship breakdowns for families affected by TLM. In fact, particularly in relation to young children, international family law practitioners have observed that it can make little difference 'if separation from a parent has been caused by forcible displacement across borders or by the parent's voluntary pursuit of opportunities abroad'.[208] Regardless, existing knowledge derived from other contexts on age-appropriate strategies for mitigating the potential risks arising from child-parent separation can be drawn upon to inform effective measures in TLM policies. Learnings from family law concerning the management of child-parent separation are discussed in Chapter 7.[209] However, it should be noted that in family law decisions governing parental relocation, 'the beacon remains the best interests of the children'.[210]

204 See Chapter 3 (Section 3.2.3).
205 Nigel Cantwell, 'Are Children's Rights Still Human?' in Antonella Invernizzi and Jane Williams (eds), *The Human Rights of Children From Visions to Implementation* (Ashgate, 2011) 37, 50; *UN High Commissioner for Refugees (UNHCR) Guidelines on Determining the Best Interests of the Child* (UNHCR, May 2008).
206 See Chapter 3 (Section 3.2.1).
207 Lu, above n 105, 3.
208 Eliahu Frank Abram, 'The Child's Right to Family Unity in International Immigration Law' (1995) 17(4) *Law and Policy* 397, 399.
209 See Chapter 7 (Section 7.3.2).
210 Sarah Gottfried, 'Virtual Visitation: The Wave of the Future in Communication Between Children and Non-Custodial Parents in Relocation Cases' (2002) 36(3)

The overarching principle of the best interests of the child must inform all actions concerning children.[211] This demands not only that children's best interests be assessed, but that measures be identified to minimise and mitigate any justifiable interferences with these interests and other specific children's rights.[212] The use of best interests assessments as a tool for understanding how children's rights and interests may be affected by State policies has been urged by the CRC Committee in statements including:

> [T]he Committee recommends that State parties ... consider using ... child impact assessments on how investments in any sector may serve 'the best interests of the child'.[213]

In relation to TLM, such assessments can draw on existing knowledge about factors that affect transnational families and their capacity to maintain relationships while separated. To this end, Zentgraf and Chinchilla have identified a spectrum of factors that should be considered in the identification of strategies to support a child before, during and after their parent's migration. These include, among other things: the characteristics of the family, their socio-economic status and the household structure; the nature of the circumstances driving the parent's migration; children's age at separation and reunification; the suitability of alternative caregivers; the quality and frequency of contact while separated; the use of remittances; the prevalence of out-migration in the community; and the nature of the institutions responsible for child protection and social welfare.[214] Best interests assessments that address children's age-related development needs in light of such factors that are specific to TLM can inform the development of appropriate support measures for children and families. Such measures can minimise the degree of interference by TLM with children's best interests and CRC rights under Art 27 by reducing the potential negative psychosocial effects for children in the event of parental migration.

In determining children's best interests, and developing measures to reduce interferences by TLM with children's best interests, children's views must be incorporated in line with their age and maturity. This accords with children's right to have their views assigned weight relative to their evolving capacity under Art 12, which is discussed in Chapter 3.[215] In this regard, Carling et al have found that older children and adolescents often express their opinions about their parent's migration and 'evaluate their care arrangements' relative to how they recall

Family Law Quarterly 475, 479 quoting *McCoy v MCoy*, 764 A 2d 449, 453 (NJ, 2001).

211 See Chapter 3 (Section 3.2.1).

212 See Chapter 3 (Section 3.2.1).

213 *Report on the Forty-sixth Session*, UN Doc CRC/C/46/3, [71.b].

214 Kristine M Zentgraf and Norma Stoltz Chinchilla, 'Transnational Family Separation: A Framework for Analysis' (2012) 38(2) *Journal of Ethnic and Migration Studies* 345, 349.

215 See Chapter 3 (Section 3.2.4).

the care provided by their parents.[216] Studies that capture children's views demonstrate a frequent desire on the part of children for their parents – particularly mothers – to return home even when children understand (and often greatly appreciate) the reasons for their migration.[217] In fact, it has been found that if children are given a choice, they would prefer to grow up in 'households that would allow for greater proximity, time together, intimacy and familiarity';[218] and that children place greater value on their parents' emotional resources than economic as 'an important part of a parents' role is to provide emotional comfort'.[219] This again demonstrates that while TLM is often framed as an opportunity for parents to provide for their children's development needs, this ignores children's desire and right to have their parents present to provide for their emotional needs; and the significance of the parental role in providing for children's psychosocial development. Both this right of children and role of parents are protected in the CRC.

4.5 Conclusion

Parental migration has been described as 'a crisis in the lives of children', with the period of separation 'likely to forever alter the nature of the child-parent relationship'.[220] This chapter has shown that while TLM does provide parents with an opportunity to earn income that *may* (but does not necessarily) improve their children's education, health and material outcomes; it simultaneously creates risks to psychosocial and emotional aspects of children's development that are protected equally under Art 27. Hence, the chapter demonstrates that it is misleading to conceive of TLM as an appropriate form of assistance to parents to enable them to provide for their children's development needs, as this prioritises children's economic needs over *all other needs* without any form of assessment. Rather, appropriate measure of parental assistance required from States under Art 27(3) must be *effective* in implementing children's right to have their physical and non-physical development needs met under Art 27; and be *consistent* with other CRC provisions that together protect parents' primary role in their children's upbringing and development.

Throughout this chapter, the significant risks that parental migration poses to children's psychosocial development and well-being have been highlighted and supported by evidence from a wide range of social science studies. These studies emphasise the heightened potential harms to children that arise when their primary caregiver, usually their mother, migrates. However, there are numerous

216 Carling, Menjivar and Schmalzbauer, above n 118, 207.
217 See, eg, Ukwatta, above n 133, 120.
218 Parrenas, 'Transnational Fathering: Gendered Conflicts, Distant Disciplining and Emotional Gaps', above n 133, 1070.
219 Carola Suarez-Orozco et al (2002) cited in Ernesto Castañeda and Lesley Buck, 'Remittances, Transnational Parenting, and the Children Left Behind' [2011] (December) *The Latin Americanist* 85, 97.
220 Castañeda and Buck, above n 219, 105.

strategies that States can adopt to reduce these potential harms to children, and the sheer failure to incorporate such strategies into TLM policies only underscores the inappropriateness of TLM as a form of assistance to parents. The CRC Committee has clearly expressed its concerns about the potential negative implications of parental migration for children's upbringing and development, urging that:

> States have a responsibility to facilitate social and family cohesion, including by ensuring adequate social safety nets and economic opportunities at a local level.[221]

Investment in the creation of local employment options is one of the policy measures identified in this chapter that could reduce the interference by TLM with children's rights under Art 27. This can occur in parallel with the continued operation of TLM to create viable alternatives for parents that would give them the option to remain with their children while still being able to provide for them financially. This would also reduce the need for parents to remigrate and promote informed-decision making as parents would have options to consider.

Other reasonably available measures identified in this chapter that would reduce potential harms to children's psychosocial development include the use of children's best interests assessments to inform age-appropriate support strategies that should be stipulated in TLM policies. These assessments and strategies must incorporate and respond to the views and experiences of affected children, which accords with the duty of States to give due consideration to children's best interests and hear the views of children in all matters affecting them under Arts 3 and 12 of the CRC respectively.[222] Moreover, the CRC and CMW Committees have urged that States facilitate the participation of children affected by migration 'in the design, implementation and evaluation of policies 'that could directly or indirectly affect them ... including in the fields of social policies and social services'. This goes to the need for children's experiences to inform measures of support that can be made available in mainstream social services during periods of parental absence.

Giving due regard to the principle of international cooperation,[223] responsibility for financing and implementing such measures should not rest solely with labour-sending countries as labour-receiving countries have greater available resources and influence over the design of TLM policies. Moreover, the sharing of responsibility between States for implementing measures to reduce harm to children is essential because, as the following chapter demonstrates, the effectiveness of such measures depends upon policies and actions taken in *both* labour-sending and labour-receiving countries.

The CRC and CMW Committees have reiterated that States have a duty to ensure for *all* children 'a standard of living adequate for their physical, mental,

221 CRC Committee, *Report of the 2012 Day of General Discussion*, above n 60 [42].
222 See Chapter 3 (Sections 3.2.1 and 3.2.4).
223 See Chapter 3 (Section 3.3).

spiritual and moral development', irrespective of their parents' migration status.[224] Going forward, if States are to reduce interferences by TLM policies with children's rights under Art 27, a broader conception of children's development that accords with Art 27 must be adopted.

224 *Joint General Comment on Children in the Context of International Migration*, UN Doc CMW/C/GC/3-CRC/C/GC/22, para 43.

5 Articles 10(2) and 5

Can TLM policies better support the maintenance of transnational child-parent relationships?

Article 10(2)

A child whose parents reside in different States shall have the ***right to maintain on a regular basis, save in exceptional circumstances personal relations and direct contacts with both parents****.*

Article 5

The ***States Parties shall respect the responsibilities, rights and duties of parents*** *or, where applicable, the members of the extended family or community as provided for by local custom, legal guardians or other persons legally responsible for the child,* ***to provide, in a manner consistent with the evolving capacities of the child, appropriate direction and guidance*** *in the exercise by the child of the rights recognized in the present Convention.*

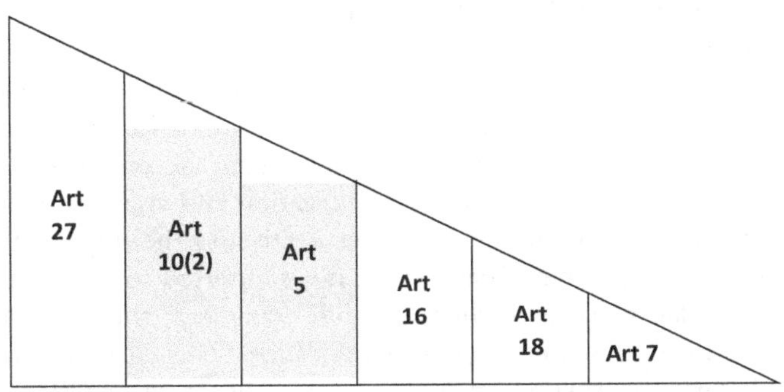

5.1 Introduction

Building on knowledge from the previous chapter about the important and protected role of parents in providing for children's psychosocial development needs, this chapter examines how TLM policies can better support parental capacity to meet children's psychosocial development needs ***during*** periods of separation. As such, this chapter moves the analysis of how TLM affects children's rights to focus on features of TLM policies that directly and indirectly interfere with children's right to maintain 'personal relations and direct contacts with both parents' on a regular basis when separated transnationally under Art 10(2) of the CRC. Given the inextricable link between the ability to maintain direct contact and personal relations and a parent's capacity to provide direction and guidance to their children, Arts 10(2) and 5 are considered together in this chapter. Under Art 5, children have a right to receive direction and guidance from their parents as they move through the different stages of childhood. Without the ability to maintain direct and regular relations and contact with their parents, children's capacity to receive guidance from their parents is thwarted. Hence, there is a significant interdependence between Arts 10(2) and 5 in the context of TLM and overlap in the challenges that it poses to the child-parent relationship.

The first and second sections in this chapter consider Art 10(2) and the structural features of low-waged TLM that interfere with the maintenance of direct contact, personal relations and communication between migrant workers and their children. It is argued that, as Kneebone explains, while these structural features result from policies in labour-sending ***and*** labour-receiving countries, they reflect the balance of power between States.[1] Hence, as previously discussed, labour-receiving States are in a significantly stronger position to adopt and resource measures that would enable the children of migrant workers to realise their right to maintain their relationship with their parents transnationally.[2] In these sections, it is argued that interferences with Art 10(2) can be *easily* reduced through a range of reasonably available and affordable measures, which makes these interferences unnecessary and unreasonable and thus they fail to constitute permissible limitations to this CRC right. These interferences remain unjustified by States, which may in part be because policymakers responsible for designing TLM programmes are unaware of children's rights under Art 10(2).

The final section in this chapter considers features of transnational family life that, if supported, would help parents to provide guidance to their children while separated in line with children's right to receive such guidance under Art 5. These include support for alternative caregivers to maintain the presence of physically absent parents in children's lives; and communication and visitation strategies that accord with children's changing development needs and the stage in the parent's migration cycle. It argues that if parents are not supported to continue providing direction and guidance to their children while separated, then the child-parent relationship can break down even upon reunification. This chapter reiterates that, as Tobin and Varadan explain, Art 5 is part of a collection of CRC rights 'that recognise and affirm the importance of the family unit and the special role of

1 Susan Kneebone, 'Migrant Workers Between States: In Search of Exit and Integration Strategies in South East Asia' (2012) 40 *Asian Journal of Social Science* 367, 375.

2 See Chapter 3 (Section 3.3) on international cooperation.

parents' in children's lives, which is significantly broader than providing for them financially.[3]

5.2 Understanding Article 10(2) in the context of TLM

5.2.1 Limitations are only permitted in exceptional circumstances

The use of the term 'shall' reflects the mandatory nature of the obligation on States to respect, protect and ensure that children are able to exercise their right to maintain direct and regular personal relations and contact with their parents if separated transnationally. This requires States to adopt positive measures to enable children to maintain direct contact and relations with their parents during periods of separation if there are barriers to children exercising this right.[4] Given that the parent resides in a different State from the child, the effectiveness of such measures will be determined by conditions in both States. While a child's right under Art 10(2) is not absolute, the limitation clause only permits interferences with this right '*in exceptional circumstances*'.[5] While the CRC and its *travaux preparatoires* do not define 'exceptional circumstances', these are to be understood in relation to the requirement to consider the best interests of the child in all circumstances.[6] That is, the exceptional circumstances must be defined by reference to a child's best interests.[7]

Moreover, policies that interfere with the protected right in Art 10(2) need to show that the 'exceptional circumstances' justify the limitation on children's rights. This requires States to show that the limitation pursues a legitimate aim, is necessary and proportionate to the aim, and adopts measures of least interference with the rights in question. For limitations based on exceptional circumstances to be considered lawful, they must meet this justification test.[8] Moreover, the

3 John Tobin and Shelia Varadan, 'Article 5. The Right to Parental Direction and Guidance Consistent with a Child's Evolving Capacities' in J Tobin (ed), *The UN Convention on the Rights of the Child: A Commentary* (OUP, 2019) 158, 160. See also John Tobin, 'Fixed Concepts but Changing Conceptions: Understanding the Relationship Between Children and Parents under the CRC' in Martin D Ruck, Michele Peterson-Badali and Michael Freeman (eds), *Handbook of Children's Rights Global and Multidisciplinary Perspectives* (Routledge, 2017) 53.

4 John Tobin and Judy Cashmore, 'Article 9. The Right Not to Be Separated from Parents' in J Tobin (ed), *The UN Convention on the Rights of the Child: A Commentary* (OUP, 2019) 305, 310; Jason M Pobjoy and John Tobin, 'Article 10. The Right to Family Reunification' in J Tobin (ed), *The UN Convention on the Rights of the Child: A Commentary* (OUP, 2019) 341, 347, 358.

5 *CRC* art 10(2).

6 *CRC* art 3. See Sharon Detrick, *A Commentary on the United Nations Convention on the Rights of the Child* (Martinus Nijhoff, 1999) 196–7.

7 American Bar Association Working Group on the United Nations Convention on the Rights of the Child, *Report of the American Bar Association Working Group on the United Nations Convention on the Rights of the Child* (1993) 48 cited in Sharon Detrick, above n 6, 197.

8 Australian Human Rights Commission, *Human Rights Brief No 4: Lawful Limits on Fundamental Freedoms* (8 March 2006) <https://www.humanrights.gov.au/publica

limitation must be applied strictly and must not impair the broader rights and freedoms that Art 10(2) guarantees for children to ensure the continuation of their relationship with their parents if separated.[9] Hence, this limitation clause is much stricter than the broad limitation clause on State obligations to reunify family members provided in Art 10(1), which is discussed in Section 5.2.3. Interferences with a child's right under Art 10(2) need to be justified on an individual basis to show that the circumstances are exceptional and that the interference is in a child's best interests. If it is not in a child's best interests, the reasons for the interference with a child's capacity to communicate with his or her parents would need to be shown to be legitimate and the interference necessary to achieve the aim and proportionate to the aim. In ordinary circumstances, the limitations that TLM policies place on children's right to communicate freely with their parents pursue no legitimate purpose. Moreover, States responsible for creating these policies have not endeavoured to provide a justification for their policies that create conditions and permit practices that interfere with a child's right under Art 10(2).

5.2.2 *Significance of Articles 9 and 10(1)*

State obligations under Art 10(2) must be informed by interdependent articles, including Arts 9 and 10(1). The significance of these articles is discussed in the following chapter in relation to children's right to have their family life respected under Art 16, which includes their relationship with their parents.[10] Briefly, Art 9 imposes a positive obligation on States to ensure that children and parents are not separated unless it is in the child's best interests. However, it has not been included in the conceptual framework because of its intended application to child-parent separation by States in a domestic setting and generally for protective reasons.[11] Article 10(1), on the other hand, imposes a positive obligation on States to reunify children and parents who are separated transnationally. However, this obligation is strongest when reunification in a family's country of origin is not possible or in a child's best interests,[12] which is generally not the case in the context of TLM. The exceptions here are labour-receiving countries that require exit visas for a migrant worker to leave their country of employment;[13] and the fact

tions/human-rights-brief-no-4#5_exceptional>; *CCPR General Comment No 27*, UN Doc CCPR/C/21/Rev.1/Add.9, paras 2, 13.

9 Ibid.

10 See Chapter 6 (Section 6.2).

11 Detrick, above n 6, 170.

12 *General Comment No 6*, UN Doc CRC/GC/2005/6 (1 September 2005), [83].

13 Harry Cook and Jane Sail, 'Migrant Well-Being in the Middle East and North Africa: A Focus on Gender in Cairo' (Working Paper for the World Migration Report 2013, IOM, 2013); International Trade Union Confederation, *Gulf Countries: Increase Migrant Worker Protection* (23 November 2013) <http://www.ituc-csi.org/gulf-countries-increase-migrant>; Migrant Forum in Asia, *Policy Brief No 2: Reform of the Kafala (Sponsorship) System* <https://www.ilo.org/dyn/migpractice/docs/132/PB2.pdf>.

that, as Jastram explains, economic realities 'keep most migrant workers firmly tied to the host country'.[14]

Nonetheless, TLM is considered a form of voluntary migration that involves a 'choice' by the parent rather than a form of child-parent separation that is forced by State actions. The notion of parental 'choice' in the context of TLM is discussed in Chapter 6.[15] However, even if TLM policies could be shown to constitute State acts of child-parent separation, Art 10 provides a broad limitation clause that significantly restricts the extent of a State's family reunification obligations. It permits States to restrict family reunification on grounds including national security, public order, public health and the rights of others.[16] As explained in the drafting of the CRC, the purpose of this broad limitation clause is to demonstrate that Art 10 'is not intended to affect the general right of States to establish and regulate their respective immigration laws'.[17] Rather, it is an attempt to balance individual rights with the sovereignty of States to determine their immigration policies.[18] The challenges that State sovereignty raises for children's rights in the context of TLM are again discussed in Chapter 6. [19] Suffice to say that it is for these reasons that Art 10(1) is not included in the conceptual framework, although it contributes to the context for interpreting other interrelated rights including Art 10(2).

5.2.3 Broad limitations on reunification obligations do not apply to Art 10(2)

Importantly, the limitation clause in Art 10 only applies in relation to the grant of reunification and *not* to State obligations to respect a child's right to maintain direct and regular relations and contact with both parents in the event of separation. The duty to respect – that is, not interfere with – this latter right is subject to a much stricter limitation clause. As discussed above, under Art 10(2), States can only limit a child's right to maintain regular relations and direct contact with their parents *in exceptional circumstances.* This is because, when read in light of other CRC articles including those identified in the conceptual framework, the CRC clearly presumes that maintenance of the child-parent relationship is in a child's best interest unless proven otherwise. Moreover, maintaining direct and regular contact and relations between children and parents who reside transnationally in no way threatens or undermines a State's control over immigration. Hence, issues of State sovereignty cannot be used to justify interferences with children's right to maintain their relationship with their parents *across* borders under Art 10(2).

14 Kate Jastram, *Family Unity: The New Geography of Family Life* (1 May 2003) Migration Policy Institute <https://www.migrationpolicy.org/article/family-unity-new-geography-family-life> 3.
15 See Chapter 6 (Section 6.3.4).
16 *CRC* art 10(2).
17 Chairman of the open-ended Working Group quoted in Detrick, above n 6, 170.
18 OHCHR, 'Family Reunification' (OHCHR Migration Papers, November 2005) 1.
19 See Chapter 6 (Section 6.3.2).

The right of the child to maintain personal relations and direct and regular contact with their parents depends upon the ability of their parents to do the same. This reflects the interdependence and indivisibility of children's rights with those of their parents. It also means that when the ability of parents to communicate freely with their children is restricted, then their children's rights are interfered with in relation to Art 10(2). This demands that those States responsible for the interference provide not only a justification but also an explicit assessment about whether there are other measures reasonably available that would reduce the degree of interference.[20] If the interference has no legitimate aim, employs measures that are unnecessary to achieve a legitimate aim, or fails to adopt measures of minimal interference, then it constitutes a violation of Art 10(2).

Evident throughout this chapter is that TLM policies both explicitly and implicitly restrict the ability of migrant workers to visit and communicate with their children; and that these restrictions by no means constitute measures of least interference, nor do they appear to pursue a legitimate aim. For example, in the context of labour-receiving countries such as Singapore and the Gulf States, migrant workers typically enter on two-year employment visas and are contractually entitled to return home to visit their family only at the end of this period.[21] While TLM regimes in countries like Canada and Australia do not explicitly restrict the return home of workers, the costs of return home visits in conjunction with low-waged employment render opportunities for visiting family during the period of employment infrequent at best. Such practices continue despite an understanding in other disciplines like family law that parents can maintain a significant role in their children's lives despite distance if communication is combined with visitation to an extent sufficient 'to maintain and nurture' the relationship between the physically absent parent and the child.[22]

In relation to the CRC, it has been observed that if direct and regular physical contact is limited for practical reasons such as geographic distance, personal relations between children and parents can still be developed and maintained through other media such as the internet and telephone.[23] Doek explains that in such

20 John Eekelaar and John Tobin, 'Article 3. The Best Interests of the Child' in J Tobin (ed), *The UN Convention on the Rights of the Child: A Commentary* (OUP, 2019) 73, 97.

21 Human Rights Watch, *Slow Reform: Protection of Migrant Domestic Workers in Asia and the Middle East* (Human Rights Watch, 2010) 9; IOM, *Labour Migration from Indonesia: An Overview of Indonesian Migration to Selected Destinations in Asia and the Middle East* (IOM, 2010) 43.

22 Sarah Gottfried, 'Virtual Visitation: The Wave of the Future in Communication Between Children and Non-Custodial Parents in Relocation Cases' (2002) 36(3) *Family Law Quarterly* 475, 482 quoting *Baures v Lewis*, 770 A 2d 214, 230 (NJ, 2001).

23 Jaap E Doek, *A Commentary on the United Nations Convention on the Rights of the Child: Article 8 The Right to Preservation of Identity, Article 9 The Right Not to Be Separated from His or Her Parents* (Martinus Nijhoff, 2006) 29–30.

instances, a child's right 'to use such means for maintaining personal relations with her/his parent(s)' could be explicitly provided for in legislation.[24] Such provisions in policies, legislation and bilateral agreements governing TLM could improve protection and support for children's rights under Art 10(2). However, as the following section demonstrates, TLM regimes currently interfere with – rather than protect and support – children's right to maintain direct and regular contact and relations with their parents.

5.3 Structural barriers to direct contact, personal relations and communication

5.3.1 Restricting opportunities for regular physical contact during the period of employment

While the CRC does not define what is meant by 'regular' contact, an ordinary understanding of the term implies contact and interaction that occurs in a frequent and routine manner so that it is constant and predictable for the child.[25] As mentioned, migrant workers are typically employed on two-year contracts (except for seasonal workers) and the period of familial separation frequently spans the length of the contract because workers cannot afford to visit their families during this period.[26] Moreover, contracts are often renewed multiple times, particularly when remittances become the main (or only) source of family income.[27] In such instances, it is not uncommon for workers to opt for an extra month's pay in lieu of a return visit, further extending the period of familial separation. To illustrate, a study from the Philippines calculated the time that parents and children spent together during the total period of employment, based on the frequency and duration of parental visits home. This study found that:

24 Ibid.

25 See, eg, Australian Institute of Family Studies, 'Parent-Child Contact and Post-Separation Parenting Arrangements' (Research Report, No 9, July 2004) figs 1(a)–1(c) citing Australian Bureau of Statistics (ABS), *Family Characteristics Report* (1997). This ABS Report considers 'regular contact' between a child and non-resident parent to be face-to-face contact that occurs at a frequency ranging from daily to at least once a month.

26 Piyasiri Wickramasekara, 'Migration Regimes and Their Linkages for Family Unity, Integrity and Development' in Marion Panizzon, Gottfried Zurcher and Elisa Fornale (eds), *The Palgrave Handbook of International Labour Migration: Law and Policy Perspectives* (Palgrave Macmillan, 2015) 146, 151.

27 Elspeth Graham and Lucy P Jordan, 'Migrant Parents and the Psychological Well-Being of Left-Behind Children in Southeast Asia' (2011) 73 *Journal of Marriage and Family* 763, 766; Maruja M B Asis, 'Living with Migration: Experiences of Left Behind Children in the Philippines' (2006) 2(1) *Asian Population Studies* 45, 45; John Bryant, 'Children of International Migrants in Indonesia, Thailand, and the Philippines: A Review of Evidence and Policies' (Innocenti Working Paper, No 2005–05, UNICEF, April 2005) 3.

> [M]igrant mothers spent an average of 23.9 weeks with their children over the course of an average of 11.42 years, while migrant fathers spent 74 weeks with their children over 13.79 years.[28]

By comparison, a study from Moldova found that proximity allowed many parents to visit their children more regularly every two to three months.[29] However, it also found that a quarter of the children in the study saw their parents less than once a year, with the frequency of visits depending on both distance and the legality of their parent's migration status.[30] Hence, as Zentgraf and Chinchilla explain, laws determining the migration status of migrant workers are an important factor facilitating or inhibiting return home visits. These laws, combined with wages and employment conditions that determine how long it takes to accumulate the money needed to return home, together 'affect the frequency and type of contacts those parents have with their children'.[31] To illustrate, the 2017 ASEAN Consensus on the Rights of Migrant Workers discussed in Chapter 3[32] recognises the right of migrant workers to be visited by their family members as a 'fundamental right'.[33] However, it simultaneously restricts this right as being 'for the purposes and length of time that the national legislations, regulations and policies of the Receiving State may allow'.[34] This reflects how migration and employment policies ***dictated by labour-receiving countries*** influence a child's capacity to realise their right under Art 10(2) to have direct physical contact with their parents.

The effect of migrant workers' limited financial resources on their capacity to visit their children during the period of employment was stressed by key informants in observations such as the following, which was made in relation to TLM between Asia and the Gulf States:

> If they have to finish a bond period because they have borrowed so much money to migrate ... then it's really difficult for them to go back if their child needs them'. *(Key Informant – Government 6)*

These observations highlight the precariousness of the financial conditions under which migrant workers operate, which include significant debts acquired to

28 Rhacel Salazar Parrenas (2005) 32 cited in Ernesto Castañeda and Lesley Buck, 'Remittances, Transnational Parenting, and the Children Left Behind' [2011] (December) *The Latin Americanist* 85, 86.

29 UNICEF Moldova, 'The Situation of Children Left Behind by Migrating Parents' (Study Report, UNICEF, 2006) 35.

30 Ibid.

31 Kristine M Zentgraf and Norma Stoltz Chinchilla, 'Transnational Family Separation: A Framework for Analysis' (2012) 38(2) *Journal of Ethnic and Migration Studies* 345, 358.

32 See Chapter 3 (Section 3.3.4.i).

33 *ASEAN Consensus on the Rights of Migrant Workers* para 8.

34 Ibid.

be able to participate in TLM programmes. Such debts restrict the capacity of migrant workers to return home regularly or in times of familial need. Regulation of recruitment agents should be a shared responsibility between labour-sending and labour-receiving countries given that they operate in both jurisdictions to source and manage migrant workers. However, other factors that serve to limit the mobility of migrant workers – such as low wages, visa restrictions, migration status and limited leave (which do not always differ from leave provisions for local workers) – are all features of TLM regimes that are determined by labour-receiving countries. Combined, these features restrict a parent's ability to have regular physical contact with their children during the period of employment. This, in turn, unnecessarily interferes with children's right to maintain direct contact and personal relations with their parents under Art 10(2).

i. Potential impact of prolonged periods of physical separation is foreseeable

Existing studies reveal, anecdotally, that children of migrant workers often experience a deep sense of loss and yearning resulting from the prolonged physical absence of their parents (particularly in relation to mothers). This is discussed in the previous chapter in relation to the impact of parental migration on children's social and emotional well-being.[35] Children's frequent desire for direct *physical* contact with their parents is captured in the following comments from the daughter of a migrant worker who participated in a study by Parreñas conducted in the Philippines:

> I would have wanted her next to me, so I could feel her love … I know she loves me because she is working hard over there … so that we could have everything we want and everything we need … But still, I want her to be with me here every day … since I was small it was only my grandparents showing me love. She was not here.[36]

It is because of the foreseeable impact of lengthy periods of child-parent separation on children that the CRC protects children's right to maintain *regular* direct contact with their parents if separated transnationally. This foreseeability is reflected in the observations of a key informant from the government sector that:

> 'I think that prolonged absence is definitely not good for the upbringing of children. Because I do believe that children need both parents … So I think if a child is separated from their parent for a long period of time, it has an impact somehow. How long is too long? That's very hard to say'. *(Key Informant – Government 1)*

35 See Chapter 4 (Section 4.3).

36 Rhacel Salazar Parrenas, *Children of Global Migration: Transnational Families and Gendered Woes* (Stanford University Press, 2005) 124.

This reflects the difficulty in determining an appropriate length of child-parent separation that will minimise harm to children given that it will vary according to the specific context of each child. However, guidance on appropriate lengths of separation, and *how they can be effectively managed*, can be drawn from other disciplines that manage child-parent separation. This is discussed in Chapters 6 and 7. [37] Suffice to say here that the ILO has reiterated the obligation on States to support opportunities for regular physical contact between migrant workers and their families in its rights-based approach to labour migration. These non-binding guidelines urge States to facilitate 'the movement of migrant workers between the country in which they work and their home country to enable them to maintain family and social ties'.[38] This reflects an understanding that without States taking positive measures to support migrant workers to visit their families, family relationships will breakdown over time. It also accords with the duty of States to protect and ensure children's right to maintain their relationship with their parents in transnational contexts under Art 10(2).

Contrary to these obligations, visa regimes in labour-receiving countries currently discourage the circulation of workers.[39] Not only does this restrict opportunities for direct contact with children, it limits parental 'choice' about the duration of the separation. Circulation-friendly visas as a measure to enhance support for direct contact between children and parents in the context of TLM is discussed further in Chapter 6. [40] The pressing need for workers to have the right to return home on a regular basis *combined with* financial assistance or adequate wages *and* sufficient holiday leave was reiterated by key informants. They stressed that as each of these factors are necessary to enable regular return visits, they must all be stipulated in contracts and *not* dependent on the goodwill of employers. This is captured in comments such as:

> 'It's down to individual employers to 'be nice' and offer such possibilities ... What has to be built into migration policies is the regular opportunity to return for a week or so to be with children for a little while. And to rethink the lengths of contracts'. *(Key Informant – R & P 3)*

This comment supports the additional observation by some key informants that the length of standard contracts should be shortened to one year or even six months (like seasonal TLM). Other observations by key informants also included that paid and/or mandatory leave would eliminate the option for employers to offer pay in lieu; and that workers should be supported to return home for events

37 See Chapter 6 (Section 6.4.1) and Chapter 7 (Section 7.2.3).

38 ILO, *ILO Multilateral Framework on Labour Migration: Non-binding Principles and Guidelines for a Rights-Based Approach to Labour Migration* (ILO, 2006) [12.9].

39 Wickramasekara, above n 26, 168.

40 See Chapter 6 (Section 6.4.3.ii).

of major significance for a family and, in particular, for children (such as religious events, graduations, serious illnesses involving close family members and so on). Each of these observations is indicative of the existence of reasonably available measures that would reduce the interference of TLM policies with children's right under Art 10(2) to have regular direct contact with their parents when their relationship is transnational.

5.3.2 Reliance on regular communication to maintain personal relations transnationally

Given the severe restrictions that TLM imposes on opportunities for direct physical contact between parents and children, migrant workers and their children rely heavily on regular communication to maintain their child-parent relationships transnationally. As Zentgraf and Chinchilla describe:

> Regular contact is the glue that keeps transnational families together and is at the centre of parenting practices from afar. The maintenance of regular, high-quality communication between absent migrant parents and their children is almost universally assumed to reduce the costs of separation on both sides.[41]

This highlights the dependency of children's ability to realise their right to regular and direct contact with their parents under Art 10(2) on measures that support regular and quality transnational communication between parents and children.

Labour-sending countries have recognised the need to invest in measures that build 'close communication between family members' in the context of TLM.[42] Moreover, international organisations such as IOM have reiterated that constant communication between migrant workers and their children can enhance the well-being of the family as a whole.[43] However, given the transnational nature of the communication, effective measures cannot be unilateral and require cooperation and shared responsibility between States. This is particularly important given that regular and quality communication enables parents who reside in labour-receiving countries to continue fulfilling important aspects of their parenting role, such as the provision of direction and guidance. This is discussed in Section 5.4.

The importance of effective measures that support regular, frequent and quality communication to sustaining transnational child-parent relationships is captured by Carling et al in their study on transnational parenthood. They observe that communication serves a dual purpose for parents who are migrant workers: to stay

41 Zentgraf and Chinchilla, above n 31, 351.

42 *Initial Report of the Republic of Indonesia on the Implementation of the International Convention on the Protection of the Rights of All Migrant Workers and Members their Families Pursuant to the Simplified Reporting Procedure* (5 March 2017) <https://tbinternet.ohchr.org/Treaties/CMW/Shared%20Documents/IDN/CMW_C_IDN_1_6902_E.pdf> 51.

43 IOM, 'Migration and Families: Background Paper' (Intersessional Workshop, International Dialogue on Migration, 7–8 October 2014) 6.

involved in their children's everyday lives by exchanging information with children and carers;[44] and to confirm the child-parent relationship itself, which relies on the act of frequent and regular communication irrespective of the information that is exchanged.[45] It is through long-distance communication that migrant workers 'strive to be socially and emotionally present while physically absent'.[46]

Labour-receiving countries share this understanding about the importance of frequent, dependable and quality communication for maintaining child-parent relationships in other contexts involving child-parent separation. To illustrate, the Australian Defence Force has identified maintaining contact with a deployed parent as key to countering feelings of sadness, abandonment, loneliness and anger that may arise in children and adolescents experiencing parental deployment.[47] They have found that children who cope well with parental deployment often have, among other things, '[d]ependable communication between the deployed parent and family'.[48] Moreover, the RAND Institute's longitudinal Deployment Life Study found that family relationships in military families in the United States were better when the deployed family member returned if the family were 'satisfied with the quantity of communication during deployment' and there were 'open lines of communication between family members during the separation'.[49] These findings again go to the foreseeability of the potential harms to children if their right to communicate freely with their parents is limited; and to learnings from other disciplines about effective measures to support this right of children in the context of transnational child-parent separation.

i. Constraints on migrant workers' communication with their children violates Art 10(2)

Constraints on the capacity of migrant workers to engage in direct and regular communication with their children vary considerably across the spectrum of TLM regimes. However, TLM policies universally fail to provide contractual stipulations that guarantee migrant workers appropriate times, private spaces and assistance with costs to enable frequent and quality communication to take place. States have provided no justifications to date as to why standard contracts that they design to

44 Jørgen Carling, Cecilia Menjivar and Leah Schmalzbauer, 'Central Themes in the Study of Transnational Parenthood' (2012) 38(2) *Journal of Ethnic and Migration Studies* 191, 203–4. See also M M B Asis, S Huang and B S A Yeoh, 'When the Light of the Home is Abroad: Unskilled Female Migration and the Filipino Family' (2004) 25(2) *Singapore Journal of Tropical Geography* 198.

45 Carling, Menjivar and Schmalzbauer, above n 44, 203–4.

46 Ibid.

47 Australian Defence Force, Joint Health Command, *Deployment Guide: A Guide to Assist Your Preparation* <www.defence.gov.au/Health/HealthPortal/docs/JHC%20Deployment%20Guide.pdf> 44–8.

48 Ibid 48.

49 RAND Arroyo Center and the National Defense Research Institute, 'Brief: How Military Families Function Before, During, and After Deployment – Findings from the RAND Deployment Life Study' (RAND Corporation, 2016) 3–4.

govern TLM fail to provide these basic measures to support migrant workers to communicate frequently and freely with their children. Moreover, as this section demonstrates, there are numerous measures ***reasonably available*** to States that are currently overlooked, which would enhance the capacity of children to realise their rights under Art 10(2). Without a legitimate aim for creating policies that hinder regular and frequent communication, and by failing to consider and adopt available measures that reduce interferences with Art 10(2), States are violating children's right to maintain regular personal relations and direct contact with their parents when separated. Importantly, to be effective, many of these measures require actions on the part of labour-receiving States given that their policies (or lack thereof) directly affect the capacity of migrant workers to communicate with their children.

For low-waged migrant workers, unlike migrants from other social classes, employer discretion continues to be associated with the elements necessary for regular and meaningful exchanges between parents and children. This reflects the reality that class and migration status remain significant factors influencing the quality of child-parent communication in the context of TLM.[50] This highlights the divergence between migration and employment regimes that enable unfettered communication (and movement) by skilled workers who operate across *fluid* borders; and the significant restrictions on communication (and movement) by migrant workers, who are governed by highly controlled migration and employment regimes and operate across *rigid* borders.[51] This is illustrated in findings from a study in the Philippines that the ability of Filipina domestic workers to communicate with their children was significantly more constrained than that of middle-class Filipina migrants, who were able to communicate closely and maintain intimacy with their children.[52]

Key informants stressed the need for contracts to stipulate workers' rights to communicate with their children on a frequent and private basis, at times and using modes of communication most suitable for their children. This goes to the need for appropriate measures to support the implementation of children's rights to accord with a child's age and capacity and be responsive to children's changing needs as they progress through the different stages of development. This is discussed in the preceding chapter in relation to Art 27.[53] As with the facilitation of return travel, States need to take active measures to support workers to be able to communicate freely with their children and measures should not be subject to employer discretion. This was reiterated by key informants in statements such as:

50 Saskia Sassen, 'Two Stops in Today's New Global Geographies: Shaping Novel Labor Supplies and Employment Regimes' (2008) 52(3) *American Behavioral Scientist* 457; Carling, Menjivar and Schmalzbauer, above n 44, 201.

51 See Saskia Sassen, 'When the Center No Longer Holds: Cities as Frontier Zones' (2012) *Cities* 1.

52 Parrenas (2005) cited in Carling, Menjivar and Schmalzbauer, above n 44, 201–2.

53 See Chapter 4 (Section 4.4).

> 'Simple things, like allowing migrants time and space for regular phone calls and using the internet for regular skyping ... These things are not costly ... One thing would be stipulating these in model contracts'. *(Key Informant – R & P 3)*

> 'It's incredibly important for the parent to have not only the right, but also the means, to be able to speak to their children on a regular, frequent basis ... It's the ability to speak and communicate not on an employer's schedule but on a schedule that makes sense to the family'. *(Key Informant – R & P 7)*

> 'They should be able to touch base and see what's going on. That would be a preventative measure, because people will know that the child is in touch with their parents ... You don't have to make that distance such a big distance if the child knows their mother is just a phone call away'. *(Key Informant – Government 6)*

These observations demonstrate the ease by which current policies and practices in the context of TLM could be improved by States to reduce interference with children's right to communicate freely with their parents. Measures such as facilitating the regular use of Skype and guaranteeing opportunities to communicate at times appropriate for children are not costly and do not impose unreasonable burdens on employers. Rather, they make strategies that assist other families to manage transnational relationships in different contexts available to low-waged migrant workers and their children. At present, TLM creates barriers to communication that are not present for families in other transnational contexts. These barriers include the confiscation of mobile phones by employers and limited access to communication technology, which could be overcome through active measures by States. These barriers are discussed in the following parts of this section.

ii. Frequent confiscation of mobile phones in particular TLM contexts

The most pronounced variation between TLM regimes in relation to direct access to communication between migrant workers and their families is access to a mobile phone. This is because, in the context of labour-receiving countries in Asia and the Gulf, the confiscation of mobile phones from domestic workers remains common practice.[54] Due to such practices, the model standard contract for women domestic workers developed by UN Women specifically identifies terms

54 Human Rights Watch, above n 21; Elizabeth Frantz, 'Jordan's Unfree Workforce: State-Sponsored Bonded Labour in the Arab Region' (2013) 49(8) *Journal of Development Studies* 1072; Amrita Pande, '"The Paper that You Have in Your Hand is My

that include that the worker 'shall be allowed to freely communicate with her/his family'[55] and that the employer 'shall not confiscate mobile phones'.[56] However, the confiscation of mobile phones still regularly occurs with, for example, the International Human Rights Clinic observing that in relation to Filipina women migrant workers employed in Kuwait:

> Because they know many stories about recruitment agencies and employers that confiscate cell phones … women have been reported to carry three cell phones, with one hidden in their underwear. Even so, agencies have been known to strip workers to confiscate the phones.[57]

Similarly, a study of 670 women domestic workers in Singapore found that 73 per cent had experienced restrictions on their communication at least once, including not being permitted by their employer of employer's family to make private phone calls.[58]

The duty in human rights law to *protect* children's rights requires States to take measures to prevent interference with CRC rights by non-State actors, which include employers. As discussed, restricting the capacity of parents to communicate with their children directly violates children's right to maintain direct contact with their parents when separated under Art 10(2). Hence, labour-receiving States have a duty to curtail the practice by employers of confiscating mobile phones, which is common in Asia and the Gulf States. Key informants reiterated the detrimental effect that this practice has on the capacity of parents to maintain personal relations with their children, observing that in the Asian and Gulf States:

> 'There should be stricter laws on the restriction of communication … For a lot of domestic workers, the employers keep their phone from them and they haven't spoken to their families in months or even a year. So how then do you keep in touch with your family?'. *(Key Informant – MLO-NGO 5)*

Freedom": Migrant Domestic Work and the Sponsorship (Kafala) System in Lebanon' (2013) 47(2) *International Migration Review* 414.

55 UN Women Asia and the Pacific, *Template on Standard Terms of Employment (STOE) for Women Migrant Domestic Workers* (UN Women, 2016) 7 cl 9.1

56 Ibid 7 cl 9.2.

57 SAIS International Human Rights Clinic interview with the Migration Policy Institute (Manila, 18 March 2013) cited in International Human Rights Clinic, *The Protection of the Rights of Migrant Domestic Workers in a Country of Origin and a Country of Destination: Case Studies of the Philippines and Kuwait* (Johns Hopkins School of Advanced International Studies (SAIS), 2013) 39.

58 Anja Wessels, 'Home Sweet Home? Work, Life and Well-being of Foreign Domestic Workers in Singapore' (Research Report, Humanitarian Organisation for Migration Economics, March 2015) 6.

These observations reiterate concerns expressed by labour-sending countries about the failure of labour laws in labour-receiving countries to protect migrant workers, particularly domestic workers who live and work in their employer's house. This is reflected in the Sri Lankan Government's view that, despite its best efforts in relation to issues such as restrictions on communication, it is necessary for 'destination countries to take legal and administrative measures to protect' the rights of these workers.[59] This demonstrates, once again, that unilateral measures in the context of TLM will be ineffective in supporting the implementation of CRC rights that protect the child-parent relationship, including Art 10(2).

Importantly, physical access to a mobile phone presents less of a challenge in liberal, democratic labour-receiving countries (with exceptional cases of worker abuse noted). This was emphasised by key informants in relation to Canada in views such as:

> 'Caregivers have their own phones here. They use their own telephones to call home ... [But] in the rural areas, workers [may need] transportation to go to a phone ... So that could at least be a basic requirement, accommodation in which there is Internet and a phone'. *(Key Informant – MLO-NGO 4)*

This highlights that, while employers in Canada generally do not prevent workers from having a mobile phone, there are no explicit policy measures in place that guarantee access to a phone or the Internet; ensure that a worker can communicate with their children at appropriate times; or support workers to meet the costs associated with long-distance communication. This is despite the fact that such basic measures of assistance to parents would help them to fulfil aspects of their parenting role irrespective of distance, and support children's capacity to realise their right to direct and regular contact with their parents under Art 10(2). Hence, in many regards, the policy void in countries like Canada resembles labour-receiving countries in Asia and the Gulf States, but *employer practices* concerning restrictions on communication are less harsh and exploitative.

Importantly, as discussed in the preceding chapter, States have a duty under the CRC to provide appropriate measures of assistance to parents to provide for their children's psychosocial and emotional needs. At present, TLM policies across the spectrum undermine rather than support the maintenance of personal relations between migrant workers and their children during the period of employment, although to varying degrees. This reflects, as Boyd argues, that TLM practices in

59 H E Ravinatha and P Aryasinha, 'Introductory Statement at the Presentation of Sri Lanka's 2nd Periodic Report (CMW/C/LKA/2) Submitted under the ICRMW' (Presented at the 25th Session of the CMW Committee, Geneva, 1 September 2016) 15.

countries like Canada appear laudable 'only because working conditions and the extension of rights in other countries are so much worse'.[60]

iii. Accessibility and affordability of communication including the Internet

While the Canadian Government does require employers to assist low-waged temporary migrant workers to secure 'suitable and affordable' accommodation, access to the Internet and telephones are not required features of the accommodation.[61] This demonstrates a lack of recognition that children's capacity to realise their rights under Art 10(2) are, in part, dependent on labour-receiving countries adopting measures to facilitate communication between migrant workers and their children. For example, the Canadian Government's standard contract for seasonal agricultural workers from Mexico requires employers to provide workers with adequate and suitable accommodation, which workers in British Columbia can be charged for daily (capped at a total of $826 during their stay in Canada).[62] The contract stipulates that workers' accommodation must include laundry facilities with 'an adequate number of washing machines' or the employer must transport the worker to the laundromat at no cost and pay five dollars each week towards laundry costs.[63] However, there are no similar provisions stipulating that, as part of the accommodation costs, the accommodation must include access to Wi-Fi and a sufficient number of computers or financial support towards meeting communication costs. Key informants from the government sector observed that Internet and telephone access could be implicitly considered to be part of reasonable accommodation, as follows:

> 'Generally speaking, I think it would be provided for in any kind of reasonable accommodation. Some of the most basic farm accommodations provides workers with access to a computer with Internet and a phone. I think if that kind of thing wasn't available, then one could question whether the accommodations are reasonable'. *(Key Informant – Government 3)*

60 Monica Boyd, 'Labour Migration for Care: Women Migrants in Canada Under the Live-in Caregiver Program' (Paper presented at the Rethinking Care and Migration in the Age of Low Fertility and Ageing Population Conference, University of Toronto, 9–10 March 2011), 25 citing Bakan and Stasiulis (1997).

61 Employment and Social Development Canada, *Labour Market Impact Assessment Application: Low-Wage Positions* (1 December 2018) <https://catalogue.servicecanada.gc.ca/apps/EForms/pdf/en/ESDC-EMP5627.pdf> 8 s 9.

62 Government of Canada, *Contract for the Employment in Canada of Seasonal Agricultural Workers from Mexico – 2019* (18 December 2018) <https://www.canada.ca/en/employment-social-development/services/foreign-workers/agricultural/seasonal-agricultural/apply/mexico.html> s 2 pt A.

63 Ibid s 2 pt A cl 1.

This observation conveys an expectation on the part of policymakers that employers will ensure access to communication technology for migrant workers as part of providing non-exploitative living conditions that are of a reasonable standard. However, given that such reasonably available measures would assist parents to maintain communication with their children, thus reducing interference with *their children's rights* under Art 10(2), they should be *explicitly* included in standard contracts to ensure that their provision is *not* employer dependent.

Moreover, researchers have noted that globally, the benefits of the Internet in transforming transnational communication are still not accessible to many migrant workers and their families, who may not have the skills or resources to use or access this technology.[64] For example, studies on children of migrant workers in South-East Asia have found that while communication via the Internet can be more cost-effective than by telephone, many migrant workers and their families are computer illiterate or cannot afford the necessary equipment.[65] This is compounded in regions in labour-sending countries that may not have this necessary infrastructure to support easy communication through the Internet. To illustrate, a recent World Bank study on Australia's Seasonal Workers Program found that only 3 per cent of workers used Skype and 4 per cent used email to communicate with their families.[66] It attributed this in part to 'the lack of access to Internet and slow speeds throughout the Pacific'.[67] The report also highlighted that communication 'is critical to mitigating the potential downside impacts on the family unit' due to 'extended absences' over six to nine month periods and found that:

> This is partly hindered by the costs of calling the Pacific and Timor-Leste from Australia — costs which are exorbitantly high by global standards.[68]

Like Canada, Australia's TLM programmes with countries in the Pacific also fail to incorporate effective measures to assist workers to maintain regular and frequent communication with their families.[69] Rather, as highlighted in the same World Bank study, workers are absorbing these significant costs to communicate with

64 Carling, Menjivar and Schmalzbauer, above n 44, 201–2. See also Leah Schmalzbauer, 'Searching for Wages and Mothering from Afar: The Case of Honduran Transnational Families' (2004) 66(5) *Journal of Marriage and Family* 1317; Leah Schmalzbauer 'Family Divided: The Class Formation of Honduran Transnational Families' (2008) 8(3) *Global Networks* 29.

65 Elspeth Graham et al, 'Transnational Families and the Family Nexus: Perspectives of Indonesian and Filipino Children Left Behind by Migrant Parent(s)' (2012) 44 *Environment and Planning* 793.

66 World Bank Group, *Maximizing the Development Impacts from Temporary Migration: Recommendations for Australia's Seasonal Worker Programme* (International Bank for Reconstruction and Development/The World Bank, 2017) 39.

67 Ibid.

68 Ibid.

69 See, eg, Australian Government Department of Foreign Affairs and Trade (DFAT), *Travel Smart – Work Smart: Pre-departure Manual for Nauru Seasonal Workers in Australia* (DFAT/ILO) 20.

their families several times a month on average, which is 'mitigating some of the potential negative consequences of family separation'.[70] However, assistance from governments and/or employers to meet communication costs would facilitate more frequent communication between parents and children, which could even occur on a daily basis at a regular time that is suitable for children. This would assist parents to be actively engaged in their children's daily lives despite being required to live separately for significant parts of the year.

Key informants emphasised that workers should be assisted by both labour-sending and labour-receiving countries to meet the costs of regular communication, including access to the Internet to facilitate the use of free services. Their comments included:

> 'Ideally, it should be provided in law, some basic entitlements for workers to be able to talk to their families every day. And if they need Wi-Fi for that, they should have access to Wi-Fi'. *(Key Informant – MLO-NGO 1)*

Such comments support the need to stipulate measures of assistance in contracts and/or relevant laws to guarantee that they are available to all migrant workers and not dependent on individual employers. These measures are reasonably available and inexpensive for States and would reduce the degree of interference by TLM policies – which are premised on child-parent separation – with children's right to maintain direct and regular contact with their parents under Art 10(2).

iv. Labour-receiving countries should assist in developing ICT infrastructure

Labour-sending countries have recognised the vital role that communication plays in maintaining familial relationships while migrant workers are employed overseas. For example, the Filipino Government has highlighted its efforts to form partnerships with large telecommunication companies so that its migrant workers 'and their families can enjoy lower rates in phone calls and internet use'.[71] However, costs associated with these types of initiatives, as well as the building of information and communications technology (ICT) infrastructure in high migration regions, are borne by labour-sending countries. This is despite labour-sending countries having more limited resources. Hence, in line with the principle of international cooperation outlined in Chapter 3, [72] the development of communication infrastructure and initiatives to support transnational communication should be a shared responsibility between labour-sending and labour-receiving

70 World Bank Group, above n 66, 39, 65.

71 Rebecca J Calzado, Department of Labor and Employment Philippines, 'Labour Migration and Development Goals: The Philippine Experience' (Paper presented at International Dialogue on Migration, Geneva, 8 October 2007) 5.

72 See Chapter 3 (Section 3.3).

countries. This is particularly so because TLM policies that source workers from specific regions and require the separation of children and parents are dictated by labour-receiving countries. At present, as Meghani explains, while labour-receiving countries, labour-sending countries and international financial institutions all encourage TLM, none provide much assistance to families to meet the challenges caused by the prolonged absence of family members.[73]

The role for labour-receiving countries to support the development of ICT infrastructure in labour-sending countries is intensified when their TLM programmes are attempting to achieve a dual development outcome, or when labour-receiving countries have parallel aid programmes with the same labour-sending countries.[74] This notion is reflected to a degree in the following observation by a key informant from the government sector:

> 'If there is anything that receiving countries could do, it is really through aid. In that sense, we certainly should and could ... as access [to technology] is not very equal ... Some people have it and others don't ... But to say receiving countries have an obligation, I wouldn't go that far. But I certainly see that programs can be put in place to help source countries in particular, like the Philippines for example'. *(Key Informant – Government 1)*

This observation captures the potential for labour-receiving countries to support measures that would assist labour-sending countries to be able to ensure that children in their jurisdiction can communicate freely with their parents working overseas. However, it also demonstrates that labour-receiving countries do not see this role as a legal obligation despite the evidence that easy and affordable access to communication significantly improves outcomes for families separated by TLM policies. These policies are defined by labour-receiving countries and completely disregard the duty of States under human rights law to not cause harm to children outside a State's jurisdiction; not enter into bilateral agreements that cause harm to children; and assist States with fewer resources to implement children's rights. Each of these is an element of the principle of international cooperation that informs the CRC and is outlined in Chapter 3. [75]

v. Supporting the capacity of workers to maintain parental presence

The above sections reveal how the capacity of migrant workers to maintain frequent and quality communication with their children is impacted heavily by

73 Zahra Meghani, 'Women on the Move' in Zahra Meghani (ed), *Women Migrant Workers: Ethical, Political and Legal Problems* (Taylor and Francis, 2015) 5, 8.

74 The connection between TLM and international development is discussed in Chapter 7 (Section 7.3).

75 See Chapter 3 (Section 3.3).

structural inequalities that determine, among other things, a family's socio-economic status.[76] Because of the precariousness associated with the migration and social status of migrant workers, it is imperative that measures to support the maintenance of their personal relations with their children are legally protected in their countries of employment. This includes time to spend with their families even if they are not physically present, time that is not subject to employer discretion. This was stressed by key informants in views such as:

> 'At the very minimum, these workers should be included under national employment standards [that] protect workers in terms of their wage, time, control over what they do outside of work, and having some separation between work and individual time. Hopefully that standard would then enable workers to have the freedom and rights to communicate via a variety of communication methods'. *(Key Informant – R & P 5)*

This view highlights the need for migrant workers to be protected by standard labour regulations that protect, among other things, a worker's personal time. The need for labour-receiving States to enforce minimum employment standards to protect the rights of migrant workers is heightened in the context of domestic workers, who are routinely excluded from national labour laws because of the nature of their employment.[77] To this end, the ILO's *Domestic Workers' Convention (2011)* (C189) entitles domestic workers to the same basic rights as other workers,[78] but it has only been ratified by 27 countries to date.[79] This is significant because, as noted in the previous chapter, there are roughly 67.1 million domestic workers worldwide, of whom 11.5 million are migrant workers (and 73.4 per cent of these migrant domestic workers are women).[80] Furthermore, the ILO's *Convention on Workers with Family Responsibilities (1981)* (C156) – which has been ratified by 44 countries including by Australia[81] – obliges States parties to:

76 Zentgraf and Chinchilla, above n 31, 353.

77 International Domestic Workers' Network, International Trade Union Confederation and Human Rights Watch, *Claiming Rights: Domestic Workers' Movements and Global Advances for Labour Reform* (Human Rights Watch, 2013) 2.

78 *Convention Concerning Decent Work for Domestic Workers* (ILO No 189), opened for signature 16 June 2011 (entered into force 5 September 2013) ('*C189*').

79 See ILO, *Ratifications of C189 - Domestic Workers Convention, 2011 (No 189)* (22 January 2019) <https://www.ilo.org/dyn/normlex/en>.

80 ILO, *ILO Global Estimates on Migrant Workers: Results and Methodology* (ILO, 2015) 6–7, 10–11; ILO, *Report VI: Towards a Fair Deal for Migrant Workers in the Global Economy*, International Labour Conference, 92nd sess, Agenda Item 6, 2004 [19]. See Chapter 4 (Section 4.3.1) on the feminisation of migration.

81 *Convention Concerning Equal Opportunities and Equal Treatment for Men and Women Workers: Workers with Family Responsibilities* (ILO No 156), opened for signature 23 June 1981 (entered into force 11 August 1983) ('*C156*'). See ILO,

> [M]ake it an aim of national policy to enable persons with family responsibilities who are engaged or wish to engage in employment to exercise their right to do so without being subject to discrimination and, to the extent possible, without conflict between their employment and family responsibilities.[82]

This highlights the importance of looking to national as well as international commitments to workers' rights in labour-receiving countries to understand the full scope of State obligations to support workers to meet their familial responsibilities. These responsibilities include those parental responsibilities that can be continued to be fulfilled if direct and regular contact between workers and their children is facilitated by States. As expressed by a key informant:

> 'It really would change the nature of the job if people could rely on that *regular* contact. It would be a different kind of separation, if they knew that they could go home once a year, could talk to their kids every day ... [on] a schedule that is regular so their kids can anticipate it'. *(Key Informant – R & P 2)*

This comment reiterates that central to managing transnational child-parent separation is that children and parents have contact and communicate on a regular, frequent and direct basis in line with the provisions in Art 10(2). The particular importance of *improved* Internet access for migrant workers and their families was stressed by key informants given the opportunity that it creates for parents to remain virtually present in children's lives.[83] The role of technology in maintaining transnational child-parent relationships has been demonstrated in the context of family law, in which it has been found that 'children benefit from both auditory and visual reminders of their absent parents'.[84] This is no different in the context of child-parent separation generated by TLM, as reflected in the following comment from a key informant:

> 'When we *see* somebody, rather than just a voice or an email, that really does make a difference. So, it's an issue of access to technology, but also access to time to be with their families'. *(Key Informant – R & P 1)*

Ratifications of C156 - Workers with Family Responsibilities Convention, 1981 (No 156) (22 January 2019) <https://www.ilo.org/dyn/normlex/en>.

82 *C156* art 3.

83 Graham and Jordan, above n 27, 781.

84 Joan B Kelly and Michael E Lamb, 'Developmental Issues in Relocation Cases Involving Young Children: When, Whether, and How?' (2003) 17(2) *Journal of Family Psychology* 193, 201.

Importantly, studies from labour-sending countries have highlighted the challenges in maintaining meaningful exchanges between children and parents through long-distance communication alone, particularly when children are young.[85] This is illustrated in UNICEF's study from Moldova, which found that while most children did communicate with their parents by phone, some considered this 'a poor substitute for real contact, which is more profound'.[86] These sentiments are captured in the following statement by a Grade 1 student who participated in the Moldovan study and whose mother had migrated for employment:

> We talk over the phone, but I want to feel her next to me; I can't see her.[87]

This supports findings that even if migrant workers communicate frequently with their children, over time 'it probably lacks the depth that parenting requires'.[88] Hence, while well-supported transnational communication can significantly enhance the capacity of children and parents to maintain personal relations over short periods, this *must* be coupled with opportunities for regular physical contact. Children have a right to both under Art 10(2) and, as discussed in Section 5.3.1, regular and direct physical contact is essential if the child-parent relationship is to be sustained transnationally over longer periods of time.

5.4 Transnational parenting and the continuation of parental guidance

Transnationalism in the context of migrant families is based on the notion that family members can remain socially present even if they are physically absent.[89] While transnational families are not new, the notion of transnational parenting is a relatively new and emerging concept used to explore and explain how the child-parent relationship is realised when children and their parents are separated transnationally.[90] It has emerged largely because of the increasing prevalence of

85 Rosemarie Edillon, *The Effects of Parent's Migration on the Rights of Children Left Behind in the Philippines* (Division of Policy and Practice Working Paper, UNICEF, August 2008) 72; Suarez-Orozco, Todorova and Louie (2002) cited in Audrey M Pottinger and Sharon Williams Brown, 'Understanding the Impact of Parental Migration on Children: Implications for Counselling Families from the Caribbean' (2006) *American Counselling Association: Vistas Online* <https://www.counseling.org/resources/library/vistas/vistas06_online-only/pottinger.pdf> 4.

86 UNICEF Moldova, above n 29, 34.

87 Ibid.

88 Edillon, above n 85, 72.

89 Carling, Menjivar and Schmalzbauer, above n 44, 192.

90 See, eg, Carling, Menjivar and Schmalzbauer, above n 44; Schmalzbauer, above n 64; Parrenas, above n 36; Rhacel Salazar Parrenas, 'Transnational Fathering: Gendered Conflicts, Distant Disciplining and Emotional Gaps' (2008) 34(7) *Journal of Ethnic and Migration Studies* 1057; J Dreby, *Divided by Borders: Mexican Migrants and Their Children* (University of California Press, 2010); J K Bernhard, P Landolt and L

transnational parenthood caused by restrictive migration regimes in labour-receiving countries that prevent (either legally or practically) family accompaniment for low-waged migrant workers.[91] Importantly, the constraints that transnational separation place on the child-parent relationship differ in the context of low-waged TLM from other forms of migration. Hence, while transnational families adopt strategies to ensure their family continues to function despite distance,[92] the ability of migrant workers to implement these strategies can be heavily restricted for reasons discussed above. These include restricted mobility, employer discretion, low wages and access to technology. Hence, without active measures from States to support strategies that transnational families in general use to maintain familial relationships, migration and employment policies that govern TLM can hinder the capacity of migrant workers to engage in transnational parenting. This, in turn, interferes with CRC provisions that protect children's right to benefit from their parents' fulfilment of all aspects of the parenting role.

As outlined in Section 5.3.2, the most effective strategies used by migrant workers to engage in transnational parenting involve the frequent and regular use of communication technology. When this technology is available, it supports their ability to continue providing direction and guidance to their children while they are physically absent. Studies have found that communication technology not only assists migrant workers to maintain family ties and familial relationships,[93] but also allows them to remain involved in their children's education,[94] be informed and provide direction about matters involving their children's well-being, provide instructions to alternative caregivers and continue to give advice, reprimands and comfort to their children.[95] However, as also discussed, communication technology is not universally accessible. Rather, social, economic and migration policies in labour-receiving and labour-sending countries can constrain the ability of the families of low-waged migrant workers to maintain familial connections while separated.[96] This is despite children having a universal right under Art 5 of the CRC to receive direction and guidance from their parents, and parents having a protected role and responsibility to provide this to their children.

Goldring, 'Transnational, Multi-Local Motherhood: Experiences of Separation and Reunification among Latin American Families in Canada' (CERIS Working Paper No 40, Latin American Research Group, York University, 2005).

91 Carling, Menjivar and Schmalzbauer, above n 44, 192.

92 Ofelia Becerril, 'Gendered Policies, Single Mothers and Transnational Motherhood: Mexican Female Migrant Farmworkers in Canada' in Zahra Meghani (ed), *Women Migrant Workers: Ethical, Political and Legal Problems* (Taylor and Francis, 2015) 154, 160.

93 Asis, above n 27, 45, 62; Gabrielle Marcelletti Rocha de Oliveira, *Transnational Care Constellations: Mexican Immigrant Mothers and their Children in Mexico and in New York City* (PhD Thesis, Columbia University, 2015) 105–6.

94 Oliveira, above n 93, 105–6.

95 Carling, Menjivar and Schmalzbauer, above n 44, 203–4. See also Asis, Huang and Yeoh, above n 44.

96 Eleonore Kofman, 'Gendered Global Migrations' (2004) 6(4) *International Feminist Journal of Politics* 643, 645.

5.4.1 Article 5 and the children of migrant workers

Article 5 recognises that children, subject to their age and maturity, will require direction and guidance from their parents in order to exercise their rights as children. It also recognises parents' 'responsibilities, rights and duties' to provide this direction and guidance to their children in ways appropriate to the child's evolving capacities. This aspect of the parental role identified in Art 5 is interdependent with the CRC's recognition that parents have the primary responsibility for their children's upbringing and development in Art 18; and parents have the primary responsibility to provide for the children's mental, spiritual, moral and social development needs in Art 27. As discussed in Chapters 4 and 7, States parties to the CRC are required to assist parents to meet these primary child-rearing responsibilities.[97]

Hence, as Tobin and Varadan explain, while Art 5 protects *children's* right to receive direction and guidance from their parents,[98] it also recognises that parents have a right to influence their children's upbringing but 'the power of parents must be exercised not for their own benefit but for the benefit of their child and the enjoyment of his or her rights'.[99] The use of the term 'shall' in Art 5 makes mandatory the obligation it imposes on States to respect – or not interfere with – the responsibilities, rights and duties of parents to provide direction and guidance to their children subject to their evolving capacity. As with other rights, if measures taken by States do limit a parent's capacity to provide direction and guidance to their children, then the limitation must be lawful, reasonable and consistent with other CRC provisions.[100] This includes the best interests of the child. Again, this involves demonstrating that the limitation is in pursuit of a legitimate aim and uses measures of least interference reasonably available to States.[101]

A parent's migration does not strip them of their responsibilities, rights and duties that are recognised and protected in Art 5 of the CRC and other interdependent articles including Arts 18 and 27. Rather, as discussed in Section 5.4.2, parents frequently (and can often successfully) exercise elements of their parental role and responsibilities from afar. This includes the continued provision of direction and guidance to their children, so long as the child-parent relationship is still intact. However, the strategies that workers (both skilled and low-waged) and their families utilise to enable the continued presence of the absent parent can be heavily constrained in the context of low-waged TLM for reasons discussed in Section 5.3. These include travel and communication costs, access to technology, time and privacy for communication, visa and employment restrictions and

97 State obligations to assist parents to fulfil their parental responsibilities are discussed in Chapters 4 and 7.

98 Tobin and Varadan, above n 3, 160. See also Garton Kamchedzera, 'Article 5 – The Child's Right to Appropriate Direction and Guidance' in Andre Alen et al, *A Commentary on the United Nations Convention on the Rights of the Child* (Martinus Nijhoff, 2012).

99 Tobin and Varadan, above n 3, 160.

100 Ibid 163–4.

101 Ibid.

employer discretion. When migrant workers can overcome these barriers, then the costs associated with implementing transnational parenting strategies are borne by the workers and their families. This is despite their low wages and the economic pressures facing these families that drives parental migration in the first instance.[102] It is also in spite of the duty that States have under the CRC to assist parents to fulfil their child-rearing roles and responsibilities.

Importantly, Art 5 recognises the potential role of members of the extended family in providing direction and guidance to a child. It is frequently argued that in the context of TLM, the children of migrant workers are primarily cared for by extended families. Difficulties with arguments that assume that extended family members can adopt the primary care giving role provided by parents prior to their migration are discussed in Section 5.4.3. Suffice to say here that the child-parent relationship is recognised and protected in the CRC *regardless* of the composition and structure of a child's family. This is outlined in Chapter 3 in relation to the fundamental role of the family in international law.[103] That is, while a child's family – be it nuclear or extended – will often play an important role in a child's upbringing, it does not replace a parent's central role (in ordinary circumstances) in providing direction and guidance to their children. This is no matter where the parent resides and particularly if that aspect of the parental role can be executed irrespective of physical distance between the parent and his or her child. In other words, the child-parent relationship is protected even when the extended family is involved in a child's care; as is a child's right to receive direction and guidance *from their parents* even if they also receive it from other family members.

Hence, Art 5 recognises that children's capacity to exercise their rights will generally be achieved in the context of their family and with guidance from their parents and, where appropriate, other family members. However, it also recognises that the guidance and direction that children need from their parents will change as they mature. As explained by the CRC Committee:

> Article 5 contains the principle that parents (and others) have the responsibility to continually adjust the levels of support and guidance they offer to a child. These adjustments take account of a child's interests and wishes as well as the child's capacities for autonomous decision making and comprehension of his or her best interests.[104]

Thus, the parental role in providing direction and guidance to children needs to be understood in light of the overarching principle of a child's right to be heard and have their views accorded weight commensurate with their age and maturity under Art 12 of the CRC. This overarching principle is outlined in Chapter 3[105]

102 The drivers of parental migration are discussed in Chapter 4 (see Sections 4.2.2 and 4.2.3).

103 See Chapter 3 (Section 3.4).

104 *General Comment No 7*, UN Doc CRC/C/GC/7/Rev.1, para 17.

105 See Chapter 3 (Section 3.2.4).

and is also discussed in relation to family decision-making in the context of TLM in Section 5.4.4.

5.4.2 Supporting transnational parental presence

Researchers have observed that migrant workers continue parenting while physically absent by, when possible, remaining actively involved in their children's everyday lives.[106] Frequent exchange of information between parents, children and alternative caregivers keeps the parent 'virtually present'[107] and facilitates the continued provision of direction and guidance by parents to their children while they are separated. This is demonstrated in a study of Mexican women seasonal workers in Canada, which found that during the average 6.5 months that mothers were away from their children in a year, the mothers engaged in 'transnational mothering' by attending to child-care obligations by phone.[108] These included advising the alternative caregiver about the child's food, schooling, health, discipline issues and the appropriate use of remittances.[109] Through frequent communication, mothers were also able to help with children's homework and 'provide love and guidance in phone conversations'.[110]

This demonstrates the potential effectiveness of measures that enable workers to engage in frequent communication with their children to assist them to maintain a continued parental presence in their children's lives. As discussed in Section 5.3.2, this potential is enhanced by new communication technologies. This was reiterated by key informants in views including:

> 'With social media and the Internet ... you can overcome barriers like location ... [and] maybe have at least a sense of some presence over distance'. *(Key Informant – MLO-NGO 5)*

However, as discussed in Section 5.3.2, frequent communication alone is insufficient for parents to maintain their relationships with their children over prolonged periods and needs to occur in tandem with opportunities for direct contact. This accords with Baldassar's research on how transnational families in general – that is, without the restrictions imposed by low-waged TLM policies – continue to provide emotional support despite distance. It found that:

> [T]ransnational family members are reliant on two types of technologies and two modes of communication to facilitate their transnational exchanges:

106 Asis, above n 27, 45; See also Parrenas, above n 36.
107 Graham and Jordan, above n 27, 781.
108 Becerril, above n 92, 163.
109 Ibid.
110 Ibid.

> *communication technologies,* which occur across distance and provide *virtual contact* ... and *travel technologies,* which allow people to visit each other (to be co-present) and have *face-to-face contact.* [111]

This emphasises the need for both regular and direct communication *and* contact to sustain transnational familial relationships. This is why the CRC has protected a child's right to *both* under Art 10(2) when they are transnationally separated from their parents. Observations by key informants supported research findings on the need for both forms of contact if parents are to sustain their role in providing emotional support to children over prolonged periods. These observations included:

> 'Telecommunications help, but it's not good for families ... The Internet is an improvement, but it's not good enough to just facilitate the transnational arrangement. The minimum is the freedom to move; for children to be with their parents, but also for parents to go back [to visit]'. *(Key Informant – MLO-NGO 4)*

This reiterates the need for measures that facilitate regular, frequent and direct communication between migrant workers and their children to be coupled with opportunities for regular *physical* contact during the period of employment. As discussed in Section 5.3, these measures would help low-waged migrant workers to overcome the challenges that they face in 'maintaining family across time and distance'.[112] This includes their capacity to continue parenting during the period of employment, which includes fulfilling their role in providing direction and guidance to their children (which their children have a right to receive under Art 5).

5.4.3 The role of the extended family

It is frequently rationalised that extended families can fill the void for children when their parents migrate for low-waged TLM, making them less vulnerable to the impact of their parents' absence. However, this assumption is based on the notion that cultural differences between labour-sending and labour-receiving countries diminish the rights of the children of migrant workers to have their relationship with their parents protected. Moreover, as Crock and Benson explain:

111 Loretta Baldassar, 'Transnational Families and the Provision of Moral and Emotional Support: The Relationship Between Truth and Distance' (2007) *Identities: Global Studies in Culture and Power* (2007) 14(4) 385, 389.

112 Carling, Menjivar and Schmalzbauer, above n 44, 192.

> Cross-cultural expectations … are particularly harmful when assumptions about agency and vulnerability interfere with acknowledging the needs of young people.[113]

Importantly, CRC rights that protect the child-parent relationship apply equally to all children regardless of the formation of their family. Arguments based on cultural diversity and cultural relativism have typically been used by States to justify cultural practices that violate CRC rights by claiming that these rights reflect 'Western' values and norms.[114] However, this is reversed in the context of TLM. This is because it is commonly held that harm to children arising from TLM policies, that strip them of rights that protect their relationship with their parents, is mitigated by the fact that they come from cultures where extended family formations may be prevalent. However, TLM policies are largely designed by 'Western' labour-receiving countries that uphold these rights for their own children, as discussed in Chapter 7. [115] The CRC Committee has observed that in relation to attempts to justify other practices on the grounds of cultural values and traditions:

> Cultural identity cannot excuse or justify the perpetuation by decision-makers and authorities of traditions and cultural values that deny the child or children the rights guaranteed by the Convention.[116]

Reliance on the notion that the extended family can fill a parent's role as primary caregiver in the event of migration is problematic for a number of reasons. Not only does it undermine the protected role of parents as children's primary caregivers; it also fails to recognise the valuable role that family members can play in facilitating transnational child-parent relationships if they are supported to do so. Moreover, it does not account for the widespread breakdown of traditional extended family arrangements due to demographic changes and increasing financial pressures on families. These are discussed in the following sections.

i. Support for alternative caregivers as facilitators of transnational child-parent relationships

Strategies that facilitate the continued presence of parents rely heavily on the child's alternative caregiver(s), particularly when children are young. These are often members of the child's extended family. Hence, effective measures on the part of States to assist parents to maintain their role transnationally must include

113 Mary Crock and Lenni B Benson, 'Central Issues in the Protection of Child Migrants' in Mary Crock and Lenni Benson (eds), *Protecting Migrant Children: In Search of Best Practice* (Elgar, 2018) 1, 11.

114 Adamantia Pollis, 'Cultural Relativism Revisited: Through a State Prism' (1996) 18 *Human Rights Quarterly* 316, 320, 322.

115 See Chapter 7 (Section 7.2.3) for discussion on the value of the child-parent relationship in labour-receiving countries.

116 *General Comment No 14*, UN Doc CRC/C/GC/14, para 57.

support for children's alternative caregiver(s) to implement strategies to preserve the presence of the parent in the child's life. This includes assistance with, among other things, the costs, technology and time associated with maintaining transnational relationships.

Support for families as 'the primary caretakers of children' has been recognised by governments as essential to the nurture and protection of children.[117] In relation to TLM, supporting families in their care of children should include assisting them in their efforts to maintain children's relationships with their parent's while they are working abroad. Such assistance should, again, be a shared responsibility between labour-sending and labour-receiving countries in line with the principle of international cooperation.[118] Moreover, the costs borne by families that take on the daily care of the children of migrant workers over prolonged periods, flow directly from policies established by labour-receiving countries that prevent family accompaniment. The prevention of family accompaniment is discussed further in Chapter 6. [119] The need for governments of both labour-sending *and* labour-receiving countries to support extended families to meet the demands (financial and other) associated with caring for the children of migrant workers was reiterated by key informants in comments such as:

> 'When the whole family is together, families deserve support raising children. So too, if one parent is away, providing care elsewhere, there needs to be support for the other parent or grandparent who is looking after the children. So it's part of a larger thing — public responsibilities for family support'. *(Key Informant – R & P 1)*

> 'If specific communities are senders of considerable numbers of migrants to the same country, then they could have programs — such as a special family support system or access to the child benefit — which the receiving government supports in return. This comes back to responsibility in the transnational sphere'. *(Key Informant – R & P 3)*

Both labour-sending and labour-receiving States should share the responsibility for supporting alternative caregiver(s), given their dependency on families to care for the dependent children of migrant workers who are not allowed to accompany their parents. As Bryant observes, the psychosocial costs to children of parental migration are often lessened when extended family becomes involved in the child's care.[120] However, extended families – and particularly grandmothers – are

117 *Declaration on the Commitments for Children in ASEAN* para 9.
118 See Chapter 3 (Section 3.3).
119 See Chapter 6 (Section 6.4.4 and 6.5).

assuming ever increasing childcare responsibilities as TLM continues to escalate.[121] Studies have shown that as a result of TLM, millions of children growing up in the absence of one or both parents are being cared for by single parents or relatives in labour-sending countries.[122] These mounting pressures on extended families are contributing to the breakdown of the traditional social support role that they may have once played and upon which governments still rely in the context of TLM.

ii. Breakdown of extended family structures

The scale of labour migration itself (both intra and intercountry) is a significant factor contributing to the breakdown of extended families.[123] As Heymann's research on transnational families across five continents found, even in countries with strong collective care traditions:

> [E]xtended care networks do not always work smoothly, because they do not remain immune to the broader effects of economic globalisation. Indeed, economic crises may affect the functioning of transnational kin networks … This, in turn, can impact the well-being of those who stay behind.[124]

Similar findings were made by Badasu and Michel in the context of West Africa (a significant labour-sending region), where the raising and care of children has traditionally been seen as a communal and not individual responsibility.[125] Their study found that:

> [T]he twin processes of modernization-migration and urbanization have undermined solidarity and family ties … The rise of boarding facilities at both the primary and secondary school level that are patronized by transnational migrant families also gives evidence of this new pattern of care.[126]

121 Delali Badasu and Sonya Michel, 'On a Collision Course: Millennium Development Goals and Mothers' Migration' in Zahra Meghani (ed), *Women Migrant Workers: Ethical, Political and Legal Problems* (Taylor and Francis, 2015) 75, 83; Bandita Sijapati, 'Women's Labour Migration from Asia and the Pacific: Opportunities and Challenges' (Issue in Brief, Issue No 12, IOM / Migration Policy Institute, March 2015) 5; Amaia Pérez Orozco, 'Global Care Chains Reshaping the Hidden Foundations of an Unsustainable Development Model' in Zahra Meghani (ed), *Women Migrant Workers: Ethical, Political and Legal Problems* (Taylor and Francis, 2015) 101, 114.

122 Lan Anh Hoang et al, 'Transnational Migration, Changing Care Arrangements and Left-behind Children's Responses in South-East Asia' (2015) 13(3) *Children's Geographies* 263, 263–4.

123 ILO and UNDP, *Decent Work in Latin America and the Caribbean: Work and Family: Towards New Forms of Reconciliation with Social Co-Responsibility* (ILO/UNDP, 2009) 70.

124 Heymann (2006) quoted in Carling, Menjivar and Schmalzbauer, above n 44, 197.

125 Badasu and Michel, above n 121, 89.

126 Ibid 90.

The emergence of new forms of care in labour-sending countries for the children of migrant workers that do not involve the extended family – such as boarding facilities at schools – reflects the reality that cultural practices are not static.[127] Hence, not only can the extended family not be assumed to replace the specialised care and attention – including direction and guidance – that children require and are entitled to from their parents;[128] the changing nature of the extended family means that it cannot be assumed to have the capacity to sufficiently nurture and protect children in the absence of their parents *without additional support.* This highlights the need for States to provide appropriate assistance to alternative caregivers if they are going to rely on family members to assume the primary caregiving role for children of migrant workers.

Furthermore, children have the right under Art 5 to receive guidance from their parents even if they are not physically present. Studies show, however, that the longer that parents are separated from their children, the more their parental authority is diminished. This undermines the capacity of parents to discharge their role in providing direction and guidance to their children. It also encourages other family members to assume this role rather than supplement it. For example, a study of Latin American mothers working in Canada found that the periods of child-parent separation were significantly longer than mothers initially expected.[129] This, in turn, affected the mothers' authority within their families despite efforts to communicate with and stay informed about their children.[130] Bernhard et al describe that for informants in this study:

> [T]he length of separation was completely unexpected. Temporary care arrangements became permanent and in the process there was a relinquishment of authority and an erosion of maternal status.[131]

This reinforces the need for States to fulfil their duty under Art 10(2) to ensure that children have both regular and direct communication and physical contact with their parents in order to sustain transnational relationships. Enabling children to realise their rights under Art 10(2) then enables parents to continue fulfilling elements of their parental role while separated, including the provision of direction and guidance. This, in turn, reduces unnecessary interference with children's right under Art 5 to receive this direction and guidance from their parents.

5.4.4 *Relevance of stage in the life cycle and migration cycle*

For parents to be able to provide direction and guidance to their children 'in a manner consistent with the evolving capacities of the child' as required by Art 5,

127 Ibid 92.
128 ILO and UNDP, above n 123, 70.
129 Judith K Bernhard, Patricia Landolt and Luin Goldring, 'Transnationalizing Families: Canadian Immigration Policy and the Spatial Fragmentation of Care-giving among Latin American Newcomers' (2009) 47(2) *International Migration* 3, 5.
130 Ibid 18.
131 Ibid.

the child's age and stage of development must be considered. This is similar to the need to consider children's age in relation to parental capacity to meet their development needs from a distance, which is examined in Chapter 4 in relation to Art 27.[132] The quality of long-distance interactions, and the ability of children to independently initiate and conduct such exchanges, are limited when children are young and increase as children mature. Nonetheless, for reasons outlined in Section 5.3.2, migrant workers tend to adopt the same communication style (primarily by phone) with each of their children irrespective of the child's age.[133] This is despite the limited capacity of young children to receive and share information with their parents by telephone. This goes to the need to ensure that measures supporting the maintenance of personal relations between parents and children while separated are age-appropriate for the child.

Moreover, appropriate assistance to alternative caregivers to facilitate the maintenance of the child-parent relationship will also vary according to a child's age and the stage in the life-cycle of the alternative caregivers themselves. That is, as Baldasssar explains, the stage in the life cycle of all family members – parents, children and alternative caregivers – determine who can take on primary care responsibilities and what those responsibilities are at a given point in time.[134] This notion was reiterated by key informants in comments such as:

> 'Everybody has ties, everybody has obligations, but some of those obligations and ties are more significant at particular times in life. So, having responsibilities for young children — and putting aside responsibilities for older parents — bringing that recognition into policy design would be the first thing'. *(Key Informant – R & P 7)*

This comment illustrates the need for TLM policies to incorporate measures to assist parents to meet their parental responsibilities, recognising that these measures need to be responsive to the changing needs that children have of their parents as children develop. Giving consideration to parental responsibilities in relation to children's stage of development in the design of TLM policies will also assist in determining the types of assistance that alternative caregivers require during the period of migration. This reflects the notion in Art 5 that the types of support and guidance that children require from their parents and families need to be continually adjusted according to children's changing needs.[135] As the CRC Committee explains, these adjustments are necessary to 'take account of a child's interests and wishes as well as the child's

132 See Chapter 4 (Section 4.4).
133 Edillon, above n 85, 25.
134 Baldassar, above n 111, 394.
135 *General Comment No* 7, UN Doc CRC/C/GC/7Rev.1, para 17.

capacities for autonomous decision-making and comprehension of his or her best interests'.[136]

i. Children's participation in pre-migration decision-making

A child's capacity to participate in decisions that affect them increases with their age and maturity, a notion embodied in Art 12 of the CRC in relation to the right to be heard. This overarching principle in the CRC is outlined in Chapter 3. [137] In the context of TLM, children frequently express a desire for their parents (particularly mothers) to return home, which is discussed in Chapter 4 in relation to Art 27 and children's psychosocial needs.[138] In fact, consultations with children in Sri Lanka on *their* priorities for post-2015 found that in high labour migration provinces, one of their top priorities was *to not have* their mothers migrate.[139] As Ukwatta observes, children often feel this way even when they recognise the sacrifices that their parents are making 'for the collective interest of the family'.[140]

However, it has been found that understanding *why* their parents migrated does assist in children's adjustment to the absence of their parent(s).[141] In this regard, child rights organisations have advocated for improving understanding among parents and caregivers about the need to involve children in decision-making about their parent's migration *and* their alternative care arrangements.[142] This would both enhance children's understanding about their parent's migration and better prepare them for the period of separation.[143] Research on military families experiencing deployment have emphasised the benefits of family readiness for the period of separation, which is discussed further in Chapter 6. [144] Moreover, it is recognised more generally that failure by parents and other adults to provide information and guidance to children about potential risks to their well-being limits children's ability to protect themselves against these potential harms, thus enhancing their vulnerability.[145]

Considering children's views in a family's decision-making concerning parental migration and alternative care arrangements, and giving these views weight appropriate to their age and maturity, accords with a child's right to be heard under Art 12. The effective implementation of children's rights under Art 12

136 Ibid.
137 See Chapter 3 (Section 3.4).
138 See Chapter 4 (Sections 4.3.1, 4.3.2 and 4.4).
139 Save the Children, *"The World We Want": Consultations with Sri Lankan Children on Their Priorities for Post 2015* (Save the Children, September 2013) 5–10, 19–25.
140 Swarna Ukwatta, 'Sri Lankan Female Domestic Workers Overseas: Mothering their Children from a Distance' 27 *Journal of Population Research* 107, 120.
141 Asis, above n 27, 61.
142 See, eg, Kusala Wettasinghe, Gethsie Shanmugam and Sarala Emmanuel, *Alternative Care Giving of Migrant Workers' Children* (Terre des Hommes, 2012) 10.
143 Ibid 9.
144 See Chapter 6 (Section 6.4.1.ii).
145 John Tobin, 'Understanding Children's Rights: A Vision Beyond Vulnerability' (2015) 84 *Nordic Journal of International Law* 155, 170.

enables children and adolescents to be more prepared for and active in addressing challenges that they face in relation to their CRC rights.[146] As Asis observes, if children are actively included in a family's management of the migration process, then they can contribute to the development of responses to the absence of a parent.[147] This involvement can enhance the appropriateness of the responses to the child, taking into account their age and maturity. In the context of TLM, it also provides parents the opportunity to direct and guide their children (in ways relative to their age and capacity) in their understanding about decisions to migrate and potential strategies for managing the separation. However, at present, while children are often cast as being 'the primary beneficiaries or "victims" of migration',[148] they are seldom consulted in decisions concerning migration and in research on the impact of TLM.[149] This is despite the CRC Committee having emphasised the need for children's views and experiences to be actively considered in matters concerning children and international migration.[150]

Moreover, children's participation (despite their age) in familial decision-making is not a cultural norm in many labour-sending countries. For example, Asis has observed that in the Philippines, cultural assumptions about the child-parent relationship bestow considerable authority upon parents to define their children's well-being, which parents largely construe in terms of basic survival and development needs such as food, shelter and education.[151] These parents did not conceive participation rights as part of children's rights or 'consider the idea of granting children greater participation as part of good parenting'.[152] Moreover, studies from Sri Lanka have found that parents rarely involve their children in pre-migration discussions and sometimes they are not even informed before their parents migrate.[153] This can leave children feeling bewildered, confused and distressed, often blaming themselves for their parent's migration in the absence of having been involved in and guided about the decision to migrate.[154]

Hence, to assist children to realise their right to be heard in matters affecting them under Art 12, States can adopt measures to support parents and families to

146 Nigel Cantwell, 'Are Children's Rights Still Human?' in Antonella Invernizzi and Jane Williams (eds), *The Human Rights of Children From Visions to Implementation* (Ashgate, 2011) 37, 56–7.
147 Asis, above n 27, 47.
148 Hoang et al, above n 122, 266.
149 Julia O'Connell Davidson and Caitlin Farrow, *Child Migration and the Construction of Vulnerability* (Save the Children, 2007) 23; Hoang et al, above n 122, 266.
150 CRC Committee, *Report of the 2012 Day of General Discussion: The Rights of All Children in the Context of International Migration* (28 September 2012) [42].
151 Asis, above n 27, 47.
152 Ong (2001) cited in Asis, above n 27, 47.
153 ILO Country Office for Sri Lanka and the Maldives, *Reintegration with Home Community: Perspectives of Returnee Migrant Workers in Sri Lanka* (ILO, 2013) 12; S T Hettige et al, *Understanding Psychosocial Issues Faced by Migrant Workers and their Families* (Sri Lankan Ministry of Foreign Employment Promotion and Welfare, 2012) 30–1.
154 Hettige et al, above n 153, 30–1.

involve children (subject to their age and capacity) in familial decision-making concerning parental migration and alternative care arrangements. Measures can include equipping parents with the skills, information and understanding necessary to prepare children for the period of separation. Investment in this type of assistance for families would support children's right to have their views considered in decisions that concern them and to receive direction and guidance from their parents in ways appropriate to their age and maturity. While the implementation of such measures would need to occur in labour-sending countries, they could be funded jointly by labour-receiving countries given that they design the TLM policies that require these periods of child-parent separation. At the very least, TLM policies could make it mandatory that such measures are in place to include, prepare and support children across the different phases associated with parental migration.

ii. Prolonged separation and child-parent relationships post-reunification

If children and parents have not been supported to maintain their relationship while separated, then it is not uncommon for parents to be unable to resume their parental role as primary caregiver, including providing advice and guidance to their children, upon reunification. Hence, the importance of adopting measures to ensure children's right to direct contact and communication with their parents under Art 10(2) during the period of transnational separation extends beyond the period of separation. That is, if the child-parent relationship breaks down because of the separation, then the parental role that is protected by Arts 5, 18 and 27 of the CRC can continue to be undermined even when the child and parent are able to reside together. As Zentgraf and Chinchilla highlight in their study on transnational family separation:

> Psychologists and other social service providers who deal with families attempting to reunite after separation confirm that the quality of contact during separation is one important factor that influences the success of those reunions.[155]

However, as discussed in Section 5.3, communication alone is insufficient to sustain child-parent relationships over prolonged periods. Hence, the duration of the child-parent separation is also a significant factor affecting whether parents are able to resume their primary role in their children's upbringing upon reunification. Studies from Canada demonstrate that labour-receiving countries are now aware of the impact of prolonged child-parent separation caused by TLM policies on children's relationships with their parents post-reunification. For example, a study of Caribbean migrant workers in Canada connected the length of child-parent

155 Artico (2003), Boss (1999), Falicov (2002) cited in Zentgraf and Chinchilla, above n 31, 346.

separation with the degree of perceived difficulties in the child-parent relationship, finding that:

> A longer period of separation was significantly related to less identification with the parent and less conformity to the parent at the time of reunification.[156]

Similarly, studies on Canada's former Live-in Caregiver Program (LCP) found that mothers were often separated from their children for five to six years prior to reunification in Canada, or even longer if mothers had been domestic workers in other countries like Hong Kong or Singapore beforehand.[157] This meant that children were often teens at the time of reunification with their mothers,[158] with their mothers having been absent for many of their children's younger years. Hence, children and parents missed out on significant transformations in each other's lives across multiple stages of the child's development.[159] As Nana explains, this type of disruption to the child-parent relationship often renders children and parents unable to re-establish intimate bonds with each other once reunified.[160] This extends the interferences caused by TLM policies with those CRC rights that protect the child-parent relationship beyond the period of separation and into the period of reunification. Hence, measures to mitigate harm to children caused by TLM policies must also support children and parents to re-establish their relationship in the post-reunification phase of parental migration.

Canadian studies have highlighted how prolonged family separation under the former LCP is one factor attributed to poorer educational and employment outcomes for the children of former live-in caregivers compared to other migrant and refugee groups.[161] This goes to children's right to have their overall development needs met under Art 27, as discussed in the previous chapter. However, it has also been attributed to the compromising of 'parents' ability to guide their children through school, especially during the teenage years', caused by the disruption to

156 Richard N Lalonde, Andrea Smith and Simone Johnson, 'Serial Migration and its Implications for the Parent-Child Relationship: A Retrospective Analysis of the Experiences of the Children of Caribbean Immigrants' (2004) 10(2) *Cultural Diversity and Ethnic Minority Psychology* 107, 107–8.

157 Geraldine Pratt, Philippine Women Centre of BC and Ugnayan ng Kabataang Pilipino sa Canada (Filipino Canadian Youth Alliance), 'Deskilling Across the Generations: Reunification Among Transnational Filipino Families in Vancouver' (Working Paper Series, No 08–06, Metropolis British Columbia, Centre of Excellence for Research on Immigration and Diversity, September 2008) 12.

158 Ibid.

159 Oishi Nana, 'Family Without Borders? Asian Women in Migration and the Transformation of Family Life' (2008) 14(4) *Asian Journal of Women's Studies* 54, 65.

160 Ibid.

161 Phillip Kelly, 'Understanding Intergenerational Social Mobility: Filipino Youth in Canada' (IRPP Study No 45, Institute for Research on Public Policy, February 2014) 22.

the child-parent relationship because of prolonged separation.[162] This undermining of parents' capacity to fulfil their role in providing guidance to their children, as protected in Art 5, is captured in the following comments from a participant in Kelly's study on the settlement of Filipino children of former live-in caregivers in Canada:

> [A] lot of the parents tell me that they don't know how to parent because they haven't seen their kids since they were four or five. So all of a sudden they're high-schoolers and the kids hate them immediately …
>
> (Female school settlement counsellor, interview, 2011)[163]

Key informants, including from the government sector, highlighted these findings from Canadian studies in comments including:

> 'The long-term separation of usually the woman from the family in their home country really affected the outcomes of their children here … They missed being with their mothers or fathers in that development stage … So we found that the children of live-in caregivers are doing relatively poorly in terms of educational attainment and their own economic and social outcomes. And the one possible explanation is that it could be because the family was separated … for quite a few years before they were able to bring them in'. *(Key Informant – Government 1)*

This comment reveals the transparency of the knowledge available to policy-makers about the potential effects to children's long-term educational and social outcomes that can arise from significant disruptions to the child-parent relationship and family unit during children's formative years. It is supported by recent findings from the United States that children who have experienced prolonged wait times before being able to join their migrant parent(s) in the United States face notable detriments to their psychosocial well-being, which make adapting to a new life (including school) significantly more challenging than for children who migrate with their parents.[164]

The complete undermining of the parental role that is caused by prolonged separation also occurs when reunification takes place in labour-sending countries, which is the norm in the context of TLM. The ILO has found that many women migrant workers experience a lack of closeness between themselves and their children upon return, find it difficult to adjust to their children having grown up in

162 Ibid.
163 Ibid 23.
164 Yao Lu, Qian He and Jeanne Brooks-Gunn, 'Diverse Experience of Immigrant Children: How Do Separation and Reunification Shape Their Development?' (2018) *Child Development* (advance).

their absence, and are frequently challenged by a lack of respect from their children.[165] Moreover, case studies have shown that parental migration can cause children to lose trust in their parents[166] and no longer follow their parents' direction, shifting their affection and attachment to the alternative caregiver.[167] This interferes with the very role of parents that is protected in Art 5, as well as potentially harming children by causing further disruptions to their primary attachment figures at the time of reunification. This risk to children is reflected in the following observation from a study of Latin American caregivers in Canada:

> Mothers and children had become strangers and the child's willingness and ability to re-attach was called into question, since the 'reunification' was, in effect, a second major rupture of the child's attachment.[168]

Importantly, in this study, Bernhard et al further found that mothers were often no longer the primary decision-makers in their children's lives.[169] Rather, they were stripped of this role, which is protected in the CRC, because of unnecessarily long periods of child-parent separation. Moreover, this study found that grandparents frequently assumed this decision-making role in children's lives and often did not exercise the same degree of discipline as the parents.[170] In turn, this resulted in the children becoming more self-directed out of necessity.[171] However, the principle in Art 5 recognises that the degree to which children can provide self-direction increases in parallel with their evolving capacities, not out of necessity because of fractured child-parent relationships that limit parental capacity to provide direction and guidance to their children.

5.5 Conclusion

Migrant workers are often able to successfully implement strategies to continue key aspects of their parenting role while abroad, including the provision of direction and guidance to their children. When this is the case, their physical absence can be compatible with their emotional presence in their children's lives.[172]

165 Lin Lean Lim et al, *Preventing Discrimination, Exploitation and Abuse of Women Migrant Workers: An Information Guide* (Booklet 5, Gender Promotion Programme, ILO, 2003) 6 quoted in Rianne Mahon and Sonya Michel, 'Not In Focus: Migrant Women Caregivers As Seen by the ILO and the OECD' in Sonya Michel and Ito Peng (eds), *Gender, Migration, and the Work of Care: A Multi-Scalar Approach to the Pacific Rim* (Palgrave Macmillan, 2017) 269, 278.

166 Maria G Hernadez, *Migrating Alone or Rejoining the Family? Implications of Migration Strategies and Family Separations for Latino Adolescents* (2013) cited in IOM, above n 43, 5.

167 Becerril, above n 92, 164–5.

168 Bernhard, Landolt and Goldring, above n 129, 20.

169 Ibid 21.

170 Ibid.

171 Ibid.

172 Carling, Menjivar and Schmalzbauer, above n 44, 192.

However, this chapter has shown how structural features of TLM policies create conditions that interfere with the capacity of children and parents to maintain a transnational relationship. This not only restricts children's right under Art 10(2) to have direct and regular contact and personal relations with their parents, but also the enjoyment of their right under Art 5 to receive direction and guidance from their parents.

This chapter has revealed the ease by which interferences with children's rights under Arts 10(2) and 5 could be reduced through reasonable measures including creating and financially supporting opportunities for more frequent return home visits for migrant workers. This must be combined with the introduction of circulation-friendly visas, which is discussed further in the following chapter. Other simple, affordable and practical measures available to States that would support regular and frequent communication between migrant workers and their children include guaranteeing workers' appropriate times, private spaces and access to technology (including Wi-Fi) to support quality communication with their children; and assisting workers and their families to meet communication costs. Labour-receiving States should also be responsible for enforcing strict penalties for the confiscation of mobile phones in contexts where this employer practice is commonly permitted.

Emphasised throughout this chapter is that for any of these measures to be implemented effectively, they *must* be legally guaranteed for workers and their families and *not* employer dependent. While these measures do not alter the transnational child-parent arrangement currently embedded in TLM policies, they remain important because they support parents to continue fulfilling elements of their parenting role from afar. This continued parental involvement in children's lives has been shown to significantly improve outcomes for the children of migrant workers both during and after the period of separation.[173]

This chapter has also highlighted the need for States to support children, parents and families (including alternative caregivers) to access and use communication modes and strategies that are *age-appropriate* for children, if long-distance communication is going to effectively assist children to maintain their relationship with their parents. This requires actions on the parts of *both* labour-sending and labour-receiving States given that the parent and child reside in different States. Moreover, in line with the principle of international cooperation – and *because* it is labour-receiving States that determine TLM policies – responsibility for resourcing measures to support direct contact and communication should be shared between States and *not* borne by families as is currently the case. An additional measure identified in this chapter, which is strongly supported by the principle of international cooperation, is the potential for labour-receiving countries to invest in

173 CHAMPSEA Philippines, *In the Wake of Parental Migration: Health and Well-being Impacts on Filipino Children* (Scalabrini Migration Center, 2011) 37; Ukwatta, above n 140, 123–5; Halahingano Rohorua et al, 'How do Pacific Island Households and Communities Cope with Seasonally Absent Members?' (2009) 24(3) *Pacific Economic Bulletin* 19, 21.

developing communication infrastructure in high migration areas from which they source workers.

The reasonable availability of these measures to States underscores the *unnecessary* nature of current interferences caused by features of TLM policies with children's rights to maintain their relationship with their parents while separated. This chapter has demonstrated the long-term effects that such undermining of the parental role can have not only on children's life outcomes but also on the child-parent relationship post-reunification. It has also reiterated the need for families and governments to *include children* in familial decision-making and policy development concerning parental migration respectively. This has been shown to increase children's preparedness for periods of separation and accords with children's right to be heard in matters affecting them under Art 12.[174]

The CRC strongly protects the child-parent relationship and various provisions reflect its presumption that it is generally in children's best interests to be with their parents. However, Art 10(2) recognises that it will not always be possible or practical for children and parents to reside together, and so it specifically protects the child-parent relationship in the event of transnational separation. This is because the child-parent relationship is considered a fundamental part of a child's family life. State policies cannot interfere with a child's family life *without justification*, as it is protected against arbitrary interference under Art 16 of the CRC. Hence, this book will now consider how children's right to family life, which includes their relationship with their parents, is impacted by TLM.

174 See Chapter 3 (Section 3.2.4).

6 Article 16

Do TLM policies generate arbitrary interferences with children's family life?

> ***Article 16***
>
> 1 No child shall be subjected to **arbitrary or unlawful interference with his or her** privacy, **family**, home or correspondence, nor to unlawful attacks on his or her honour and reputation.
>
> 2 The child has the right to the protection of the law against such interference or attacks.

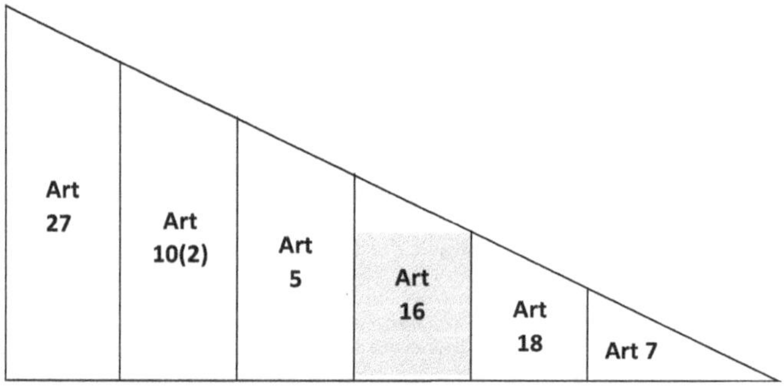

6.1 Introduction

This chapter explores how features of TLM policies interfere with children's family life, in particular with the child-parent relationship, which comprises a significant component of a child's family life. While it is frequently assumed that voluntary migration does not constitute an interference with family life because of the choice to migrate, the decision by parents to migrate in the context of TLM is often made in the face of few viable alternatives and the prolonged periods of child-parent separation that often result are determined by factors outside the control of migrant workers. Both of these issues are discussed in preceding chapters.[1] Hence, this chapter argues that restrictive features of TLM policies that cause significant disruption to the child-parent relationship create arbitrary interferences with children's family life *because* these features are unnecessary and unreasonable and have yet to be shown by States as being proportionate to a legitimate aim.[2] The chapter is framed by the duty of States under Art 16 to protect against arbitrary and unlawful interferences with children's family life,[3] with those CRC provisions focused on in previous and following chapters all demonstrating the centrality of the child-parent relationship to children's family life. It highlights a number of reasonably available measures that could reduce the degree to which TLM policies interfere with children's right to have their family life and relationship with their parents protected.

The CRC Committee has stressed the connection between the maintenance of familial relations (which includes child-parent relations) and the preservation of a child's family environment.[4] In contrast, TLM reflects a growing trend that disrupts and fractures children's family life.[5] This chapter demonstrates the challenges that this presents to the family's protected status in human rights law, including under Art 17 of the ICCPR that also requires States to ensure that 'no one shall be subjected to arbitrary or unlawful interference with his … family'.[6] The protected role of the family as the fundamental group unit in society is outlined in Chapter 3[7] and contributes significantly to the context for interpreting Art 16 of the CRC. Importantly, Art 16 imposes a *positive* obligation on States' parties to protect against arbitrary interferences with children's family life, with the obligation to *protect* requiring States to 'take all appropriate measures within the scope of their available resources to ensure children enjoy their article 16 rights'.[8]

This chapter argues that while States have a degree of discretion concerning the measures that they take to fulfil their obligations under Art 16, related CRC rights that protect the child-parent relationship *must* inform an understanding of the measures necessary to protect against arbitrary interferences with a child's family

1 See Chapter 4 (Section 4.2) and Chapter 5 (Section 5.3).
2 *Siracusa Principles*, UN Doc E/CN.4/1985/4, annex pt I A paras 10–12.
3 The CRC Committee has reiterated that the child's right to family life is protected under Art 16 in addition to the CRC's recognition of the family as the fundamental unit of society and natural environment for children's growth and well-being in its Preamble. See *General Comment No 14*, UN Doc CRC/C/GC/14, [59].
4 Ibid.
5 Reddock and Bobb-Smith (2008) 28–9 cited in Rianne Mahon and Sonya Michel, 'Not In Focus: Migrant Women Caregivers As Seen by the ILO and the OECD' in Sonya Michel and Ito Peng (eds), *Gender, Migration, and the Work of Care: A Multi-Scalar Approach to the Pacific Rim* (Palgrave Macmillan, 2017) 269, 277.
6 *ICCPR* art 17.
7 See Chapter 3 (Section 3.4).
8 John Tobin and Sarah M Field, 'Article 16. The Right to Protection of Privacy, Family, Home, Correspondence, Honour, and Reputation' in J Tobin (ed), *The UN Convention on the Rights of the Child: A Commentary* (OUP, 2019) 550, 554.

life.[9] This includes those CRC articles identified in the conceptual framework as well as Arts 9 and 10(1), which together reflect the presumption in the CRC that it is in a child's best interests not to be physically separated from their parents in ordinary circumstances. The first part of this chapter considers the significance of Arts 9 and 10(1) in the context of TLM and a child's right to have their family life protected.[10]

In the second part of this chapter it is argued that while States have the right to control immigration, features of TLM policies that prevent family accompaniment and prolong periods of parental absence are aimed at minimising costs for labour-receiving countries. Hence *this* is the aim that States need to justify as being *legitimate* for policies that cause potentially significant harms to a *particular* group of children (that is, the children of low-waged migrant workers). It highlights the challenges this presents to the principle of international cooperation, which requires States to not cause harm, or enter into agreements that cause harm, to children outside their own jurisdiction.[11] This section also argues that while parents may 'choose' to participate in TLM, parental choice alone does not absolve States of their obligation to justify interferences with children's family life caused by State policies. This is because children are rights-bearers in their own right.[12]

The third part of this chapter demonstrates how specific features of TLM policies unnecessarily and unreasonably prolong child-parent separation. Features discussed in this section include the deliberate encouragement of the remigration of migrant workers and the failure to adopt circulation-friendly visas to facilitate frequent visitation between parents and children. It argues that the duration of child-parent separation created by these features is unnecessary to pursue both the avoidance of settlement costs associated with family accompaniment and the desire by labour-receiving countries to encourage migrant workers to return home at the end of their contracts. This section considers learnings from other professions that regularly manage child-parent separation to identify the types of reasonably available measures that could reduce the degree of interferences by TLM policies with children's family life.

The final section of this chapter argues that permitting family accompaniment for *other* categories of temporary migrants directly discriminates against the children of low-waged migrant workers *without justification*. It highlights how adopting measures to protect the family life of 'skilled' migrants has resulted in children's family *rights* being reframed by labour-receiving States as *privileges* granted on grounds such as nationality, class and their parent's levels of education.[13] While it is recognised that CRC rights are generally not absolute, rights

9 Ibid 554, 578–9. This goes to the need for 'appropriate' measures to be consistent with other CRC provisions as discussed in Chapter 4 (see Section 4.2.1).

10 Reasons for not including Arts 9 and 10(1) in the conceptual framework are provided in Chapter 2 (see Section 2.1.1).

11 The principle of international cooperation is discussed in Chapter 3 (see Section 3.3).

12 See, eg, *General Comment No 7*, UN Doc CRC/C/GC/7/Rev.1, para 3.

13 Eliahu Frank Abram, 'The Child's Right to Family Unity in International Immigration Law' (1995) 17(4) *Law and Policy* 397, 404; Stephen Castles, 'The Forces Driving Global Migration' (2013) 34(2) *Journal of Intercultural Studies* 122, 131.

restrictions *cannot* be arbitrary and *must* be justified by law as being for a legitimate purpose.[14] This reflects the substantive dimension of the requirement under Art 16 that State-sanctioned interferences with family life be lawful.[15] Hence, this section argues that, without justification, discriminatory practices that limit *only* the rights of children of *low-waged* migrant workers amount to an arbitrary, and therefore unlawful, interference with these children's right to have their family life protected.

6.2 Articles 9 and 10(1) in relation to TLM and children's right to family life

6.2.1 The child-parent relationship is protected as part of a child's family life

Importantly, human rights and immigration law presume that the family unit, in its narrowest conception, includes parents and their dependent children.[16] This is reflected in provisions in the ICRMW, which reflect an assumption that migrant workers are able to migrate with their dependent children (and spouse) and protects their right to move and reside as a family unit.[17] The CRC, however, adopts a broader interpretation of the family to include members of a child's extended family, as reflected in Art 5. This broader definition and the role of the extended family in a child's life are discussed in Chapters 3 and 5. [18] Moreover, the CRC Committee has recognised that family patterns vary and there is significant diversity in family arrangements for the purposes of raising children.[19] This means that for some children, grandparents and other extended family members may have a particularly significant role as carers in children's lives.[20]

As discussed in Chapter 3, European human rights law helps define the concept of 'family life' as entailing the existence of strong or close personal ties between individuals.[21] This is reflected in the view of the Human Rights Committee that minimal requirements for a family include living together, economic ties and a regular and intense relationship.[22] The European Court of Human Rights has

14 Katherine Covell, R Brian Howe and Anne McGillivray, 'Implementing Children's Education Rights in Schools' in Martin D Ruck, Michele Peterson-Badali and Michael Freeman (eds), *Handbook of Children's Rights Global and Multidisciplinary Perspectives* (Routledge, 2017) 296, 306.
15 Tobin and Field, above n 8, 557.
16 See Chapter 3 (Section 3.4).
17 *ICRMW* arts 29, 30, 44, 45.
18 See Chapter 3 (Section 3.4.1) and Chapter 5 (Section 5.4.3).
19 *General Comment No 7*, UN Doc CRC/C/GC/7/Rev.1, para 19.
20 Ibid.
21 Article 8 of the *ECHR* enshrines the right to respect for, and non-interference with, family life. See Helene Lambert, 'Family Unity in Migration Law: The Evolution of a More Unified Approach in Europe' (Research Paper No 13–06, University of Westminster School of Law, 2013). See also Chapter 3 (Section 3.3.4).
22 Human Rights Committee, *Views: Communication No 417/1990*, 51st sess, UN Doc CCPR/C/51/D/417/1990 (27 July 1994) [10.2].

held that critical to the State ensuring *respect* for family life is the right of family members to live together to enable family relationships to 'develop normally'.[23] European jurisprudence has also stressed that the 'mutual enjoyment' of each other's company – including between parents and children – is 'a fundamental element of family life'.[24] Accordingly, Art 16 protects children against arbitrary interferences with *their* family life, which may comprise of extended family members. However, as discussed in Chapter 3, both broad and narrow definitions of the family include the child-parent relationship and the close and particular ties that this relationship entails. It is the arbitrary interference with this specific relationship, which is a significant part of a child's family life in ordinary circumstances, that is the focus of this chapter.

The CRC reiterates existing rights in general human rights law that protect the family from arbitrary interference and obligate States to provide assistance to families to perform their child-rearing responsibilities.[25] The Human Rights Committee has explained that the right to found a family in human rights law[26] implies the possibility to live together which, in turn:

> … implies the adoption of appropriate measures … in cooperation with other States, to ensure the unity or reunification of families, particularly when their members are separated for political, economic or similar reasons.[27]

The CRC has also established additional rights that complement provisions in general human rights law to specifically protect the child-parent relationship as a central part of a child's family, including Arts 7, 9 and 10. At present, parents are driven to engage in TLM for economic reasons and are governed by State-designed TLM policies that disrupt the child-parent relationship because of the family's socio-economic status. A child's family life is interfered with by disruptions to their relationship with their parents. Features of TLM policies that interfere with this relationship include the denial of family accompaniment, restrictions on the mobility of migrant workers and encouragement of remigration. These are discussed in this chapter. They also include the interferences cause by prolonged parental absence and limits on communication with the parental role in providing guidance and emotional support to children. These are discussed in the previous chapters in relation to Arts 10(2) and 27. As these chapters show, the limitations – caused by TLM policies – on children's rights that protect the child-parent relationship are unnecessary and unreasonable as there are less harmful measures available to States that would achieve the same aim. This aim is to prevent the permanent migration and settlement of families, as discussed in Section 6.3.1.

23 *Marckx v Belgium* [1979] Eur Court HR 2, [31], [45]; Ben Saul, 'Indefinite Security Detention and Refugee Children and Families in Australia: International Human Rights Law Dimensions' (2013) 20 *Australian International Law Journal* 55, 58.

24 *Gul v Switzerland* [1996] Eur Court HR 5 [C.6] (Judge Martens).

25 *ICCPR* arts 17, 23; *ICESCR* arts 10, 11.

26 *ICCPR* art 23(2).

27 *CCPR General Comment No 19*, UN Doc HRI/GEN/1/Rev.1, [5].

Moreover, they apply only to the children of low-waged temporary migrant workers for no legitimate reason, the discriminatory nature of which is discussed in Section 6.5. For these reasons, they constitute arbitrary interferences with these children's relationship with their parents, despite the obligation on States under Art 16 to take positive measures to protect children from arbitrary interference with their family life. Hence, while it is recognised that 'the integrity of the family unit is not inviolable', State-sanctioned interferences with a child's family unit must be justified.[28]

Both labour-sending and labour-receiving States have failed to provide a justification for features of TLM policies that arbitrarily interfere with child-parent relations, particularly by prolonging the periods of parental absence unnecessarily. These policies have been developed by States despite the CRC's strong presumption that it is in a child's best interests to be with and raised primarily by their parents in ordinary circumstances and as part of their family life. As Detrick explains, 'Article 9(1) and Article 10(2) embody the principle of family unity, as they share the aim of protecting children against separation from their parents'.[29]

6.2.2 Articles 9 and 10(1) in the context of TLM

Article 9 requires that States 'ensure that a child shall not be separated from his or her parents against their will'.[30] It has not been explicitly included in the conceptual framework for this book because of its intended application to the removal of children from their parents by the State in *domestic settings.* [31] This generally relates to child protection in cases of abuse and neglect, or determining a child's place of residence when parents live separately.[32] Art 10(1), however, imposes a positive obligation on States to facilitate the reunification of parents and children who are separated transnationally. This is discussed in Chapter 5 in relation to Art 10(2).[33] However, as Art 10(1) makes direct reference to Art 9(1) in defining the obligation of States,[34] it is necessary to recognise the duty of States under Art 9(1) to not separate children from their parents unless it is in their best interests. As Art 10(1) provides, it is in accordance with the obligation on States under Art 9 that States are required to facilitate the reunification of children and parents who are

28 John Tobin, 'Fixed Concepts but Changing Conceptions: Understanding the Relationship Between Children and Parents under the CRC' in Martin D Ruck, Michele Peterson-Badali and Michael Freeman (eds), *Handbook of Children's Rights Global and Multidisciplinary Perspectives* (Routledge, 2017) 53, 56.

29 Sharon Detrick, *A Commentary on the United Nations Convention on the Rights of the Child* (Martinus Nijhoff, 1999) 195.

30 *CRC* art 9(1).

31 Detrick, above n 29, 170.

32 *CRC* art 9(1).

33 See Chapter 5 (Section 5.2.2).

34 Art 10(1) states that: 'In accordance with the obligation of States Parties under article 9, paragraph 1, applications by a child or his or her parents to enter or leave a State Party for the purpose of family reunification shall be dealt with by States Parties in a positive, humane and expeditious manner…'

separated transnationally under Art 10(1). This demonstrates the intention that these articles inform one another. Hence, the positive obligation on States under Art 9 to ensure that children are not separated from their parents extends to State actions concerning the reunification of parents and children separated transnationally, with the significant difference being the scope of the limitation clauses that apply to Arts 9 and 10(1).[35]

Children's right not to be separated from their parents under Art 9 is subject to a very strict limitation clause – it can be interfered with *only* when it is 'necessary for the best interests of the child'.[36] Article 10(1), on the other hand, has a broad limitation clause that permits restrictions that are by law and in the public interest.[37] The discrepancy between these limitation clauses is based on the notion that States have the right to control the entry and residence of non-citizens. The Courts have considered that securing a country's economic well-being is likely to be considered a legitimate aim for not permitting the stay of someone with no right to remain in a country.[38] Hence, labour-receiving States can readily rely on their economic interests to deny the family accompaniment and reunification rights of migrant workers and their families. However, as the rest of this chapter shows, this becomes more difficult when the measures used to achieve these economic aims are shown to be unnecessary, unreasonable and disproportionate to the potential harms that they cause to children and families. It is also challenged by the fact that for *other* groups, their 'right to remain in the country' increases over time, giving them greater access to their family reunification rights under Art 10(1). TLM policies, on the other hand, deliberately fail to recognise the length of time that migrant workers have resided in a country, assigning them an indefinite temporary status to ensure that they do not acquire residency rights that would entitle them to family reunification. This is discussed in Section 6.4.

Nonetheless, the obligation on labour-receiving States to facilitate the reunification of children and parents who are both non-citizens are significantly weakened when they can be reunified in their country of nationality. This goes to the notion that States do not have an obligation to facilitate family reunification in their territory if it can be achieved in their country of origin, particularly without significant rupture to their family life.[39] This involves consideration of factors including the nationality of family members, the best interests of children and the

35 Jason M Pobjoy and John Tobin, 'Article 10. The Right to Family Reunification' in J Tobin (ed), *The UN Convention on the Rights of the Child: A Commentary* (OUP, 2019) 341, 348–9. See also Abram, above n 13, 421.

36 *CRC* art 9(1).

37 Art 10(2) restricts the extent of a State's family reunification obligations across borders, permitting 'restrictions as are prescribed by law and which are necessary to protect the national security, public order (ordre public), public health or morals or the rights and freedoms of others'.

38 *ZH (Tanzania) v Secretary of State for the Home Department* [2011] UKSC 4 [18] (Lady Hale) ('*ZH (Tanzania)*').

39 *Rodrigues da Silva and Hoogkamer v The Netherlands* (2007) 44 EHRR 729, [39]; *ZH (Tanzania)* [2011] UKSC 4 [19] (Lady Hale).

extent of social, cultural and familial ties with both countries.[40] In the context of TLM, as children have continued residing in their country of nationality, they have not themselves established ties with the labour-receiving country. This is a deliberate intention of preventing them from accompanying their parents. Hence, the obligation on labour-receiving States to reunify migrant workers and their children within their territory is weak, which is why Art 10(1) has not been included in the conceptual framework. However, labour-receiving countries retain a duty to justify policies that deny family accompaniment rights only to low-waged workers and generate unreasonably and unnecessarily long periods of separation between parents and their dependent children. In this vein, the CRC and CMW Committees have together urged States to *prevent* transnational child-parent separation in the first instance by encouraging them 'to develop policies that enable migrants to regularly be accompanied by their families in order to avoid separation'.[41]

6.2.3 Role of labour-receiving countries in protecting the family life of children in labour-sending countries

The CRC and CMW Committees have highlighted a positive duty for labour-receiving countries to adopt procedures that 'seek to facilitate family life and ensure that any restrictions are legitimate, necessary and proportionate'.[42] They have emphasised that while the right to family unity may intersect with legitimate State interests to control immigration, the separation of a family by refusing a family member entry into a State party's territory may arbitrarily or unlawfully interfere with children's family life if the refusal is unjustified.[43]

As State obligations to facilitate family reunification are frequently understood as a measure to protect the right to family life,[44] labour-receiving countries argue that they do not arise in the context of TLM as family life can take place in a migrant worker's home country at their choosing. However, this ignores the structural barriers associated with TLM that prevent frequent reunification between children and parents during the period of employment. These are outlined in Chapter 5 and include low wages, employer discretion and restrictive visa regimes.[45] Moreover, it fails to give *any* consideration to the best interests of the child, despite the CRC Committee having urged that:

40 *⊠ner v The Netherlands* (2007) 45 EHRR 421, [57]–[58]; *ZH (Tanzania)* [2011] UKSC 4 [17] (Lady Hale).

41 *Joint General Comment on Children in the Context of International Migration*, UN Doc CMW/C/GC/4-CRC/C/GC/23, para 37.

42 Ibid.

43 Ibid para 28.

44 Ibid; OHCHR, 'Family Reunification' (OHCHR Migration Papers, November 2005) 17.

45 See Chapter (Section 5.3.1).

> When the child's relations with his or her parents are interrupted by migration … preservation of the family unit should be taken into account when assessing the best interests of the child in decisions on family reunification.[46]

The OHCHR has raised specific concerns about the failure to address the right of children impacted by parental migration to be reunified with their parents in immigration policies in receiving countries. This clearly extends to the need for labour-receiving States to reconsider their reunification policies in the context of TLM, particularly in relation to their impact on the best interests of children in labour-sending countries and their relationship with their parents. To this end, the OHCHR has stated that:

> The situation of children left behind in the context of migration is also of relevance to family reunification policies in countries of destination. Where possible and in their best interests, States should enable children to join their parents who have migrated.[47]

The OHCHR has stressed that opportunities for reunification between these children and their parents should not be dependent on their parents' migration status.[48] However, at present, TLM policies interfere with children's right to family unity based on not only their parents' temporary migration status, but also on their family's socio-economic status. As discussed in Chapter 4, labour-sending and labour-receiving countries promote parental migration *without* dependent children as a way for parents to provide for their children in the face of poverty.[49] This is despite the CRC and CMW Committees making clear that poverty alone is not sufficient grounds to justify the separation of a child from his or her parents.[50] Rather, the Committees instruct that when poverty renders parents unable to meet the material and financial needs of their children then:

> States should provide appropriate assistance to parents … in the performance of their childrearing responsibilities, including by providing social benefits and child allowances and other social support services regardless of the migration status of the parents or the child.[51]

This returns to the need for appropriate measures that assist parents to fulfil their parenting obligations in ways that do not, or at least minimally, interfere with

46 *General Comment No 14*, UN Doc CRC/C/GC/14, [66].

47 *OHCHR Study on the Protection of the Rights of the Child in the Context of Migration*, UN Doc A/HRC/15/29 (5 July 2010) [78].

48 Ibid.

49 See Chapter 4 (Section 4.2.2).

50 *Joint General Comment on State Obligations Regarding the Human Rights of Children in Countries of Origin, Transit, Destination and Return*, UN Doc CMW/C/GC/4-CRC/C/GC/23, para 30.

51 Ibid.

children's right to family life. Even if labour-receiving countries can justify not permitting the entry of children as being legitimate on economic grounds, they retain their duty to ensure that the measures employed to prevent family accompaniment constitute measures of least interference with children's right to have their family life protected.

6.3 Immigration control as a justification for prolonged child-parent separation

6.3.1 Immigration control is not the primary reason for denying family accompaniment

It can be argued that the denial of family accompaniment to the children of low-waged migrant workers falls within the purview of a State's right to limit immigration. Scholars have referred to this as 'the mother of all trump rights'[52] and 'one of the last bastions of individual states'.[53] It is this right that gives rise to the broad limitation clause in Art 10 permitting States to not facilitate family reunification on grounds of national security and public order. However, as Crock and Benson observe:

> [F]ew nations, if any, have fully integrated norms of child welfare law into their migration laws and policies. Too often, immigration enforcement trumps the values and systems designed to promote the welfare of children.[54]

The CRC and CMW Committees have recognised that a migrant's right to family unity 'may intersect with States' legitimate interests in making decisions on the entry or stay of non-nationals'.[55] However, they have also explained that the CRC requires States to take *positive* measures to protect and maintain the family unit, of which family accompaniment is only one possible measure. In this vein, the Committees have reiterated that:

> Protection of the right to a family environment frequently requires that States must not only refrain from actions that could result in family separation or other arbitrary interference in the right to family life but also take positive

52 Catherine Dauvergne, 'Irregular Migration, State Sovereignty and the Rule of Law' in Vincent Chetail and Céline Bauloz (eds), *Research Handbook on International Law and Migration* (Edward Elgar, 2014) 75, 90.

53 Nicola Piper, 'Gender and Migration: A Paper Prepared for the Policy Analysis and Research Programme of the Global Commission on International Migration' (GCIM, September 2005) 41.

54 Mary Crock and Lenni B Benson, 'Central Issues in the Protection of Child Migrants' in Mary Crock and Lenni Benson (eds), *Protecting Migrant Children: In Search of Best Practice* (Elgar, 2018) 1, 9.

55 *Joint General Comment on State Obligations Regarding the Human Rights of Children in Countries of Origin, Transit, Destination and Return*, UN Doc CMW/C/GC/4-CRC/C/GC/23, para 28.

measures to maintain the family unit, including reunion of separated family members.[56]

In practice, TLM policies epitomise the opposite of States refraining 'from actions that could result in family separation' and taking 'positive measures to maintain the family unit'. Rather, they regularise the separation of parents and dependent children, employing a State's right to restrict immigration to prevent family accompaniment by dependent children. However, using 'immigration control' to justify mandatory child-parent separation is problematic for a number of reasons. First, TLM regimes encourage – in fact, recruit – the entry of foreign nationals into labour-receiving countries.[57] Hence, they do not seek to limit the entry of migrant workers, but to limit their *rights* upon entry under highly regulated migration regimes. Second, by denying family accompaniment, labour-receiving countries endeavour to maintain a flexible source of low-waged labour that: a) can be brought into and removed from their territory according to *labour market demands* [58] (not national security and public order as framed by some countries[59]); and b) avoid the costs associated with having the children of migrant workers reside (even temporarily) in the labour-receiving country. In fact, savings on costs associated with migrant integration is frequently advanced as a gain for labour-receiving countries in relation to TLM.[60] These costs include costs to the State (such as in relation to education and healthcare) and to the employer (as children's presence would reduce the unfettered flexibility of workers and generate a need for improved standards in accommodation and/or wages). As observed by a key informant in relation to migrant women careworkers:

> 'That is why they are desired — they are cheaper on so many levels. So, if the goal is to keep costs low, then bringing their children into the equation is not part of the logic of outsourcing social reproduction costs'. *(Key Informant – R & P 2)*

56 Ibid para 27.

57 Rachel Silvey, 'Transnational Rights and Wrongs: Moral Geographies of Gender and Migration' (2009) 37(2) *Global Gender Justice* 75, 76; Piper, above n 53.

58 Piyasiri Wickramasekara, 'Migration Regimes and Their Linkages for Family Unity, Integrity and Development' in Marion Panizzon, Gottfried Zurcher and Elisa Fornale (eds), *The Palgrave Handbook of International Labour Migration: Law and Policy Perspectives* (Palgrave Macmillan, 2015) 146, 149–50, 170.

59 The framing of migrant workers as 'security risks' and threats to public order is commonplace in Asian labour-receiving countries, particularly Singapore and Malaysia. See Susan Kneebone, 'Migrant Workers Between States: In Search of Exit and Integration Strategies in South East Asia' (2012) 40 *Asian Journal of Social Science* 367, 373–4.

60 Wickramasekara, above n 58, 163; Susan Kneebone, 'Transnational Labour Migrants: Whose Responsibility?' in Fiona Jenkins, Mark Nolan and Kim Rubenstein (eds), *Allegiance and Identity in a Globalised World* (Cambridge University Press, 2014) 426, 428.

This observation reveals how the goal of TLM policies is ultimately to keep costs low for labour-receiving countries by sourcing workers to fill low-waged jobs with poor working conditions (rather than raising wages and improving conditions to entice local workers); and avoiding costs to employers and the State that would arise from the presence of immediate family members. As labour-receiving countries dictate the parameters of TLM regimes, it is unsurprising that they operate largely in their favour. However, by failing to consider children as part of the equation in policies that are premised on child-parent separation, labour-receiving States are blatantly ignoring their obligation under Art 3 to give due consideration to children's best interests in policies that affect them. This obligation is strengthened by the principle of international cooperation, which means that States cannot just ignore harm caused to children by their policies if the children affected reside outside of their jurisdiction. Rather, they maintain a duty to justify interferences with children's rights and best interests caused by their policies and actions. In relation to TLM, this means demonstrating that the actual aim of denying family accompaniment – that is, to ensure that costs to labour-receiving countries and employers remain low – is legitimate and that the measures used to pursue this aim are necessary, reasonable and of minimal interference.

To date, even if labour-receiving countries have attempted to justify their TLM policies on economic grounds, they have failed to address the fact that there are measures available that would reduce the degree of interference by TLM policies with children's right to have their family life protected. For example, the Canadian Government's rationale for its Temporary Foreign Worker Program (TFWP), through which Canada has been sourcing foreign labour since 1973, states that the TFWP:

> is designed to facilitate economic growth by responding to labour market needs, while ensuring a balance is kept between the interests of businesses and those of the Canadian workforce.[61]

This highlights the aim of TLM policies for labour-receiving countries, which is that they benefit their economies, employers and labour markets. It also reflects the desire on the part of labour-receiving countries to create a flexible labour force that is unencumbered by the costs and responsibilities associated with children's presence.

By deliberately ensuring that children remain outside their jurisdiction, labour-receiving countries attempt to avoid State duties that would arise if children were permitted to reside with their parents. The social costs of TLM to children's well-being and development is then framed as the responsibility of labour-sending countries, in whose jurisdiction these children continue to reside. This is premised on the notion, as Carens explains, that within the existing international order,

61 Standing Committee on Human Resources, Skills and Social Development and the Status of Persons with Disabilities, Parliament of Canada, *Temporary Foreign Worker Program* (2016) 1.

'states are much more responsible for what goes on in their own jurisdictions than they are for what goes on elsewhere'.[62] This approach, typical of labour-receiving States, is reflected in the following observation by a key informant from the government sector:

> 'You can theoretically argue that when the parent leaves for another country for work, the home country, the State, is actually responsible to fill in that blank that is left by the parent ... It is hard to do it cross-jurisdictionally. How can the host country be responsible for that part of it? I find it hard to imagine a legal framework that would cover that'. *(Key Informant – Government 1)*

However, in contrast to this observation, the CRC does just that: it provides a legal framework for understanding children's rights as a *shared responsibility between States* that requires them to take cooperative measures to support the realisation of children's rights globally. The shared duty of labour-receiving countries to address the impact of TLM on children is discussed in Section 6.3.3. Additionally, the recent non-binding New York Declaration,[63] and subsequent Global Compact for Migration,[64] reflect a recognition by the international community of the pressing need to develop a cross-jurisdictional framework for realising the rights of migrants and their children in contemporary migration circumstances. These instruments have been developed *because* of the fact that the implementation of rights in the context of migration depends on actions taken not only by sending but also by receiving and transit countries. The Declaration and Compact are discussed in Chapter 7 in relation to the emerging framework for the global governance of migration.[65] At present, the rationale behind TLM policies – to meet employer demands for low-waged labour with few additional costs to the labour-receiving State[66] – *is at odds* with the notion of shared responsibility within an international framework for protecting the rights of migrant workers and their families.

6.3.2 The significance of citizenship in labour-receiving countries

By encouraging migrant workers into their territory temporarily and without their children, labour-receiving countries are able to avoid commitments to workers and their families that would otherwise arise on the basis of their status as foreign nationals.[67] As a result, the movement of workers made possible by globalisation

62 Joseph Carens, *The Ethics of Immigration* (Oxford University Press, 2013) 117.
63 *New York Declaration*, UN Doc A/RES/71/1.
64 *Global Compact for Migration*, UN Doc A/RES/73/195.
65 See Chapter 7 (Section 7.3.4).
66 Castles, above n 13, 131.
67 Nicola Piper, 'Global Governance of Labour Migration: From "Management" of Migration to an Integrated Rights-based Approach' in Peter Drahos (ed), *Regulatory Theory: Foundations and Applications* (ANU Press, 2017) 375, 377.

has meant that, as Kneebone explains, 'individual rights have become detached from the protective mechanisms provided by citizenship'.[68] This is of particular significance in the context of low-waged TLM, where notions of citizenship and sovereignty are selectively employed by labour-receiving States to restrict the rights of workers while encouraging their entry. Hence, as Ball and Piper have argued, our conception of sovereignty in the context of labour migration is in need of transformation 'to accommodate and protect those whose rights are undermined by virtue of their employment outside the country of their citizenship'.[69] The need to revisit the degree to which State sovereignty and citizenship determine the capacity of migrant workers and their families to realise their rights is of particular significance, given the sheer scale of TLM. This was reiterated by key informants in views including:

> 'Now that labour markets are so integrated, our legal regimes need to be more integrated ... There is a moral obligation to recognise that this worker has a whole life that they are being expected to leave behind'. *(Key Informant – R & P 2)*

This view highlights the current gap between labour market policies that encourage TLM and the protective function of citizenship, access to which migrant workers are denied. For migrant workers who are parents, this directly impacts the rights of their children in that it allows States to deny family accompaniment and other family support entitlements that are attached to citizenship and migration status. Bhaba captures this connection between citizenship and a child's capacity to exercise their family rights in the following observation:

> [T]he fact of belonging to a country fundamentally affects the manner of exercise of a child's family and private life, during childhood and well beyond.[70]

Hence, in denying citizenship (or State protections associated with citizenship) to migrant workers in a deliberate effort to limit their rights, labour-receiving States are failing to recognise and justify the interferences that this causes with those children's rights that are interdependent with, and inseparable from, their parents' rights.

68 Kneebone, above n 60, 445–6. See Chapter 1 (Section 1.3) for discussion on state sovereignty and transnationalism.

69 Rochelle Ball and Nicola Piper, 'Globalisation of Asian Labour Migration: Implications for the Nation-State, Citizenship and Human Rights' (Unpublished paper, no date) 6 (footnote omitted) quoted in Kneebone, above n 60, 448.

70 Jacqueline Bhaba, 'The "Mere Fortuity of Birth"? Children, Mothers, Borders and the Meaning of Citizenship' in Seyla Benhabib and Judith Resnik (eds), *Migrations and Mobilities: Citizenship, Borders and Gender* (NYU Press, 2009) 187, 193.

6.3.3 Labour-receiving countries share a duty to address the impact of TLM on children

i. The duty is informed by the principle of international cooperation

Even if labour-receiving States continue to restrict the entry of the children of migrant workers, they retain multiple obligations under the CRC. First, given that their TLM policies inevitably affect children because of the required child-parent separation, they must inform TLM policies with a proper consideration of the best interests of children. Second, they are required to justify any interferences with children's best interests and specific familial rights caused by TLM policies, which involves showing that these interferences are in pursuit of a legitimate aim using necessary, reasonable and proportionate measures. Finally, in line with the principle of international cooperation, they share responsibility with labour-sending countries to take active measures to minimise harm to children affected by TLM.

The duty of all States parties under the CRC to engage in international cooperation and shared responsibility to realise children's rights is outlined in Chapter 3. [71] This duty is informed by the CRC Committee's direction to States that:

> Upon ratification of the Convention, States bear upon themselves the obligation not only to implement the Convention within their respective territorial jurisdiction, but also to contribute, through international cooperation, to global implementation.[72]

Moreover, the CRC Committee has directed that cooperation between States should 'not impact negatively on children, especially those who are most vulnerable'.[73] Bilateral agreements governing TLM are a form of cooperation between States and hence should not have a negative impact on children in labour-sending countries. As discussed in Chapter 4, the vulnerabilities of these children by virtue of being children from poorer families in developing countries is heightened when their parents migrate.[74] A parent's migration will not *always* cause direct harm to the child, however, parental absence certainly heightens the risk of potential harms to these children.[75] Thus, the failure by labour-receiving States to accept shared responsibility for the impact of TLM on children in labour-sending countries is not only convenient, it also runs contrary to the principle of international cooperation agreed in the CRC.

Multilateral organisations have emphasised that *because* TLM is a transnational process, the issues that it generates cannot be effectively managed without *genuine*

71 See Chapter 3 (Section 3.3). See also *Report on the Forty-sixth Session*, UN Doc CRC/C/46/3, [92].
72 *General Comment No 5*, UN Doc CRC/GC/2003/5, para 7.
73 *General Comment No 19*, UN Doc CRC/C/GC/19, para 38.
74 See Chapter 4 (Section 4.3).
75 See Chapter 4 (Section 4.3) and Chapter 5 (Section 5.4).

international cooperation by – and to the benefit of – *all* involved States.[76] Most recently, the UN General Assembly has urged that in the context of migration:

> International cooperation and, in particular, cooperation among countries of origin or nationality, transit and destination, has never been more important.[77]

Key informants across all sectors reiterated the need for labour-receiving countries to recognise the social impacts that TLM has on the children and families of migrant workers; and ideally share responsibility for minimising these impacts. Their views included:

> 'I do think that there is an obligation on receiving States to think of individual workers not just as units of labour but human beings with family and community ties that should be respected for moral reasons but also for reasons to do with the UN Convention on the Rights of the Child and other conventions around civil and political rights'. *(Key Informant – R & P 7)*

Key informants (excluding from the government sector) aligned the burden on labour-receiving countries to assist in minimising the social impacts of TLM with the difference in their available resources compared to labour-sending countries. This was emphasised in comments such as:

> 'People aren't travelling from poor country to poor country. They are travelling from poor to rich, and therefore the receiving countries have more responsibility'. *(Key Informant – R & P 1)*

This comment recognises, just as the CRC does, that States with greater resources (which are labour-receiving States) should assist States with fewer resources (that is, labour-sending States) to implement and protect children's rights. This accords with the principle of international cooperation discussed in Chapter 3. [78] Hence, although labour-sending States may have stronger obligations towards these children by virtue of them being their citizens and resident within their jurisdiction; in reality, they do not have the capacity to meet the additional social support needed to mitigate harms to children and communities

76 IOM, *Labour Migration from Indonesia: An Overview of Indonesian Migration to Selected Destinations in Asia and the Middle East* (IOM, 2010) Preface.
77 *New York Declaration*, UN Doc A/RES/71/1, para 11.
78 See Chapter 3 (Section 3.3).

caused by widespread parental absence. Key informants stressed this reality in observations including:

> 'Sending countries have a responsibility to both those who are going and those who are left behind. They simply don't have the capacity ... to fulfil that responsibility adequately ... So then the question is whether receiving countries take on some additional responsibility. And yes, I think they should'. *(Key Informant – R & P 4)*

This highlights the contradiction between the principle in international human rights law that developed countries should *assist* developing countries, and the structure of TLM policies, which operate in favour of labour-receiving countries and create social costs that labour-sending countries have neither the resources nor power to mitigate alone. In fact, as Silvey argues, TLM policies have created a form of 'subsidization of wealthy nations by poor nations' of those costs related to social reproduction.[79] This includes costs associated with raising children in the absence of their primary caregivers, which are then borne by families (predominantly women) in *less-resourced* countries.[80]

ii. Ethical obligations become legal under the CRC

Short of acknowledging the legal obligation under the CRC to consider the impact of TLM on children in labour-sending countries, key informants from the government sector did recognise an ethical obligation to give consideration to the issue. This was particularly so if the TLM policy purported to have a dual international development objective. This is illustrated in comments including:

> 'It's an ethical obligation ... For many people, the connection is broken at the border. The ethical obligation finishes because they only have a domestic focus ... But if it's run as a development program, then we will necessarily be thinking about it'. *(Key Informant – Government 4)*

However, the legal principles and rights in question *all* have ethical underpinnings, but their inclusion in the CRC makes these shared morals into *legal norms and standards* to which States parties *agree to be bound*. As Dauvernge explains in the comparative context of the Refugee Convention:

79 Silvey, above n 57, 77.
80 See Chapter 4 (Section 4.3.2.i) and Chapter 5 (Section 5.4.3).

> It takes on rule of law characteristics as the international community recognizes, in spite of all politics to the contrary, its ethical core.[81]

Hence, ratification of human rights treaties elevates the duty of labour-receiving countries to consider the rights of the children of migrant workers in their TLM policies from a moral or ethical one to a legal one. This was reiterated by key informants in observations such as:

> 'If a government truly lives by its commitments to human rights, it needs to acknowledge that the worker's human rights extends to their children and families, regardless of whether they live with the worker or not'. *(Key Informant – R & P 5)*

> 'The actions of a State even outside its jurisdiction should conform to the spirit of [human rights] law, which means the impact on foreign populations should be strongly included in the valuation of a foreign policy ... Sometimes a government may decide that they are violating children's rights but there is a higher reason, but that should be taken into consideration for a policy to be legally adopted'. *(Key Informant – MLO-NGO 4)*

The latter comment goes to the central issue that States responsible for TLM policies that separate children and parents as a matter of course must justify the separation as a necessary measure that is in pursuit of a legitimate aim. A State's right to control its borders does not negate its obligations to give due consideration to children's best interests and to justify interferences with children's rights arising from its policies and actions. This includes interferences that may be sustained by children outside a State's jurisdiction and that arise from foreign policies and bilateral agreements between States.

6.3.4 *Parental 'choice' does not negate State duties to justify interferences with CRC rights*

Similarly, State policies that interfere with children's rights must still be justified by the States responsible for the policies even if parents 'consent' to the interference. In the context of TLM, it is frequently claimed that parents 'choose' to leave their children and 'consent' to their own familial rights being diminished as a prerequisite for participation in TLM regimes. For example, Ruhs argues that workers make a choice – albeit within the constraints of larger structural factors – to tolerate restrictions on their rights in exchange for the opportunity to earn higher

81 Dauvergne, above n 52, 92.

incomes abroad.[82] The failure of labour-sending countries to demand equal rights for their workers is seen as an acceptance of this trade-off between the rights of their citizens and access to foreign labour markets.[83] However, this argument is highly problematic in relation to children's rights for multiple reasons.

i. Children are individual rights-bearers

First and foremost, as discussed in Chapter 3, the CRC casts children as rights-bearers in their *own* right.[84] Hence, interferences with rights pertaining to the child-parent relationship and a child's family life that are *held by the child* must be assessed and justified in relation to the child. Parental consent does not absolve States from their obligation to consider children's best interests in matters affecting them nor from other duties to children under the CRC.[85] That is, individual contracts between a migrant worker and an employer in a labour-receiving country cannot waive the universal rights of the children of migrant workers, even if the contract is sanctioned by the labour-sending State. This is particularly important in light of the pivotal role of the child-parent relationship in a *child's* life and development.[86] In fact, courts have recognised that the right to family life is of more immediate importance to children than adults, precisely because of its relationship with children's development. As explained by Lady Hale of the UK Supreme Court:

> The family rights of children are of a different order from those of adults … Children need a family life in a way that adults do not … their emotional needs can only be fully met within a functioning family. Depriving a child of her family life is altogether more serious than depriving an adult of his … the effect upon the child's interests is always likely to be more severe than the effect upon an adult's.[87]

Hence, even if parents 'consent' to their own human rights being restricted, interferences with the interdependent rights of children still need to be justified.

82 Martin Ruhs, 'Protecting the Rights of Temporary Migrant Workers: Ideals Versus Reality' in Joanna Howe and Rosemary Owens (eds), *Temporary Labour Migration in the Global Era* (Hart Publishing, 2016) 299, 307–8.

83 Ibid.

84 See Chapter 3 (Section 3.2).

85 This is because States have a duty to consider children's best interests in *all* matters affecting them under art 3 of the CRC as discussed in Chapter 3 (see Section 3.2.1). For example, parental consent can be overridden in relation to the medical treatment of a child if the parent's decision is not considered to be in a child's best interests. See Rita Shackel, 'The UN Convention on the Rights of the Child: Tracing Australia's Implementation of the Provisions Relating to Family Relations' in O Cvejić Jan⊠ić (ed), *The Rights of the Child in a Changing World* (Springer, 2016) 37, 56.

86 See Chapter 4 (Sections 4.3.1 and 4.3.2) on the potential harms of child-parent separation to children's development and Chapter 7 (Section 7.2.2) on the benefits of strong child-parent relationships to children's development.

87 *ZH (Tanzania)* [2011] UKSC 4.

However, at present, TLM policies entirely overlook subsequent implications for the rights of children that arise from restrictions on their parents' rights. This was reiterated by key informants in views such as:

> 'Temporary foreign worker programs are premised on individualising the workers, separating them out from their relationships with their families'. *(Key Informant – R & P 2)*

This view demonstrates the complete failure in TLM policies to contemplate the interdependence between the rights of parents and children.[88] The importance of realising how *children's* rights are impacted by limitations on their parents' rights is amplified when we recognise, as Freeman explains, that addressing children's vulnerability and meeting their particular needs is not possible if children's rights are recognised 'on a par with adults'.[89] Hence, the assumption that if adults agree to have their own rights restricted in the context of TLM, this permits restrictions on their children's interdependent rights by States, goes against the requirement for States to justify interferences with children's rights, which are *held by children* as individual rights-bearers.

ii. The choice to migrate is often not genuine or informed

Secondly, there is the very real question about the degree to which a parent's choice to be separated from his or her children for *prolonged* periods in the context of TLM is genuine and informed. Global inequalities, rigid immigration regimes and limited viable employment opportunities have left many parents with few options other than to migrate without their children in order to provide for them.[90] Hence, as Wickramasekara states, given the costs of TLM to families, it is a fallacy to equate TLM with 'migration by choice'.[91] Similarly, Lenard and Straehle have observed that in the Canadian context:

> That they choose guest-work in developed countries over poverty in their home countries is not unreasonable … but it is a mistake to conclude from this choice that they would then choose guest-work over full membership if this choice was made available to them instead.[92]

88 The interdependence of the rights of children and parents is discussed in Chapter 2 (see Section 2.1).
89 Michael Freeman, 'The Value and Values of Children's Rights' in Antonella Invernizzi and Jane Williams (eds), *The Human Rights of Children: From Visions to Implementation* (Ashgate, 2011) 21, 29.
90 See Chapter 4 (Section 4.2).
91 Wickramasekara, above n 58, 171.
92 Patti Tamara Lenard and Christine Straehle, 'Temporary Labour Migration, Global Redistribution and Democratic Justice' (2011) 11(2) *Politics, Philosophy and Economics* 206, 214.

This highlights the limited options from which low-waged migrant workers have to 'choose' if they pursue employment overseas in the face of poverty or unemployment at home. Poverty and unemployment as key drivers for TLM are discussed in Chapter 4, as is the need to invest in the creation of employment opportunities in labour-sending countries to generate *real* choices for workers.[93] Key informants emphasised the need for labour-receiving countries to recognise their role in creating conditions that reduce options for parents that would enable them to be viably employed *without* having to leave their children. Their comments included:

> 'The grinding poverty and feeling of not having many choices other than to go to earn their money this way, is a moral failing at an international level in terms of deep inequality ... Receiving states don't see a moral responsibility to that larger inequality. In fact, they aggrandise their own moral superiority by saying that they wouldn't have had a job at home otherwise, so we are offering them this opportunity'. *(Key Informant – R & P 2)*

This comment again highlights the contradiction between the approach to TLM taken by labour-receiving countries and the principle of international cooperation;[94] which requires States with greater resources to take positive measures to respond to (rather than take advantage of) global inequalities between countries. Importantly, as discussed in Chapter 4, the migration of parents is not only *encouraged* by labour-receiving and labour-sending States, it is frequently incentivised, which creates an environment for uninformed decision-making.[95] This concern is reiterated by findings in the recent World Happiness Report that people's migration decisions are frequently based on 'limited and positively biased information' with limited knowledge about the consequences of their migration.[96]

Key informants, including from the government sector, recognised that when migrant workers 'choose' to leave young children, they are making a 'conflicted' choice in the belief that *leaving* their child for employment is in their child's best interests. This is captured in views such as:

> 'We all want opportunities, but if you're having to leave in situations where you are leaving young kids behind, it's kind of different. I think most people would feel that's a conflicted choice they are being forced to make'. *(Key Informant – Government 4)*

93 See Chapter 4 (Sections 4.2.2 and 4.2.3).
94 See Chapter 3 (Section 3.3).
95 See Chapter 4 (Section 4.2.3.i).
96 John F Helliwell, Richard Layard and Jeffrey D Sachs (eds), *World Happiness Report 2018* (Sustainable Development Solutions Network, 2018) 46–7.

Furthermore, prior to migration, parents often do not foresee how long they will be apart from their children.[97] In the context of low-waged TLM, numerous factors that are beyond the worker's control frequently prolong the duration of the child-parent separation. These are addressed in Section 6.4 and include the immobility of migrant workers during their period of employment due to rigid immigration regimes;[98] limited resources to enable frequent reunification with their children if their movement is not legally restricted;[99] and the development of familial dependence on remittances demanding the worker's perpetual remigration, which is generally unforeseen and unintended.[100]

iii. Consent is not always sufficient to limit rights

Lastly, even if it is held that parents make a conscious and informed choice to have their rights restricted by labour-receiving countries, States regularly do not accept consent as the *only* factor relevant in the limitation of a person's rights. This was emphasised by key informants in statements including:

> 'We have all kinds of situations where we don't just take simple consent, where we try to restrict the reach of consent ... The Children's Convention is articulating a set of principles that asks us to pay attention to something beyond the simple transaction between individuals. What underlies the Children's Convention is recognition that a simple contractual model of human relationships is insufficient'. *(Key Informant – R & P 4)*

This statement reiterates the notion that *even if* parents enter into contracts that limit their own familial rights, if these contracts are developed or endorsed by States, then States must still *justify* significant interferences with children's rights that arise from contractual limitations on their parents' rights. That is, States are still required to show that the limitations on children's rights caused by standard contracts that feature in TLM policies are in pursuit of a legitimate aim and use reasonably available measures that will minimise interference with children's rights.

It is recognised that *some* aspects of immigration control contribute to the rationale for child-parent separation in the context of TLM. This includes labour-receiving States attempting to reduce the risks of migrant workers

97 Joanna Dreby and Tim Adkins, 'The Strength of Family Ties: How US Migration Shapes Children's Ideas of Family' (2011) 19(2) *Childhood* 169, 171.

98 Jørgen Carling, Cecilia Menjivar and Leah Schmalzbauer, 'Central Themes in the Study of Transnational Parenthood' (2012) 38(2) *Journal of Ethnic and Migration Studies* 191, 199.

99 Ibid 201. See also Chapter 5 (Section 5.3.1).

100 See Section 6.4.2.

absconding, knowing that they will want to return to their dependent children.[101] However, this same objective could be achieved with shorter periods of separation, which reflects the fact that prolonged child-parent separation is not a necessary nor reasonable feature of existing TLM regimes. This is the focus of the following section. Suffice to say that more frequent opportunities for child-parent reunification during the period of employment would increase costs for States. This is contrary to the primary aim of separating these workers from their dependent children – that is, to minimise the costs of low-waged TLM to labour-receiving countries. However, as labour-receiving countries are sourcing migrant workers to meet their labour shortages, they should bear (or at least share) the costs of supporting the children of these workers to realise their right to family life. That is, the pursuit of cheaper labour by labour-receiving States is not grounds for the unnecessary and thoughtless violation of children's right to have their family life protected under Art 16.

6.4 Prolonged child-parent separation is not a *necessary* feature of TLM

As discussed in Section 6.2, the legal obligation on labour-receiving States to facilitate the reunification of workers and their children *within* their territories is significantly limited. However, policies that routinely separate dependent children from their parents still amount to an interference with children's right to have their family life respected and protected from arbitrary interference. Hence, under human rights law, States responsible for such interferences with children's rights must justify these interferences by demonstrating that they are in pursuit of a legitimate aim *and* use measures to ensure minimal interference with the rights in question.[102]

Consideration of the duty to adopt least restrictive measures has been *completely neglected* in the context of TLM. This is despite the numerous measures reasonably available to States that would reduce the cumulative period and negative effects of child-parent separation currently generated by TLM. These measures are the focus of this section. For example, as discussed in Chapter 5 in relation to children's right to have direct contact with their parents under Art 10(2), it would not be difficult for States to support more frequent return home visits for workers.[103] Ideally, these costs would be absorbed by labour-receiving countries given their greater resources and failure to share in the burden of managing social costs associated with TLM policies that operate in their favour.[104] This would bring low-waged TLM in line with other

101 See Section 6.4.2.

102 *Siracusa Principles*, UN Doc E/CN.4/1985/4, annex pt I A paras 10–12.

103 See Chapter 5 (Section 5.3.1).

104 For example, income tax collected by labour-receiving countries from low-waged temporary migrant workers could be used to subsidise more frequent opportunities for return travel. At present, not only do these workers pay income tax on wages earned

professions that routinely manage child-parent separation, where governments or employers subsidise frequent return travel for workers in return for their willingness to work in, for example, remote locations. Learnings from other disciplines is discussed in Section 6.4.1.

Even those advocating for the restriction of migrant workers' family rights recognise that rights-restrictions should be temporary, time-limited, evidenced-based and *justified* as a measure to avoid specific costs to labour-receiving countries that would arise from fulfilment of these rights.[105] Ruhs suggests the period of limitation be four years.[106] However, in terms of children's development, a four-year separation between children and parents can have significant impacts for both the child and child-parent relationship unless properly managed.[107] Should States be able to justify such a period of separation, then it is essential to children's well-being that opportunities for child-parent reunification during this period are incorporated into and supported by TLM policies. This would adhere more closely to what labour-receiving States themselves consider reasonable and necessary for their own (citizen) children's development and well-being if they are separated from their parents.

At present, the different standards applied to the children of migrant workers, and the reduced value placed on their child-parent relationships, are grounded in their nationality and their family's socio-economic status. As Hacker explains, policies governing children in developed countries construct children as being 'in need of intense contact with both parents'; whereas TLM policies construct children from labour-sending countries as not needing their parents and takes their separation for granted.[108] Hence, practices from professions *within* labour-receiving countries that address parental deployment and child-parent separation offer invaluable learnings on how TLM policies can minimise harm to children by actively mitigating risks associated with child-parent separation.

in the labour-receiving country despite not having their families with them to benefit from social services, they also have all or part of their return airfare deducted from their wages depending on their country of employment. To illustrate, workers in Australia's Seasonal Worker Program, which is framed as also being an international development programme, are taxed 15 cents on every dollar that they earn, have costs for private health insurance deducted from their wages and are required to pay half of their return airfare (and a full return airfare if they need to return home 'to attend to an urgent family matter'). See Australian Government Department of Jobs and Small Business, *Frequently Asked Questions about the Seasonal Worker Programme for Seasonal Workers* (20 August 2018) <https://www.jobs.gov.au/frequently-asked-questions-seasonal-workers>.

105 Ruhs, above n 82, 308.

106 Ibid.

107 See Chapter 7 (Section 7.2).

108 Daphna Hacker, *Legalized Families in the Era of Bordered Globalization* (Cambridge University Press, 2017), 212.

6.4.1 Opportunities to learn from other fields that manage child-parent separation

i. Separation in family law

In fields such as family law, acceptable lengths of child-parent separation and necessary protective strategies in the event of separation have been established over time, based on extensive research and child development expertise. Courts recognise that each case of child-parent separation is context-specific, however their decisions will always be informed by the best interests of the child.[109] Learnings from family law are discussed in the following chapter in relation to children's right to be cared for by their own parents under Art 7.[110] Where separation is inevitable, TLM regimes can draw on the principles and knowledge established in family law about how to minimise harm to children and maintain child-parent bonds at a distance. For example, as Kelly and Lamb urge, in family separation cases involving parental relocation, it is important that travel arrangements be specified and modified as children mature and become more able to manage longer periods between parental visits.[111] This notion of adaptable arrangements based on the age, capacity and life stage of the child is discussed in Chapters 4 and 5. [112] Interestingly, in the context of family law, practitioners consider significantly shorter periods of separation (ranging from a few days to a few weeks) as being in the best interests of children than those currently generated by TLM.[113]

ii. Military deployment

Numerous professions require the deployment of workers who are also parents, most notably military service. As Castaneda and Buck observe, for the families of low-waged migrant workers, much like for military families:

> [T]he family must adjust to the ambiguity of having one of their own away, not knowing when, or if, that person will return.[114]

109 See, eg, *McCoy v MCoy*, 764 A 2d 449, 453 (NJ, 2001) cited in Sarah Gottfried, 'Virtual Visitation: The Wave of the Future in Communication Between Children and Non-Custodial Parents in Relocation Cases' (2002) 36(3) *Family Law Quarterly* 475, 479; Helen Rhoades, 'Revising Australia's Parenting Laws: A Plea for a Relational Approach to Children's Best Interests' (2010) 22(2) *Child and Family Law Quarterly* 172, 172; Hacker, above n 108, 210.
110 See Chapter 7 (Section 7.2.3).
111 Joan B Kelly and Michael E Lamb, 'Developmental Issues in Relocation Cases Involving Young Children: When, Whether, and How?' (2003) 17(2) *Journal of Family Psychology* 193, 201.
112 See Chapter 4 (Section 4.4) and Chapter 5 (Section 5.4.4).
113 Kelly and Lamb, above n 111, 201.
114 Ernesto Castañeda and Lesley Buck, 'Remittances, Transnational Parenting, and the Children Left Behind' [2011] (December) *The Latin Americanist* 85, 105.

The Australian Defence Force has identified a need for additional support for children during times of transition such as parental deployment. To this end, they have initiated programmes such as the Defence School Transition Aides program, which assists children to manage the different phases of their parent's deployment.[115] The mainstreaming of support in schools and other settings that have frequent contact with children whose parents are deployed is also needed in the context of TLM. This is discussed in Chapter 4.[116] Similarly, other strategies to support defence force families experiencing deployment could be considered in the context of TLM, such as telephone support lines to connect family members with psychology, medical, social work and chaplaincy services; and tailored seminars for defence families to teach skills to effectively manage the stresses and challenges arising from military life.[117] These reflect reasonably available measures that could assist children to manage the period of child-parent separation in the context of TLM.

Key informants reiterated the need to inform TLM policies with existing knowledge from labour-receiving countries about the effective management of familial separation in reflections such as:

> 'Once you recognise that it is a human problem, then the fact that these are temporary workers, how decisive is that as compared to these commitments to maintaining family relationships and what is good for children'. *(Key Informant – R & P 4)*

This reflects the reality that the children of migrant workers experience their separation from their parents *in the same way* as would children who are citizens of labour-receiving countries. Hence, TLM policies can not only be informed by practices from other fields, but also by longitudinal studies on the effects of child-parent separation in labour-receiving countries arising from a parent's deployment. This is particularly so in the absence of any large-scale longitudinal studies on the impact of TLM on children's familial relationships and psychosocial well-being. For example, the RAND Institute's recent longitudinal study on the impact of military deployment on families in the United States examined the impact of deployment on the quality of parental relationships and child well-being.[118] Findings from such studies can inform TLM policies (acknowledging the similarities

115 Gail Macdonald, 'School-based Support for Students with a Parent on Military Deployment' (2016) 42(1) *Children Australia* 57, 57.

116 See Chapter 4 (Section 4.3.3.iv).

117 Australian Defence Force, Joint Health Command, *Deployment Guide: A Guide to Assist Your Preparation* <www.defence.gov.au/Health/HealthPortal/docs/JHC%20Deployment%20Guide.pdf> 91, 97–8.

118 RAND Arroyo Center and the National Defense Research Institute, 'Brief: How Military Families Function Before, During, and After Deployment – Findings from the RAND Deployment Life Study' (RAND Corporation, 2016) 1.

and differences between military and non-military contexts). To illustrate, an important finding from this Deployment Life Study (DLS) is that the promotion of family readiness by the military prior to the period of separation vastly improved outcomes for families. Moreover, by understanding a family's degree of readiness prior to parental deployment, support services are able to best target those families most in need. This is observed in the DLS Study as follows:

> Families that have been prepared successfully (i.e., those that have high family readiness) presumably weather the stresses of deployment more successfully than families that are less prepared (i.e., those that have low family readiness). Thus, assessments of family readiness, prior to deployments, can play a role in allocating resources for families most likely to need them.[119]

Family readiness involves families having knowledge about the challenges associated with deployment, being equipped with the necessary skills to address such challenges and being aware of available support resources.[120] As Meadows et al explain, families are considered 'crisis-prone' if their resources for dealing with stress are inadequate but are considered 'crisis-proof' if they have adequate resources for managing the stresses associated with deployment.[121] This approach to family support and the building of family readiness and resilience is directly transferrable in the comparative context of TLM.

iii. Fly-in-fly-out workers

Strategies that 'skilled' workers use to maintain transnational familial relationships can also be drawn upon, as many of these strategies could be made available to low-waged workers with not too onerous support from States and employers. In the Australian context, the significant growth in fly-in-fly-out workers has given rise to the longitudinal study *Working Away*. This study is examining the impact of mobile work on Australian households and family well-being with a view to identifying 'the kinds of multifaceted support that might be required for this practice to flourish without negative impacts'.[122] It is noteworthy that the periods of child-parent separation in this context are significantly shorter (that is, days or weeks at a time[123]). However, they are still perceived as having potentially negative social impacts on families and children that need to be proactively managed, given that separation is a feature of this type of employment, which is essential to

119 Terri Tanielian et al, *The Deployment Life Study: Methodological Overview and Baseline Sample Description* (RAND Arroyo Center and the National Defence Research Institute, 2014) 2.

120 Sarah O Meadows et al, *Family Resilience in the Military: Definitions, Models, and Policies* (RAND Corporation, 2015) 2.

121 Ibid 6.

122 Australian Research Council Project, *Working Away: How Working Away is Changing Home* <https://www.workingaway.net/the-project/>.

123 Ibid.

the Australian economy.[124] The study, which is underway, will offer learnings on how family life can be maintained using new forms of technology and travel, and will provide recommendations for the effective management of mobile work to reduce social impacts on families.[125] These lessons are invaluable in the context of low-waged TLM, where families are separated for significantly longer periods of time with markedly fewer resources, compounding the potential for negative social effects including familial breakdown. As Carling et al observe in their study on transnational parenthood:

> [T]he longer the parents remain unable to reunite with their children, the higher the likelihood that family members will grow apart.[126]

The more that children and parents grow apart because of protracted periods of separation caused by State policies, the greater the degree of interference with children's right to family life; and the more difficult the separation is to justify as a necessary and reasonable feature of TLM policies.

6.4.2 Remigration exacerbates the period of parental absence over the course of a childhood

i. Encouraging remigration in TLM policies

TLM across the spectrum encourages the remigration of migrant workers. This is because employers prefer to rehire people who they know and have already trained. For example, the explicit policy objective of the Australian Seasonal Workers Program (SWP) includes that it assists:

> Australian employers who are unable to source enough local Australian workers to meet their seasonal labour needs by providing access to a reliable workforce, able to return in future seasons.[127]

It is recognised that by capping the period of participation in seasonal TLM programmes to six or eight months per year, workers are able to spend part of each year with their children and families.[128] However, Canada's comparative Seasonal Agricultural Workers Program (SAWP) – which has been operating for decades –

124 Ibid.
125 Ibid.
126 Carling, Menjivar and Schmalzbauer, above n 98, 200.
127 Commonwealth, *Australian Government Response to the Joint Standing Committee on Migration Report: Seasonal Change – Inquiry into the Seasonal Worker Programme* (February 2017) 1.
128 Nic Maclellan and Peter Mares, 'Labour Mobility in the Pacific: Creating Seasonal Work Programs in Australia' in Stewart Firth (ed), *Globalisation and Governance in the Pacific Islands: State, Society and Governance in Melanesia* (ANU Press, 2006) 137, 159.

offers insights into the issues that arise when workers are encouraged to remigrate over successive years. As Becerril has found, many workers in Canada's SAWP Program 'live and work longer in Canada than in their nation of origin' and this employment is their family's primary source of income.[129] When families become dependent on the foreign income generated by the worker, whatever element of 'choice' that existed in their initial decision to migrate is often removed. Moreover, their continued remigration means that parents become separated from their children for cumulatively long and often ***unintended*** periods of time, which can have a profound impact on the children's well-being and the child-parent relationship as discussed in Chapters 4 and 5. [130]

The prevalence of the remigration of low-waged migrant workers in the Canadian context is highlighted by Faraday as follows:

> There is no limit to how many years a SAWP worker can return to work in Canada. Between 70% and 80% of SAWP workers return year after year to the same farms.[131]

Faraday further notes that a survey of 600 Mexican workers conducted in 2010 found that 'on average they participate in the SAWP for 7 to 9 years' and almost 'a quarter return to Canada for more than 10 years, with many returning for more than 25 years'.[132] Hence, a single (or even once repeated) period of six to eight months of parental absence during a child's life may constitute a manageable period of separation. However, when it is multiplied over a decade or more, then the parent becomes absent for a significant part of their child's childhood. This unnecessarily protracts the cumulative period of child-parent separation, which heightens the potential for children and parents to grow apart. Importantly, it also reduces the availability of parents to meet their children's non-material development needs across not one, but multiple, stages of their development.

ii. The intention behind circular migration

As discussed in Chapter 4, potential negative impacts on children are compounded when it is their primary caregiver who migrates.[133] In this light, TLM regimes that deliberately target the remigration of primary caregivers must address how these potential effects will be minimised in line with the duty to not cause harm to

129 Ofelia Becerril, 'Gendered Policies, Single Mothers and Transnational Motherhood: Mexican Female Migrant Farmworkers in Canada' in Zahra Meghani (ed), *Women Migrant Workers: Ethical, Political and Legal Problems* (Taylor and Francis, 2015) 154, 171.

130 See Chapter 4 (Section 4.3) and Chapter 5 (Section 5.4.4.ii).

131 Fay Faraday, 'Made in Canada: How the Law Constructs Migrant Workers' Insecurity' (Summary Report, Metcalfe Foundation, September 2012) 15.

132 Ibid.

133 See Chapter 4 (Section 4.3.2).

children through State actions. For example, Spain requires that migrant workers recruited from Morocco to work in its strawberry industry on a seasonal basis *must* be women *with* dependent children.[134] This policy is seen to create 'ideal guest workers' who are anchored to their home countries and will therefore willingly return at the end of each season.[135] This demonstrates that the aim of separating parents and dependent children is to benefit labour-receiving countries by reducing the risks of workers absconding and avoiding settlement costs. This was reiterated by key informants in observations such as:

> 'That is not really the objective ... Circular migration occurs because they don't want people to settle ... If you look at Canada's program ... people come and go from Mexico for 20 years but have *no* settlement rights at all'. *(Key Informant – MLO-NGO 6)*

This observation underscores the fact that although seasonal migration does permit more frequent opportunities for physical contact between parents and children, this is incidental and is ***not the aim*** being pursued by seasonal TLM policies. Rather, the aim that States need to justify as being legitimate to pursue through child-parent separation again goes to reducing costs associated with TLM to labour-receiving States, as discussed in Section 6.3.

iii. Remigration of non-seasonal migrant workers

The prolonged nature of child-parent separation characteristic of TLM is amplified in relation to the remigration of non-seasonal low-waged workers. In the context of Asia and the Gulf States, these workers are typically employed on two-year contracts that can be continually renewed. As with seasonal migration, their remigration is encouraged as employers prefer to rehire workers who have already been trained. This is demonstrated in relation to the Philippines, one of the largest labour-sending countries, where an increase in rehiring Filipino migrant workers over the past few decades has been attributed to employer preference 'to hire workers who already have international experience'.[136]

The remigration of migrant workers has also been aligned with the failure of States to develop workers' skills in ways that would open up viable employment

134 Christy M Glass, Susan Mannon and Peggy Petrzelka, 'Good Mothers as Guest Workers: Constructing the Trope of Compliant Maternity in Spain's Strawberry Industry' (2014) 44(3) *International Journal of Sociology* 8, 9.

135 Ibid.

136 Aniceto C Orbeta Jr and Michael R M Abrigo, 'Managing International Labor Migration: The Philippine Experience' (2011) 38(1–2) *Philippine Journal of Development* 57, 60.

options when they return home. The UN Special Rapporteur on the Human Rights of Migrants raised this concern in the context of Sri Lanka, stating that:

> As their skills are not recognized in Sri Lanka, this often leads to re-migration. Most Sri Lankan migrants go overseas initially for a two-year contract period, but the Special Rapporteur met with returned migrants who had been away for as long as 30 years, with little to show for it in terms of savings, improved housing, skills, etc.[137]

This comment highlights the valuable lessons that countries like Australia, which are only now developing non-seasonal low-waged TLM programmes, can learn from countries that have been exporting labour for decades. The need to build in measures that reduce the propensity to remigrate over many years is even more vital in TLM policies that pursue an international development objective, as is the case in Australia. Not only does perpetual remigration limit the potential economic benefits of TLM to a particular group, these workers are then away from their families for unnecessary and cumulatively long periods, and families become dependent on their continued remigration for income.

6.4.3 Regional proximity and circulation-friendly visas together reduce periods of separation

i. Regional proximity

Regional proximity lends itself to more frequent opportunities for migrant workers to visit their families due to reduced travel costs and time. In a study of pre-school children from over 4000 households in a rural region of Nicaragua, it was found that the absence of parents (mothers and/or fathers) for seasonal work did not cause negative effects for the early childhood development of these young children.[138] Importantly, parents were migrating to other Central American countries or regions within Nicaragua and were away from their children for an average of three months at a time.[139] The view that three months appears to be a manageable period of separation – if separation is necessary – was expressed by key informants in the context of seasonal TLM in comments such as:

> 'In terms of family disruption, it is less unmanageable to go for three months than to go for three years'. *(Key Informant – Government 4)*

137 *Special Rapporteur on the Human Rights of Migrants – Mission to Sri Lanka*, UN Doc A/HRC/29/36/Add.1, [55].

138 Karen Macours and Renos Vakis, 'Seasonal Migration and Early Childhood Development' (Social Protection Discussion Paper, No 0702, The World Bank, March 2007).

139 Ibid 6.

'With seasonal workers ... there is almost no pressure for family reunification because ... the idea is that people will go back every year ... So if it's three months, then that's not unreasonable, if it's 8 months then it is. What about 6 months? I don't know'. *(Key Informant – R & P 4)*

These comments reflect the recognition that even if child-parent separation is justified in the context of TLM, it is *short* periods of separation that could be considered reasonable. As periods become more protracted, they become less reasonable and necessary making them difficult to justify as non-arbitrary measures needed to prevent the settlement costs associated with family accompaniment.

ii. Circulation-friendly visas

While the possibility for frequent returns home is enhanced by regional proximity, this must be coupled with circulation-friendly visas that encourage the free movement of workers between their place of employment and family. As Piper observes:

> What is important for such groups is to obtain the kind of visa that would allow them to move easily backwards and forwards between origin and destination countries ... With temporary migration schemes becoming more and more significant, an infrastructure needs to be created (backed up by policy) that facilitates transnational family life.[140]

The German seasonal workers programme has been highlighted in that regard, as it sources workers from nearby Eastern European countries (predominantly Poland) to work for up to six months in industries such as agriculture and hospitality.[141] As EU citizens, workers can move freely between Germany and their home countries. Hence, the sheer proximity combined with the ease of travel between Poland and Germany means that workers can frequently return home for short visits during the period of their employment contracts.[142] While the structure of the programme is based on meeting the seasonal needs of German industries (and has not been designed with reducing the social costs to families in mind),[143] the benefits of a model that enables free and easy circulation of workers is that the social costs to children, families and labour-sending countries are minimised. It has also enabled many people to combine their seasonal employment in Germany with permanent employment in Poland,[144] which reduces a family's dependence on the remigration of the worker as the sole source of family income.

140 Piper, above n 53, 22.
141 Wickramasekara, above n 58, 159.
142 European Policy Centre (2011) cited in Wickramasekara, above n 58, 160.
143 Ibid.
144 Kaczmarczyk and Tyrowicz (2008) cited in Wickramasekara, above n 58, 159.

Such models enable job-sharing arrangements in a fashion more similar to other professions where workers rotate and fly-in-fly-out for work. This reduces periods of child-parent separation to lengths that are considered reasonable in other professions that require people to work away from home. The potential for rotational models to reduce the impact of TLM on families was emphasised by key informants in comments such as:

> 'The easy thing here is the geographic closeness. So, for a Polish woman, it is of course much easier to work for two weeks in Germany and return for one week, be with her family, and then go back'. *(Key Informant – R & P 3)*

A recent study on Australia's SWP found that some participants, particularly Samoan, were adopting job-sharing arrangements within extended families, where a family member would cover the worker's responsibilities at home for six months. When the worker returned from Australia after six months, the two extended family members would exchange roles.[145] The formalisation of rotational models, which some families are adopting informally, would extend and encourage this possibility more broadly within TLM and even beyond seasonal work and/or countries that are in close proximity. This presents a reasonably available measure for States to facilitate transnational family life, which is more in line with other professions that manage familial separation for employment purposes.

Presently, for low-waged migrant workers, rigid visa restrictions that stifle circulation significantly limit the capacity of parents to make regular return visits to their children.[146] In fact, Oliveria has found that in relation to Mexican migrant workers in the United States, fear of losing their rights if they leave, or being denied re-entry, is leading to an increase in the number of years that mothers are staying separated from their children in Mexico.[147] This was stressed by key informants in views including:

> 'Frequent visits are important, but if migrant workers don't have the right of return, sometimes they'll stay absent for years'. *(Key Informant – MLO-NGO 6)*

Hence, the UN Special Rapporteur on the Human Rights of Migrants has recently reiterated the global need for '[r]ecognizing real labour needs and

145 World Bank Group, *Maximizing the Development Impacts from Temporary Migration: Recommendations for Australia's Seasonal Worker Programme* (International Bank for Reconstruction and Development/The World Bank, 2017) 42.

146 Julia O'Connell Davidson and Caitlin Farrow, *Child Migration and the Construction of Vulnerability* (Save the Children, 2007) 51.

147 Gabrielle Marcelletti Rocha de Oliveira, *Transnational Care Constellations: Mexican Immigrant Mothers and their Children in Mexico and in New York City* (PhD Thesis, Columbia University, 2015) 15.

opening up considerably more visa opportunities or visa-free travel programmes for migrant workers at all skill levels'.[148]

In the Australian context, the Lowy Institute has gone further to model the economic benefits of the free movement of workers between the Pacific and Australia. It found that under an uncapped model, the economic benefits to the Pacific would be 'around 40 times Australia's current aid budget to the region';[149] and a capped model requiring an annual quota of around 2850 workers would still provide a benefit to Pacific Island countries 'three times the value of [Australia's] existing aid program'.[150] Key informants, except from the government sector, repeatedly emphasised the importance of circulation-friendly visas to the maintenance of transnational family life and sustainability of TLM policies that separate children and parents. Their reflections included:

> 'The only policy as important as the right to family unity is the right to leave the country without losing all of your rights. So that implies multiple entry visas [and] you have to know that the employer is not going to fire you'. *(Key Informant – MLO-NGO 4)*

This reflection, again, goes to the interconnectedness of the rights of migrant workers and their children. Under the CRC, parents are entitled to receive appropriate assistance to fulfil their parenting responsibilities, particularly under Arts 27 and 18.[151] In the context of TLM, this must include protection of workers' employment rights while they are tending to parental duties, which includes returning home to visit their children. Without such protection, even if measures such as circulation-friendly visas are made available to parents, they will not constitute *effective* measures as parents will be discouraged from using them.

6.4.4 Shifts away from permanent settlement increase the likelihood and foreseeability of disruption to family units

i. Australia's opportunity to learn from Canadian experiences

Unlike Canada, Australia has historically resisted *dedicated* low-waged labour migration programmes.[152] However, facing pressure to provide TLM pathways to

148 *Report of the Special Rapporteur on the Human Rights of Migrants on a 2035 Agenda for Facilitating Human Mobility*, UN GAOR, 35th sess, Agenda Item 3, UN Doc A/HRC/35/25 (28 April 2017) [37] ('*2035 Agenda for Facilitating Human Mobility*').

149 Leon Berkelmans and Jonathan Pryke, 'The Development Benefits of Expanding Pacific Access to Australia's Labour Market' (Lowy Institute Analyses Paper, December 2016).

150 Ibid 13–14.

151 Article 27 is discussed in Chapter 4, which defines 'appropriate assistance' (see Section 4.2.1); and Article 18 is discussed in Chapter 7.

152 Laurie Berg, *Migrant Rights at Work: Law's Precariousness at the Intersection of Immigration and Labour* (Routledge, 2016) 6.

fill low-waged positions including in care work,[153] hospitality and non-seasonal agriculture, the Australian Government announced a new Pacific Labour Scheme in 2017.[154] The Scheme seeks to employ Pacific Islanders for up to three years in 'low and semi-skilled' positions in the Northern Territory and rural and regional areas.[155] This represents a significant shift away from Australia's traditional approach to migration that has typically permitted family accompaniment for both temporary and permanent migrants.[156] Key informants reiterated the significance of this shift in Australia's approach to labour migration in views including:

> 'We need to think about why we are moving towards policies that by their very nature separate dependent children from their parents ... Australia has really prided itself on *not* having guest worker programs ... on having migration policies and strategies that are based on permanency and settlement'. *(Key Informant – R & P 7)*

One reason that Australia has historically shunned dedicated 'low-skilled' temporary labour migration programmes[157] is that it has traditionally recognised the benefits of the permanent settlement of migrants to building Australia and the Australian economy.[158] In relation to TLM, the benefits of maintaining family unity between migrants and their dependent children – which is assumed in the context of permanent settlement – are evident not only for children but also for labour-receiving countries. This was stressed by key informants in comments such as:

> 'Allowing children to co-reside with parents ... would make these parents better workers because they would have much less to worry about, and healthier and happier families can contribute more than unhappy parents separated from their children'. *(Key Informant – R & P 5)*

This comment highlights how child-parent separation can unsurprisingly affect the health and well-being of workers, which can not only impact their productivity

153 Elizabeth Adamson et al, 'Social Care and Migration Policy in Australia: Emerging intersections?' (2017) 52(1) *Australian Journal of Social Issues* 78.

154 Department of Foreign Affairs and Trade (DFAT), *Pacific Labour Scheme* (November 2018) <https://dfat.gov.au/geo/pacific/engagement/Documents/pacific-labour-scheme.pdf>.

155 Ibid.

156 Wickramasekara, above n 58, 148.

157 Deborah Brennan and Elizabeth Adamson, 'Care and Migration' in Sheila Shaver (ed), *Handbook on Gender and Social Policy* (Elgar, 2018) 253, 258.

158 Mary E Crock, 'Contract or Compact: Skilled Migration and the Dictates of Politics and Ideology' (2001) (16) *Georgetown Immigration Law Journal* 133.

but also their parenting capacity. It underscores the need for countries like Australia to learn from the Canadian experience about the impact of prolonged child-parent separation prior to reunification, which is discussed in Chapter 5. [159] This is particularly so since it has been suggested that the Canadian approach to caregiver migration offers a good model for countries like Australia to meet labour needs in the care sector.[160] However, even advocates for this approach in an Australian context have recognised that:

> Adverse family and community impacts of labour mobility can be minimized by avoiding long-term family separations.[161]

ii. Canadian recognition of the detrimental effects of prolonged family separation

The detrimental effects of family disruption caused by Canada's former Live-in Caregiver Program are discussed in Chapter 5[162] and stemmed largely from the length of time between a worker acquiring permanent residency (PR) and reunification with their children, which could take between five to ten years.[163] In response to these concerns, the Canadian Government reformed the programme in 2014 to introduce, among other things, an annual cap on the number of caregivers able to apply for PR to reduce processing times,[164] and removal of the requirement for caregivers to live with their employers.[165] The annual cap has removed a feature of the programme that was frequently touted as best practice – that is, a direct pathway to PR in recognition that the worker is filling a permanent gap in the Canadian labour market.[166] However, as caregivers entering under the new caregiver pathways are still required to work in Canada for two years before being eligible to apply for PR,[167] the removal of the 'live-in' requirement opens

159 See Chapter 5 (Section 5.4.4.ii).

160 Richard Curtain, Matthew Dornan, Jesse Doyle and Stephen Howes, *Pacific Possible: Labour Mobility: The Ten Billion Dollar Prize* (Pacific Possible Series, World Bank, July 2016) v–vi, 22–4.

161 Ibid ix–x, 37.

162 See Chapter 5 (Section 5.4.4.ii).

163 Monica Boyd, 'Labour Migration for Care: Women Migrants in Canada Under the Live-in Caregiver Program' (Paper presented at the Rethinking Care and Migration in the Age of Low Fertility and Ageing Population Conference, University of Toronto, 9–10 March 2011) 22.

164 Applications will be capped at a total of 5500 per year, with spouses and dependent children not included in the cap. See Government of Canada, *Improving Canada's Caregiver Program* (31 October 2014) <https://www.canada.ca/en/news/archive/2014/10/improving-canada-caregiver-program.html>.

165 Ibid.

166 Caregivers can still apply for permanent residency under two caregiving streams (the Caring for Children Pathway and the Caring for People with High Medical Needs Pathway) but only 2750 applications will be processed under each stream per year.

167 Government of Canada, *Caregivers – Options for Permanent Residence* (3 October 2018) <https://www.canada.ca/en/immigration-refugees-citizenship/services/immigrate-canada/caregivers.html>.

up the possibility for workers to be accompanied by their children during this period. Whether this will occur, however, is yet to be seen and may not be viable for many workers given the low-waged nature of the work and high costs of living.

Significantly, the benefits of allowing children and parents to migrate together has been recognised in certain Canadian provinces that want to encourage the permanent settlement of migrant workers in low-waged jobs where there is a *permanent* labour market need.[168] These provinces have recognised that supporting the settlement of the family *as a unit* is central to the well-being of workers and their families, which is pivotal to retaining workers in these provinces. This was highlighted by key informants in relation to the retention of migrants in Canada's Atlantic provinces in comments including:

> 'We are asking employers when they are doing their selection to see if they can try and hire a husband and wife, especially in the low-skilled [sector]. Because this way, the wife will have a job and the husband will have a job and the school system is ready ... It's a very integrated approach to ensure that the family will stay'. *(Key Informant – Government 5)*

This comment demonstrates the reasonable measures available to labour-receiving countries to support the unity of migrants and their families, which are already adopted in some regions that are in need of population growth. These include identifying employment opportunities that allow both parents to be employed in the same business or area so that the family can migrate together and have sufficient income to support the whole family. Such measures limit the interference caused by migration with children's family life by enabling children to continue residing with their parents. Importantly, these measures are available to other groups of *temporary* migrants, which highlights that family accompaniment does not necessarily have to be associated with PR. This is the focus of the following final section.

6.5 Children's right to family unity is upheld if their parents are 'skilled' migrants

The children of 'skilled'[169] temporary workers *are* permitted to migrate with their parents if their parents so choose. This is because labour-receiving countries wish

168 For example, Manitoba encourage workers of *all* skills levels to transition to permanent residence, which then enables them to sponsor their spouses and children and settle in the province. See Delphine Nakache and Leanne Dixon-Perera, 'Temporary or Transitional? Migrant Workers' Experiences with Permanent Residence in Canada' (IRPP Study No 55, Institute for Research on Public Policy, October 2015) 7.

169 'Skilled' migrants are selected by the labour-receiving country based on factors including education, qualifications, work experience, language ability and potential economic contribution to the labour-receiving country based on earning capacity.

to encourage the entry of 'wanted' temporary migrants (which also includes international students), while simultaneously discouraging not the entry but the settlement of 'unwanted' low-waged migrant workers.[170] This is done by ensuring that low-waged, or 'low-skilled',[171] migrant workers have the most limited rights of all temporary foreign workers, which includes restrictions (legal and/or practical) on their right to family accompaniment.[172] This was stressed by key informants in observations such as:

> 'Do these states allow students to bring their families in? ... Why do they do that? Because you can't expect people to come for longer than a few weeks, or maybe a few months, without their families'. *(Key Informant – R & P 4)*

This observation reiterates the discriminatory nature of permitting family accompaniment to some temporary migrants and not others based on the nature of the employment alone. It reflects, as Ong observes, the different 'latitudes of citizenship' that entitle temporary skilled migrants to the benefits of citizenship based on their sought-after skills, benefits that are denied to 'low-skilled' workers.[173] It also reflects how those with the greatest needs for measures to protect their rights, essential to enable their children's realisation of interdependent CRC rights, are those who get the least assistance from labour-receiving States.

They are predominantly categorised as 'professionals' in their occupational fields. See, eg, Australian Bureau of Statistics, *3416.0 – Perspectives on Migrants, 2009: Skilled Migration* (15 April 2009) <http://www.abs.gov.au/AUSSTATS/abs@.nsf/Lookup/3416.0Main+Features32009>.

170 Castles, above n 13, 126, 130.

171 'Low-skilled' migrant workers are filling low-waged positions but may have substantial educational qualifications and employment experience. For example, Kelly has found that while Filipino immigrants in Canada are highly educated, 'they have tended to enter low-paying and low-status segments of the labour force' (such as healthcare, hospitality, manufacturing and caregiving). See Phillip Kelly, 'Understanding Intergenerational Social Mobility: Filipino Youth in Canada' (IRPP Study No 45, Institute for Research on Public Policy, February 2014) 11. Similarly, as 2001 survey of Filipino domestic workers in Hong Kong found that 62 per cent had completed tertiary studies. See Asato (2003) cited in Nicole J Sayers, 'An Analysis of the Situation of Filipino Domestic Workers' (Working Paper, ILO, 14 December 2007) 10.

172 Graeme Hugo, 'Best Practice in Temporary Labour Migration for Development: A Perspective from Asia and the Pacific' (2009) 47(5) *International Migration* 23, 27.

173 Aihwa Ong, 'Latitudes of Citizenship: Membership, Meaning and Multiculturalism' in Alison Brysk and Gershon Shafir (eds), *People Out of Place: Globalisation, Human Rights, and the Citizenship Gap* (Routledge, 2004) 53; Kneebone, above n 60, 431.

6.5.1 Children of 'low-skilled' temporary migrants are discriminated against in terms of family rights

i. Differential treatment must be proportionate to a legitimate aim

While differential treatment itself is not unlawful, it becomes unlawful when States fail to provide a justification for such distinction. In the context of TLM, the differential treatment between skilled and 'low-skilled' migrants has been attributed to the belief that skilled workers are of a higher value to labour-receiving countries, will integrate more readily and will cost less to the State given their higher earning capacity.[174] These beliefs support the rationale for denying family accompaniment to low-waged migrant workers, which, as discussed in Section 6.3, is that costs to labour-receiving countries should be minimised.

However, *even if* the reduction of costs to labour-receiving countries can be considered a *legitimate* aim pursued by TLM policies, States must still demonstrate that the measures used to achieve this aim are reasonable and proportionate. This has been stressed by the CRC and CMW Committees in the context of children and migration as follows:

> Any differential treatment of migrants shall be lawful and proportionate, in pursuit of a legitimate aim and in line with the child's best interests and international human rights norms and standards.[175]

Hence, States *must* show that the serious potential harms to children arising from prolonged child-parent separation,[176] and the significant disruption that it causes to children's family life, is *proportionate* to the aim of reducing costs to labour-receiving countries. This is particularly given the constraints on workers returning home for frequent visits during the period of employment, as discussed in Section 6.4 and Chapter 5 in relation to Art 10(2),[177] and the duty of States to not cause harm to children in other countries.[178]

ii. Discrimination can be unintended

Under the CRC, arbitrary discrimination against children based on shared characteristics is prohibited, even if there is no *intended* purpose to cause harm.[179] That is, discrimination includes harm that is unintended but caused to members of a particular group because of differential treatment.[180] The denial of family rights

174 Piper, above n 53, 20.
175 *Joint General Comment on Children in the Context of International Migration*, UN Doc CMW/C/GC/3-CRC/C/GC/22, para 22.
176 See Chapter 4 (Section 4.3).
177 See Chapter 5 (Section 5.3.1).
178 See Chapter 3 (Section 3.3).
179 See Chapter 3 (Section 3.2.2).
180 Bruce Abramson, *Article 2: The Right of Non-Discrimination* (Martinus Nijhoff, 2008) 71.

to migrant workers in the context of TLM disrupts children's family life *because* of their parent's skill level, socio-economic status and country of origin. Hence, while the overt and intended discrimination is against their parents, the interdependent rights of the children of these workers is interfered with on the same prohibited grounds (which include socio-economic status and nationality). The CRC and CMW Committees have reiterated that in the context of children affected by migration, the non-discrimination principle embodied in Art 2 of the CRC (as outlined in Chapter 3[181]) obliges States to respect and ensure the rights of all children regardless of their parents' migration status.[182] The Committees have also urged that this principle 'be at the centre of all migration policies and procedures ... regardless of the migration status of children or their parents'.[183]

The fact that TLM policies have completely failed to consider the impact of denying family rights to migrant workers on their children's interdependent rights reflects that the discrimination against these children is likely to be unintended. This is both when family accompaniment is legally barred (amounting to overt discrimination), and when family accompaniment is prevented by practical constraints attached to low-waged TLM (amounting to 'de facto' discrimination). Importantly, de facto (in fact) discrimination against the worker (that is, the parent) can still be intended, as discussed in Chapter 3.[184] However, again, the discriminatory effect on their children is likely to be unintended given that it has generally not even been considered. Hence, the overt or de facto discrimination against migrant workers unintentionally interferes with their children's CRC rights on discriminatory grounds (that is their parent's migration status, country of origin and family's socio-economic status). Without justifying this discrimination against children as being proportionate and in pursuit of a legitimate aim, States are in violation of Art 2.

While the obligation on States to not discriminate against children under the CRC applies to children within the State's jurisdiction, States also have a duty to assist other States to fulfil their CRC obligations in accordance with the principle of international cooperation.[185] However, by preventing family accompaniment while actively sourcing workers who are likely to have dependent children, labour-receiving States are undermining (rather than enhancing) the capacity of labour-sending States to implement the CRC rights of the children of migrant workers. Moreover, as discussed in Section 6.2, labour-receiving States retain a duty to justify TLM policies that deliberately keep these children outside their jurisdiction as these policies directly affect these children. Part of this justification must necessarily involve demonstrating that the differential affording of family rights based on parents' skill levels, socio-economic status and nationality is in pursuit of a legitimate aim. Part of the aim that needs to be justified is the deliberate attempt to

181 See Chapter 3 (Section 3.2.2).
182 *Joint General Comment on Children in the Context of International Migration*, UN Doc CMW/C/GC/3-CRC/C/GC/22.
183 Ibid para 22.
184 See Chapter 3 (Section 3.2.2).
185 See Chapter 3 (Section 3.3).

avoid costs associated with meeting CRC obligations that would arise if children could accompany parents. This needs to be evaluated in light of the fact that labour-receiving countries benefit from the low costs associated with their parents' labour.

iii. Discriminatory practices are inconsistent with additional legal commitments

In justifying interferences with children's CRC rights, labour-receiving countries also need to consider the challenges that discriminatory practices in TLM present to their domestic and regional legal commitments to preserve and support the family unit. Examples of regional legal commitments that strengthen State obligations in relation to the protection of family rights are discussed in Chapter 3. [186] In a domestic sense, TLM practices in the Canadian context create conditions for low-waged migrant workers that are incompatible with Canadian domestic human rights law[187] and labour regulations for local workers. These include, for example, provisions in the *Canadian Charter of Rights and Freedoms* that afford migrant workers 'equal protection and equal benefit of the law without discrimination' including on grounds of national or ethnic origin;[188] and the *Canadian Human Rights Act*, which establishes the principle that people should have an equal opportunity:

> … to make for themselves the lives that they are able and wish to have and to have their needs accommodated, consistent with their duties and obligations as members of society, without being hindered in or prevented from doing so by discriminatory practices based on race, national or ethnic origin…[189]

Importantly, the CRC recognises that part of people's 'duties and obligations as members of society' are their parental duties and responsibilities towards their children. A 2006 review of Canada's Federal Labour Standards highlighted the need for labour regulation to respect international obligations to effectively protect the rights of migrant workers,[190] including labour rights related to a worker's capacity to attend to family obligations and needs.[191] While the review discussed the human rights challenges faced by migrant workers in a domestic context, the very nature of TLM policies that prevent family accompaniment create transnational familial relationships. Therefore, for measures supporting workers to meet familial and parental obligations to be effective, they must account for the fact that a migrant worker's dependent children are overseas *because* of TLM policies. This

186 See Chapter 3 (Section 3.3.4).
187 Faraday, above n 131, 5.
188 *Canada Act 1982* (UK) c 11, sch B pt I ('*Canadian Charter of Rights and Freedoms*') s 15(1).
189 *Canadian Human Rights Act*, RSC 1985, c H-6, s 2.
190 Brian B McArthur, *In Praise of the Arthurs Report on Canadian Federal Labour Standards* (Canadian Centre for Policy Alternatives, March 2007) 8, 10.
191 Ibid 15.

accentuates the need for labour-receiving States to look to their international commitments to govern the protection of the rights of workers and their families in the context of TLM.

Only by recognising the essential connection between domestic labour regulation and a migrant worker's ability to realise their human rights protected under international law, which includes their right to appropriate assistance to meet parental responsibilities, can TLM hope to be consistent with human rights law. This is reflected in Commissioner Arthur's statement in the abovementioned review that:

> It is widely understood that people who are poor and insecure tend to suffer more violations of their rights than those who are not, and that such people are at a disadvantage when they have to claim or defend their legal rights in general, and their human rights in particular.[192]

In this vein, the CRC and CMW Committees have highlighted the pressing need for States to respond to the de facto discrimination that is routinely endured by children as a result of their parents' migration status and strict migration regimes.[193] This includes States fulfilling their CRC obligations 'by adopting positive measures to prevent, diminish and eliminate the conditions and attitudes that cause or perpetuate de facto discrimination' towards children affected by migration.[194]

6.6 Conclusion

TLM regimes are part of a parallel process where the movement of labour is increasingly transnational but only skilled workers are truly mobile, being able to move freely without restrictions on their rights and the rights of their families.[195] This chapter has demonstrated how features of TLM policies interfere with children's specific right to have their family life protected against *arbitrary* interference under Art 16 of the CRC, recognising that their relationship with their parents is a significant part of their family life. It has argued that the nature of these interferences is arbitrary for two reasons. First, explicit and implicit features of TLM policies that restrict the free movement of migrant workers between their country of employment and country of their children's residence *unnecessarily* and *unreasonably* prolong the period of child-parent separation. Second, these

192 Harry Arthurs, *Fairness at Work: Federal Labour Standards for the 21st Century* (Publication Services, Human Resources Development Canada, 2006) 95; See also McArthur, above n 190, 12.

193 *Joint General Comment on Children in the Context of International Migration*, UN Doc CMW/C/GC/3-CRC/C/GC/22.

194 Ibid para 26.

195 Castles, above n 13, 131; Eric Neumayer, 'Unequal Access to Foreign Spaces: How States Use Visa Restrictions to Regulate Mobility in a Globalised World' (2006) 31(1) *Transactions of the Institute of British Geographers* 72, 81.

restrictive features *as well as* the denial of the right to family accompaniment affect *only* the children of migrant workers and are therefore discriminatory in their effect.

This chapter has reiterated that *even if* labour-receiving States can demonstrate that the intended purpose of minimising economic costs to labour-receiving countries is a legitimate aim for denying family accompaniment, they must still *justify* the measures that they use to maximise their economic gains as being necessary, reasonable and proportionate. This chapter has highlighted that there is *absolutely no need* for the periods of separation between children and parents to be so long under TLM regimes. It has identified reasonably available measures that could reduce prolonged periods of child-parent separation *without* forcing States to address their discriminatory practice of denying family accompaniment to only this group of temporary migrants. These include introducing circulation-friendly visas; encouraging regional initiatives that increase proximity between workers and their families (combined with the right to move freely and the protection of workers' employment rights when they return home for visits); reducing the deliberate encouragement of remigration by equipping workers with skills during their period of employment that will reduce their need to remigrate (combined with investment in local employment opportunities in labour-sending countries); and formalising rotational or job-sharing models that align with practices in other sectors that require workers to work away from their families.

This chapter has stressed the benefits of drawing on learnings from other disciplines and professions that regularly manage child-parent separation, including in family law, for military deployment and with fly-in-fly-out workers in regional locations. These fields can offer guidance in the development of TLM policies on appropriate lengths of child-parent separation; on how families can be supported to prepare for and manage periods of separation; and on suitable care, communication and travel plans that can be modified according to children's ages and changing needs. Importantly, these strategies will need to be subsidised by States if migrant workers are to have the capacity to implement them given their low wages and limited available resources.

Resourcing such measures should be a shared responsibility between labour-receiving and labour-sending States given that labour-sending States bear *all* the social costs associated with the unnecessarily restrictive features of TLM policies that are designed to keep costs low for labour-receiving countries. This chapter has emphasised how this approach completely undermines the principle of international cooperation, which requires States with resources to assist those with fewer resources rather than capitalise on the global inequalities between States. The inconsistency of current TLM practices with the principle of international cooperation could be addressed by labour-receiving countries funding and supporting measures to significantly reduce the periods of child-parent separation experienced by the children of migrant workers. At present, the restrictions on the rights of migrant workers and their children that are based on their country of origin, migration status and perceived human capital has meant that TLM is, as Castles describes, 'more a result of inequality than a tool to alleviate it'.[196]

Importantly, prolonged physical separation not only interferes with a child's right to family life under Art 16, but also interferes with parents' protected role as their children's primary caregivers and the right of children to be cared for by their parents as far as possible, which are fundamental elements of a child's family life protected in Arts 18 and 7 respectively.[197] The CRC and CMW Committees have stressed the interconnectedness, in relation to children affected by migration, between children's family life, parental entitlements to assistance and child development, urging that:

> a comprehensive approach to the child's right to a family environment in the context of migration should contemplate measures directed at enabling parents to fulfil their duties with regard to child development.[198]

This highlights the pivotal role of parents in a child's family life and the interconnectedness of CRC provisions that protect the child-parent relationship and recognise its centrality to children's development and well-being. The significant interference by TLM policies with the parental role and responsibility for the upbringing and development of children, and children's right to be cared for by their parents, is the focus of the next chapter that examines the impact of TLM on children's rights under Arts 7 and 18 of the CRC.

196 Castles, above n 13, 127.

197 Jaap E Doek, *A Commentary on the United Nations Convention on the Rights of the Child: Article 8 The Right to Preservation of Identity, Article 9 The Right Not to Be Separated from His or Her Parents* (Martinus Nijhoff, 2006) 24–5.

198 *Joint General Comment on Children in the Context of International Migration*, UN Doc CMW/C/GC/3-CRC/C/GC/22, para 31.

7 Articles 18 and 7

State obligations to protect the child-parent relationship: Securing a place for children's rights in TLM

Article 18

1. States Parties shall use their best efforts to ensure recognition of the principle that both parents have common responsibilities for the upbringing and development of the child. ***Parents*** *or, as the case may be, legal guardians,* ***have the primary responsibility for the upbringing and development of the child****. The best interests of the child will be their basic concern.*
2. For the purpose of guaranteeing and promoting the rights set forth in the present Convention, ***States Parties shall render appropriate assistance to parents and legal guardians in the performance of their child-rearing responsibilities*** *and shall ensure the development of institutions, facilities and services for the care of children.*

Article 7

1. 'The child shall ... have ... as far as possible, ***the right to*** *know and* ***be cared for by his or her parents****.'*
2. States Parties ***shall ensure the implementation of these rights*** *in accordance with their national law and their obligations under the relevant international instruments in this field...*

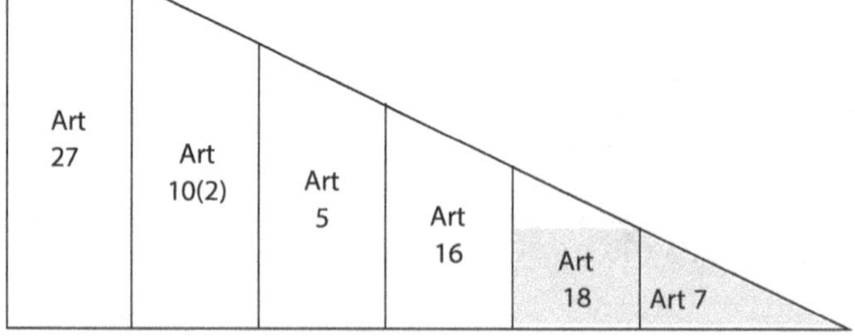

7.1 Introduction

As the final chapter in Part B, this chapter uses Arts 18 and 7 of the CRC to underscore the centrality of the child-parent relationship in human rights law *and* to children's development and well-being. Articles 18 and 7 are the last of the CRC rights being considered in this book across a spectrum of rights that protect the child-parent relationship in the context of TLM. Hence, this chapter is heavily premised on the issues raised in the preceding chapters in Part B that have each illuminated how different aspects of the child-parent relationship are impacted by restrictive features of TLM policies.

This chapter argues that assisting parents to fulfil their protected role as their children's *primary* carers is not only *legally* required by States parties to the CRC under Art 18, but also necessary to: a) minimise potential harms to and maximise the potential well-being of children; and b) introduce coherence with the international development aims that many States and multilateral organisations use to promote TLM. Regarding the former, this chapter demonstrates that labour-receiving countries recognise and espouse the importance of the child-parent relationship in numerous domestic settings, including in family law and child development disciplines. It argues that the importance of the child-parent relationship to children's development and well-being is universal and protected for *all* children no matter where they reside. Concerning the latter, this chapter highlights the significant inconsistencies between TLM policies that pursue international development goals, while promoting the separation of children and parents. It argues that development goals are obscured by measures focused primarily on remittances and the efficient management of migration. The chapter concludes that without more comprehensive measurement of social impacts on children and familial relationships, States cannot make informed decisions about how best to promote TLM without significantly interfering with children's right to be cared for by their parents and the protected role of parents as primary caregivers in international human rights law.

This chapter reflects the interconnectedness of the CRC rights that have been considered throughout this book. Importantly, Art 18 *entitles* parents to State assistance to fulfil their child-rearing responsibilities as those adults charged with the primary responsibility for their children's upbringing and development. Appropriate assistance is defined in Chapter 4 in relation to Art 27 and involves assistance that is *effective* in implementing the right in question and *consistent* with all other CRC provisions.[1] The CRC Committee has directed that appropriate support for parents in their role as primary caregivers necessitates that States do not separate children from their parents *unless* it is in the child's best interests.[2] Hence, the primary responsibility for a child's upbringing and development implies that, in ordinary circumstances, parents and children will be entitled to reside together. The preceding chapter on Art 16 demonstrates that this

1 See Chapter 4 (Section 4.2.1).

2 *General Comment No 7*, UN Doc CRC/C/GC/7/Rev.1, para 18.

assumption is completely undermined in the context of TLM. Moreover, while Art 18 does not define the child-rearing responsibilities that pertain to the parental role as primary caregiver, the CRC provisions previously examined illustrate that these responsibilities include the securing of living conditions (with State assistance) necessary for children's physical, mental, spiritual, moral and social development as identified in Art 27; and the provision of direction and guidance to children as embodied in Art 5.

Parents having primary responsibility for their children's upbringing and development is also inextricably linked with children's right to be cared for by their own parents as far as possible under Art 7. Hence, Arts 18 and 7 are considered together in this chapter. Combined, all of the articles considered in Part B reflect, as the CRC Committee has highlighted, the crucial role that parents play in children's capacity to realise their rights.[3] Moreover, each of the measures identified in relation to specific articles in previous chapters present States with an opportunity to *increase the extent* to which children can be cared for by their parents by enhancing parents' capacity to remain actively involved in children's care and upbringing, even if they must migrate for employment.

7.2 Recognition of the importance of supporting parents as primary carers

7.2.1 The significance of Articles 18 and 7 to children's well-being

Articles 18 and 7 together protect the primary role of parents in children's upbringing and care, premised on knowledge that strong and healthy child-parent relationships are critical to children's well-being, development and best interests.[4] In this light, these articles must be understood in relation to other CRC articles that protect more specific aspects of the child-parent relationship, including Arts 27, 10, 5 and 16 as identified in the normative and conceptual framework outlined in Chapter 2. [5]

i. Article 18

Article 18(2) specifies that the *purpose* of State assistance to parents is to guarantee and promote children's CRC rights. Hence, if TLM is considered a measure by States to assist parents to provide for their children, then it must not undermine or impede other CRC rights, such as children's rights to have direct and regular contact with their parents and have their family life protected. As Tobin and Seow explain, while States maintain a degree of discretion regarding the nature of the

3 Ibid para 15.
4 See Chapter 2 (Section 2.3.1).
5 See Chapter 2 (Section 2.3).

assistance provided to parents, 'such assistance must still be effective and consistent with the provisions of the Convention'.[6]

The CRC Committee has reiterated that the appropriate assistance to parents required from States under Art 18 is interconnected with State duties to assist parents to secure living conditions necessary for their children's development under Art 27.[7] The Committee has also recognised that economic pressures can force parents to work far away from their families, directly impacting their children.[8] Hence, it has urged States to provide assistance that responds to the reality that many parents often have no choice but to combine poorly paid employment with their parental responsibilities; and that the realisation of children's rights depends largely on their carers' available resources and own well-being.[9] The Committee has also emphasised that negative impacts on young children are potentially at their greatest when children experience disrupted relationships with their parents/primary caregivers, including through separation.[10]

Additionally, Article 18(1) demands that States 'shall use their best efforts' to *ensure* that *both* parents share common responsibilities for their children's upbringing and development. This imposes a positive obligation on States to proactively encourage and support parents to share child-rearing responsibilities. It is recognised that States cannot force parents to allocate parental responsibilities in a particular way. However, this positive obligation implies that State policies should, at the least, not undermine the capacity of parents to share child-rearing responsibilities. Rather, States should be taking reasonable measures to support, educate, and incentivise parents to act in accordance with this principle of shared parental responsibility.[11] Hence, together with a child's right to maintain direct and regular contact with *both* parents if separated under Art 10(2),[12] Art 18 protects children's right to be raised by *both* parents, unless it is not in their best interests.

However, parental capacity to share day-to-day child-rearing responsibilities is undermined by TLM policies that encourage the migration of one or both parents. As discussed in Chapters 4 and 5, children are frequently left with alternative caregivers who assume primary responsibility for their upbringing and development.[13] Even if these caregivers are other family members, as discussed, these arrangements cannot be presumed to adequately or rightfully replace a parent's role in a child's life.[14] Rather, the recognition of the family in human rights law as

6 John Tobin and Florence Seow, 'Article 18. Parental Responsibilities and State Assistance' in J Tobin (ed), *The UN Convention on the Rights of the Child: A Commentary* (OUP, 2019) 646, 651.
7 *General Comment No 7*, UN Doc CRC/C/GC/7/Rev.1, para 20.
8 Ibid para 19.
9 Ibid paras 20–1.
10 Ibid para 18.
11 Tobin and Seow, above n 6, 650.
12 See Chapter 5 on Art 10(2).
13 See Chapter 4 (Section 4.3.2) and Chapter 5 (Section 5.4.3).
14 See Chapter 5 (Section 5.4.3).

the most significant environment for children's growth and development,[15] which is entitled to the 'widest possible protection and assistance',[16] provides the broader context within which Art 18 should be understood.[17] To this end, the CRC and the CRC Committee recognise that the extended family can complement but does not displace the child-parent relationship in children's upbringing, which is a protected relationship regardless of a family's structure.[18]

ii. Article 7

The CRC recognises that children's right to be cared for by their own parents is limited to what is 'possible' both in terms of practical limitations and in considering the rights of parents themselves.[19] However, this limitation does not absolve States of their duty to take all reasonable measures within available resources to assist parents to be able to care for their children if they want to be their children's carers.[20] In the context of parents migrating *because* they want to provide for their children, the desire to care for their children is clearly evident.[21] Regardless, States require these parents to sacrifice their day-to-day role in their children's upbringing, by requiring their physical separation and failing to adopt measures to enable migrant workers to continue their parenting role during the period of employment. Measures that are reasonably available and would assist migrant workers to engage in transnational parenting are discussed in Chapter 5 in relation to Arts 10 (2) and 5.[22]

The principle in Art 7 – that children should be cared for by their own parents to the greatest extent possible – has long been recognised as an important notion in children's development and rights. For example, the earlier non-binding *Declaration of the Rights of the Child (1959)* articulated the principle that '[t]he child … shall, wherever possible, grow up in the care and under the responsibility of his parents'.[23] Similarly, the non-binding *Declaration on Social and Legal Principles relating to the Protection and Welfare of Children (1986)* held that '[t]he first priority for a child is to be cared for by his or her own parents'.[24] These

15 *CRC* Preamble.
16 *ICESCR* art 10.
17 See Chapter 3 (Section 3.4) on the fundamental role of the family in human rights law.
18 *General Comment No 7*, UN Doc CRC/C/GC/7/Rev.1, para 15. See, eg, *CRC* art 5 of the CRC. See also Chapter 5 (Section 5.4.3).
19 John Tobin and Florence Seow, 'Article 7. The Rights to Birth Registration, a Name, Nationality, and to Know and Be Cared for By Parents' in J Tobin (ed), *The UN Convention on the Rights of the Child: A Commentary* (OUP, 2019) 236, 271–2.
20 Ibid 271–2, 277–8.
21 This is discussed in relation to parental motivations for migrating in Chapter 4 (see Section 4.2).
22 See Chapter 5.
23 *Declaration of the Rights of the Child*, UN Doc A/RES/14/1386, principle 6.
24 *Declaration on Social and Legal Principles relating to the Protection and Welfare of Children, with Special Reference to Foster Placement and Adoption Nationally and*

Declarations not only provide context for understanding Art 7, but also demonstrate that States are cognisant of the importance to children's well-being that they are cared for by their own parents whenever possible. Hence, the CRC Committee has stressed the primary role that parents play in promoting a child's development and well-being in its guidance to States on implementing rights in early childhood.[25]

7.2.2 Benefits of supporting the child-parent relationship to children's development

It is recognised that parental care and parental presence are not the sole factors contributing to the quality of the environment in which children are raised.[26] As discussed in Chapter 5, many families are able to raise children when parents migrate for employment without significant detriment to the children's well-being and development.[27] However, as also discussed, this is achieved with little assistance from States and depends largely on a family's available resources, the capacity of alternative caregivers, employer discretion and a parent's migration status.[28] Hence, as Edillon observes in her study on the effects of parental migration on the rights of children in the Philippines, while individual families decide what is best for children, government policies are needed to support these families in their decisions and protect the rights of these children.[29]

i. Early childhood development

To date, labour-receiving States have failed to acknowledge the potential impacts of TLM on child-parent relationships, including the impact that disruptions to the child-parent attachment may have for children's early childhood development (ECD).[30] This is symptomatic of a tendency in policy-making to overlook the importance of ECD to children's well-being and the effective realisation of their rights.[31] The risks of this oversight are particularly significant given that ECD sets

Internationally, GA Res 41/85, UN GAOR, 95th plen mtg, UN Doc A/RES/41/85 (3 December 1986) art 3.

25 Ineta Ziemele, *A Commentary on the United Nations Convention on the Rights of the Child, Article 7: The Right to Birth Registration, Name and Nationality, and the Right to Know and Be Cared for by Parents* (Brill, 2007) 1; *General Comment No 7*, UN Doc CRC/C/GC/7/Rev.1.

26 Rosemarie Edillon, *The Effects of Parent's Migration on the Rights of Children Left Behind in the Philippines*, August 2008, UNICEF, ii.

27 See Chapter 5 (Section 5.4).

28 See Chapter 5 (Sections 5.3 and 5.4).

29 Edillon, above n 26, ii.

30 Early childhood development (ECD) generally occurs between the prenatal period and eight years of age. See Emma Pearson and Jennifer Tan Poh Sim, 'Fulfilling Child Rights Through Early Childhood Development' (South-South Cooperation for Child Rights Working Paper, No 3, UNICEF, September 2013) 10.

31 Ibid 14.

patterns for children's later development and future as adults.[32] Nonetheless, TLM policies have failed to incorporate measures to assess and mitigate the potential impacts of child-parent separation on children's ECD, despite labour-receiving countries understanding the importance of early childhood experiences on children's brain development.[33] These experiences include children's interaction and relationships with their primary caregivers.[34] The failure of TLM policies to respond to children's heightened need for their parents to be physically co-present during early childhood was reiterated by key informants in views including:

> 'I even think governments rationalise it a little bit by saying, well they can go back home at the end and be with their kids later, they can have that later'. *(Key Informant – R & P 2)*

This view highlights the failure in TLM policies to comprehend the *changing* needs that children have from their parents as they grow and develop, many of which are specific to a stage of development and cannot be met at a later stage. Moreover, in the context of TLM, it has been found that even if the child-parent relationship is later restored, children often continue to experience a void that they are unable to forget.[35] Moreover, disruption to important attachment relationships can affect young children's behaviour and development and erode child-parent relationships, making it hard to re-establish relationships after the disruption.[36] This is particularly so in the absence of regular and frequent parental contact,[37] which is often constrained in the context of TLM as discussed in Chapter 5. [38] Put simply, as stated by a key informant, 'years matter when the kids are

32 UNICEF, 'The Structural Determinants of Child Well-being' (Expert Consultation Hosted by the UNICEF Office of Research, Florence, 22–23 June 2012) 6.

33 World Bank, 'Early Childhood Development' in *World Development Report 2015: Mind, Society, and Behavior* (World Bank, 2015) 98; Center on the Developing Child, Harvard University, *Brain Architecture* <http://developingchild.harvard.edu/science/key-concepts/brain-architecture>; National Scientific Council on the Developing Child, *The Science of Early Childhood Development: Closing the Gap Between What We Know and What We Do* (Center on the Developing Child, Harvard University, January 2007); Anthony Lake and Margaret Chan, 'Putting Science into Practice for Early Child Development' (2014) 385(9980) *The Lancet* 1816–17.

34 Ibid.

35 Artico (2003) cited in Ernesto Castañeda and Lesley Buck, 'Remittances, Transnational Parenting, and the Children Left Behind' [2011] (December) *The Latin Americanist* 85, 85.

36 Joan B Kelly and Michael E Lamb, 'Developmental Issues in Relocation Cases Involving Young Children: When, Whether, and How?' (2003) 17(2) *Journal of Family Psychology* 193, 195. See also John Bowlby, *Child Care and the Growth of Love: Abridged and Edited by Margery Fry. With Two New Chapters by Mary D Salter Ainsworth* (Penguin Books, 1965).

37 Ibid.

38 See Chapter 5 (Section 5.3).

young'.[39] This goes to the need for TLM policies to adopt measures that are appropriate and modifiable according to children's age and capacity, to assist parents and children to maintain their relationship, as discussed in Chapters 4 and 5. [40]

The importance of child-parent relationships to children's emotional, social, personal and cognitive development, and the potential adverse effects of disrupted child-parent relationships on children's development and well-being, have both been widely acknowledged.[41] In relation to ECD, it is understood that young children need regular contact with and caregiving from their attachment figures for attachment formation to occur and for relationships to be fostered, maintained and strengthened.[42] For young children in particular, loss of an important attachment figure, if that person was actively involved in the child's care, is considered a central risk factor.[43] As discussed in Chapter 4, TLM policies are encouraging the migration of women migrant workers, particularly in the care and health sectors, many of whom are their children's primary attachment figure prior to migration.[44] Hence, the known potential impacts to a child's development and well-being of a major disruption to the relationship with a primary attachment figure demonstrates the foreseeable interferences caused by TLM policies with children's rights under Arts 7 and 18 as well as Art 27 (as discussed in Chapter 4).

While it may be argued that 'attachment theory' in child psychology is a 'Western' concept,[45] there is sufficient evidence demonstrating that children universally – which includes from labour-sending countries – experience loss when separated from their parents/primary caregivers.[46] This is demonstrated in Chapter 4 in relation to the impact of parental absence on children's psychosocial development needs,[47] and highlighted in Castenada and Buck's study on remittances and transnational parenting as follows:

> It becomes more difficult to justify being left behind in exchange for remittances given what is known about the profound impact the relationship with the primary caregiver has on one's life course … the choice between emotional and economic well-being becomes an impossible one.[48]

39 Interview with Key Informant (R & P 4).
40 See Chapter 4 (Section 4.4) and Chapter 5 (Section 5.4.4).
41 Kelly and Lamb, above n 36, 194–5; See also Bowlby, above n 36; M E Lamb et al, 'Parent-Child Relationships: Development in the Context of the Family' in M H Bornstein and M E Lamb (eds), *Developmental Psychology: An Advanced Textbook* (Lawrence Erlbaum Associates Publishers, 1999) 411.
42 Ibid.
43 Kelly and Lamb, above n 36, 195, 197–8.
44 See Chapter 4 (Section 4.3.2.i).
45 See Chapter 2 (Section 2.3).
46 See Chapter 4 (Section 4.3).
47 See Chapter 4 (Section 4.3).
48 Castaneda and Buck, above n 35, 85.

As the World Bank has observed in relation to ECD, all children go through the same sequence of physical, emotional and cognitive growth and development.[49] Hence, the centrality of a child's relationship with his or her primary caregiver to their development and well-being is of equal importance to the children of migrant workers as to any child at all stages of child development.

ii. Assisting parents across children's developmental stages

As discussed in Chapter 5, effective measures to support children's relationships with their parents will be influenced by both the child's stage in the life-course and their parent's stage in the migration cycle.[50] UNICEF has reiterated that adopting a 'life-course' approach to policy-making enables child-centred interventions to be tailored to children's key development stages.[51] As parenting support is intended to assist parents to execute their caregiving role in a functional sense,[52] necessary measures of assistance will inevitably vary depending on their child's stage of development. In addition to age, other social structural variables (such as gender and culture) need to be considered *together with* individual variations specific to the child and family, in order to understand a child's particular needs and identify measures that are in that child's best interests.[53] This can be achieved through the use of best interests assessments as outlined in Chapter 4, which are currently omitted from TLM policies.[54]

As well as being a legal obligation on States under Arts 18 and 27, the need to provide parental assistance is grounded in recognition that enhanced parental capacity reduces risks to children and optimises their development in both the immediate and long term.[55] This reflects the reality that children's ability to enjoy their development rights depends largely on the situation of their parents (and families). As Crock and Benson explain:

> The children's rights will be determined often by the rights of adults with whom they are associated by relationship or responsibility.[56]

49 World Bank, *Early Childhood Development* (24 October 2017) <http://www.worldbank.org/en/topic/earlychildhooddevelopment#1>. See also Rianne Mahon, 'After Neo-Liberalism?: The OECD, the World Bank and the Child' (2010) 10(2) *Global Social Policy* 172, 180.

50 See Chapter 5 (Section 5.4.4).

51 UNICEF, above n 32, 6.

52 UNICEF Office of Research (Innocenti), *Family and Parenting Support: Policy and Provision in a Global Context* (UNICEF, 2015) 12.

53 Jeanette Lawrence and Agnes Dodds, 'Developmental Science, Child Development and the Law' in Lisa Young, Mary Anne Kenny, Geoffrey Monahan (eds), *Children and the Law in Australia* (LexisNexis Butterworths, 2nd ed, 2017) 83.

54 See Chapter 4 (Section 4.4.1.i).

55 UNICEF, above n 32, 1.

56 Mary Crock and Lenni B Benson, 'Central Issues in the Protection of Child Migrants' in Mary Crock and Lenni Benson (eds), *Protecting Migrant Children: In Search of Best Practice* (Elgar, 2018) 1, 20.

However, rather than strengthening parental capacity, current TLM policies limit the ability of migrant workers to fulfil many of the parental rights, roles and responsibilities associated with their children's upbringing and development. Moreover, by encouraging remigration, the period of child-parent separation is often prolonged and spans multiple stages of their children's development. The issue of remigration is discussed in Chapter 6. [57] Reducing remigration is one of a number of measures identified in previous chapters that could effectively support parents to fulfil their child-rearing responsibilities. The complete undermining of the parental role by TLM policies, which fail to support migrant workers to continue fulfilling their child-rearing responsibilities, was captured in the observations of key informants including:

> 'When a kid is brought up, he needs his parents and he needs attention from many others as well. If something is missing, there is always an effect ... even if you don't see negative results for the kid, from the parent's perspective, it's a loss in life when you have to separate from your children. Because the joy of having children is really to watch them grow up'. *(Key Informant – Government 1)*

This observation supports the presumption in the CRC, and particularly in Arts 9 and 10, that children and parents should not be separated *unless* it is in the child's best interests. Together with a child's right to be cared for by his or her parent's as far as possible under Art 7, the CRC's presumption in favour of non-separation implies that important aspects of the child-parent relationship require parents to be *physically with* their children as they grow and develop. Importantly, in the event of child-parent separation, factors that are recognised to contribute to the likelihood of children achieving their psychological potential include their ability to maintain *meaningful* relationships with both parents.[58] This once again demonstrates that the CRC rights that protect the child-parent relationship are steeped in an understanding about the importance, to overall development and well-being, of children's strong and healthy relationships with their parents and primary caregivers.

7.2.3 The value of the child-parent relationship in labour-receiving countries

The vast discrepancy between support for citizens in their role as primary caregivers in labour-receiving countries and the failure to assist migrant workers to fulfil their parental responsibilities is evident in multiple domestic settings, including family law and employment regulation. In countries like Canada and Australia, measures taken by governments to support parents include the provision of paid

57 See Chapter 6 (Section 6.4.2).
58 Kelly and Lamb, above n 36, 196.

parental leave to enable children to be cared for primarily by one parent in their first year of life, and carers leave to enable parents to care for sick children. These types of leave provisions comprise reasonable measures that are not available to migrant workers but could be adopted to reduce the degree of interference with a child's right to be cared for by his or her parents.

Granted that it is unlikely that migrant workers would ever be extended the same family leave provisions as citizens of labour-receiving countries, more limited paid leave provisions could include funded return home visits (including at times of major significance for families) as discussed in Chapter 5.[59] That is, the gap between current TLM practices and the family rights and support for citizens in labour-receiving countries is so great that labour-receiving States could easily improve their support for families in the context of TLM in ways that would not be too onerous and would allow TLM to remain economically beneficial for labour-receiving States. For example, as mentioned in Chapter 6, the costs associated with a return home visit could be met at least in part by labour-receiving countries, possibly utilising the taxes that they collect from low-waged migrant workers.[60] Moreover, if governments are unwilling to absorb these costs through their TLM programs, measures could be funded through overseas development assistance programs in the same countries from which labour-receiving countries source labour.[61]

Either way, costs associated with paid leave provisions should be shared between labour-receiving and labour-sending States, given that parents work in one State and children are intentionally made to reside in the other. The failure to recognise the benefit of such parental assistance to the well-being of children and families was stressed by key informants in comments such as the following, which was made in the Canadian context:

> 'Family leave is provided because of the recognition of the needs of the family to be together when you have a new baby. You have the right to have your job back ... [and] get paid 75 or 80 percent of your salary for that year. So, recognition of the child, family, motherhood is so much greater for the Canadian citizen than it is for people who aren't citizens'. *(Key Informant – R & P 2)*

This observation reflects how rights that protect and support familial relationships are attached to citizenship, which is one of the reasons why labour-receiving States are reluctant to grant such rights to temporary migrant workers. It is also

59 See Chapter 5 (Section 5.3.1).
60 See Chapter 6 (Section 6.4) n 100.
61 See, eg, Chapter 5 (Section 5.2.3.iv) about the possibility of linking overseas development assistance with the development of ICT infrastructure in labour-sending countries.

used by labour-receiving countries as a basis for explaining and justifying the denial of family rights in existing TLM structures, as discussed in Chapter 6.[62] The different value placed on the child-parent relationship for citizens, as opposed to migrant workers, is most evident in family law in relation to the measures considered necessary by labour-receiving States to support parents and children to maintain their relationship in the event of divorce and parental relocation. These measures, combined with measures to support family life in employment regulation, can inform measures that could be incorporated into TLM policies to reduce interference with rights protecting the child-parent relationship.

i. The child-parent relationship in family law as compared to TLM

An understanding of the importance of strong child-parent relationships to children's development (in ordinary circumstances) informs domestic practices in relation to family law in countries like Australia and Canada. This reflects an accepted understanding about the potential implications of disrupting children's primary attachments, particularly when children are young. As expressed by Judge Robyn Sexton:

> It seems generally accepted that serious disruption to the child's primary attachments can lead to adverse outcomes, including subsequent mental health issues, throughout that child's life span.[63]

However, while strong child-parent relationships are important for *all* children – and the CRC protects this relationship for *all* children – labour-receiving countries assign a lesser importance to this relationship for the children of migrant workers than for children who are their citizens. For example, in relation to post-divorce relocation, psychologists have argued that '[y]oung children are not designed to cope with the separation from their parents'[64] and that 'optimal outcomes for most children do not start with separated parents'.[65] They have therefore emphasised the need for decision-makers to understand the consequences of disrupting children's attachment relationships[66] and how to best achieve 'tolerable' outcomes for children upon separation.[67] In this context, significant physical distances between parents and children are considered to be a barrier to maintaining a close

62 See Chapter 6 (Section 6.3.2).

63 Federal Magistrate Robyn Sexton, 'Parenting Arrangements for the 0–4 Year Age Group' (Paper presented at the Legal Aid NSW Family Law Conference, Hanoi, 13–15 September 2011) 30–1.

64 James G Byrne et al, 'Practitioner Review: The Contribution of Attachment Theory to Child Custody Assessments' (2005) 46(2) *Journal of Child Psychology and Psychiatry* 115, 118.

65 Richard Bowlby and Jennifer McIntosh, 'John Bowlby's Legacy and Meanings for the Family Law Field: In Conversation with Sir Richard Bowlby' (2011) 49(3) *Family Court Review* 549, 549.

66 Kelly and Lamb, above n 36, 193.

67 Bowlby and McIntosh, above n 65, 549.

and continuing relationship.[68] Moreover, lengthy periods of separation comprising months or years at a time are understood to increase the likelihood 'that relationships will weaken or become nonexistent over time'.[69] This highlights the inconsistences between the value ascribed to the child-parent relationship in relation to divorce in labour-receiving countries, as compared to the TLM policies in labour-receiving countries that assume the prolonged separation of children and parents.[70] This blatant contrast reflects how the children of migrant workers are denied CRC rights that protect the child-parent relationship based on a lack of citizenship and belonging to the country in which their parents are employed, as discussed in Chapter 6.[71]

It is recognised that families can mitigate the barriers presented by physical distances, particularly in relation to older children, through frequent travel and communication. However, as with migrant workers, this necessitates that the family have a certain level of available resources and the flexibility and freedom to travel. This contrasts with the constraints on travel and communication faced by many migrant workers that are discussed in Chapter 5 in relation to Art 10(2). The dependence on access to resources to maintain transnational child-parent relationships in any context was reiterated by key informants in statements including:

> 'There must be lots of cases of divorced families with parents living in two different countries ... Obviously, they have to have money to do this kind of back-and-forth, so we're talking about middle-class families. So, *class* always plays a role'. *(Key Informant – R & P 4)*

This echoes the findings in Chapter 5 that migrants from other social classes, such as skilled migrants, have significantly greater available resources than low-waged migrant workers to adopt strategies to maintain child-parent relationships transnationally *without* State assistance.[72] Hence, reasonable measures to assist parents to maintain transnational relationships with their children can look to those strategies used by families with resources and endeavour to make these available to low-waged migrant workers. Such measures are identified in Chapters

68 Patrick Parkinson, Judy Cashmore and Judi Single, 'The Need for Reality Testing in Relocation Cases' (2010) 44(1) *Family Law Quarterly* 1, 1; Kelly and Lamb, above n 36, 199–200.

69 Kelly and Lamb, above n 36, 200.

70 For a detailed comparison of specific differences in how family law values the child-parent relationship in the context divorce compared to how this relationship is devalued in the context of TLM, see Daphna Hacker, *Legalized Families in the Era of Bordered Globalization* (Cambridge University Press, 2017) 210–11.

71 See Chapter 6 (Section 6.3.2).

72 See Chapter 5 (Section 5.3).

5 and 6 and include, for example, subsidisation of travel costs and circulation-friendly visas to facilitate easy movement between the different States in which the parent and child reside.[73]

ii. Considerations for courts in decisions on relocation are ignored in TLM

When children and parents are separated in domestic settings in countries like Australia and Canada, the Court's paramount consideration must be the best interests of the child, which requires a determination to be made based on the particulars of a case.[74] This returns to the necessity to understand the specific development needs of a child, as discussed in Section 7.2.2. As Judge Robyn Sexton explains in the context of Australian family law:

> The question will be how long can this particular child's absence from an attachment figure be sustained before attachment formation will be damaged and/or the child will experience a sense of loss?[75]

However, in the context of TLM, the best interests of the children of migrant workers are ***not even considered as a group***, let alone on a case-by-case basis. In Australian family law, determining a child's best interests requires courts to consider whether 'children have the benefit of both of their parents having a meaningful involvement in their lives'.[76] Like the CRC, Australian family law legislation recognises that it is not always possible for parents to share equally in the care of their children. However, it holds that where shared care is not practical, then courts should consider ordering that the child spend 'substantial and significant time' with each parent if it is reasonably practical to do so.[77] In comparison to the duration of child-parent separation generated by TLM, 'substantial and significant time' with a parent is understood in a domestic setting to be time that allows for the parent's involvement in the child's daily routine and in events of significance to the child; and allows for the child's involvement in events of significance to the parent.[78] This represents the degree of parental involvement that governments in labour-receiving countries perceive as being necessary for children who are their citizens to exercise their right to maintain relations with both parents.

Importantly, in family law, it is recognised that 'virtual visitation' is increasing opportunities for parents and children to maintain contact when physical visits are

73 See Chapter 5 (Section 5.3) and Chapter 6 (Section 6.4).

74 Helen Rhoades, 'Revising Australia's Parenting Laws: A Plea for a Relational Approach to Children's Best Interests' (2010) 22(2) *Child and Family Law Quarterly* 172. See, eg, *Family Law Act 1975* (Cth) s 60CA (in Australia).

75 Judge Sexton, above n 63, 34.

76 *Family Law Amendment (Shared Parental Responsibility) Act 2006* (Cth) s 60B(1)(a).

77 *Family Law Act 1975* (Cth) s 65DAA(2).

78 Ibid s 65DAA(3).

rendered impossible or impracticable due to distance.[79] However, this continues to be viewed as a measure to *supplement* the direct contact that is achieved through physical visits.[80] This is reflected in the view of the Family Law Council of Australia that:

> [C]ommunication over the telephone and internet does have a place, but is not sufficient for the child to maintain a meaningful relationship with a parent who lives elsewhere at some distance.[81]

This highlights the interconnectedness between the need for measures to support children to realise their right to direct and regular contact and personal relations with their parents under Art 10(2) and effective measures to assist parents to fulfil their parenting role in the context of TLM.

7.2.4 Parental care is recognised as protective for the child

Active parental involvement in a child's life is generally considered to be a protective factor for the child. This is reflected in the fact that in relation to TLM, it has been found that parental absence can heighten children's risk of abuse.[82] This is particularly so if children are not subject to the same degree of oversight that would have been provided by the absent parent.[83] In this context, the absence of a child's primary caregiver creates an additional risk factor for the child that may be compounded by other factors including poverty and suitability of alternative caregivers. This should be viewed in light of the serious child protection challenges continuing to be faced in labour-sending regions.[84] For example, countries in the Asia-Pacific have declared the need to adopt preventative 'policies that focus on safeguarding children from potential harm'.[85] Encouraging the prolonged absence of children's primary caregivers runs counter to a preventative approach to child protection. Moreover, given the prevalence of TLM, it is necessary for States to adopt measures to address these heightened risks to children, such as the mainstreaming of support for the children of migrant workers in education, health and justice systems, as discussed in Chapter 4. [86]

79 Sarah Gottfried, 'Virtual Visitation: The Wave of the Future in Communication Between Children and Non-Custodial Parents in Relocation Cases' (2002) 36(3) *Family Law Quarterly* 475, 476.
80 Ibid 477.
81 Family Law Council, *Relocation: A Report to the Attorney-General Prepared by the Family Law Council* (Commonwealth of Australia, May 2006) 3.
82 Rasika Jayasuriya and Brian Opeskin, 'The Migration of Women Domestic Workers from Sri Lanka: Protecting the Rights of Children Left Behind' (2015) 48 *Cornell International Law Journal* 579, 613–15.
83 Ibid.
84 UNICEF, *The Beijing Declaration on South-South Cooperation for Child Rights in the Asia Pacific Region*, High-Level Meeting on Cooperation for Child Rights in the Asia Pacific Region (Beijing, 4–6 November 2010) [11].
85 Ibid [13].
86 See Chapter 4 (Section 4.3.3.iv).

As Isaksen et al explain, when children's primary caregivers migrate, children often harbour private and profound doubts about why their parent(s) left and these feelings can undermine the child-parent relationship.[87] This is irrespective of whether children are well cared for by extended families.[88] This is because the child-parent relationship is of equal value, and entitled to equal protection, regardless of a child's nationality. While parental migration impacts each family unit differently, it is in the context of TLM that 'we see how the distorted and eroded family ties of the South support the market of the North'.[89] Current TLM policies systematically disrupt child-parent relationships in labour-sending countries by creating protracted periods of separation and simultaneously failing to assist parents to maintain their role as their children's primary carer during (and after) separation.

7.3 Creating coherence with international development and migration governance agendas going forward

The undermining of the family unit through low-waged TLM is occurring simultaneously with research that confirms that sustainable economic development is only achievable through the strengthening of stable family units.[90] Discounting the known benefits to children of strong child-parent relationships, labour-receiving countries continue to employ TLM policies that deliberately separate children and parents for prolonged periods. This is to meet their own desire to keep wages low in certain sectors and limit costs associated with the employment of migrant workers by restricting their rights and entitlements.[91] As discussed in Chapter 6, by keeping migrant workers on a temporary migration status and not permitting family accompaniment, labour-receiving States are able to 'off-shore' costs usually associated with workers and their families, such as healthcare, education, childcare and aged care.[92] Hence, children's rights are compromised so that labour-receiving countries can benefit economically; and labour-sending countries are left to bear the costs associated with a worker's family that would normally be met by the State of employment if children were permitted to move with their parents. As Silvey highlights, this amounts to a direct 'development subsidy from poor to wealthy countries'.[93] It also reflects, as Freeman explains, 'the way the powerful

87 Lise Widding Isaksen, Sambasivan Uma Devi and Arlie Russell Hochschild, 'Global Care Crisis: A Problem of Capital, Care Chains, or Commons?' (2008) 52(3) *American Behavioral Scientist* 405, 419.

88 See Chapter 4 (Section 4.3) and Chapter 5 (Section 5.4.3).

89 Isaksen, Devi, and Hochschild, above n 87, 419.

90 Savitri Goonesekere, 'Human Rights as a Foundation for Family Law Reform' (2000) 8 *The International Journal of Children's Rights* 83, 83–4.

91 Fiona Williams, 'Markets and Migrants in the Care Economy' (2011) 47 *Soundings* 22, 29.

92 See Chapter 6 (Section 6.3.1). See also Rachel Silvey, 'Transnational Rights and Wrongs: Moral Geographies of Gender and Migration' (2009) 37(2) *Global Gender Justice* 75, 78–9.

93 Silvey, above n 92, 79.

regulate space (social, political, geographical), define participation, marginalise significance and frustrate development',[94] which is discussed in the following section.

7.3.1 Low-waged TLM presents challenges to commitments by labour-sending countries

As less-powerful countries, labour-sending States frequently agree to TLM policies that undermine their own commitments to their nationals to protect the family unit. This is in spite of the principle of international cooperation that requires countries with greater resources to assist those with fewer to implement their CRC obligations, which include protecting children's family life.[95] To demonstrate, Sri Lanka's National Labour Migration Policy recognises that 'low-skilled' labour migration continues to pose the greatest protection issues for migrant workers and their families, including social costs to families and children left behind.[96] Hence, the policy highlights how balancing the promotion of labour migration with the protection of workers and their families remains a continuous challenge for labour-sending countries.[97] TLM policies that demand prolonged child-parent separation constrain not only the capacity of the Sri Lankan Government to fulfil its obligations to protect the child-parent relationship under the CRC, but also under domestic law that incorporates CRC rights and principles. For example, Sri Lanka's Charter on the Rights of the Child requires that:

> The State shall ensure the recognition of the parental right to the care, custody, guardianship and development of a child by providing support through its economic policies.[98]

Directly incorporating Art 18 of the CRC, the Charter further holds that 'parents or guardians of a child shall have the primary responsibility of maintaining, upbringing and developing the child'; and that 'the State shall render appropriate assistance to parents or guardians of the child in the performance of the child rearing responsibilities'.[99] Similarly, Filipino domestic legislation – enacted over two decades ago – recognises that while remittances contribute significantly to the national economy, the State does not promote overseas employment as a means to sustain economic growth and achieve national development.[100] Rather, the State shall 'create local employment opportunities'[101] in pursuit of the ideal that

94 Michael Freeman, 'The Value and Values of Children's Rights' in Antonella Invernizzi and Jane Williams (eds), *The Human Rights of Children From Visions to Implementation* (Ashgate, 2011) 21, 21.

95 The principle of international cooperation in discussed in Chapter 3 (Section 3.3) and Chapter 6 (Section 6.3.3.i).

96 Sri Lankan Ministry for Foreign Employment Promotion and Welfare, *National Labour Migration Policy for Sri Lanka* (Government of Sri Lanka, October 2008) 2.

97 Ibid.

98 Government of Sri Lanka, *Charter on the Rights of the Child* (1992) art 19.

99 Ibid.

100 *Migrant Workers and Overseas Filipinos Act of 1995* (Republic Act No 8042) s 2(c).

101 Ibid.

'overseas employment no longer becomes the only recourse for families to have better lives, and instead simply becomes one of the options'.[102]

These commitments in domestic law and policy reflect an understanding in labour-sending countries that it is not ideal for families to have their primary source of income dependent on family members migrating and re-migrating. In this regard, human rights institutions have encouraged governments in the Asia-Pacific region to reject attempts to formalise the 'export of workers' as a strategy to sustain national economic growth and development.[103] However, despite a duty under the CRC to support less resourced countries in their efforts to reduce interferences with children's rights, the policy goals of labour-sending countries to reduce low-waged TLM are unsupported by and incompatible with the actions of labour-receiving countries. Rather, labour-receiving countries are increasingly demanding more low-waged migrant workers in a growing number of sectors. This conflict in objectives was reiterated by key informants in views such as:

> 'These are mostly unilateral measures, because governments [in labour-sending countries] know that nothing happens at the other end. The destination countries will not do anything'. *(Key Informant – MLO-NGO 6)*

This view reveals the lack of genuine international cooperation in the context of TLM, which would involve the sharing of responsibility for managing the social costs of TLM policies between labour-receiving and labour-sending countries.[104] Hence, the legitimate objective in the national policies of labour-sending countries of attempting to reduce low-waged TLM in recognition that it is not good for children and families accords with State obligations under the CRC to protect the family unit, children's family life and the parental role as primary caregiver. However, it conflicts with the aim by labour-receiving States, responsible for determining TLM policies, to keep filling their labour needs with a continual flow of cheaper labour. Efforts to prove that the latter aim is also legitimate focus on propagating the 'migration–development nexus', which is based on remittance-based measures that do not assess the social impacts of TLM that are generated in parallel for children and families. This is discussed in Section 7.3.4 in relation to the need for improved data collection to inform decision-making and the identification of effective protective strategies for children. Moreover, the separation of children and parents (recognised by labour-sending States as being problematic)

102 Rebecca J Calzado, Department of Labor and Employment Philippines, 'Labour Migration and Development Goals: The Philippine Experience' (Paper presented at International Dialogue on Migration, Geneva, 8 October 2007) 4.

103 SEANF, '2010 South East Asia National Human Rights Institutions Forum (SEANF) Paper on Migrant Workers' (2010) 11(1) *Asia-Pacific Journal on Human Rights and the Law* 63.

104 See Chapter 3 (Section 3.3) on the principle of international cooperation.

clearly interferes with a number of CRC rights and principles and these interferences have not been justified by labour-receiving States to date.

7.3.2 Perceived willingness in labour-receiving States to engage with these challenges

Limiting the rights of migrant workers should be understood in the context of the broader reduction of labour rights for *all* workers in the pursuit of cheaper labour that is characteristic of neoliberalism and economic globalisation.[105] This was emphasised by key informants across all sectors in observation such as:

> 'Employers and governments rarely think about children even in the domestic policy context [in labour-receiving countries] ... Employers and government don't think about the working conditions, working hours, quality of wages, all those things that affect families and their children'. *(Key Informant – R & P 7)*

In the context of TLM, the failure to recognise and address the impact of employment policies on children is compounded by the absence of political will to protect the rights of children affected by migration.[106] Hence, inadequate provisioning by States to assist workers to meet their parental responsibilities is heightened for migrant workers and access to measures remains almost entirely employer-dependent, as discussed in Chapter 5 in relation to Art 10(2).

i. Protecting children's rights against interferences arising from employer practices

In human rights law, the duty to 'protect' from harm imposes an obligation on States to prevent non-State actors from interfering with individual rights.[107] This is essential because of the increasing privatisation of many areas of State activity, including in the provision of care, and is a necessary means to hold employers accountable for practices that impede human rights.[108] The CRC Committee has stressed the importance of States developing legal and institutional frameworks to ensure that children's rights are protected in relation to business activities.[109]

105 Nicola Piper, 'Global Governance of Labour Migration: From "Management" of Migration to an Integrated Rights-based Approach' in Peter Drahos (ed), *Regulatory Theory: Foundations and Applications* (ANU Press, 2017) 375, 379.

106 Julia O'Connell Davidson and Caitlin Farrow, *Child Migration and the Construction of Vulnerability* (Save the Children, 2007) 22.

107 See Chapter 3 (Section 3.2.2).

108 Goonesekere, above n 90, 96.

109 CRC Committee, *General Comment No 16 (2013) on State Obligations Regarding the Impact of the Business Sector on Children's Rights*, UN Doc CRC/C/GC/16 (17 April 2013) para 4 ('*General Comment No 16*').

This is because of the potential 'lifelong, irreversible and even transgenerational consequences' that business practices can have on children; and the imbalance between the significant influence that the business sector has on government decision-making as compared to the often disregarded impact on children.[110]

In relation to respecting, protecting and fulfilling children's rights impacted by business activities, the CRC Committee has held that the duty to respect requires States to not be directly or indirectly involved in the infringement of children's rights. This demands that business-related decision-making, laws and policies 'be transparent, informed and include full and continuous consideration of the impact on the rights of the child'.[111] The Committee has further directed that the duty to protect requires States to 'take all necessary, appropriate and reasonable measures to prevent business enterprises from causing or contributing to abuses of children's rights', including introducing, monitoring and enforcing regulatory measures.[112] Failure to take reasonable measures to prevent businesses from infringing children's rights renders States responsible for these infringements and in breach of their general obligation to protect children's rights under Art 4 of the CRC.[113] Finally, State obligations to fulfil children's rights requires States to take positive measures to facilitate, promote and provide for the enjoyment of children's rights that are impacted by business practices.[114]

In addition to directions from the CRC Committee, there is significant guidance available to States and employers on incorporating human rights into business practices that could inform measures to reduce interference with children's rights in the context of TLM.[115] Such guidance includes the UN's Guiding Principles on Business and Human Rights[116] and the draft *Legally Binding Instrument to Regulate, in International Human Rights Law, the Activities of Transnational Corporations and Other Business Enterprises.*[117] The former reiterates that businesses have a duty to 'avoid infringing on the human rights of others' and to

110 Ibid.

111 Ibid para 26.

112 Ibid para 28.

113 Ibid.

114 Ibid para 29.

115 See, eg, UNICEF, *Children's Rights and Business Principles* (UNICEF, 2012); UNICEF and Save the Children, *Children's Rights in Policies and Codes of Conduct: A Tool for Companies* (UNICEF 2013).

116 *Report of the Special Representative of the Secretary General on the Issue of Human Rights and Transnational Corporations and Other Business Enterprises, John Ruggie: Guiding Principles on Business and Human Rights: Implementing the United Nations "Protect, Respect and Remedy" Framework*, 17th sess, Agenda Item 3, UN Doc A/HRC/17/31 (21 March 2011) ('*Guiding Principles on Business and Human Rights*').

117 Open-ended Intergovernmental Working Group on Transnational Corporations and Other Business Enterprises with Respect to Human Rights, *Zero Draft: Legally Binding Instrument to Regulate, in International Human Rights Law, the Activities of Transnational Corporations and Other Business Enterprises* (16 July 2018) ('*Zero Draft*').

'address adverse human rights impacts with which they are involved'.[118] The latter is currently being developed to strengthen the protection of human rights in business practices of a transnational nature, including advancing international cooperation in the fulfilment of State obligations in transnational business contexts.[119] It will be of particular relevance to understanding how States and businesses can better protect children's rights in the context of TLM given its transnational nature. Importantly, the CRC Committee has urged States to ensure that transnational business activities are sufficiently regulated to prevent adverse impacts on children's rights and rights violations *in foreign jurisdictions.* [120] The connection between human rights, responsibility for supply chains and TLM was stressed by key informants in comments such as:

> 'One thing would be to look at the debate around global supply chains from the point of view of global care chains and the concept of due diligence ... saying there is such thing as due diligence and it feeds down the global care chain – there is such thing as responsibility'. *(Key Informant – R & P 3)*

This highlights the potential for TLM policies to be informed by developments in the business sector's engagement with human rights and ethical supply chain management. The CRC Committee has held that measures to ensure the realisation of children's rights impacted by business practices should include awareness-raising 'aimed at challenging and eradicating discriminatory attitudes towards all children, especially those in vulnerable situations'.[121] As discussed in Section 7.2.4, children are particularly vulnerable when their parents have migrated for employment in the context of TLM. Moreover, UNICEF's guidance to companies on supporting children's rights as part of their corporate responsibility includes that businesses provide working conditions that support workers 'in their roles as parents or caregivers'.[122] As an example of good practice in a transnational context, it has highlighted a partnership between a UK multinational company and Chinese women's NGO to provide telephone cards for use between migrant workers and their children.[123] These so-called 'love cards' are seen by the company as a measure to support distance parenting by facilitating regular communication between parents, children and families.[124] The CRC Committee has stressed the importance of 'family-friendly workplace policies', including in relation to working hours and remuneration, on children's development at all ages

118 *Guiding Principles on Business and Human Rights*, UN Doc A/HRC/17/31, annex pt 2 [11].
119 *Zero Draft*, above n 117, art 2.
120 *General Comment No 16*, UN Doc CRC/C/GC/16, para 42.
121 Ibid para 14.
122 UNICEF, above n 115, 21.
123 Ibid.
124 Ibid.

and stages.[125] This again highlights the interconnectedness of measures to support parents in the performance of their familial responsibilities with children's overall development and well-being.

ii. Costs and responsibilities can be shared between States and employers

Presently, instead of demanding employer practices that better protect the rights of migrant workers and their families, TLM policies focus on providing employers with a source of *cheap labour* that has as limited associated costs to the employer as possible. As Williams explains, by employing workers with the least bargaining power wages can be kept low and labour kept 'affordable to individual employers, efficient to the state or profitable to private sector employers'.[126] This is compounded by the fact that these workers come from labour-sending States that also have limited negotiating power in the development of bilateral agreements that govern their workers.

However, as it is employers who benefit from low-waged labour, employers should share in the responsibility for supporting migrant workers to maintain connections with children and family. Nana has emphasised this in relation to the transformation of family life in Asia due to women's increasing migration, stating:

> [E]mployers of migrant women should consider sharing the direct responsibility for transnational parenthood … After all, they are the ones who benefit the most from this international division of reproductive labor. The employers can share responsibility by guaranteeing the time and resources for migrant women … to remain in communication with their family, and not only allow but also pay for their home visits whenever necessary.[127]

Hence, labour-receiving States can either directly subsidise or share with employers the costs of reasonably available measures to support workers to maintain direct regular communication and contact with their children. The ILO have encouraged the sharing of responsibility between States *and* employers to enable work-family reconciliation in the context of migrant workers by adopting the notion of social 'co-responsibility'.[128] This involves measures to support the maintenance of child-parent relationships and family life that reflect those measures identified in Chapters 5 and 6 in relation to Arts 10(2) and 16. To illustrate, the ILO's recommendations concerning co-responsibility for enabling migrant workers to reconcile their work and family commitments include: the creation of

125 *General Comment No 16*, UN Doc CRC/C/GC/16, para 20.

126 Williams, above n 91, 30.

127 Oishi Nana, 'Family Without Borders? Asian Women in Migration and the Transformation of Family Life' (2008) 14(4) *Asian Journal of Women's Studies* 54, 72.

128 Rianne Mahon and Sonya Michel, 'Not In Focus: Migrant Women Caregivers As Seen by the ILO and the OECD' in Sonya Michel and Ito Peng (eds), *Gender, Migration, and the Work of Care: A Multi-Scalar Approach to the Pacific Rim* (Palgrave Macmillan, 2017) 269, 278.

viable local employment opportunities so that families do not have to separate to meet financial needs; facilitating the return and reintegration of migrant workers to prevent remigration; reducing regulatory barriers to opportunities for families to reunite; ensuring equal labour rights for migrant workers; and making employers co-responsible for protecting the legal rights of working parents.[129] As discussed in Chapter 5, these measures will not be effective if they are not stipulated in contracts and regulations and *enforced* by labour-receiving States to remove employer discretion. This is particularly so given that labour-sending countries are extremely limited in their ability to enforce protection measures for their workers residing and employed in labour-receiving countries.

iii. Willingness will be relative to the associated costs for labour-receiving countries

In view of the commitments by countries like Canada and Australia to human rights norms and standards, and Australia's dual development objective in its TLM policies, such countries may be more open to supporting improved communication measures between migrant workers and their children. This is particularly so since such measures do not require permitting children into their jurisdiction and because the associated costs are minimal. Contrary to supporting improved communication measures, it is foreseeable that States will be more reluctant to support measures that involve family accompaniment given the more substantial associated costs. This was captured in observations by key informants including:

> 'With virtual connection, you have to spend some money on the infrastructure and make sure people on both ends have access, but in the modern world that doesn't look too difficult ... and could be something that people would be willing to invest in and see some benefit from. If you get into control over hours, and vacation times, you start to interfere with the dynamics of the labour market, and that's going to be more difficult. If you get into moving people, that's more difficult still'. *(Key Informant – R & P 4)*

While this observation demonstrates the likely connection between the willingness of labour-receiving States to support measures being *relative to the costs* that they will incur, it also reiterates that *even those measures with fewer costs* would reduce interferences with children's rights to a significant degree.

Given the availability of reasonable measures that could reduce interference with CRC rights for very little cost, it is likely that these have not been considered in TLM policies because policymakers have not drawn a connection between labour market programs and children's rights. This notion was expressed by key informants in comments such as:

129 ILO and UNDP (2009) 128 cited in Mahon and Michel, above n 128, 280.

'A lot of policy makers would be aware of the Convention on the Rights of the Child, but its relevance to their policy making about labour market programs would not even occur to them ... I think it's partly because the status of children, both in national domestic and international policy making, is negligible'. *(Key Informant – R & P 7)*

This reflects a general failure in policymaking to consider how employment policies and practices that govern workers affect their children and can limit children's capacity to realise their individually held rights, many of which are interdependent with their parents' rights.[130] However, States have a *duty* to ensure – through information provision, training and support – that government departments and agencies are aware of human rights obligations and observe them both in relation to their own actions and in relation to employment practices that they influence.[131]

As demonstrated in Section 7.2.3, labour-receiving States are well aware of the potential harms to children arising from child-parent separation. They are also aware of the duty to justify potential harms to children arising from State policies, by establishing that such policies are in pursuit of a legitimate aim and use measures that are necessary, proportionate and the least harmful reasonably available to achieve that aim. Moreover, concerns about the impact of parental migration have been widely and publicly raised by the governments of labour-sending countries (as discussed in Section 7.3.1) as well as non-government and international organisations. Hence, denying knowledge of the degree of interferences with children's rights caused by TLM, and possible harms that it creates for children, does not absolve labour-receiving States of their duty to justify these interferences. As expressed by a key informant:

'Even for receiving governments that want to acknowledge their legal obligations to families left behind, I think a big barrier is how to translate that into concrete policy measures and the fiscal implications of such obligations ... That's very tough, and I think that's why there's total inaction – because it's so much easier to simply say we don't know about this'. *(Key Informant – R & P 5)*

This observation stresses the tendency towards inaction and denial when recognising and addressing human rights obligations in complex policy settings appears too difficult and carries unknown financial implications for States. However, this book has endeavoured to break down particular children's rights in the

130 See Chapter 2 (Section 2.1) on the interdependence of children's and parents' rights.
131 *Guiding Principles on Business and Human Rights*, UN Doc A/HRC/17/31, annex pt 1 [8].

context of TLM to highlight the many reasonably available measures that States could adopt to support children who are separated from their parents because of TLM policies.

A summary of these measures in relation to the specific CRC rights and principles is provided in Appendix I. They include, for example, incorporating children's best interests assessments into all stages of TLM policy development, implementation and evaluation; supporting migrant workers to engage in more frequent return home visits, including by providing financial assistance and introducing circulation-friendly visas; ensuring that migrant workers and their children (and alternative caregivers) have access to the technology and privacy needed to engage freely in communication with each other at times suitable for the family; supporting families to prepare for periods of separation, including encouraging parents to involve their children in discussions about parental migration and alternative care arrangements; mainstreaming support for children of migrant workers in education, health and justice sectors to create protective and supportive environments while parents are absent; reducing the deliberate encouragement of remigration in TLM policies and investing in creating viable employment opportunities in labour-sending countries to reduce parents' need to remigrate; prioritising children's rights and best interests in the implementation of the emerging framework for the global governance of migration (which is discussed in Section 7.3.4); and investing in collecting comprehensive, disaggregated and longitudinal data on the social impacts of TLM including on children (which is discussed in Section 7.3.5).

Such measures vary in their associated financial implications, but each would reduce to a different degree the current level of interference caused by TLM with children's rights. Adopting such measures is essential if TLM policies are to comply with State obligations under the CRC to support parents to fulfil their parental responsibilities and to not cause harm to children in other countries. They are also essential if TLM is to genuinely contribute to any sustainable development for communities in labour-sending countries.

7.3.3 Migration, family and the Sustainable Development Agenda

The inextricable connection between TLM policies and children's rights should be absolutely clear in the context of TLM regimes that pursue an international development objective. As the CRC Committee has stated, international aid programs should 'ensure that child rights are respected and protected in all sectors covered by State parties' bilateral and multilateral development cooperation'.[132] Moreover, the Committee has advised States parties that:

> [T]he Convention should form the framework for international development assistance related directly or indirectly to children and that programmes of donor States should be rights-based.[133]

132 *Report on the Forty-sixth Session*, UN Doc CRC/C/46/3, [93.b].
133 *General Comment No 5*, UN Doc CRC/GC/2003/5, para 61.

In the 2030 Sustainable Development Goals (SDGs), States have recognised an inherent connection between migration policy, fair employment practices and sustainable development. Simultaneously, they have recognised a connection between strong family units and sustainable development. Importantly, the SDG goals that do make explicit mention of migrants and migration have been developed in favour of the continuation and growth of labour migration, despite the connection between migration and development not yet being fully proven or accepted.[134] As the Asia Pacific Mission for Migrants highlighted in 2014, countries that have been exporting low-waged labour for decades (such as the Philippines) have not yet 'experienced leaps in their development' or the transformation of economic fundamentals that continue to fuel social disadvantage.[135] Rather, the Mission observed that remittance-based development has serious and far-reaching social impacts and fails to address the underlying economic, social and political challenges associated with underdevelopment in labour-sending countries.[136] This is in spite of the UN General Assembly having resolved that migration policies must promote and protect human rights, especially of children, and avoid 'approaches that might aggravate their vulnerability'.[137]

i. Sustainable Development Goals

SDG targets that explicitly mention migrants and migration ***make no mention*** of measuring or addressing the social costs of labour migration. They instead encourage commitment to protect the labour rights of workers;[138] promote the facilitation of orderly, safe and regular migration through planned and well-managed migration policies; and set targets to reduce remittance transaction costs.[139] The focus by States on measuring the 'success' of TLM based on remittance and efficiency measures was highlighted by key informants in statements including:

> 'They look only at the quantifiable issues ... not the more critical issues – wages, how to improve working conditions and the effects on children left behind'. *(Key Informant – MLO-NGO 6)*

134 See Chapter 4 (Section 4.2) and the Introduction (Research Context) for discussion on the contested role of remittances in international development. See also Deborah Brennan and Elizabeth Adamson, 'Care and Migration' in Sheila Shaver (ed), *Handbook on Gender and Social Policy* (Elgar, 2018) 253, 263; Migration and Development Civil Society Network (MADE), 'Migration and SDG Implementation: The Real Challenge Starts Now' (Briefing Paper, MADE, 18 December 2015) 2.

135 Asia Pacific Mission for Migrants, *Labour Export Program and Further Commodification of Migrants as Prescriptions for Development* (19 September 2014) <http://aprnet.org/?p=196>.

136 Ibid.

137 *Resolution on International Migration and Development*, UN Doc A/RES/71/237, para 5.

138 See *Sustainable Development Agenda*, UN Doc A/RES/70/1, 20 (Goal 8, target 8.8).

139 Ibid 21 (Goal 10, targets 10.7 and 10.10).

This illustrates how measuring the social impacts of TLM is not adequately addressed in the international development agenda including the SDGs, in part because they are not as easily quantified and therefore more difficult to measure. However, the migration-related SDG targets that encourage the more efficient migration of low-waged workers are being pursued *in parallel* with development goals that promote the value of parents and strong families to children's development. This is reflected in IOM's observation that:

> The United Nations General Assembly has recognised the crucial role of the family in fostering human development and has called for due consideration to be given to promoting family policy development when setting the post-2015 development agenda.[140]

To this end, a UN Expert Group on Family policies and the Sustainable Development Agenda found that the degree of parents' availability affects the level of *preventative care* that children receive, which directly relates to 'ensuring healthy lives and promoting well-being for all at all ages' (that is, SDG 3).[141] Moreover, the Group held that:

> [P]olicies promoting children's health must involve families as primary caregivers responsible for their development. Such policies should promote safe and stable family environments and positive parenting.[142]

However, TLM policies that separate parents and dependent children undermine parents' role as primary caregivers and reduce parental availability to children. Reasonable measures that have been identified in relation to supporting the implementation of SDG 3[143] include family-oriented policies and programs that promote children's physical and mental well-being, including programs that boost parental capacity to deliver positive health outcomes for their children.[144] Such

140 IOM, 'Migration and Families: Background Paper' (Intersessional Workshop, International Dialogue on Migration, 7–8 October 2014) 1 citing *Preparations for and Observance of the Twentieth Anniversary of the International Year of the Family*, UN GAOR, 68th sess, Agenda Item 27(b), UN Doc A/C.3/68/L.16/Rev.1 (29 October 2013).

141 *Report of the United Nations Expert Group Meeting: Family Policies and 2030 Sustainable Development Agenda* (UN Department of Economic and Social Affairs, New York, 12–13 May 2016) [14] ('UN Expert Group on Family Policies and Sustainable Development Agenda').

142 UN Expert Group on Family Policies and Sustainable Development Agenda, above n 141, [14] citing *Implementation of the Objectives of the International Year of the Family and its Follow-up Processes: Report of the Secretary-General*, UN ESCOR, 71st sess, UN Doc A/71/61–E/2016/7 (19 November 2015).

143 SDG 3 is for States to 'Ensure healthy lives and promote well-being for all at all ages'. See *Sustainable Development Agenda*, UN Doc A/RES/70/1, 16 (Goal 3).

144 UN Expert Group on Family Policies and Sustainable Development Agenda, above n 141, [16].

policies and programs should be considered in conjunction with TLM policies if they are to be effectively implemented in the context of TLM. At present, as the CMW Committee has observed, stakeholders in many States demonstrate a lack of understanding about the 'innumerable links between migration-related challenges and the SDGs',[145] which 'hampers the implementation of the SDGs overall'.[146]

In relation to SDG 3, it has also been found that children's health and survival is directly affected by their parents' work environments and is improved if parents have supportive workplaces.[147] This highlights the interconnectedness of children's rights, including to health, survival and development, with their parents' workplace rights and entitlements. It is amplified in the context of TLM, where the workplace rights and entitlements of migrant workers are severely restricted given their lack of citizenship and temporary status; and the interconnected rights of their children severely limited because they must reside in a different jurisdiction from their parents. In fact, the CMW Committee has stated that policies that exclude migrant workers from participating in and belonging to the host society in which they live 'based on their status limits the opportunities to implement the SDGs'.[148] In this vein, the CMW Committee has urged that integrating migrant workers and their families into host societies 'is a precondition for the full implementation of the SDGs'.[149]

The UN Expert Group has further highlighted the indisputable benefits to children of *both* parents being actively involved in their children's lives. Under Art 18, States have a duty to support the involvement of both parents in the fulfilment of child-rearing responsibilities, should both parents wish to undertake them. This is interconnected with children's right to have their psychosocial development needs met by their parents under Art 27, with it being found that parental involvement by both mothers *and* fathers, in ordinary circumstances, benefits children socially, psychologically and behaviourally.[150] This highlights how policies that undermine one parent's role in their children's lives can negatively impact children's development and well-being, as discussed in Chapter 4 in relation to Art 27.

Moreover, support for parental involvement in children's education has been found to be important to the implementation of SDG 4, which involves 'ensuring inclusive and equitable quality education and promoting lifelong opportunities for all'.[151] This is because of the established link between parental involvement and

145 CMW Committee, *Contribution to the 2030 Sustainable Development Goals in Response to a Call for Inputs by the High-Level Political Forum on Sustainable Development (HLPF)* (19 April 2018) 1 pt 1 ('*Contribution to the 2030 Sustainable Development Goals*').

146 Ibid 6 pt 4.

147 UN Expert Group on Family Policies and Sustainable Development Agenda, above n 141, [95].

148 CMW Committee, *Contribution to the 2030 Sustainable Development Goals*, above n 145, 3 pt 1.

149 Ibid.

150 UN Expert Group on Family Policies and Sustainable Development Agenda, above n 141, [98].

151 Ibid [21].

improved educational outcomes for children, reduced behavioural problems and dropout rates and improved transitions to adulthood.[152] The Expert Group highlights that parental ability to be actively involved in children's education is often affected by parents' working conditions,[153] which again is heightened in the context of TLM. This reiterates the importance of States adopting measures in TLM policies that facilitate the continued involvement of parents in their children's daily lives to counter some of the negative impacts of a parent's physical absence on their children's development outcomes both in the short and long term.

ii. Investment in children for sustainable development

While it has been recognised that parental employment is central to alleviating poverty, the abovementioned Expert Group has warned of the risks of interfering with children's family life by failing to support parents in their role as children's carers as follows:

> Family life is important for cognitive and behavioural outcomes of children … time constraints to personal care provided by parents at too early an age can hamper child development and family functioning.[154]

The conflict that the undermining of families by TLM poses to the notion of the migration-development nexus was stressed by key informants in views including:

> 'The talk about human development is still not linked to migration policy. You cannot have real development that is going to be sustainable when you break up communities'. *(Key Informant – MLO-NGO 4)*

Hence, in implementing the Sustainable Development Agenda, measures are needed to reconcile the conflicting goals of promoting parental migration as a development strategy; and supporting parental involvement in children's lives to improve their development outcomes.

Beyond the SDGs, UNICEF has stressed the connection between achieving sustainable growth and the need to invest in children, which includes building the capacity and competence of their parents to engage effectively in their development.[155] For example, it has argued that the need to put children at the heart of development strategies is essential because the realisation of children's rights is

152 Ibid.
153 Ibid.
154 Ibid [153].
155 Michael Samson (Economic Policy Research Institute), *Cognitive Capital: Investing in Children to Generate Sustainable Growth* (UNICEF East Asia and the Pacific, October 2016) 24; UNICEF Office of Research (Innocenti), above n 52, 8–9.

'instrumental in achieving long-term developmental impacts'.[156] Furthermore, the CRC Committee has urged that better links be made between children's rights and both migration and international development policies.[157] Even the World Bank – a strong advocate for TLM – has, as Mahon observes, 'embraced early childhood development as a key part of its broader "investing in people" strategy'.[158]

Hence, the conflict between remittance-based development strategies – premised on parental migration – and development strategies focused on enhancing parental involvement in children's growth and development is clearly evident and yet to be reconciled. The emerging framework for the global governance of migration – that features the Global Compact for Migration – is an opportunity to begin reconciling the migration for development agenda with the need to support parents and families in the fulfilment of their child-rearing roles and responsibilities, as envisaged in the CRC and the SDGs discussed above.

7.3.4 Emerging framework for the global governance of migration

As highlighted by the ILO, poorly governed labour migration can generate risks and challenges for low-waged workers and their countries of origin, which include hindering sustainable development.[159] In recognition of the pressing need for improved mechanisms for the governance of migration at a global level, the New York Declaration was adopted by States in 2016.[160] The Declaration laid the foundation for the Global Compact for Migration, which was adopted in December 2018.[161] It is the first-ever framework for international cooperation on migration to be negotiated by States across a spectrum of migration issues that impact countries of origin, transit and migration, as well as migrants themselves and communities impacted by migration.[162]

i. New York Declaration

The New York Declaration identifies a need to implement 'planned and well-managed migration policies' to protect the rights of all migrants and facilitate the safe and regular movement of people in line with the Sustainable Development Agenda.[163] However, it also expresses a commitment by States (noting its non-

156 Samson, above n 155, 24.
157 CRC Committee, *Report of the 2012 Day of General Discussion: The Rights of All Children in the Context of International Migration* (28 September 2012) [42].
158 Mahon, above n 49, 173.
159 ILO, *Reports of the Committee for Labour Migration: Resolutions and Conclusions Submitted for Adoption by the Conference*, 106th sess, Agenda Item 4, Provisional Record 12–1 (15 June 2017) [I.3].
160 *New York Declaration*, UN Doc A/RES/71/1.
161 *Global Compact for Migration*, UN Doc A/RES/73/195.
162 Kathleen Newland, 'Will International Migration Governance Survive the COVID-19 Pandemic?' (MPI Policy Brief, October 2020) 4.
163 *New York Declaration*, UN Doc A/RES/71/1, paras 16, 41.

binding legal status) to address the drivers behind large movements of people by creating conditions that allow people to live in their countries of origin.[164] The Declaration acknowledges that the drivers of migration include 'poverty, underdevelopment, lack of opportunities, poor governance and environmental factors'.[165] Additionally, UN resolutions both preceding and subsequent to the New York Declaration recognise that the sustainable development impact of migration can only be understood if the social and human rights dimensions are considered along with the economic.[166] Moreover, the General Assembly's Resolution on International Migration and Development that followed the New York Declaration reaffirmed that:

> States have the duty to comply with their obligations under international law, including international human rights law, in order to ensure full respect for the human rights of migrants, regardless of their migration status.[167]

The New York Declaration goes further in affirming State commitments to comply with CRC obligations.[168] In this regard, it affirms State commitments to 'giving primary consideration at all times to the best interests of the child'; providing for children's basic needs including their 'psychosocial development'; and striving to provide 'children with a nurturing environment for the full realization of their rights and capabilities'.[169] It also recognises that migration processes can compound children's vulnerability and hence children's best interests must be 'a primary consideration in all relevant policies' as part of State commitments to protect the rights of children impacted by migration.[170]

The General Assembly has declared in the Declaration that '[m]igration should be a choice, not a necessity'.[171] To reduce people's necessity to migrate, it urges States to commit to enhancing employment opportunities for people in their home countries.[172] However, in relation to improving the management of migration, its focus – like the SDGs – is on improving the efficiency of, rather than reducing dependency on, labour migration.[173] Nonetheless, the Declaration appears more measured than the SDGs in relation to promoting labour migration

164 Ibid para 43.
165 Ibid annex II para 7.
166 *Declaration on the High-level Dialogue on International Migration and Development*, GA Res 68/4, UN GAOR, 68th sess, Agenda Item 21(e), UN Doc A/RES/68/4 (21 January 2014) para 1; *Resolution on International Migration and Development*, UN Doc A/RES/71/237, para 2.
167 *Resolution on International Migration and Development*, UN Doc A/RES/71/237, para 8.
168 *New York Declaration*, UN Doc A/RES/71/1, para 32.
169 Ibid.
170 Ibid para 59.
171 Ibid para 43.
172 Ibid para 44.
173 Ibid para 46.

as a development strategy, recognising some of the associated costs and risks as well as limitations to its development potential.

The New York Declaration establishes welcome principles for an international framework for the governance of migration. However, its strengths are limited by its non-binding legal status and its gravitational pull back to a State's sovereign right to exercise immigration control. This is reflected in the Declaration's linking of State commitments 'to protecting the safety, dignity and human rights and fundamental freedoms of all migrants' with the facilitation of 'safe, orderly and regular migration, including return and readmission, taking into account national legislation'.[174] Despite its limitations, however, as Aleinikoff and Martin observe, the emergence of, and agreement to, the Declaration in itself reflects a growing consensus among States around the pressing need for governance measures that transcend State boundaries and are based on international cooperation.[175]

ii. Global Compact for Migration

The recently adopted Global Compact for Migration emerged from the New York Declaration and is considered part of a 15-year agenda that complements the SDGs and is 'aimed primarily at implementing targets 10.7 and 8.8 of the Sustainable Development Goals'.[176] As stated by the UN Special Rapporteur on the human rights of migrants:

> On the basis primarily of targets 10.7 and 8.8, the Special Rapporteur intends to recommend that States and other stakeholders develop long-term strategies to fulfil their obligations towards all migrants, including migrants in a precarious situation, as set out in the Sustainable Development Goals.[177]

However, as discussed in Section 7.3.3, these SDG targets actively promote labour migration as both a development strategy for labour-sending countries and a livelihood strategy for families. This is despite TLM currently requiring families to separate for long periods even if they have dependent children. Without reading these SDG goals in conjunction with those that support the importance of parental involvement and stable family units to children's development, the potential for migration to deliver sustainable development outcomes is severely limited.

Importantly, the Global Compact recognises that low-waged migrant workers face particular barriers to family life and family unity and suggests policy measures to address some of these barriers.[178] These include that new human rights-based and gender-sensitive model agreements be developed to govern the labour

174 Ibid para 41.
175 T Alexander Aleinikoff and Susan Martin, 'Making the Global Compacts Work: What Future for Refugees and Migrants?' (Policy Brief, No 6, Kaldor Centre for International Refugee Law, April 2018) 26.
176 *2035 Agenda for Facilitating Human Mobility*, UN Doc A/HRC/35/25, [83].
177 Ibid [41].
178 *Global Compact for Migration*, UN Doc A/RES/73/195, [21.i].

mobility of people of all skill levels; and that States reduce bars to family reunification for migrants of all skill levels by, for example, eliminating restrictions based on income requirements, language prerequisites, length of residency and type of employment.[179]

However, while such measures have potential to significantly reduce interferences with the family rights of migrant workers and their children, the Compact's non-binding legal status means that States are not compelled to adopt these measures in their TLM policies. This is compounded by the Compact's recognition that while it is a cooperative framework, it 'upholds the sovereignty of States'.[180] Nonetheless, it reiterates State obligations under international law[181] and identifies a child-sensitive approach as one of its guiding principles.[182] In relation to the latter, the Compact states that:

> The Global Compact promotes existing international legal obligations in relation to the rights of the child, and upholds the best interests of the child at all times, as a primary consideration in all situations concerning children in the context of international migration, including unaccompanied and separated children.[183]

Hence, even if States justify encouraging labour migration on the grounds of isolated SDGs, the Compact reaffirms State commitments to consider children's best interests in all migration policies. Moreover, the New York Declaration upon which the Compact is premised commits States parties to implementing 'planned and well-managed migration policies'.[184] This necessitates that States address *foreseeable* interferences with children's rights and potential harms to children arising from their migration policies, an obligation under international law.

Thus, as the Compact builds on human rights and other obligations that are already established in international law, it has the potential to have legal effects even if non-binding.[185] Moreover, even as soft law, it reinforces norms in global governance and transnational social protection standards that are fundamental in efforts to advance the rights of migrant workers and their families.[186] As Folbre argues, measures to 'establish stronger norms of social responsibility' are critical to breaking down 'unfair structures of constraint' – such as gender, class and nationality – to increase social spending on children and families in need of

179 Aleinikoff and Martin, above n 175, 18.
180 *Global Compact for Migration*, UN Doc A/RES/73/195, [7].
181 Ibid.
182 Ibid [15.h].
183 Ibid.
184 *New York Declaration*, UN Doc A/RES/71/1, para 16.
185 Costello (2019) and Guild, Basaran and Allinson (2019), cited in Elaine Lebon-McGregor, 'A History of Global Migration Governance: Challenging Linearity' (International Migration Institute, Working Paper 167, September 2020) 21.
186 Thomas Faist, *The Transnationalized Social Question: Migration and the Politics of Social Inequalities in the Twenty-First Century* (Oxford University Press, 2019) 125, 129.

support.[187] Importantly, the Compact has not only articulated a shared set of commitments by States but has also identified specific measures required to meet its objectives. That is, it has brought 'the existing normative framework governing international migration within a cooperative framework for achieving effective migration governance', which includes practical actions needed to generate policy guidance and best practices.[188] As Asis and Feranil explain, good practices that have been implemented in line with the Compact – including its overarching principle of child-sensitivity – provide a template for translating the Compact's 'objectives into action to ensure that the full protection and best interests of migrant children [and] the left-behind children of migrant workers … remain a priority.'[189]

7.3.5 Data collection, informed decision-making and effective risk management

The management of risks associated with child-parent separation should feature in all TLM policies that separate parents and children. However, this relies upon an understanding of the risks to children's interests that requires, in addition to best interests assessments, the collection of comprehensive data on the social impacts of migration. The Special Rapporteur on the human rights of migrants has deemed the increased collection and analysis of disaggregated migration-related data to be critical to the capacity of States to 'develop a human rights- and evidence-based governance framework for international migration and mobility'.[190] This must necessarily include the collection of longitudinal data on the social impacts of TLM on children and families, which has not been invested in by States, to date. Without this information, States are failing to facilitate informed decision-making by parents, families and policymakers alike.

i. Need for the assessment of social impacts

The need for evaluations that examine social impacts accords with the commitment by States in the New York Declaration to 'consider reviewing our migration policies with a view to examining their possible unintended negative consequences'.[191] In its rights-based framework for labour migration, the ILO has also espoused the principle that:

187 Nancy Folbre, *Who Pays for the Kids?: Gender and the Structures of Constraint* (Routledge, 1994) 255.

188 UN Network on Migration (UNNM), 'The Global Compact for Migration (GCM): Well Governed Migration as an Essential Element of Effective COVID-19 Response' (UNNM Policy Brief, 2020) 4–5.

189 Maruja M B Asis and Alan Feranil, 'Not for Adults Only: Toward a Child's Lens in Migration Policies in Asia' (2020) 8(1) *Journal on Migration and Human Security* 68, 68.

190 *2035 Agenda for Facilitating Human Mobility*, UN Doc A/HRC/35/25, [8].

191 *New York Declaration*, UN Doc A/RES/71/1, para 45.

> [K]nowledge and information are critical to formulate, implement and evaluate labour migration policy and practice, and therefore its collection and application should be given priority.[192]

The ILO and CMW Committee have argued that without reliable evidence and disaggregated data that addresses context-specific challenges arising from labour migration – including in relation to regions, gender and employment sectors – effective policy responses cannot be generated.[193] Researchers and policymakers have long drawn attention to the lack of disaggregated data in the context of labour migration, arguing that it hinders a proper understanding of the social and longer-term impacts of low-waged migration on communities and countries of origin over time.[194] It has been urged that disaggregated data needs to be systematically collected to better understand the development impacts of TLM on labour-sending countries and trends over time in relation to children whose parents migrate.[195] Researchers have continued to call for empirical data that measures the social impacts of remittance-based development strategies, arguing that aggregate data and current measures – that focus primarily on quantifying financial gains to economies – conceal social impacts.[196] Hence, only by tracking social impacts over time, and documenting lessons from labour-sending countries, can the real effects of the normalisation of family separation on children and communities be understood.[197] These concerns were stressed by key informants across all sectors in observations including:

> 'It is more difficult to quantify social impacts versus the economic, which is why I think it is attractive to say this represents X number of dollars in remittances. When you actually look at what some of the potential negative

192 ILO, *ILO Multilateral Framework on Labour Migration: Non-binding Principles and Guidelines for a Rights-Based Approach to Labour Migration* (ILO, 2006) 9; CMW Committee, *Contribution to the 2030 Sustainable Development Goals*, above n 145, 5 pt 2.

193 ILO, above n 159, [II.5], [II.12].

194 See, eg, Macha Farrant, Anna MacDonald and Dhananjayan Sriskandarajah, 'Migration and Development: Opportunities and Challenges for Policymakers' (IOM Migration Research Series, No 22, April 2006) 46; John Bryant, 'Children of International Migrants in Indonesia, Thailand, and the Philippines: A Review of Evidence and Policies' (Innocenti Working Paper, No 2005–05, UNICEF, April 2005) 17.

195 Ibid.

196 Rosalia Cortes, 'Remittances and Children's Rights: An Overview of Academic and Policy Literature' (Division of Policy and Practice Working Paper, UNICEF, January 2007) 1; Robert E B Lucas (ed), *International Handbook on Migration and Development* (Edward Elgar Publishing, 2014) 1.

197 Kristine M Zentgraf and Norma Stoltz Chinchilla, 'Transnational Family Separation: A Framework for Analysis' (2012) 38(2) *Journal of Ethnic and Migration Studies* 345, 346; Rosalia Cortes, 'Children and Women Left Behind in Labor Sending Countries: An Appraisal of Social Risks' (Division of Policy and Practice Working Paper, UNICEF, August 2008); Pearson and Sim, above n 30, 16.

impacts of the schemes are, it is more difficult to quantify' *(Key Informant – MLO-NGO 7)*

Key informants from the government sector also reiterated the need to measure social impacts alongside economic in relation to policymaking in general in views such as:

'Social impact is not independent of economic — the social and economic cannot be separated. [Social impact] is much more difficult to track but it is not to say that it is not as important as the economic. In fact, our research shows that they are very much interconnected'. *(Key Informant – Government 1)*

The OHCHR has also highlighted that a 'lack of disaggregated data is one of many challenges in formulating and implementing child-sensitive migration policies'.[198] This reinforces the widespread arguments by researchers about the urgent need for more data and analysis on the impact of parental migration on children's overall development and well-being.[199]

ii. Effective measures must be informed

The CRC Committee has reiterated that ensuring that children's best interests are a primary consideration 'demands a continuous process of child impact assessment' and evaluation of 'the actual impact of implementation'.[200] It directs States that this process of monitoring the implementation of children's rights 'needs to be built into government at all levels and as early as possible in the development of policy'.[201] As Tobin explains, this accords with the obligation on States to take *effective* measures to implement children's rights under Art 4 of the CRC.[202] The nature of 'effective' measures is outlined in Chapter 4 in relation to appropriate assistance to parents and includes, among other things, that measures be evidence-

198 *OHCHR Study on the Protection of the Rights of the Child in the Context of Migration*, UN Doc A/HRC/15/29, [7].

199 See, eg, Rodolfo de la Garza, De la Garza, 'Migration, Development and Children Left Behind: A Multidimensional Perspective' (Social and Economic Policy Working Paper, UNICEF, May 2010) x; Kolitha Wickramage, Chesmal Siriwardhana and Sharika Peiris, 'Promoting the Health of Left-Behind Children of Asian Labour Migrants: Evidence for Policy and Action' (Issue in Brief, IOM / Migration Policy Institute, Issue No 14, September 2015) 1.

200 *General Comment No 5*, UN Doc CRC/GC/2003/5, para 45.

201 Ibid.

202 John Tobin, 'Article 4. A State's General Obligation of Implementation' in J Tobin (ed), *The UN Convention on the Rights of the Child: A Commentary* (OUP, 2019) 108, 113.

based.[203] This involves data collection as well as the development of indicators and benchmarks, establishment of independent monitoring systems and undertaking of child impact assessments (which analyse the impact of policies on children's capacity to enjoy their rights).[204] To this end, the Committee has highlighted the connection between child-specific indicators and improvements to State policy formulation, monitoring and evaluation concerning the implementation of children's rights.[205] Moreover, it has reiterated the essential role that the collection of reliable and disaggregated data on children plays in implementation as it allows for the 'identification of discrimination and/or disparities in the realization of rights'.[206] Specifically in the context of children affected by migration, the CRC and CMW Committees have urged that:

> States parties should develop a systematic rights-based policy on the collection and public dissemination of qualitative and quantitative data on all children in the context of international migration in order to inform a comprehensive policy aimed at the protection of their rights.[207]

This should be considered in light of the UN Secretary-General's recommendation, reiterated by the UN Expert Group on Family Policies and the Sustainable Development Agenda, that in confronting family poverty:

> Governments ... should be encouraged to support data collection and research on family issues and the impact of public policy on families and invest in family-oriented policy and programme design, implementation and evaluation.[208]

Even scholars in favour of restricting the family-related rights of migrant workers have emphasised the need for improved measurement and analysis of the impact of migration policies on the rights of migrants (both de jure and de facto) over time, between countries and across groups of migrants.[209] This is because, as Ruhs explains, only by developing a longitudinal understanding about the impact of rights restrictions can there be informed policymaking, based on a critical

203 See Chapter 4 (Section 4.2.1.i).

204 Tobin, above n 202, 121–2.

205 CRC Committee, *Report on the Forty-sixth Session*, UN Doc CRC/C/46/3, [80].

206 *General Comment No 5*, UN Doc CRC/GC/2003/5, para 48.

207 *Joint General Comment on Children in the Context of International Migration*, UN Doc CMW/C/GC/3-CRC/C/GC/22, para 16.

208 *Celebration of the Twentieth Anniversary of the International Year of the Family in 2014: Report of the Secretary-General*, UN ESCOR, 70th sess, UN Doc A/70/61–E/2015/3 (18 November 2014) [70.c]; UN Expert Group on Family Policies and Sustainable Development Agenda, above n 141, [26].

209 Martin Ruhs, 'Protecting the Rights of Temporary Migrant Workers: Ideals Versus Reality' in Joanna Howe and Rosemary Owens (eds), *Temporary Labour Migration in the Global Era* (Hart Publishing, 2016) 299, 321.

assessment of international experience and a proper understanding of the effectiveness of policy interventions.[210]

7.4 Conclusion

Building on findings from preceding chapters in Part B, this chapter has reiterated the importance of investment by States in developing and supporting strong child-parent relationships to children's well-being. It has argued that the CRC protects the rights and entitlements of children and parents under Arts 18 and 7 *universally*. That is, parents are entitled to State assistance to fulfil their broad child-rearing responsibilities under Art 18, and children have the right to be cared for by their parents *as far as possible* under Art 7, *irrespective* of their country of residence, cultural background or family formation. This chapter has highlighted how the intrinsic value of the child-parent relationship to children's development outcomes is well-founded in *labour-receiving* countries and children who are citizens in *these* countries have this relationship strongly respected and protected in family law. By contrast, TLM policies that physically separate dependent children from their parents for prolonged periods undermine this relationship for children who come from countries with *fewer* resources and generally poor families.

Hence, this chapter has highlighted the absolute contradiction that TLM policies – premised on prolonged child-parent separation and the undermining of the family unit – create for the international development agenda that the international community is simultaneously pursuing. It argues that without adopting measures to reconcile this contradiction, TLM will be unable to generate sustainable development outcomes for communities in labour-sending countries. Such measures identified in this chapter include the incorporation of strategies informed by other disciplines that regularly manage child-parent separation (such as family law) to mitigate potential impacts of disruptions to children's attachment figures on children's development; regulation of employer practices to guarantee that the ability of migrant workers to maintain contact and communication with their children is not hindered; reconciliation of SDGs that promote support for families and positive parenting with SDGs that promote TLM; development of new model TLM agreements that are human-rights based and child-sensitive (as recommended in the Global Compact for Migration); and prioritisation of the rights and best interests of children in the implementation of State commitments under the New York Declaration and Global Compact for Migration. These measures must be considered in light of the CRC Committee's concerns about the breakdown of family structures being caused by poverty and unemployment and the adverse impact that this has on parents' capacity to care for their children.[211] Moreover, the Committee has stressed that investment in children's rights is essential to

210 Ibid 322.

211 Tobin and Seow, above n 6, 673–4 citing, eg, CRC Committee, CO Niger, CRC/C/15/Add.179, para 36.

achieving lasting positive outcomes in relation to economic growth and sustainable development.[212]

Importantly, the CRC and existing knowledge on child development reflect an understanding that in ordinary circumstances it will be in children's best interests to be primarily cared for by their parents in a stable family environment. This presumption is undermined by TLM policies that result in the lengthy separation of children and parents. Given that child-parent separation inevitably and foreseeably affects children, it is essential – and *legally* required under the CRC – that the development and implementation of TLM policies include the assessment of potential impacts on children's best interests and rights; justification of interferences with children's rights that protect the child-parent relationship; and adoption of measures to reduce interferences with these rights. This chapter has argued that each of these processes *must* be informed by comprehensive data that assesses the *social impacts* of TLM on children, families and communities. Without investment in the collection of longitudinal and disaggregated data, the true extent of how children's rights are impacted by TLM cannot be accurately gauged and the development of appropriate policy responses will be stifled.

This chapter has reiterated that central to reducing interferences by TLM with the child-parent relationship is the incorporation into TLM policies of effective measures to assist migrant workers to continue fulfilling their primary role in their children's upbringing and development. Such measures, identified throughout this book, are collated in Appendix I and examples provided in Section 7.3.2(iii). This chapter has highlighted the opportunity that the emerging framework for the global governance of migration presents to States to identify, incorporate and implement such measures to reduce the 'unintended negative consequences'[213] for children currently being generated by unnecessarily restrictive TLM policies. It has also stressed that for measures of parental assistance to be *effective* in the context of TLM, they must account for and respond to how *transnational* separation affects parental capacity to fulfil child-rearing responsibilities. That is, they must support migrant workers to continue being actively involved in their children's care, even if they are employed under and governed by TLM policies that continue to deny them the right to family accompaniment.

Of utmost significance, this book has shown that *any* measures that improve the capacity of parents to remain actively involved in their children's upbringing and development will inevitably enhance the extent of the possibility ('as far as possible') by which their children can be cared for by their own parents, which is the right of *all* children under the CRC.

212 *General Comment No 19*, UN Doc CRC/C/GC/19, para 12.
213 *New York Declaration*, UN Doc A/RES/71/1, para 45.

Conclusion

This book has demonstrated how restrictive features of existing TLM policies create unnecessary and unjustified interferences with children's rights that protect the child-parent relationship under the CRC. Drawing on evidence from social science studies and the knowledge of key informants from multiple sectors engaged in TLM, it has shown how the effects of protracted periods of child-parent separation caused by TLM policies can interfere with numerous CRC rights. These are children's rights to: be cared for by their parents as far as possible under Art 7; maintain direct and regular contact and personal relations with their parents if separated under Art 10(2); have their family life (which includes their relationship with their parents) protected against arbitrary interference under Art 16; and have their parents assisted by the State to fulfil their child-rearing roles and responsibilities as their children's primary caregivers under Art 18, which includes to meet their children's *overall* development needs under Art 27.

While it is frequently argued that parents 'choose' to migrate to advance their children's interests, this book recognises that genuine and informed choices in the context of TLM are heavily constrained by factors beyond the control of many migrant workers.[1] These include poverty and limited viable livelihood options in labour-sending countries; a family's financial debt and/or dependency on remittances; misinformation about the potential positive and negative effects of parental migration (particularly on children); and lack of foreseeability about the *length* of child-parent separation that often follows a parent's initial migration.[2] This length is compounded by the frequent remigration of migrant workers, driven by the same factors that are, again, often beyond a family's control.[3]

Hence, irrespective of whether TLM is considered economically beneficial for migrant workers and their families (which remains a contested view),[4] this book has shown that the protracted lengths of child-parent separation that are a

1 See Chapter 4 (Section 4.2) and Chapter 6 (Section 6.3.4).
2 See Chapter 4 (Section 4.2) and Chapter 6 (Section 6.3.4).
3 See Chapter 6 (Section 6.4.2).
4 See Chapter 4 (Section 4.2), Chapter 7 (Section 7.3.3) and Introduction – Research Context (Section i. The contested role of remittances).

structural feature of TLM can have potentially harmful *non-economic* impacts on children's rights, best interests and well-being.[5] It has stressed the need for further research on the *social* impacts of parental migration to properly understand the true benefits of TLM for children and communities in labour-sending countries and to identify appropriate strategies to mitigate detrimental effects.[6] The findings in this book are buttressed by the knowledge that:

> When we invest wisely in children and families, the next generation will pay that back through a lifetime of productivity and responsible citizenship.[7]

The book has not explored *all* of the possible measures that could reduce potential harms to children, families and communities arising from TLM, nor examined how they could be implemented. Further investigation on other possible measures and methods for implementation should be the focus of future research, which *must* be designed to consider social impacts (both short- *and* long-term) on a par with remittance-based outcomes.[8] Instead, this book has sought to bring children's rights into global debates about TLM, with a focus on those rights that protect the child-parent relationship given its *recognised* value and importance to children's development and well-being.[9] It accords with Bhabha's view that:

> Children need to become a central focus of migration policy, not an afterthought, and active participants in contestation over rights not invisible dependent variables, if the promise of the ambitious normative regime is to be concretized in practice.[10]

To date, children's rights and children's voices have been overlooked in dominant discourses and policymaking processes concerning TLM, which focus heavily on its perceived economic benefits to both labour-receiving and labour-sending countries.[11] Moreover, when human rights are considered in the context of TLM, it is largely in relation to addressing rights violations against migrant workers in labour-receiving countries.[12] This has meant that, as observed by the CMW Committee:

5 See Chapter 4 (Section 4.3) and Chapter 5 (Section 5.4.4.ii).
6 See Chapter 7 (Section 7.3.5).
7 National Scientific Council on the Developing Child, *The Science of Early Childhood Development: Closing the Gap Between What We Know and What We Do* (Center on the Developing Child, Harvard University, January 2007) 3.
8 See Chapter 7 (Section 7.3.5).
9 See Chapter 2 (Section 2.3.1) and Chapter 7 (Section 7.2).
10 Jacqueline Bhabha, '"More Than Their Share of Sorrows": International Migration Law and the Rights of Children' (2003) 22(2) *Saint Louis University Public Law Review* 253, 275.
11 See Chapter 4 (Sections 4.2.2 and 4.2.4).
12 See Introduction – Scope (Section ii. Rights Violations against Migrant Workers).

> While migration remains a much-discussed topic, some groups … such as … family members of migrants who stay in countries of origin, receive insufficient attention.[13]

Hence, it has been attempted here to redress this in part by ***giving attention*** to the rights of children who remain in labour-sending countries when their parents migrate under TLM policies that do not permit accompaniment by dependent children. The book has demonstrated that States have a ***duty*** under human rights law to consider how such policies, which clearly and foreseeably affect children, impact children's rights and best interests.[14] This duty stands ***regardless*** of the purported economic benefits of TLM in its current forms, with the CRC demanding that policymakers consider children's rights and best interests in ***all*** processes and decision-making that affects children.[15]

However, when we pause to examine TLM, it becomes evident that TLM policies disregard many of the pivotal aspects of the child-parent relationship that the CRC protects and presumes to be in children's best interests in ordinary circumstances. These include parents' role in providing for their children's psychosocial and emotional development needs (Art 27), providing their children with direction and guidance (Art 5) and being primarily responsible for their children's upbringing and development (Art 18).[16] Using qualitative research informed by social science studies, key informant interviews and primary national, regional and global policy documents, this book has demonstrated how TLM frequently undermines each of these protected aspects of the parental role, not only in theory but in reality. This evidence-based and grounded approach clearly reflects that the ***degree*** of disruption to child-parent relationships caused by restrictive features of TLM policies is ***unnecessary*** and could be easily reduced without abandoning TLM altogether.

If States listened to the children of migrant workers, as they are required to do under the CRC,[17] they would hear that these children need their parents for *so much more than remittances.* If States heeded the advice of the CRC Committee they would recognise that children, particularly young children, 'are especially vulnerable to adverse consequences' arising from child-parent separation 'because of their physical dependence on and emotional attachment to their parents/primary caregivers'.[18] And, if States assigned *even half* of the value and protection to

13 CMW Committee, *Contribution to the 2030 Sustainable Development Goals in Response to a Call for Inputs by the High-Level Political Forum on Sustainable Development (HLPF)* (19 April 2018) 1 pt 1.

14 *CRC* art 3.

15 *CRC* art 3. See also Mary Crock and Hannah Martin, 'First Things First: International Law and the Protection of Migrant Children' in Mary Crock and Lenni Benson (eds), *Protecting Migrant Children: In Search of Best Practice* (Elgar, 2018) 75, 89.

16 See Chapters 4, 5 and 7 on Arts 27, 5 and 18 respectively.

17 See Chapter 3 (Section 3.2.4) on children's right to be heard under Art 12 of the CRC.

18 *General Comment No 7*, UN Doc CRC/C/GC/7/Rev.1, para 18.

the child-parent relationship as is given to children who are citizens in *labour-receiving* countries,[19] then they would design TLM policies differently. That is, they would be designed in ways that enhance, rather than hinder, the capacity of children and parents to maintain meaningful relationships *even if* parents are employed transnationally.

Thus, this book has focused largely on the role that labour-receiving States should assume in reducing the potential harms of TLM to children. This is because these States are primarily responsible for determining TLM policies, which makes them central to prospects for achieving policy reforms.[20] Moreover, labour-sending countries have expressed desires to reduce their dependency on low-waged TLM.[21] For example, Filipino government officials have recognised that investment in maintaining strong family ties and developing sustained livelihoods in the labour-sending country is needed so that 'overseas employment no longer becomes the only recourse for families to have better lives, and instead simply becomes one of the options'.[22]

Hence, in line with the principle of international cooperation,[23] it has been argued that labour-receiving countries should assist labour-sending countries in their efforts to create alternatives to migration for parents *at least* by reducing deliberate attempts in TLM policies to encourage continuous remigration.[24] Importantly, the principle of international cooperation requires States with greater resources to assist those with fewer resources to implement CRC rights.[25] This entails that the protection of children's rights in the context of TLM is a shared responsibility between (poorer) labour-sending countries *and* (wealthier) labour-receiving countries. It also involves the duty under international human rights law to not cause harm to children in other countries,[26] which must be considered by labour-receiving countries when they are designing TLM policies.

However, even if labour-receiving States choose to disregard their obligations in accordance with the principle of international cooperation in the context of TLM, it is stressed that *all* countries – labour-receiving and labour-sending – are legally obligated under the CRC to properly consider *how* children's rights and best interests are affected by State policies that affect them.[27] The degree of foreseeability that policies premised on the separation of children and parents will affect

19 See Chapter 7 (Section 7.2.3) on the value of the child-parent relationship in labour-receiving countries.
20 See methodology in Chapter 1 (Section 1.2.3).
21 See, eg, *Migrant Workers and Overseas Filipinos Act of 1995* (Republic Act No 8042) s 2(g); Sri Lankan Ministry for Foreign Employment Promotion and Welfare, *National Labour Migration Policy for Sri Lanka* (Government of Sri Lanka, October 2008) iv.
22 Rebecca J Calzado, Department of Labor and Employment Philippines, 'Labour Migration and Development Goals: The Philippine Experience' (Paper presented at International Dialogue on Migration, Geneva, 8 October 2007) 4.
23 See Chapter 3 (Section 3.3).
24 See Chapter 6 (Section 6.4.2).
25 See Chapter 3 (Section 3.3).
26 See Chapter 3 (Section 3.3) on the principle of international cooperation.
27 See Chapter 3 (Section 3.2.1).

children, makes it exceptionally difficult for States to deny their legal duty to consider children's rights and best interests in the development of TLM policies.

While it is recognised that children's rights can be limited and their best interests outweighed by other policy considerations, States retain a *legal duty to justify* any interferences with children's rights and best interests arising from their policies and actions. This book has stressed that, to date, *no* State has done this in the context of TLM. That is, it has not been shown that the restrictive features of TLM policies that prolong periods of child-parent separation and significantly disrupt the child-parent relationship are in pursuit of a legitimate aim and use necessary and reasonable measures of *least interference* to pursue that aim.[28] It has argued that the lack of justification, together with the failure to adopt reasonably available measures that would reduce interferences with children's rights, leads to the conclusion that the limitations on CRC rights caused by TLM policies are unnecessary and unreasonable and violate those provisions of the CRC that protect the child-parent relationship.[29]

Views captured throughout this book reflect a growing awareness on the part of *both* labour-receiving and labour-sending States about the potential negative impacts of TLM on children, families and communities. However, at present, this awareness is accompanied by a failure to act for fear of costs associated with addressing features of TLM that are particularly harmful to children and families. As stated by a key informant:

> Even for receiving governments that want to acknowledge their legal obligations to families left behind, I think a big barrier is how to translate that into concrete policy measures and the fiscal implications of such obligations … That's very tough, and I think that's why there's total inaction — because *it's so much easier to simply say we don't know about this* [emphasis added].[30]

However, *we do know* about the potential harms of child-parent separation to children's development and well-being, and a wealth of evidence about the potential harms to children arising from parental migration has been provided in Part B of this book.

Nonetheless, this book does not argue for the discontinuation of TLM. Rather, it accepts its inevitable continuation in coming decades and argues that there is a spectrum of *reasonably available measures* that could reduce interferences with children's rights, making TLM less harmful and potentially more sustainable going forward. This approach accords with the notion that respecting human rights and restricting immigration are not necessarily mutually exclusive.[31] Hence, each of

28 *Siracusa Principles*, UN Doc E/CN.4/1985/4, annex pt I A paras 10–12.
29 These provisions are Arts 27, 10(2), 5, 16, 18 and 7, each of which is examined in Part B of this book.
30 Interview with Key Informant (R & P 5).
31 Mary Crock and Lenni B Benson, 'Central Issues in the Protection of Child Migrants' in Mary Crock and Lenni Benson (eds), *Protecting Migrant Children: In Search of Best Practice* (Elgar, 2018) 1, 19.

the measures identified in Part B of this book (and summarised in Appendix I) offers States an opportunity to *begin to reduce* the potential harms to children's rights caused by parental migration without dismantling TLM as a system that is favoured and promoted in the current global order.

Measures identified that can co-exist with TLM include, for example: the use of children's best interests assessments in TLM policy development; supporting the movement of migrant workers between their country of employment and their children; guaranteeing migrant workers and their families access to the technology, privacy and time needed for parents to communicate effectively with their children; supporting children's preparedness for periods of separation including by involving them in discussions about parental migration; providing support for children in mainstream services (such as in the education, health and justice sectors) during periods of parental absence; reducing the encouragement of remigration including by creating viable livelihood options in labour-sending countries; prioritising children's rights and best interests in the implementation of the New York Declaration and Global Compact for Migration; and investing in future research and data collection on the *social* impacts of TLM on children.

The book has highlighted how investing in developing a proper understanding of the types and extent of risks to children posed by TLM, and understanding how the likelihood of these risks eventuating are affected by different variables (such as a child's age, whether a migrant worker is a child's primary caregiver and protective factors present in different communities), can help States determine the amount of resources to invest in different measures.[32] Importantly, because of the interconnectedness of the CRC rights being examined, *any* measure adopted will inevitably reduce the degree of interference with the other interrelated rights and increase the extent ('as far as possible') to which children can be cared for by their own parents (Art 7).[33] The book also demonstrates that some of these measures would not be financially onerous on States.[34] For example, ensuring that parents can speak with their children at times that are *suitable for their children* is a simple measure that addresses the situation for many migrant workers that is poignantly captured by poet Nayyirah Waheed in a line from her poem *The Maid*:

> set her hours
> past her own children's bed time.[35]

The relatively low costs associated with implementing such measures that support (rather than challenge the necessity of) transnational child-parent relationships in the context of TLM strengthen the reasonableness of the expectation that States should invest in these measures. As Tobin explains:

32 See Chapter 4 (Section 4.4.1) and Chapter 7 (7.3.2).
33 See Chapter 2 (Section 2.3) on the interconnectedness of these CRC rights.
34 See, eg, Chapter 5 (Section 5.3.2 and Section 5.4.4.i) on communication measures to support transnational child-parent relationships and involving children in pre-migration discussions to increase preparedness for periods of separation respectively.
35 Nayyirah Waheed, 'The Maid' in *Salt* (Createspace, 2013).

> If a relatively low level of resources is required to protect against the interference with a child's right, a state will be under a greater burden to allocate the necessary resources to protect the child especially where the consequences of the interference are significant.[36]

Importantly, assessing the impact of TLM policies on children's rights can also encourage States to recognise limits on the degree of harm they are willing to cause to children, no matter the economic gains. For example, in a parallel observation on the protection of migrant workers in Canada, Commissioner Arthurs recognised that just as child labour is rejected on ethical grounds, even if it is economically attractive, migrant workers should not have to live in poverty in affluent societies.[37] Similarly, a children's rights-based approach in the context of TLM can help States to identify limits on the degree to which they are willing to interfere with the child-parent relationships of non-citizen children for their own economic gains. This supports the notion that 'some conditions are simply too oppressive to be imposed by a society' regardless of whether they are agreed to by labour-sending countries or migrant workers themselves in the face of limited alternatives.[38] It also, once again, accords with the principle of international cooperation that requires labour-receiving countries to not cause harm to children in other countries and to assist in the global implementation of children's rights,[39] rather than capitalise from global inequalities that exist between States and people.

It must not be forgotten that these people are mothers and fathers *with children who need their mothers and fathers*. In this vein, this book has stressed the need to look to other professions and disciplines that regularly manage child-parent separation to identify strategies that are used to maintain child-parent relationships when families have access to support and resources. It has argued that States that are encouraging parental migration, while simultaneously denying family accompaniment, need to invest in making these strategies available to low-waged migrant workers and their families. These types of non-legal policy measures can support the effective implementation of children's rights,[40] and can also be informed by the body of knowledge and principles on balancing business interests with human rights.[41]

The importance of non-legal policy measures in addressing the drivers and managing the social impacts of TLM cannot be stressed enough in view of the

36 John Tobin, 'Article 4. A State's General Obligation of Implementation' in J Tobin (ed), *The UN Convention on the Rights of the Child: A Commentary* (OUP, 2019) 108, 130.

37 Harry Arthurs, *Fairness at Work: Federal Labour Standards for the 21st Century* (Publication Services, Human Resources Development Canada, 2006) 247.

38 Laurie Berg, *Migrant Rights at Work: Law's Precariousness at the Intersection of Immigration and Labour* (Routledge, 2016) 41.

39 See Chapter 3 (Section 3.3).

40 Laura Lundy, Ursula Kilkelly and Bronagh Byrne, 'Incorporation of the United Nations Convention on the Rights of the Child in Law: A Comparative Review' (2013) 21(3) *International Journal of Children's Rights* 442.

41 See Chapter 7 (Section 7.3.2.i).

emerging legally non-binding policy framework for the global governance of migration. Together, the New York Declaration and the Global Compact for Migration offer a significant opportunity to incorporate policy measures to reduce the degree of interference caused by TLM with children's rights. They also represent the most recent recognition by States of the centrality of the principle of international cooperation in State responses to complex policy challenges, emerging at the intersection between migration, poverty and human rights. However, as a number of countries (including Australia) failed to sign the Global Compact for Migration, the strength of understanding TLM from a children's rights perspective is that *all* States (except the United States) are *legally* bound to fulfil their obligations towards children under the CRC.[42]

This book has argued that in considering children's rights in the context of TLM, States and multilateral organisations that characterise TLM as an international development strategy should heed findings by the UN Expert Group on Family Policies and the Sustainable Development Agenda, that social protection measures and support for families should *not be linked* to the labour market.[43] This is particularly since 'the traditional social protection role of families is weakening due to a number of demographic changes', and because poverty reduction in developing countries cannot be achieved without addressing structural challenges.[44] This reflects the reality that without addressing the drivers of TLM, remittances alone are unlikely to generate sustainable development outcomes in labour-sending countries.[45] Instead, TLM will continue to disrupt child-parent relationships, families and communities – perpetuating inequalities for children who already face heightened vulnerabilities given that their parents' migration is primarily driven by poverty.

States, labour-receiving and labour-sending alike, are well aware of the potential negative impacts on children's life courses when heightened vulnerabilities experienced by children are not effectively mitigated in the early stages of life. This is stressed in the 2016 State of the World's Children Report, which has reiterated that without States adopting effective measures to address inequities experienced by children globally:

> [I]nequities in childhood and adolescence will continue to generate unequal outcomes for families around the world, fuelling intergenerational cycles of disadvantage that threaten the strength and stability of societies everywhere.[46]

42 Introduction – Research Context (Section i. The significance of the CRC).

43 *Report of the United Nations Expert Group Meeting: Family Policies and 2030 Sustainable Development Agenda* (UN Department of Economic and Social Affairs, New York, 12–13 May 2016) para 47.
See also Chapter 7 (Section 7.3.3).

44 Ibid.

45 Hein de Haas, 'The Migration and Development Pendulum: A Critical View on Research and Policy' (2012) 50(3) *International Migration* 8, 19–20.

46 UNICEF, *The State of the World's Children 2016: A Fair Chance for Every Child* (UNICEF, 2016) 89.

This book has shown how TLM policies currently fuel inequalities in children's capacity to enjoy their CRC rights in ways that are unnecessarily harmful and disruptive to their relationship with their parents and family life. It has endeavoured to identify reasonable measures to mitigate *some* of the potential harms to children associated with parental migration; and ground these measures in universal norms and State obligations towards children under international human rights law. It is hoped that it makes a timely and positive contribution to the emerging conversation about *how* and *why* States should act to better address the social impacts of TLM given its global scale and projected future growth.

Appendix I

Summary of policy measures to reduce interferences caused by TLM with CRC provisions and general legal principles that protect the child-parent relationship in international human rights law

Overarching CRC principles: These inform all specific CRC rights and obligations of States parties	**The best interests of the child shall be a primary consideration** in all State actions concerning children (Art 3). **There must be no arbitrary discrimination against children** (including due to their parents' social or migration status) (Art 2). **The survival *and development* of the child must be ensured by States** to the maximum extent possible (Art 6). **Children's views must be heard and given due weight** according to their age and maturity in matters affecting them (Art 12).
General principles in human rights law: These are advanced in the CRC	**International cooperation between States parties is necessary to implement children's rights** and improve living conditions for children globally and particularly in developing countries (CRC, Art 4 and Preamble). **States should** respect people's rights within their territories *and* extraterritorially and **refrain from conduct that directly and indirectly interferes with the rights of people outside their territories** (Maastricht Principles 19, 20, 21). **The family is the fundamental group unit in society and natural environment for children's growth and well-being** and must be protected and assisted by States to assume its responsibilities toward children (CRC, Preamble; ICCPR, Art 23; ICSECR, Art 10).
Relevant definitions in human rights law:	**Appropriate measures are effective** in implementing the right in question **and consistent with all CRC provisions** and principles. **Arbitrary interferences** are limitations on rights that **are not necessary, reasonable and proportionate to a legitimate aim.** The principle of **proportionality requires a rational connection between a legitimate aim and the measures adopted** to achieve the aim; **and the adoption of measures of least interference** reasonably available to States.

Policy measures to support interconnected CRC provisions that protect the child-parent relationship

Children's rights	*State obligations*	*Social issues*	*Policy measures*
Article 27: Right to a standard of living adequate for their physical, mental, spiritual, moral and social development	Parents are entitled to *appropriate* measures of assistance from States to secure living conditions necessary to meet children's physical ***and*** psycho-social development needs	1. TLM undermines parental role in providing for children's social and emotional development needs	a) Invest in creating local employment options to enable parents to provide financially for their children while continuing to reside with them b) Promote informed and well-considered decision-making about parental migration including through the provision of non-biased information
		2. Prolonged parental absence increases risks to children's psycho-social well-being and development in the short and long term	a) Adopt broader child development measures in evaluating TLM that are beyond economic and material to include psychosocial well-being b) Include *best interests assessments* and consider children's views at all stages of policy development, implementation and evaluation processes c) Consider children's age and capacity in the development and adoption of measures to assist migrant workers to fulfil their parenting role d) Mainstream support for children of migrant workers in education, health and justice sectors if there are high rates of parental migration
Article 10(2): Right to maintain regular and direct personal relations and contact with both parents in the event of transnational separation	States must respect, protect and fulfil children's right to maintain their relationship with their parents if separated transnationally unless there are ***exceptional circumstances***	1. Limited opportunities for direct physical contact prolongs the period of parental absence	a) Provide financial assistance or adequate wages to support regular return travel (and ideally paid leave), which must be combined with circulation-friendly visas – see Art 16 [Measure 4(a)] b) Ensure adequate (possibly mandatory) leave provisions (which could include leave for events of major significance for children and families)
		2. Conditions associated with low-waged TLM can constrain regular, frequent and quality communication between children and parents	a) Include contractual stipulations that guarantee workers time (at times of the day that are suitable for their children and alternative caregivers) and private spaces to enable regular and frequent communication with their children (without employer discretion) b) Provide access to age appropriate communication modes and strategies for children including support for alternative caregivers to access these modes and implement these strategies c) Subsidise communication costs (phone and internet) for migrant workers, their families and alternative caregivers d) Ensure access to Wi-Fi for migrant workers and their families e) Invest in developing communication infrastructure in high migration areas in labour-sending countries (with costs shared with labour-receiving countries that source workers from these areas / countries) f) Enforce strict penalties for the confiscating of mobile phones

Policy measures to support interconnected CRC provisions that protect the child-parent relationship

Children's rights	*State obligations*	*Social issues*	*Policy measures*
Article 5: Right to receive direction and guidance from their parents in a manner consistent with their age and capacity	States must not interfere with rights, responsibilities and duties of parents to provide direction and guidance to their children to enable them to exercise their rights	1. Constraints on communication unnecessarily restrict parental capacity to continue providing direction and guidance to children	As above in relation to Art 10(2) [Measures 2 (a)–(f)]
		2. Unfounded presumption that the extended family can replace parents as their children's primary caregivers without effect to the child	a) Recognise loss experienced by children from parental migration even when they are well cared for by alternative caregivers b) Develop appropriate measures of support for alternative caregivers to enable them to assist in facilitating transnational child-parent relationships (including assistance with care-related costs)
		3. Exclusion of children from familial decision-making about parental migration for employment	a) Provide support for parents and families to understand and adopt processes to include children in decision-making about parental migration and their alternative care arrangements b) Engage children and families in 'family readiness' strategies to prepare for periods of separation – see Art 16 [Measure 2(b)]
		4. Breakdown of child-parent relationship post-reunification due to length of separation	a) Adopt measures to reduce periods of separation – See Art 10(2) [Measures 1 (a)–(b)] and Art 16 [Measures 2, 3 and 4]

Policy measures to support interconnected CRC provisions that protect the child-parent relationship

Children's rights	*State obligations*	*Social issues*	*Policy measures*
Article 16: Right to protection against arbitrary interference with their family life, which includes their relationship with their parents	States have a positive obligation (i.e. must take active measures) to protect children against arbitrary interference with their family life	1. Labour-receiving countries attach family rights (including family accompaniment) to citizenship, permanent residency and/or an adult's skill level to deny these rights to low-waged migrant workers and their children	a) Examine how rights that are protected on the basis of citizenship (including family rights) can be extended to workers who are sourced from overseas and thus inevitably have transnational family relationships b) Consider making family accompaniment available to migrant workers who have dependent children as it is for other groups of temporary migrants (such as skilled temporary migrants and international students) c) Recognise children as rights-bearers in their own right, which demands that States justify interferences by TLM policies with *children's* rights that result from limitations on their parents' interdependent rights
		2. Labour-receiving countries assign less value to the child-parent relationship for children in labour-sending countries than for their own citizens	a) Incorporate learnings from fields that manage child-parent separation (eg, family law/military) into TLM policies including guidance on lengths of separation, suitable care plans and communication and travel plans (these must be modifiable according to a child's age and changing needs) b) Promote 'family readiness' by equipping families with knowledge about the challenges of parental migration, skills to address these challenges and making support services available and accessible to families c) Subsidise costs to make strategies that 'skilled' workers use to maintain transnational family relationships available to low-waged workers – see Art 10(2) [Measures 1(a) and 2(b)–(e)]
		3. Remigration protracts the period of parental absence, which increases detriment to the child-parent relationship	a) Address the deliberate encouragement of remigration in TLM policies and consider limiting the times a worker can participate in TLM schemes b) Invest in equipping migrant workers with skills during their period of employment that will reduce their need to remigrate c) Create viable employment opportunities in labour-sending countries to reduce a worker's need to remigrate – see Art 27 [Measure 1(a)]
		4. Rigid immigration regimes and employment conditions restrict parents from visiting children	a) Introduce circulation-friendly visas that facilitate the free movement of workers between their country of employment and their children b) Promote regional initiatives to increase proximity between workers and their families (combined with the right to move freely) c) Formalise rotational / job-sharing models that align with practices in other sectors that require workers to work away from their families d) Protect workers' employment rights when they return home for visits

Policy measures to support interconnected CRC provisions that protect the child-parent relationship

Children's rights	*State obligations*	*Social issues*	*Policy measures*
		5. Child-parent separation prior to permanent migration hinders settlement outcomes for children and families	a) Avoid two-step migration processes that require an initial period of child-parent separation and allow children to accompany workers who are on a pathway to permanent residency (if the family chooses this) b) Identify opportunities where both parents can be employed in the same business or in close proximity to each other
Articles 18 and 7 (considered together) ***Article 18:*** Right to have their parents be the adults with the primary responsibility for their upbringing and development	Parents are entitled to *appropriate* State assistance to perform their child-rearing responsibilities	1. TLM undermines strong child-parent attachments and relationships, and parents' protected role as their children's primary caregivers	a) Adopt strategies to mitigate impacts of disruptions to children's attachment figures including on children's early childhood development (this can be informed by disciplines such as family law, which regularly manage child-parent separation – see Art 16 [Measures 2(a)–(c)]) b) Make (at least some) of the family-related leave entitlements in domestic employment regulations available to migrant workers (eg, parental and carers' leave) to support parents to fulfil parenting duties
Article 7: Right to be cared for by their parents as far as possible	States shall ensure implementation of this right in accordance with national law and international obligations	2. Parental migration removes the protective function of strong parental presence and involvement in children's lives	a) Incorporate measures to address heightened risks to children during periods of parental absence including the mainstreaming of support – see Art 27 [Measure 2(d)] – and preparing children for periods of separation – see Art 5 [Measures 3(a)–(b)] and Art 16 [Measure 2(b)]
		3. States fail to protect against unjustified interferences with CRC rights by non-State actors (ie, employers)	a) Regulate employer practices to ensure uniformity and guarantee that workers' ability to maintain relationships with their children is not hindered or discretionary – see Art 10(2) [Measures (a) and (f)] b) Costs associated with measures that involve employers could be shared between employers and labour-receiving States, or subsidised by labour-receiving States if they want to continue to keep employer costs minimal

Policy measures to support interconnected CRC provisions that protect the child-parent relationship			
Children's rights	*State obligations*	*Social issues*	*Policy measures*
		4. Disruption to child-parent relationships is inconsistent with the need to strengthen families and communities to achieve sustainable international development	a) Reconcile Sustainable Development Goals (SGDs) that promote support for families and positive parenting with SDGs that promote TLM b) Recognise the centrality of investing in early childhood development (ECD) to long-term development strategies, and how parental migration conflicts with the importance of parental involvement to children's ECD
		5. Emerging framework for global governance of migration (including the New York Declaration, Global Compact for Migration and 2035 Agenda for Facilitating Human Mobility) is heavily premised on SDGs that promote TLM	a) Incorporate children's rights and best interests in relation to TLM and parental migration into the goals, targets and indicators being developed for the *UN 2035 Agenda for Facilitating Human Mobility* b) Prioritise children's rights and best interests in the implementation of the New York Declaration and Global Compact for Migration c) Develop new human-rights based, child-sensitive and gender-sensitive model TLM agreements (a measure in the Global Compact for Migration) d) Recognise that international cooperation in the context of TLM demands that labour-receiving countries share responsibility for measures to support children in countries from which they source labour
		6. Informed decision-making about TLM policies and measures to support children is stifled by failure to invest in comprehensive data collection	a) Invest in collecting and assessing comprehensive, disaggregated and longitudinal data on children impacted by TLM including on social impacts b) Base measures to mitigate harm to children arising from parental migration on multi-disciplinary evidence (including social science studies and studies in child development, parental deployment and family law)

Appendix II

Breakdown of key informants

A semi-structured interview was conducted by the researcher (in English) with all key informants between December 2016 and March 2018. These interviews were approved by the University of Melbourne's Law Human Ethics Advisory Group.

Breakdown of Key Informants

Canada	*Sector*	*Code*
1	Federal Government	Government 1
2	Federal Government	Government 2
3	Federal Government	Government 3
4	Provincial Government	Government 5
5	Research and Policy Institute	R & P 1
6	Research and Policy Institute	R & P 2
7	Research Institute	R & P 4
8	Research and Policy Institute	R & P 5
9	Research Institute	R & P 6
10	Non-government Organisation (Service Provision)	MLO-NGO 3
11	Non-government Organisation (Research)	MLO-NGO 4
Asia-Pacific	*Sector*	*Code*
12	Federal Government	Government 4
13	Federal Government	Government 6
14	Research Institute	R & P 3
15	Research and Policy Institute	R & P 7
16	Non-government Organisation (Service Provision)	MLO-NGO 1
17	Multilateral Organisation (Research and Policy)	MLO-NGO 2
18	Non-government organisation (Research)	MLO-NGO 5
19	Multilateral Organisation (Research and Policy)	MLO-NGO 6
20	Multilateral Organisation (Research and Policy)	MLO-NGO 7

Bibliography

A) Articles

Abram, Eliahu Frank, 'The Child's Right to Family Unity in International Immigration Law' (1995) 17(4) *Law and Policy* 397

Adamson, Elizabeth, Natasha Cortis, Deborah Brennan, Sara Charlesworth, 'Social Care and Migration Policy in Australia: Emerging Intersections?' (2017) 52(1) *Australian Journal of Social Issues* 78

Amuedo-Dorantes, Catalina, 'The Good and the Bad in Remittance Flows: Remittances Have the Potential to Lift up Developing Economies' (2014) 97*IZA World of Labor* 1

Asis, M M B, S Huang and B S A Yeoh, 'When the Light of the Home is Abroad: Unskilled Female Migration and the Filipino Family' (2004) 25(2) *Singapore Journal of Tropical Geography* 198

Asis, Maruja M B, 'Living with Migration: Experiences of Left Behind Children in the Philippines' (2006) 2(1) *Asian Population Studies* 45

Asis, Maruja M B and Alan Feranil, 'Not for Adults Only: Toward a Child's Lens in Migration Policies in Asia' (2020) 8(1) *Journal on Migration and Human Security* 68

Baldassar, Loretta, 'Transnational Families and the Provision of Moral and Emotional Support: The Relationship Between Truth and Distance' (2007) 14(4)*Identities: Global Studies in Culture and Power* 385

Battistella, Graziano and Cecilia Conaco, 'The Impact of Labour Migration on the Children Left Behind: A Study of Elementary School Children in the Philippines' (1998) 13 (2) *Sojourn: Journal of Social Issues in Southeast Asia* 220

Bernhard, Judith K, Patricia Landolt and Luin Goldring, 'Transnationalizing Families: Canadian Immigration Policy and the Spatial Fragmentation of Care-giving among Latin American Newcomers' (2009) 47(2) *International Migration* 3

Bhabha, Jacqueline, '"More Than Their Share of Sorrows": International Migration Law and the Rights of Children' (2003) 22(2) *Saint Louis University Public Law Review* 253

Biao, Xiang, 'How Far are the Left Behind Left Behind? A Preliminary Study in Rural China' (2007) 13(3) *Population, Place and Space* 179

Bowlby, Richard and Jennifer McIntosh, 'John Bowlby's Legacy and Meanings for the Family Law Field: In Conversation with Sir Richard Bowlby' (2011) 49(3) *Family Court Review* 549

Bretherton, Inge, 'The Origins of Attachment Theory: John Bowlby and Mary Ainsworth' (1992) 28*Developmental Psychology* 759

Byrne, James G, Thomas G O'Connor, Robert S Marvin and William F Whelan, 'Practitioner Review: The Contribution of Attachment Theory to Child Custody Assessments' (2005) 46(2) *Journal of Child Psychology and Psychiatry* 115

Carling, Jørgen, Cecilia Menjivar and Leah Schmalzbauer, 'Central Themes in the Study of Transnational Parenthood' (2012) 38(2) *Journal of Ethnic and Migration Studies* 191

Castañeda, Ernesto and Lesley Buck, 'Remittances, Transnational Parenting, and the Children Left Behind' [2011] (December) *The Latin Americanist* 85

Castañeda, Ernesto, 'Living in Limbo: Transnational Households, Remittances and Development' (2012) (51) *International Migration* 13

Castles, Stephen, 'The Forces Driving Global Migration' (2013) 34(2) *Journal of Intercultural Studies* 122

Cohen, Jeffrey H, 'Remittance Outcomes and Migration: Theoretical Contests, Real Opportunities' (2005) 40(1) *Studies in Comparative International Development* 88

Connell, John, 'From Blackbirds to Guestworkers in the South Pacific: Plus ça Change…?' (2010) 20*Economic and Labour Relations Review* 111

Crock, Mary E, 'Contract or Compact: Skilled Migration and the Dictates of Politics and Ideology' (2001) (16) *Georgetown Immigration Law Journal* 133

Daiute, Colette, 'The Rights of Children, the Rights of Nations: Developmental Theory and the Politics of Children's Rights' (2008) 64(4) *Journal of Social Issues* 701

Dawson, Hannah, 'The Role of Canada in the International Promotion of Human Rights', *McGill Blogs* (6 March 2016)

Dreby, Joanna and Tim Adkins, 'The Strength of Family Ties: How US Migration Shapes Children's Ideas of Family' (2011) 19(2) *Childhood* +

Frantz, Elizabeth, 'Jordan's Unfree Workforce: State-Sponsored Bonded Labour in the Arab Region' (2013) 49(8) *Journal of Development Studies* 1072

Gamburd, Michelle R, 'Advocating for Sri Lankan Migrant Workers: Obstacles and Challenges' (2009) 41(1) *Critical Asian Studies* 61

Gibson, John and David McKenzie, 'The Development Impact of a Best Practice Seasonal Worker Policy' (2014) 96(2) *The Review of Economics and Statistics* 229

Glass, Christy M, Susan Mannon and Peggy Petrzelka, 'Good Mothers as Guest Workers: Constructing the Trope of Compliant Maternity in Spain's Strawberry Industry' (2014) 44(3) *International Journal of Sociology* 8

Goonesekere, Savitri, 'Human Rights as a Foundation for Family Law Reform' (2000) 8*The International Journal of Children's Rights* 83

Gottfried, Sarah, 'Virtual Visitation: The Wave of the Future in Communication Between Children and Non-Custodial Parents in Relocation Cases' (2002) 36(3) *Family Law Quarterly* 475

Graham, Elspeth and Lucy P Jordan, 'Migrant Parents and the Psychological Well-Being of Left-Behind Children in Southeast Asia' (2011) 73*Journal of Marriage and Family* 763

Graham, Elspeth, Brenda S A Yeoh, Theodora Lam, Maruja Asis, Su-kamdi, 'Transnational Families and the Family Nexus: Perspectives of Indonesian and Filipino Children Left Behind by Migrant Parent(s)' (2012) 44*Environment and Planning* 793

de Haas, Hein, 'Migration and Development: A Theoretical Perspective' (2010) 44(1) *International Migration Review* 227

de Haas, Hein, 'The Migration and Development Pendulum: A Critical View on Research and Policy' (2012) 50(3) *International Migration* 8

Hanson, Karl and Laura Lundy, 'Does Exactly What it Says on the Tin? A Critical Analysis and Alternative Conceptualisation of the So-called "General Principles" of the

Convention on the Rights of the Child' (2017) 25(2) *The International Journal of Children's Rights* 285

Hart, Jason, 'Children's Participation and International Development: Attending to the Political' (2008) 16*International Journal of Children's Rights* 407

Harris-Short, Sonia, 'International Human Rights Law: Imperialist, Inept and Ineffective? Cultural Relativism and the UN Convention on the Rights of the Child' (2003) 25(1) *Human Rights Quarterly* 130

Hennebry, Jenna and Kerry Preibisch, 'A Model for Managed Migration? Re-Examining Best Practices in Canada's Seasonal Agricultural Worker Program' (2012) 50(1) *International Migration* 49

Hess, Julia Meredith and Diana Shandy, 'Kids at the Crossroads: Global Childhood and the State' (2008) 81(4) *Anthropological Quarterly* 765

Heymann, Jody, Francisco Flores-Macias, Jeffrey A Hayes, Malinda Kennedy, Claudia Lahaie and Alison Earle, 'The Impact of Migration on the Well-being of Transnational Families: New Data from Sending Communities in Mexico' (2009) 12(1) *Community, Work and Family* 91

Hoang, Lan Anh, Theodora Lam, Brenda S A Yeoh and Elspeth Graham, 'Transnational Migration, Changing Care Arrangements and Left-behind Children's Responses in South-East Asia' (2015) 13(3) *Children's Geographies* 263

Horton, Sarah, 'Consuming Childhood: "Lost" and "Ideal" Childhoods as a Motivation for Migration' (2008) 81(4) *Anthropological Quarterly* 925

Hugo, Graeme, 'Best Practice in Temporary Labour Migration for Development: A Perspective from Asia and the Pacific' (2009) 47(5) *International Migration* 23

Hugo, Graeme, 'Care Worker Migration, Australia and Development' (2009) 15 *Population, Space and Place* 189

Hutchinson, Terry, 'Developing Legal Research Skills: Expanding the Paradigm' (2008) 32 *Melbourne University Law Review* 1065

Hutchinson, Terry, 'The Doctrinal Method: Incorporating Interdisciplinary Methods in Reforming the Law' (2015) 3 *Erasmus Law Review* 130

Isaksen, Lise Widding, Sambasivan Uma Devi and Arlie Russell Hochschild, 'Global Care Crisis: A Problem of Capital, Care Chains, or Commons?' (2008) 52(3) *American Behavioral Scientist* 405

Jampaklay, Aree, 'Parental Absence and Children's School Enrolment: Evidence from a Longitudinal Study in Kanchanaburi, Thailand' (2006) 2(1) *Asian Population Studies* 93

Jayasuriya, Rasika and Brian Opeskin, 'The Migration of Women Domestic Workers from Sri Lanka: Protecting the Rights of Children Left Behind' (2015) 48*Cornell International Law Journal* 579

Kelly, Joan B and Michael E Lamb, 'Developmental Issues in Relocation Cases Involving Young Children: When, Whether, and How?' (2003) 17(2) *Journal of Family Psychology* 193

Kessler, Christl, 'Democratic Citizenship and Labour Migration in East Asia: Mapping Fields of Enquiry (2009) 8(2) *European Journal of East Asian Studies* 181

Kneebone, Susan, 'Migrant Workers Between States: In Search of Exit and Integration Strategies in South East Asia' (2012) 40*Asian Journal of Social Science* 367

Kofman, Eleonore, 'Gendered Global Migrations' (2004) 6(4) *International Feminist Journal of Politics* 643

Lake, Anthony and Margaret Chan, 'Putting Science into Practice for Early Child Development' (2014) 385(9980) *The Lancet* 1816

Lalonde, Richard N, Andrea Smith and Simone Johnson, 'Serial Migration and its Implications for the Parent-Child Relationship: A Retrospective Analysis of the Experiences of the Children of Caribbean Immigrants' (2004) 10(2) *Cultural Diversity and Ethnic Minority Psychology* 107

Lenard, Patti Tamara and Christine Straehle, 'Temporary Labour Migration, Global Redistribution and Democratic Justice' (2011) 11(2) *Politics, Philosophy and Economics* 206

Lu, Yao, 'Parental Migration and Education of Left-Behind Children: A Comparison of Two Settings' (2014) 76(5) *Journal of Marriage and Family* 1082

Lu, Yao, Qian He and Jeanne Brooks-Gunn, 'Diverse Experience of Immigrant Children: How Do Separation and Reunification Shape Their Development?' (2018) *Child Development* (advance)

Lundy, Laura, Ursula Kilkelly and Bronagh Byrne, 'Incorporation of the United Nations Convention on the Rights of the Child in Law: A Comparative Review' (2013) 21(3) *International Journal of Children's Rights* 442

Macdonald, Gail, 'School-based Support for Students with a Parent on Military Deployment' (2016) 42(1) *Children Australia* 57

Mahon, Rianne, 'After Neo-Liberalism?: The OECD, the World Bank and the Child' (2010) 10(2) *Global Social Policy* 172

Mazzucato, Valentina, Victor Cebotari, Angela Veale, Allen White, Marzia Grassi and Jeanne Vivet, 'International Parental Migration and the Psychological Well-being of Children in Ghana, Nigeria, and Angola' (2015) 132*Social Science and Medicine* 215

Merla, Laura, Majella Kilkey and Loretta Baldassar, 'Introduction to the Special Issue "Transnational care: Families Confronting Borders"' (2020) (Early View) *Journal of Family Research* 1

Nana, Oishi, 'Family Without Borders? Asian Women in Migration and the Transformation of Family Life' (2008) 14(4) *Asian Journal of Women's Studies* 54

Neumayer, Eric, 'Unequal Access to Foreign Spaces: How States Use Visa Restrictions to Regulate Mobility in a Globalised World' (2006) 31(1) *Transactions of the Institute of British Geographers* 72

Nwaogu, Waoma G and Michael J Ryan, 'FDI, Foreign Aid, Remittance and Economic Growth in Developing Countries' (2015) 19(2) *Review of Development Economics*, 19(1) (2015) 100

O'Connell Davidson, Julia, 'Moving Children? Child Trafficking, Child Migration, and Child Rights' (2011) 31(3) *Critical Social Policy* 454

Orbeta, Jr, Aniceto C and Michael R M Abrigo, 'Managing International Labor Migration: The Philippine Experience' (2011) 38(1–2) *Philippine Journal of Development* 57

Orellana, Marjorie Faulstich, Barrie Thorne, Anna Chee and Wan Shun Eva Lam, 'Transnational Childhoods: The Participation of Children in Processes of Family Migration' (2001) 48(4) *Social Problems* 572

Pande, Amrita, '"The Paper that You Have in Your Hand is My Freedom": Migrant Domestic Work and the Sponsorship (Kafala) System in Lebanon' (2013) 47(2) *International Migration Review* 414

Parkinson, Patrick, Judy Cashmore and Judi Single, 'The Need for Reality Testing in Relocation Cases' (2010) 44(1) *Family Law Quarterly* 1

Parrenas, Rhacel Salazar, 'Transnational Fathering: Gendered Conflicts, Distant Disciplining and Emotional Gaps' (2008) 34(7) *Journal of Ethnic and Migration Studies* 1057

Parrenas, Rhacel Salazar, 'Transnational Mothering: A Source of Gender Conflicts in the Family' (2010) 88 *North Carolina Law Review* 1825

Pellecer, Sonia (IOM Guatemala), 'Short-term Temporary Labour Migration Yields Long-Term Results' (July 2007) *Migration* 19

Piore, Michael J, 'Comment' (1980) 33(3) *Industrial and Labor Relations Review* 312

Piper, Nicola, 'The "Migration-Development Nexus" Revisited from a Rights Perspective' (2008) 7(3) *Journal of Human Rights* 282

Piper, Nicola and Matt Withers, 'Forced Transnationalism and Temporary Labour Migration: Implications for Understanding Migrant Rights' (2018) 15(5) *Identities* 558

Piper, Nicola and Stefan Rother, 'Editorial: Migration and Democracy: Citizenship and Human Rights from a Multi-level Perspective' (2015) 53(3) *International Migration* 3

Pollis, Adamantia, 'Cultural Relativism Revisited: Through a State Prism' (1996) 18 *Human Rights Quarterly* 316

Pottinger, Audrey M and Sharon Williams Brown, 'Understanding the Impact of Parental Migration on Children: Implications for Counselling Families from the Caribbean' (2006) *American Counselling Association: Vistas Online* <https://www.counseling.org/resources/library/vistas/vistas06_online-only/pottinger.pdf>

Pratt, Geraldine, 'Between Homes: Displacement and Belonging for Second-Generation Filipino-Canadian Youths' [2003–2004] (Winter) 140*BC Studies* 41

Razavi, Shahra and Laura Turquet, 'Progress of the World's Women 2015–2016: Transforming Economies, Realizing Rights' (2016) 16(1) *Global Social Policy* 86

Rhoades, Helen, 'Revising Australia's Parenting Laws: A Plea for a Relational Approach to Children's Best Interests' (2010) 22(2) *Child and Family Law Quarterly* 172

Rohorua, Halahingano, John Gibson, David McKenzie and Pilar Garcia Martinez, 'How do Pacific Island Households and Communities Cope with Seasonally Absent Members?' (2009) 24(3) *Pacific Economic Bulletin* 19

Rosewarne, Stuart, 'Temporary International Labour Migration and Development in South and Southeast Asia' (2012) 18(2) *Feminist Economics* 63

Sassen, Saskia, 'Two Stops in Today's New Global Geographies: Shaping Novel Labor Supplies and Employment Regimes' (2008) 52(3) *American Behavioral Scientist* 457

Sassen, Saskia, 'When the Center No Longer Holds: Cities as Frontier Zones' (2012) *Cities* 1

Saul, Ben, 'Indefinite Security Detention and Refugee Children and Families in Australia: International Human Rights Law Dimensions' (2013) 20*Australian International Law Journal* 55

Sawyer, Adam, 'Is Money Enough?: The Effect of Migrant Remittances on Parental Aspirations and Youth Educational Attainment in Rural Mexico' (2016) 50(1) *International Migration Review* 231

Schmalzbauer, Leah, 'Searching for Wages and Mothering from Afar: The Case of Honduran Transnational Families' (2004) 66(5) *Journal of Marriage and Family* 1317

Schmalzbauer, Leah 'Family Divided: The Class Formation of Honduran Transnational Families' (2008) 8(3) *Global Networks* 29

Silvey, Rachel, 'Transnational Rights and Wrongs: Moral Geographies of Gender and Migration' (2009) 37(2) *Global Gender Justice* 75

Somaiah, Bittiandra Chand, Brenda S A Yeoh and Silvia Mila Arlini, 'Cukup for Me to be Successful in this Country: 'Staying' Among Left-Behind Young Women in Indonesia's Migrant-Sending Villages' (2020) 20(2) *Global Networks* 237

South East Asia National Human Rights Institutions Forum (SEAFN), '2010 South East Asia National Human Rights Institutions Forum (SEANF) Paper on Migrant Workers' (2010) 11(1) *Asia-Pacific Journal on Human Rights and the Law* 63

Thronson, David B, 'You Can't Get Here from Here: Toward More Child-Centered Immigration Law' (2006) 14(1) *Virginia Journal of Social Policy and the Law* 58

Tobin, John, 'Understanding Children's Rights: A Vision Beyond Vulnerability' (2015) 84 *Nordic Journal of International Law* 155

Tobin, John, 'Seeking to Persuade: A Constructive Approach to Human Rights Treaty Interpretation' (2018) 23 *Harvard Human Rights Journal* 201

Ukwatta, Swarna, 'Sri Lankan Female Domestic Workers Overseas: Mothering their Children from a Distance' 27 *Journal of Population Research* 107

Williams, Fiona, 'Markets and Migrants in the Care Economy' (2011) 47 *Soundings* 22

Withers, Matt, 'Temporary Labour Migration and Underdevelopment in Sri Lanka: The Limits of Remittance Capital' (2019) 8(3) *Migration and Development*, 418

Wolf, Giovanna I, 'Preserving Family Unity: The Rights of Children to Maintain the Companionship of Their Parents and Remain in Their Country of Birth' (1996) 4(1) *Indiana Journal of Global Legal Studies* 207

Zentgraf, Kristine M and Norma Stoltz Chinchilla, 'Transnational Family Separation: A Framework for Analysis' (2012) 38(2) *Journal of Ethnic and Migration Studies* 345

B) Books

Abramson, Bruce, *Article 2: The Right of Non-Discrimination* (Martinus Nijhoff, 2008)

Berg, Laurie, *Migrant Rights at Work: Law's Precariousness at the Intersection of Immigration and Labour* (Routledge, 2016)

Bowlby, John, *Child Care and the Growth of Love: Abridged and Edited by Margery Fry. With Two New Chapters by Mary D Salter Ainsworth* (Penguin Books, 1965)

Bowlby, John, *Attachment and Loss, Vol 1: Attachment* (Basic Books, 1969)

Bowlby, John, *Attachment and Loss, Vol 2: Separation* (Basic Books, 1973)

Calavita, Kitty, *Immigrants at the Margins: Law, Race, and Exclusion in Southern Europe* (Cambridge University Press, 2005)

Carens, Joseph, *The Ethics of Immigration* (Oxford University Press, 2013)

Crock, Mary and Lenni Benson (eds), *Protecting Migrant Children: In Search of Best Practice* (Elgar, 2018)

Detrick, Sharon (ed), *The United Nations Convention on the Rights of the Child: A Guide to the 'Travaux Préparatoires'* (Martinus Nijhoff Publishers, 1992)

Detrick, Sharon, *A Commentary on the United Nations Convention on the Rights of the Child* (Martinus Nijhoff, 1999)

Doek, Jaap E, *A Commentary on the United Nations Convention on the Rights of the Child: Article 8 The Right to Preservation of Identity, Article 9 The Right Not to Be Separated from His or Her Parents* (Martinus Nijhoff, 2006)

Dreby, Joanna, *Divided by Borders: Mexican Migrants and Their Children* (University of California Press, 2010)

Ehrenreich, Barbara and Arlie Russell Hochschild (eds), *Global Woman: Nannies, Maids and Sex Workers in the New Economy* (Metropolitan Books, 2003)

Faist, Thomas, *The Transnationalized Social Question: Migration and the Politics of Social Inequalities in the Twenty-First Century* (Oxford University Press, 2019)

Folbre, Nancy, *Who Pays for the Kids?: Gender and the Structures of Constraint* (Routledge, 1994)

Gertel, Jörg and Sarah Ruth Sippel (eds), *Seasonal Workers in Mediterranean Agriculture: The Social Costs of Eating Fresh* (Routledge, 2014)

Global Knowledge Partnership on Migration and Development (KNOMAD), *Migration and Remittances Factbook 2016* (World Bank Group, 3rd ed, 2016)

Hacker, Daphna, *Legalized Families in the Era of Bordered Globalization* (Cambridge University Press, 2017)

Howard-Hassmann, Rhoda E, *Compassionate Canadians: Civic Leaders Discuss Human Rights* (University of Toronto Press, 2003)

Howe, Joanna and Rosemary Owens (eds), *Temporary Labour Migration in the Global Era: The Regulatory Challenges* (Hart Publishing, 2016)

Lucas, Robert E B (ed), *International Handbook on Migration and Economic Development* (Edward Elgar Publishing, 2014)

Mason, Jennifer, *Qualitative Researching* (SAGE Publications, 2nd ed, 2002)

Meghani, Zahra (ed), *Women Migrant Workers: Ethical, Political and Legal Problems* (Taylor and Francis, 2015)

Michel, Sonya and Ito Peng (eds), *Gender, Migration, and the Work of Care: A Multi-Scalar Approach to the Pacific Rim* (Palgrave Macmillan, 2017)

National Children's Commissioner, *Children's Rights Report 2017* (Australian Human Rights Commission, 2017)

Nazario, Sonia, *Enrique's Journey* (Random House, 2006)

Nowak, Manfred, *The UN Covenant on Civil and Political Rights: CCPR Commentary* (Engel, 2nd ed, 2005)

OECD, *Geographical Distribution of Financial Flows to Developing Countries 2018: Disbursements, Commitments, Country Indicators* (OECD Publishing, 2018)

Parrenas, Rhacel Salazar, *Children of Global Migration: Transnational Families and Gendered Woes* (Stanford University Press, 2005)

Suárez-Orozco, Carola and Marcelo M Suarez-Orozco, *Children of Immigration* (Harvard University Press, 2001)

Tobin, J (ed), *The UN Convention on the Rights of the Child: A Commentary* (OUP, 2019)

Withers, Matt, *Sri Lanka's Remittance Economy: A Multiscalar Analysis of Migration-Underdevelopment* (Routledge, 2019)

Yin, Robert K, *Qualitative Research from Start to Finish* (The Guilford Press, 2nd ed, 2016)

Ziemele, Ineta, *A Commentary on the United Nations Convention on the Rights of the Child, Article 7: The Right to Birth Registration, Name and Nationality, and the Right to Know and Be Cared for by Parents* (Brill, 2007)

C) Book chapters

Badasu, Delali and Sonya Michel, 'On a Collision Course: Millennium Development Goals and Mothers' Migration' in Zahra Meghani (ed), *Women Migrant Workers: Ethical, Political and Legal Problems* (Taylor and Francis, 2015) 75

Baldassar, Loretta and Laura Merla, 'Locating Transnational Care Circulation in Migration and Family Studies' in Loretta Baldassar and Laura Merla (eds), *Transnational Families, Migration and the Circulation of Care: Understanding Mobility and Absence in Family Life* (Routledge, 2014) 25

Becerril, Ofelia, 'Gendered Policies, Single Mothers and Transnational Motherhood: Mexican Female Migrant Farmworkers in Canada' in Zahra Meghani (ed), *Women Migrant Workers: Ethical, Political and Legal Problems* (Taylor and Francis, 2015) 154

Ben-Arieh, Asher and Noam Tarshish, 'Children's Rights and Well-being' in Martin D Ruck, Michele Peterson-Badali and Michael Freeman (eds), *Handbook of Children's Rights Global and Multidisciplinary Perspectives* (Routledge, 2017) 68

Besson, Samantha and Eleonor Kleber, 'Article 2. The Right to Non-discrimination' in J Tobin (ed), *The UN Convention on the Rights of the Child: A Commentary* (OUP, 2019) 41

Bhaba, Jacqueline, 'The "Mere Fortuity of Birth"? Children, Mothers, Borders and the Meaning of Citizenship' in Seyla Benhabib and Judith Resnik (eds), *Migrations and Mobilities: Citizenship, Borders and Gender* (NYU Press, 2009) 187

Bonifacio, Glenda Tibe, 'Live-in Caregivers in Canada: Servitude for Promissory Citizenship and Family Rights' in Maria Kontos and Glenda Tibe Bonifacio (eds), *Migrant Domestic Workers and Family Life* (Palgrave Macmillan, 2015) 145

Brennan, Deborah and Elizabeth Adamson, 'Care and Migration' in Sheila Shaver (ed), *Handbook on Gender and Social Policy* (Elgar, 2018) 253

Cantwell, Nigel, 'Are Children's Rights Still Human?' in Antonella Invernizzi and Jane Williams (eds), *The Human Rights of Children From Visions to Implementation* (Ashgate, 2011) 37

Cholewinski, Ryszard, 'Migration for Employment' in SirRichardPlender (ed), *Issues in International Migration Law* (Brill Nijhoff, 2015) 28

Covell, Katherine, R Brian Howe and Anne McGillivray, 'Implementing Children's Education Rights in Schools' in Martin D Ruck, Michele Peterson-Badali and Michael Freeman (eds), *Handbook of Children's Rights Global and Multidisciplinary Perspectives* (Routledge, 2017)

Cox, David, 'Children of Migrant Workers: A Family Relationship Issue' in Graziano Battistella and Cecilia Conaco (eds), *Children and Migration: A New Challenge for World-Wide Social Services* (International Social Service Hong Kong Branch, 1990)

Crock, Mary and Lenni B Benson, 'Central Issues in the Protection of Child Migrants' in Mary Crock and Lenni Benson (eds), *Protecting Migrant Children: In Search of Best Practice* (Elgar, 2018) 1

Crock, Mary and Hannah Martin, 'First Things First: International Law and the Protection of Migrant Children' in Mary Crock and Lenni Benson (eds), *Protecting Migrant Children: In Search of Best Practice* (Elgar, 2018) 75

Dauvergne, Catherine, 'Irregular Migration, State Sovereignty and the Rule of Law' in Vincent Chetail and Céline Bauloz (eds), *Research Handbook on International Law and Migration* (Edward Elgar, 2014) 75

Eekelaar, John and John Tobin, 'Article 3. The Best Interests of the Child' in J Tobin (ed), *The UN Convention on the Rights of the Child: A Commentary* (OUP, 2019) 73

Flyvbjerg, Bent, 'Case Study' in Norman K Denzin and Yvonna S Lincoln (eds), *The Sage Handbook of Qualitative Research* (SAGE Publications, 4th ed, 2011) 301

Freeman, Michael, 'The Value and Values of Children's Rights' in Antonella Invernizzi and Jane Williams (eds), *The Human Rights of Children From Visions to Implementation* (Ashgate, 2011) 21

Gibson, John and David McKenzie, 'Development through Seasonal Worker Programs: The Case of New Zealand's RSE Program' in Robert E B Lucas (ed), *International Handbook on Migration and Economic Development* (Edward Elgar Publishing, 2014) 186

Haagsman, Karlijn and Valentina Mazzucato, 'The Well-Being of Stay Behind Family Members in Migrant Households' in Tanja Bastia and Robert Skeldon (eds), *Routledge Handbook of Migration and Development* (Routledge, 2020) 181

Hochschild, Arlie Russell, 'Global Care Chains and Emotional Surplus Value' in Will Hutton and Anthony Giddens (eds), *On the Edge: Living with Global Capitalism* (Jonathan Cape, 2000) 130

Kamchedzera, Garton, 'Article 5 – The Child's Right to Appropriate Direction and Guidance' in Andre Alenet al, *A Commentary on the United Nations Convention on the Rights of the Child* (Martinus Nijhoff, 2012)

Kneebone, Susan, 'Transnational Labour Migrants: Whose Responsibility?' in Fiona Jenkins, Mark Nolan and Kim Rubenstein (eds), *Allegiance and Identity in a Globalised World* (Cambridge University Press, 2014) 426

Lamb, Michael E, C Philip Hwang and Robert D Ketterlinus, 'Parent-Child Relationships: Development in the Context of the Family' in Marc H Bornstein and Michael E Lamb (eds), *Developmental Psychology: An Advanced Textbook* (Lawrence Erlbaum Associates Publishers, 1999) 411

Lambert, Helene, 'Family Unity in Migration Law: The Evolution of a More Unified Approach in Europe' in Vincent Chetail and Céline Bauloz (eds), *Research Handbook on International Law and Migration* (Edward Elgar Publishing Ltd, 2014) 194

Lawrence, Jeanette and Agnes Dodds, 'Developmental Science, Child Development and the Law' in Lisa Young, Mary Anne Kenny, Geoffrey Monahan (eds), *Children and the Law in Australia* (LexisNexis Butterworths, 2nd ed, 2017) 83

Lester, Eve, 'Socioeconomic Rights, Human Security and Survival Migrants: Whose Rights? Whose Security?' in Alice Edwards and Carla Ferstman (eds), *Human Security and Non-Citizens: Law, Policy and International Affairs* (Cambridge University Press, 2010) 314

Lucas, Robert E B, 'Migration and Economic Development: An Introduction and Synopsis' in Robert E B Lucas (ed), *International Handbook on Migration and Development* (Edward Elgar Publishing, 2014)

Maclellan, Nic and Peter Mares, 'Labour Mobility in the Pacific: Creating Seasonal Work Programs in Australia' in Stewart Firth (ed), *Globalisation and Governance in the Pacific Islands: State, Society and Governance in Melanesia* (ANU Press, 2006) 137

Mahon, Rianne and Sonya Michel, 'Not In Focus: Migrant Women Caregivers As Seen by the ILO and the OECD' in Sonya Michel and Ito Peng (eds), *Gender, Migration, and the Work of Care: A Multi-Scalar Approach to the Pacific Rim* (Palgrave Macmillan, 2017) 269

Meghani, Zahra, 'Women on the Move' in Zahra Meghani (ed), *Women Migrant Workers: Ethical, Political and Legal Problems* (Taylor and Francis, 2015) 5

Ong, Aihwa, 'Latitudes of Citizenship: Membership, Meaning and Multiculturalism' in Alison Brysk and Gershon Shafir (eds), *People Out of Place: Globalisation, Human Rights, and the Citizenship Gap* (Routledge, 2004) 53

Pérez Orozco, Amaia, 'Global Care Chains Reshaping the Hidden Foundations of an Unsustainable Development Model' in Zahra Meghani (ed), *Women Migrant Workers: Ethical, Political and Legal Problems* (Taylor and Francis, 2015) 101

Piper, Nicola, 'Global Governance of Labour Migration: From "Management" of Migration to an Integrated Rights-based Approach' in Peter Drahos (ed), *Regulatory Theory: Foundations and Applications* (ANU Press, 2017) 375

Pobjoy, Jason M and John Tobin, 'Article 10. The Right to Family Reunification' in J Tobin (ed), *The UN Convention on the Rights of the Child: A Commentary* (OUP, 2019) 341

Ruhs, Martin, 'Protecting the Rights of Temporary Migrant Workers: Ideals Versus Reality' in Joanna Howe and Rosemary Owens (eds), *Temporary Labour Migration in the Global Era* (Hart Publishing, 2016) 299

Setien, Maria Luisa and Elaine Acosta, 'Care and Feminized North-South and South-South Migration Flows: Denial of Rights and Limited Citizenship' in Laura Oso and Natalia Ribas-Mateos (eds), *The International Handbook on Gender, Migration and Transnationalism: Global and Development Perspectives* (Edward Elgar, 2013) 397

Shackel, Rita, 'The UN Convention on the Rights of the Child: Tracing Australia's Implementation of the Provisions Relating to Family Relations' in O Cvejić Jančić (ed), *The Rights of the Child in a Changing World* (Springer, 2016) 37

Taran, Patrick A, 'Clashing Worlds: Imperatives for a Rights-Based Approach to Labour Migration in the Age of Globalization' in Vincent Chetail (ed), *Globalization, Migration and Human Rights: International Law Under Review* (Bruylant, 2007) vol 2, 405

Tobin, John, 'Understanding a Human Rights Based Approach to Matters Involving Children: Conceptual Foundations and Strategic Considerations' in Antonella Invernizzi and Jane Williams (eds), *The Human Rights of Children: From Visions to Implementation* (Ashgate, 2011) 61

Tobin, John, 'Taking Children's Rights Seriously: The Need for a Multilingual Approach' in Alison Diduck, Noam Peleg and Helen Reece (eds), *Law in Society: Reflections on Children, Family, Culture and Philosophy* (Brill, 2015) 125

Tobin, John, 'Fixed Concepts but Changing Conceptions: Understanding the Relationship Between Children and Parents under the CRC' in Martin D Ruck, Michele Peterson-Badali and Michael Freeman (eds), *Handbook of Children's Rights Global and Multi-disciplinary Perspectives* (Routledge, 2017) 53

Tobin, John, 'Article 4. A State's General Obligation of Implementation' in J Tobin (ed), *The UN Convention on the Rights of the Child: A Commentary* (OUP, 2019) 108

Tobin, John and Judy Cashmore, 'Article 9. The Right Not to Be Separated from Parents' in J Tobin (ed), *The UN Convention on the Rights of the Child: A Commentary* (OUP, 2019) 305

Tobin, John and Sarah M Field, 'Article 16. The Right to Protection of Privacy, Family, Home, Correspondence, Honour, and Reputation' in J Tobin (ed), *The UN Convention on the Rights of the Child: A Commentary* (OUP, 2019) 550

Tobin, John and Florence Seow, 'Article 7. The Rights to Birth Registration, a Name, Nationality, and to Know and Be Cared for By Parents' in J Tobin (ed), *The UN Convention on the Rights of the Child: A Commentary* (OUP, 2019) 236

Tobin, John and Florence Seow, 'Article 18. Parental Responsibilities and State Assistance' in J Tobin (ed), *The UN Convention on the Rights of the Child: A Commentary* (OUP, 2019) 646

Tobin, John and Shelia Varadan, 'Article 5. The Right to Parental Direction and Guidance Consistent with a Child's Evolving Capacities' in J Tobin (ed), *The UN Convention on the Rights of the Child: A Commentary* (OUP, 2019) 158

Wickramasekara, Piyasiri, 'Migration Regimes and Their Linkages for Family Unity, Integrity and Development' in Marion Panizzon, Gottfried Zurcher and Elisa Fornale (eds), *The Palgrave Handbook of International Labour Migration: Law and Policy Perspectives* (Palgrave Macmillan, 2015) 146

Withers, Matt and Nicola Piper, 'Transnationalism and Temporary Labour Migration' in Brenda S A Yeoh and Francis Collins (eds), *Handbook on Transnationalism* (Edward Elgar, 2021) (forthcoming)

Waheed, Nayyirah, 'The Maid' in *Salt* (Createspace, 2013)

D) Reports, papers and briefs

Reports

Arthurs, H W, 'Law and Learning: Report to the Social Sciences and Humanities Research Council of Canada by the Consultative Group on Research and Education in Law' (Social Sciences and Humanities Research Council of Canada, 1983)

Campbell, John and Olivia Warrick, *Climate Change and Migration Issues in the Pacific* (UN Economic and Social Commission for Asia and the Pacific, 2014)

CHAMPSEA Philippines, *In the Wake of Parental Migration: Health and Well-being Impacts on Filipino Children* (Scalabrini Migration Center, 2011)

Costa, Daniel, and Philip Martin, 'Temporary Labor Migration Programs: Governance, Migrant Worker Rights, and Recommendations for the UN Global Compact for Migration' (Economic Policy Institute Report, 1 August 2018)

Crush, Jonathan, Belinda Dodson, John Gay, Thuso Green and Clement Leduka, *Migration, Remittances and 'Development' in Lesotho* (Southern African Migration Programme, 2010)

Curtain, Richard, Matthew Dornan, Jesse Doyle and Stephen Howes, *Pacific Possible: Labour Mobility: The Ten Billion Dollar Prize* (Pacific Possible Series, World Bank, July 2016)

Enríquez, Carmen González and Miquel Reynés Ramón, 'Circular Migration Between Spain and Morocco: Something More than Agricultural Work?' (METOIKOS Project, European University Institute, 2011)

Faraday, Fay, 'Made in Canada: How the Law Constructs Migrant Workers' Insecurity' (Summary Report, Metcalfe Foundation, September 2012)

Ghosh, Bimal, *Migrants' Remittances and Development: Myths, Rhetoric and Realities* (IOM, 2006)

Hein, Catherine, *Reconciling Work and Family Responsibilities: Practical Ideas from Global Experience* (ILO, 2005)

Helliwell, John F, Richard Layard and Jeffrey D Sachs (eds), *World Happiness Report 2018* (Sustainable Development Solutions Network, 2018)

Hettige, S T, Evangeline S Ekanayake, Ramani Jayasundere, Anula Rathnayake and Push-parani Figurado, *Understanding Psychosocial Issues Faced by Migrant Workers and their Families* (Sri Lankan Ministry of Foreign Employment Promotion and Welfare, 2012)

Human Rights Watch, *Exported and Exposed: Abuses against Sri Lankan Domestic Workers in Saudi Arabia, Kuwait, Lebanon, and the United Arab Emirates* (Human Rights Watch, 2007)

Human Rights Watch, *Slow Reform: Protection of Migrant Domestic Workers in Asia and the Middle East* (Human Rights Watch, 2010)

Initial Report of the Republic of Indonesia on the Implementation of the International Convention on the Protection of the Rights of All Migrant Workers and Members their Families Pursuant to the Simplified Reporting Procedure (5 March 2017) <https://tbinternet.ohchr.org/Treaties/CMW/Shared%20Documents/IDN/CMW_C_IDN_1_6902_E.pdf>

International Domestic Workers' Network, International Trade Union Confederation and Human Rights Watch, *Claiming Rights: Domestic Workers' Movements and Global Advances for Labour Reform* (Human Rights Watch, 2013)

International Human Rights Clinic, *The Protection of the Rights of Migrant Domestic Workers in a Country of Origin and a Country of Destination: Case Studies of the Philippines and Kuwait* (Johns Hopkins School of Advanced International Studies, 2013)

Kelly, Phillip, 'Understanding Intergenerational Social Mobility: Filipino Youth in Canada' (IRPP Study No 45, Institute for Research on Public Policy, February 2014)

McArthur, Brian B, *In Praise of the Arthurs Report on Canadian Federal Labour Standards* (Canadian Centre for Policy Alternatives, March 2007)

Meadows, Sarah O, Megan K Beckett, Kirby Bowling, Daniela Golinelli, Michael P Fisher, Laurie T Martin, Lisa S Meredith, Karen Chan Osilla, *Family Resilience in the Military: Definitions, Models, and Policies* (RAND Corporation, 2015)

Nakache, Delphine and Leanne Dixon-Perera, 'Temporary or Transitional? Migrant Workers' Experiences with Permanent Residence in Canada' (IRPP Study No 55, Institute for Research on Public Policy, October 2015)

National Scientific Council on the Developing Child, *The Science of Early Childhood Development: Closing the Gap Between What We Know and What We Do* (Center on the Developing Child, Harvard University, January 2007)

O'Connell, Julia Davidson and Caitlin Farrow, *Child Migration and the Construction of Vulnerability* (Save the Children, 2007)

OECD, *International Migration Outlook 2019* (OECD, 2019)

de Oliveira, Gabrielle Marcelletti Rocha, *Transnational Care Constellations: Mexican Immigrant Mothers and their Children in Mexico and in New York City* (PhD Thesis, Columbia University, 2015)

Omelaniuk, Irena, *Gender, Poverty Reduction and Migration* (World Bank, 2005)

Oxford Policy Management, 'Impact of Labour Migration on "Children Left Behind" in Tajikistan' (Research Report to UNICEF Tajikistan, November 2011)

Reyes, Melanie M, *Migration and Filipino Children Left-Behind: A Literature Review* (UNICEF, 2007).

Samson, Michael(Economic Policy Research Institute), *Cognitive Capital: Investing in Children to Generate Sustainable Growth* (UNICEF East Asia and the Pacific, October 2016)

Save the Children Sri Lanka and Kishali Pinto-Jayawardena, *Left Behind, Left Out: The Impact on Children and Families of Mothers Migrating for Work Abroad* (Save the Children Sri Lanka, 2006)

Save the Children, *"The World We Want": Consultations with Sri Lankan Children on Their Priorities for Post 2015* (Save the Children, September 2013)

Tanielian, Terri, Benjamin R Karney, Anita Chandra, Sarah O Meadows and Deployment Life Study Team, *The Deployment Life Study: Methodological Overview and Baseline Sample Description* (RAND Arroyo Center and the National Defence Research Institute, 2014)

Wessels, Anja, 'Home Sweet Home? Work, Life and Well-being of Foreign Domestic Workers in Singapore' (Research Report, Humanitarian Organisation for Migration Economics, March 2015)

Wettasinghe, Kusala, Gethsie Shanmugam and Sarala Emmanuel, *Alternative Care Giving of Migrant Workers' Children* (Terre des Hommes, 2012)

World Bank, 'Early Childhood Development' in *World Development Report 2015: Mind, Society, and Behavior* (World Bank, 2015)

World Bank, *Expanding Employment Pathways for Pacific Islanders in the Australian and New Zealand Aged Care Sectors* (The World Bank Group, 2017)

World Bank Group, *Maximizing the Development Impacts from Temporary Migration: Recommendations for Australia's Seasonal Worker Programme* (International Bank for Reconstruction and Development/World Bank, 2017)

Research and working papers

Amnesty International, 'Abusive Labour Migration Policies' (Submission to the UN Committee on Migrant Workers' Day of General Discussion on Workplace Exploitation and Workplace Protection, 7 April 2014)

Andersson, Lisa and Melissa Siegel, 'Empirical Assessments of the Development Impacts of Migration' (MIGNEX Background Paper, Peace Research Institute Oslo, 2019)

Antman, Francisca, 'The Impact of Migration on Family Left Behind' (*Institute for the Study of Labor Discussion Paper* No. 6374, March 2012)

Australian Institute of Family Studies, 'Parent-Child Contact and Post-Separation Parenting Arrangements' (Research Report, No 9, July 2004)

Berkelmans, Leon and Jonathan Pryke, 'The Development Benefits of Expanding Pacific Access to Australia's Labour Market' (Lowy Institute Analyses Paper, December 2016)

Bernhard, J K, P Landolt and L Goldring, 'Transnational, Multi-Local Motherhood: Experiences of Separation and Reunification among Latin American Families in Canada' (CERIS Working Paper No 40, Latin American Research Group, York University, 2005)

Bradshaw, John, Petra Hoelscher and Dominic Richardson, 'Comparing Child Well-being in OECD Countries: Concepts and Methods' (Innocenti Working Paper, UNICEF, 2006)

Bryant, John, 'Children of International Migrants in Indonesia, Thailand, and the Philippines: A Review of Evidence and Policies' (Innocenti Working Paper, No 2005–05, UNICEF, April 2005)

Center on the Developing Child, Harvard University, *Brain Architecture* <http://developingchild.harvard.edu/science/key-concepts/brain-architecture>

Cook, Harry and Jane Sail, 'Migrant Well-Being in the Middle East and North Africa: A Focus on Gender in Cairo' (Working Paper for the World Migration Report 2013, IOM, 2013)

Cortes, Rosalia, 'Remittances and Children's Rights: An Overview of Academic and Policy Literature' (Division of Policy and Practice Working Paper, UNICEF, January 2007)

Cortes, Rosalia, 'Children and Women Left Behind in Labor Sending Countries: An Appraisal of Social Risks' (Division of Policy and Practice Working Paper, UNICEF, August 2008)

Dias, Malsiri and Ramani Jayasundere, 'Sri Lanka: Good Practices to Prevent Women Migrant Workers From Going into Expolitative Forms of Labour' (GENPROM Working Paper No 9, Series on Women and Migration, Gender Promotion Program, ILO, 1 December 2002)

Edillon, Rosemarie, *The Effects of Parent's Migration on the Rights of Children Left Behind in the Philippines* (Division of Policy and Practice Working Paper, UNICEF, August 2008)

Farrant, Macha, Anna MacDonald and Dhananjayan Sriskandarajah, 'Migration and Development: Opportunities and Challenges for Policymakers' (IOM Migration Research Series, No 22, April 2006)

de la Garza, Rodolfo, 'Migration, Development and Children Left Behind: A Multidimensional Perspective' (Social and Economic Policy Working Paper, UNICEF, May 2010)

Global Alliance Against Traffic in Women (GAATW), 'Female Temporary Labour Migration and Rights Protection in the Strawberry Sector in Huelva, Spain' (Research Report, GAATW, 2009)

Jastram, Kate, *Family Unity: The New Geography of Family Life* (1 May 2003) Migration Policy Institute <https://www.migrationpolicy.org/article/family-unity-new-geography-family-life>

Lambert, Helene, 'Family Unity in Migration Law: The Evolution of a More Unified Approach in Europe' (Research Paper No 13–06, University of Westminster School of Law, 2013)

Lebon-McGregor, Elaine, 'A History of Global Migration Governance: Challenging Linearity' (International Migration Institute, Working Paper 167, September 2020)

Macours, Karen and Renos Vakis, 'Seasonal Migration and Early Childhood Development' (Social Protection Discussion Paper, No 0702, The World Bank, March 2007)

Pearson, Emma and Jennifer Tan Poh Sim, 'Fulfilling Child Rights Through Early Childhood Development' (South-South Cooperation for Child Rights Working Paper, No 3, UNICEF, September 2013)

Perera, Nirasha and Madhubhashini R Rathnayaka, *Sri Lanka's Missing Mothers: A Working Paper on the Effects of Mother Migration on Children* (Save the Children Sri Lanka, November 2013)

Piper, Nicola, 'Gender and Migration: A Paper Prepared for the Policy Analysis and Research Programme of the Global Commission on International Migration' (GCIM, September 2005)

Piper, Nicola, 'Contributions of Migrant Domestic Workers to Sustainable Development' (Policy Paper for the Pre-GFMD VI High-Level Regional Meeting on Migrant Domestic Workers at the Interface of Migration and Development, UN Women, 2013)

Pratt, Geraldine, Philippine Women Centre of BC and Ugnayan ng Kabataang Pilipino sa Canada (Filipino Canadian Youth Alliance), 'Deskilling Across the Generations: Reunification Among Transnational Filipino Families in Vancouver' (Working Paper Series, No 08–06, Metropolis British Columbia, Centre of Excellence for Research on Immigration and Diversity, September 2008)

Reddock, Rhoda and Yvonne Bobb-Smith, 'Reconciling Work and Family: Issues and Policies in Trinidad and Tobago' (Conditions of Work and Employment Series, No 18, ILO, 2008)

Sayers, Nicole J, 'An Analysis of the Situation of Filipino Domestic Workers' (Working Paper, ILO, 14 December 2007)

World Bank, *Early Childhood Development* (24 October 2017) <http://www.worldbank.org/en/topic/earlychildhooddevelopment#1>

Policy briefs and conference papers

Aleinikoff, T Alexander and Susan Martin, 'Making the Global Compacts Work: What Future for Refugees and Migrants?' (Policy Brief, No 6, Kaldor Centre for International Refugee Law, April 2018)

Asia Pacific Mission for Migrants, *Labour Export Program and Further Commodification of Migrants as Prescriptions for Development* (19 September 2014) <http://aprnet.org/?p=196>

Australian Human Rights Commission, *Human Rights Brief No 4: Lawful Limits on Fundamental Freedoms* (8 March 2006) <https://www.humanrights.gov.au/publications/human-rights-brief-no-4#5_exceptional>

Bailey, Rochelle, 'Using Material Remittances from Labour Schemes for Social and Economic Development: Case Study Vanuatu' (In Brief 2015/15, State, Society and Governance in Melanesia Program (SSGM), ANU, 2015)

Boyd, Monica, 'Labour Migration for Care: Women Migrants in Canada Under the Live-in Caregiver Program' (Paper presented at the Rethinking Care and Migration in the Age of Low Fertility and Ageing Population Conference, University of Toronto, 9–10 March 2011)

Human Rights Council of Australia (HRCA), 'Australian Ratification of the Migrant Worker Conventions – Responses to Concerns Raised by the Australian Government' (Briefing Paper, HRCA, 2012)

International Trade Union Confederation, *Gulf Countries: Increase Migrant Worker Protection* (23 November 2013) <http://www.ituc-csi.org/gulf-countries-increase-migrant>

Migrant Forum in Asia, *Policy Brief No 2: Reform of the Kafala (Sponsorship) System* <https://www.ilo.org/dyn/migpractice/docs/132/PB2.pdf>

Migration and Development Civil Society Network (MADE), 'Migration and SDG Implementation: The Real Challenge Starts Now' (Briefing Paper, MADE, 18 December 2015)

Newland, Kathleen, 'Will International Migration Governance Survive the COVID-19 Pandemic?' (*MPI Policy Brief*, October 2020)

RAND Arroyo Center and the RAND National Defense Research Institute, 'Brief: How Military Families Function Before, During, and After Deployment – Findings from the RAND Deployment Life Study' (RAND Corporation, 2016)

Ratha, Dilip, Christian Eigen-Zucchi, Sonia Plaza, Hanspeter Wyss and Soonhwa Yi, 'Migration and Remittance Flows: Recent Trends and Outlook, 2013–2016' (Migration and Development Brief No 21, Migration and Remittances Team, Development Prospects Group, World Bank, 2 October 2013)

Sexton, Judge Robyn, 'Parenting Arrangements for the 0–4 Year Age Group' (Paper presented at the Legal Aid NSW Family Law Conference, Hanoi, 13–15 September 2011)

Sijapati, Bandita, 'Women's Labour Migration from Asia and the Pacific: Opportunities and Challenges' (Issue in Brief, Issue No 12, IOM / Migration Policy Institute, March 2015)

Wickramage, Kolitha, Chesmal Siriwardhana and Sharika Peiris, 'Promoting the Health of Left-Behind Children of Asian Labour Migrants: Evidence for Policy and Action' (Issue in Brief, IOM / Migration Policy Institute, Issue No 14, September 2015)

World Bank Migration and Remittances Team, 'Phase II: COVID-19 Crisis Through a Migration Lens' (*KNOMAD, Migration and Development Brief 33*, October 2020)

Yanovich, Liza, *Children Left Behind: The Impact of Labor Migration in Moldova and Ukraine* (23 January 2015) Migration Policy Institute <http://www.migrationpolicy.org/article/children-left-behind-impact-labor-migration-moldova-and-ukraine>

E) Treaties and treaty bodies

International treaties and declarations

Convention on the Elimination of All Forms of Discrimination Against Women, opened for signature 18 December 1979, 1249 UNTS 13 (entered into force 3 September 1981)

Convention Concerning Decent Work for Domestic Workers (ILO No 189), opened for signature 16 June 2011 (entered into force 5 September 2013)

Convention Concerning Equal Opportunities and Equal Treatment for Men and Women Workers: Workers with Family Responsibilities (ILO No 156), opened for signature 23 June 1981 (entered into force 11 August 1983)

Convention on the Rights of the Child, opened for signature 20 November 1989, 1577 UNTS 3 (entered into force 2 September 1990)

Declaration of the Rights of the Child, League of Nations Res (adopted on 26 September 1924), *League of Nations Official Journal*, Special Supp No 21, 43

Declaration of the Rights of the Child, GA Res 1386(XIV), UN GAOR, 14th sess, 841st plen mtg, Agenda Item 64, UN Doc A/RES/14/1386 (20 November 1959)

Declaration on the High-level Dialogue on International Migration and Development, GA Res 68/4, UN GAOR, 68th sess, Agenda Item 21(e), UN Doc A/RES/68/4 (21 January 2014)

Declaration on Social and Legal Principles relating to the Protection and Welfare of Children, with Special Reference to Foster Placement and Adoption Nationally and Internationally, GA Res 41/85, UN GAOR, 95th plen mtg, UN Doc A/RES/41/85 (3 December 1986)

ILO, *Ratifications of C156 - Workers with Family Responsibilities Convention, 1981 (No 156)* (22 January 2019) <https://www.ilo.org/dyn/normlex/en>

International Convention on the Protection of the Rights of All Migrant Workers and Members of their Families, opened for signature 18 December 1990, 2220 UNTS 3 (entered into force 1 July 2003)

International Covenant on Civil and Political Rights, opened for signature 16 December 1966, 999 UNTS 171 (entered into force 23 March 1976)

International Covenant on Economic, Social and Cultural Rights, opened for signature 16 December 1966, 993 UNTS 3 (entered into force 3 January 1976)

New York Declaration for Refugees and Migrants, GA Res 71/1, UN GAOR, 71st sess, Agenda Items 13 and 117, UN Doc A/RES/71/1 (3 October 2016)

Universal Declaration of Human Rights, GA Res 217A (III), UN Doc A/810 (10 December 1948)

UN treaty body documents

i. Committee on the Rights of the Child ('CRC Committee')

CRC Committee, *Report on the Fifth Session*, 5th sess, 130th mtg, UN Doc CRC/C/24 (8 March 1994)

CRC Committee, *Report on the Seventh Session*, UN Doc CRC/C/34 (8 November 1994)

CRC Committee, *General Comment No 5 on General Measures of Implementation for the Convention on the Rights of the Child*, 34th sess, UN Doc CRC/GC/2003/5 (3 October 2003)

CRC Committee, *General Comment No 6: Treatment of Unaccompanied and Separated Children Outside their Country of Origin*, 39th sess, UN Doc CRC/GC/2005/6 (1 September 2005)

CRC Committee, *General Comment No 7: Implementing Child Rights in Early Childhood*, 40th sess, UN Doc CRC/C/GC/7/Rev.1 (20 September 2006)

CRC Committee, *Report on the Forty-sixth Session*, UN Doc CRC/C/46/3

CRC Committee, *Concluding Observations: Sri Lanka*, UN Doc CRC/C/LKA/CO/3–4 (19 October 2010)

CRC Committee, *Report of the 2012 Day of General Discussion: The Rights of All Children in the Context of International Migration* (28 September 2012)

CRC Committee, *General Comment No 16 (2013) on State Obligations Regarding the Impact of the Business Sector on Children's Rights*, UN Doc CRC/C/GC/16 (17 April 2013)

CRC Committee, *General Comment No 14 (2013): The Right of the Child to have His or Her Best Interests Taken as a Primary Consideration (Art 3, Para 1)*, 62nd sess, UN Doc CRC/C/GC/14 (29 May 2013)

CRC Committee, *General Comment No 19 (2016) on Public Budgeting for the Realization of Children's Rights (art 4)*, UN Doc CRC/C/GC/19 (20 July 2016)

ii. Committee on the Protection of the Rights of all Migrant Workers and Members of Their Families ('CMW Committee')

CMW Committee, *Working Paper: Terminology in the International Convention on Migrant Workers: A Comparison With Other International and Regional Instruments*, 2nd sess, UN Doc CMW/C/2/L.1 (22 March 2005)

CMW Committee, *General Comment No 1 on Migrant Domestic Workers*, 13th sess, UN Doc CMW/C/GC/1 (23 February 2011)

CMW Committee, *Contribution to the 2030 Sustainable Development Goals in Response to a Call for Inputs by the High-Level Political Forum on Sustainable Development (HLPF)* (19 April 2018)

CMW and CRC Committees, *Joint General Comment No. 3 (2017) of the Committee on the Protection of the Rights of All Migrant Workers and Members of Their Families and No. 22 (2017) of the Committee on the Rights of the Child on the General Principles Regarding the Human Rights of Children in the Context of International Migration*, UN Doc CMW/C/GC/3-CRC/C/GC/22 (16 November 2017)

CMW and CRC Committees, *Joint General Comment No 4 (2017) of the Committee on the Protection of the Rights of All Migrant Workers and Members of Their Families and No 23 (2017) of the Committee on the Rights of the Child on State Obligations Regarding the Human Rights of Children in the Context of International Migration in Countries of Origin, Transit, Destination and Return*, UN Doc CMW/C/GC/4-CRC/C/GC/23 (16 November 2017)

CMW Committee and UN Special Rapporteur on the human rights of migrants, *Joint Guidance Note on the Impacts of the COVID-19 Pandemic on the Human Rights of Migrants* (26 May 2020)

iii. Other

Committee on Economic, Social and Cultural Rights Committee, *General Comment No 3: The Nature of States Parties' Obligations (Art. 2, Para. 1, of the Covenant)*, 5th sess, UN Doc E/1991/23 (14 December 1990)

Committee on Economic, Social and Cultural Rights Committee, *General Comment No 14: The Right to the Highest Attainable Standard of Health (Art 12 of the Covenant)*, 22nd sess, UN Doc E/C.12/2000/4 (11 August 2000)

Human Rights Committee, *General Comment No 19: Article 23 (The Family) Protection of the Family, the Right to Marriage and Equality of the Spouses*, 39th sess, UN Doc HRI/GEN/1/Rev.1 (27 July 1990)

Human Rights Committee, *Views: Communication No 417/1990*, 51st sess, UN Doc CCPR/C/51/D/417/1990 (27 July 1994)

Human Rights Committee, *CCPR General Comment No 27: Freedom of Movement (Article 12)*, 67th sess, 1783rd mtg, UN Doc CCPR/C/21/Rev.1/Add.9 (1 November 1999)

Human Rights Committee, *General Comment No 31: The Nature of the General Legal Obligation Imposed on States Parties to the Covenant*, 80th sess, 2187th mtg, UN Doc CCPR/C/21/Rev.1/Add.13 (26 May 2004)

Human Rights Committee, *Views: Communication No 1052/2002*, 89th sess, UN Doc A/62/40 (Vol.II) (20 March 2007)

F) UN Official documents and other international materials

UN official documents

Celebration of the Twentieth Anniversary of the International Year of the Family in 2014: Report of the Secretary-General, UN ESCOR, 70th sess, UN Doc A/70/61–E/2015/3 (18 November 2014)

Global Compact for Safe, Orderly and Regular Migration, GA Res 73/195, UN GAOR, 73rd sess, Agenda Items 14 and 119, UN Doc A/RES/73/195 (11 January 2019)

Implementation of the Objectives of the International Year of the Family and its Follow-up Processes: Report of the Secretary-General, UN ESCOR, 71st sess, UN Doc A/71/61–E/2016/7 (19 November 2015)

Resolution on International Migration and Development, GA Res 71/237, UN GAOR, 71st sess, Agenda Item 21(b), UN Doc A/RES/71/237 (23 January 2017)

Question of a Convention on the Rights of the Child, UN ESCOR, 36th sess, Agenda Item 13, UN Doc E/CN.4/1349 (17 January 1980)

Preparations for and Observance of the Twentieth Anniversary of the International Year of the Family, UN GAOR, 68th sess, Agenda Item 27(b), UN Doc A/C.3/68/L.16/Rev.1 (29 October 2013)

Report of the Special Rapporteur on the Human Rights of Migrants, François Crépeau: Addendum – Mission to Sri Lanka, UN GAOR, 29th sess, Agenda Item 3, UN Doc A/HRC/29/36/Add.1 (2 April 2015)

Report of the Special Rapporteur on the Human Rights of Migrants, François Crépeau: Banking on Mobility Over a Generation: Follow-up to the Regional Study on the Management of the External Borders of the European Union and its Impact on the Human Rights of Migrants, UN GAOR, 29th sess, Agenda Item 3, UN Doc A/HRC/29/36 (8 May 2015)

Report of the Special Rapporteur on the Human Rights of Migrants on a 2035 Agenda for Facilitating Human Mobility, UN GAOR, 35th sess, Agenda Item 3, UN Doc A/HRC/35/25 (28 April 2017)

Report of the Special Rapporteur on the Human Rights of Migrants on His Mission to Nepal, UN GAOR, 38th sess, Agenda Item 3, UN Doc A/HRC/38/41/Add.1 (30 April 2018)

Report of the Special Representative of the Secretary General on the Issue of Human Rights and Transnational Corporations and Other Business Enterprises, John Ruggie: Guiding Principles on Business and Human Rights: Implementing the United Nations "Protect, Respect and Remedy" Framework, 17th sess, Agenda Item 3, UN Doc A/HRC/17/31 (21 March 2011)

Report of the Working Group on the Universal Periodic Review: Canada, UN GAOR, 24th sess, Agenda Item 6, UN Doc A/HRC/24/11 (28 June 2013)

Report of the Working Group on the Universal Periodic Review: Canada: Addendum: Views on Conclusions and/or Recommendations, Voluntary Commitments and Replies Presented by the State under Review, UN GAOR, 24th sess, Agenda Item 6, UN Doc A/HRC/24/11/Add.1 (17 September 2013)

Special Rapporteur on the Human Rights of Migrants, *Promotion and Protection of All Human Rights, Civil, Political, Economic, Social and Cultural Rights, including the Right to Development*, 11th sess, UN Doc A/HRC/11/7 (14 May 2009)

Study of the Office of the United Nations High Commissioner for Human Rights on Challenges and Best Practices in the Implementation of the International Framework for the Protection of the Rights of the Child in the Context of Migration, UN GAOR, 15th sess, Agenda Items 2 and 3, UN Doc A/HRC/15/29 (5 July 2010)

Siracusa Principles on the Limitation and Derogation Provisions in the International Covenant on Civil and Political Rights, UN ESCOR, 41st sess, UN Doc E/CN.4/1985/4 (28 September 1984)

Transforming Our World: The 2030 Agenda for Sustainable Development, GA Res 70/1, UN GAOR, 70th sess, Agenda Items 15 and 116, UN Doc A/RES/70/1 (21 October 2015)

UN-INSTRAW, *Gender, Migration, Remittances and Development*, UN Doc UN/POP/MIG-5CM/2006/02 (9 November 2006)

Other international materials

i. International Labour Organisation (ILO)

ILO, *Labour Migration: Facts and Figures* (26 March 2014) <http://www.ilo.org/global/about-the-ilo/media-centre/issue-briefs/WCMS_239651/lang–en/index.htm>

ILO, *Report VI: Towards a Fair Deal for Migrant Workers in the Global Economy*, International Labour Conference, 92nd sess, Agenda Item 6, 2004

ILO, *ILO Multilateral Framework on Labour Migration: Non-binding Principles and Guidelines for a Rights-Based Approach to Labour Migration* (ILO, 2006)

ILO, *ILO Global Estimates on Migrant Workers: Results and Methodology* (ILO, 2015)

ILO, *Report IV: Addressing Governance Challenges in a Changing Labour Migration Landscape*, International Labour Conference, 106th sess, 2017

ILO, *Reports of the Committee for Labour Migration: Resolutions and Conclusions Submitted for Adoption by the Conference*, 106th sess, Agenda Item 4, Provisional Record 12–11 (15 June 2017)

ILO, *Care Work and Care Jobs for the Future of Decent Work* (ILO, 2018)

ILO, *Ratifications of C189 - Domestic Workers Convention, 2011 (No 189)* (22 January 2019) <https://www.ilo.org/dyn/normlex/en>

International Labour Organization (ILO), 'Seasonal Migrant Workers' Schemes: Rethinking Fundamental Principles and Mechanisms in light of COVID-19' (*ILO Brief*, May 2020)

ILO and United Nations Development Program (UNDP), *Decent Work in Latin America and the Caribbean: Work and Family: Towards New Forms of Reconciliation with Social Co-Responsibility* (ILO/UNDP, 2009)

ILO Country Office for Sri Lanka and the Maldives, *Reintegration with Home Community: Perspectives of Returnee Migrant Workers in Sri Lanka* (ILO, 2013)

ii. International Organisation for Migration (IOM)

IOM, 'Section 2.5: Migration and Family' in *Essentials of Migration Management Volume Two: A Guide for Policy Makers and Practitioners* (IOM, 2004)

IOM, *World Migration 2008: Managing Labour Mobility in the Evolving Economy* (IOM-World Migration Report Series, 2008)

IOM, 'Family Migration' in *World Migration Report 2008: Managing Labour Mobility in the Evolving Global Economy* (IOM World Migration Report Series, 2008)

IOM, *Labour Migration from Indonesia: An Overview of Indonesian Migration to Selected Destinations in Asia and the Middle East* (IOM, 2010)

IOM, 'Migration and Families: Background Paper' (Intersessional Workshop, International Dialogue on Migration, 7–8 October 2014)

IOM, *International Dialogue on Migration (No 24): Migration and Families* (IOM, 2015)

iii. UN Children's Fund (UNICEF)

United Nations (UN) Children's Fund (UNICEF), *Children and Migration* (13 October 2017) Global Forum on Migration and Development <https://www.gfmd.org/unicef-children-and-migration>

UNICEF, *Children and Migration* (2007) Global Forum on Migration and Development <https://www.gfmd.org/unicef-children-and-migration>

UNICEF, *Children's Rights and Business Principles* (UNICEF, 2012)

UNICEF, 'The Structural Determinants of Child Well-being' (Expert Consultation Hosted by the UNICEF Office of Research, Florence, 22–23 June 2012)

UNICEF, *The State of the World's Children 2016: A Fair Chance for Every Child* (UNICEF, 2016)

UNICEF Moldova, 'The Situation of Children Left Behind by Migrating Parents' (Study Report, UNICEF, 2006)

UNICEF and Save the Children, *Children's Rights in Policies and Codes of Conduct: A Tool for Companies* (UNICEF, 2013)

UNICEF Office of Research (Innocenti), *Family and Parenting Support: Policy and Provision in a Global Context* (UNICEF, 2015)

iv. Other

Maastricht Principles on Extraterritorial Obligations of States in the Area of Economic, Social and Cultural Rights (ETO Consortium, January 2013)

OECD, *Official Development Assistance: Definition and Coverage* (2018) <http://www.oecd.org/dac/stats/officialdevelopmentassistancedefinitionandcoverage.htm>

Office of the High Commissioner for Human Rights (OHCHR), 'Family Reunification' (OHCHR Migration Papers, November 2005)

Open-ended Intergovernmental Working Group on Transnational Corporations and Other Business Enterprises with Respect to Human Rights, *Zero Draft: Legally Binding Instrument to Regulate, in International Human Rights Law, the Activities of Transnational Corporations and Other Business Enterprises* (16 July 2018)

Report of the United Nations Expert Group Meeting: Family Policies and 2030 Sustainable Development Agenda (United Nations Department of Economic and Social Affairs, New York, 12–13 May 2016)

UN High Commissioner for Refugees (UNHCR) Guidelines on Determining the Best Interests of the Child (UNHCR, May 2008)

UN Department of Economic and Social Affairs, *International Migration Report 2013* (UN, 2013)

UN Development Programme (UNDP), *Human Development Report 2009: Overcoming Barriers – Human Mobility and Development* (UNDP, 2009)

UN Network on Migration (UNNM), 'The Global Compact for Migration (GCM): Well Governed Migration as an Essential Element of Effective COVID-19 Response' (UNNM Policy Brief, 2020)

UN Network on Migration (UNNM) and The International Fund for Agricultural Development (IFAD), 'The Impact of COVID-19 on Family Remittances: A Lifeline Cut for Migrant Families' (*UNNM Policy Brief*, June 2020).

UN Population Fund, *State of World Population 2006: A Passage to Hope: Women and International Migration* (UNFPA, 2006)

UN Women, *Review of Laws, Policies and Regulations Governing Labour Migration in Asian and Arab States: A Gender and Rights Based Perspective* (UN Women, 2013)

UN Women Asia and the Pacific, *Template on Standard Terms of Employment (STOE) for Women Migrant Domestic Workers* (UN Women, 2016)

World Health Organization (WHO), *Women on the Move: Migration, Care Work and Health* (WHO, 2017)

G) Regional and domestic policies, legislation and cases

Regional

i. Asia

ASEAN Consensus on the Protection and Promotion of the Rights of Migrant Workers, 31st ASEAN Summit (14 November 2017)

ASEAN Declaration on the Protection and Promotion of the Rights of Migrant Workers, 12th ASEAN Summit (13 January 2007)

ASEAN Parliamentarians for Human Rights (APHR), *Regional MPs: ASEAN Consensus on Migrant Workers Does Not Provide Adequate Protections* (24 November 2017) <https://aseanmp.org/2017/11/24/regional-mps-asean-consensus-on-migrant-workers-does-not-provide-adequate-protections/>

Declaration on the Commitments for Children in ASEAN, 4th Meeting of ASEAN Ministers Responsible for Social Welfare (2 August 2001)

UNICEF, *The Beijing Declaration on South-South Cooperation for Child Rights in the Asia Pacific Region*, High-Level Meeting on Cooperation for Child Rights in the Asia Pacific Region (Beijing, 4–6 November 2010)

ii. Europe

Convention for the Protection of Human Rights and Fundamental Freedoms, opened for signature 4 November 1950, 213 UNTS 221 (entered into force 3 September 1953)

Council Directive 2003/86/EC of 22 September 2003 on the Right to Family Reunification [2003] OJ L 251/12

European Commission, 'Communication from the Commission to the European Parliament, the Council, the European Economic and Social Committee and the Committee of the Regions on a New Pact on Migration and Asylum' (Brussels, 23 September 2020)

Gul v Switzerland [1996] Eur Court HR 5

HH v Deputy Prosecutor of the Italian Republic, Genoa [2012] UKSC 25

Marckx v Belgium [1979] Eur Court HR 2

ZH (Tanzania) v Secretary of State for the Home Department [2011] UKSC 4

Australia

Australian Agency for International Development (AusAID), 'Labour Mobility Initiative: Independent Progress Report' (AusAID, March 2013)

Australian Bureau of Statistics, *3416.0 – Perspectives on Migrants, 2009: Skilled Migration* (15 April 2009) <http://www.abs.gov.au/AUSSTATS/abs@.nsf/Lookup/3416.0Main+Features32009>

Australian Defence Force, Joint Health Command, *Deployment Guide: A Guide to Assist Your Preparation* <www.defence.gov.au/Health/HealthPortal/docs/JHC%20Deployment%20Guide.pdf>

Australian Government Department of Foreign Affairs and Trade (DFAT), *Pacific Labour Mobility* (November 2018) <https://dfat.gov.au/geo/pacific/engagement/pacific-labour-mobility/Pages/default.aspx>

Australian Government Department of Jobs and Small Business, *Frequently Asked Questions about the Seasonal Worker Programme for Seasonal Workers* (20 August 2018) <https://www.jobs.gov.au/frequently-asked-questions-seasonal-workers>

Australian Government Department of Foreign Affairs and Trade (DFAT), *Travel Smart – Work Smart: Pre-departure Manual for Nauru Seasonal Workers in Australia* (DFAT/ILO)

Australian Research Council Project, *Working Away: How Working Away is Changing Home* <https://www.workingaway.net/the-project/>

Commonwealth, *Australian Government Response to the Joint Standing Committee on Migration Report: Seasonal Change – Inquiry into the Seasonal Worker Programme* (February 2017)

Department of Foreign Affairs and Trade (DFAT), *Pacific Labour Scheme* (November 2018) <https://dfat.gov.au/geo/pacific/engagement/Documents/pacific-labour-scheme.pdf>

*Family Law Act*1975 (Cth)

*Family Law Amendment (Shared Parental Responsibility) Act*2006 (Cth)

Family Law Council, *Relocation: A Report to the Attorney-General Prepared by the Family Law Council* (Commonwealth of Australia, May 2006)

Canada

Employment and Social Development Canada, *Labour Market Impact Assessment Application: Low-Wage Positions* (1 December 2018) <https://catalogue.servicecanada.gc.ca/apps/EForms/pdf/en/ESDC-EMP5627.pdf>

Harry Arthurs, *Fairness at Work: Federal Labour Standards for the 21st Century* (Publication Services, Human Resources Development Canada, 2006)

Government of Canada, *Improving Canada's Caregiver Program* (31 October 2014) <https://www.canada.ca/en/news/archive/2014/10/improving-canada-caregiver-program.html>

Government of Canada, *Contract for the Employment in Canada of Seasonal Agricultural Workers from Mexico – 2019* (18 December 2018) <https://www.canada.ca/en/employment-social-development/services/foreign-workers/agricultural/seasonal-agricultural/apply/mexico.html>

Government of Canada, *Caregivers – Options for Permanent Residence* (3 October 2018) <https://www.canada.ca/en/immigration-refugees-citizenship/services/immigrate-canada/caregivers.html>

Standing Committee on Human Resources, Skills and Social Development and the Status of Persons with Disabilities, Parliament of Canada, *Temporary Foreign Worker Program* (2016)

Philippines

Calzado, Rebecca J, Department of Labor and Employment Philippines, 'Labour Migration and Development Goals: The Philippine Experience' (Paper presented at International Dialogue on Migration, Geneva, 8 October 2007)

Migrant Workers and Overseas Filipinos Act of 1995 (Republic Act No 8042)

Sri Lanka

Government of Sri Lanka, *Charter on the Rights of the Child* (1992)

H.E. Ravinatha P Aryasinha, 'Introductory Statement at the Presentation of Sri Lanka's 2nd Periodic Report (CMW/C/LKA/2) Submitted under the International

Convention on the Protection of the Rights of All Migrant Workers and Members of Their Families (CMW)' (Presented at the 25th Session of the CMW Committee, Geneva, 1 September 2016)

Shadow Report – Sri Lanka: To the UN Committee on the Protection of the Rights of All Migrant Workers and Members of their Families (CMW) for Consideration During the 25th Session (presented by 20 Civil Society Organisations, August 2016)

Sri Lankan Ministry for Foreign Employment Promotion and Welfare, *National Labour Migration Policy for Sri Lanka* (Government of Sri Lanka, October 2008)

Sri Lankan Ministry of Foreign Employment, *Ministerial Circular 2015/1: Obtaining a Report on the Family Background of Women Who Expect to Migrate for Employment*, Circular No. MFE/RAD/10/13 (June 2015)

Index